D1565724

LUTHER: WITNESS TO JESUS CHRIST

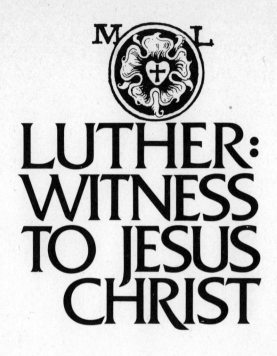

LUTHER: WITNESS TO JESUS CHRIST

MARC LIENHARD

Translated by Edwin H. Robertson

*Stages and Themes of
the Reformer's Christology*

AUGSBURG Publishing House • Minneapolis

LUTHER: WITNESS TO JESUS CHRIST

CONTENTS

TRANSLATOR'S PREFACE

The task of translating anything by Marc Lienhard is sheer joy, because of the clarity of his French, the logic of his thought, and the discipline of his material. He never leaves you in any doubt about what he means, nor are his arguments ever confused.

But there is more than Marc Lienhard in this material. There are hundreds of quotations, from Luther's Latin and German, from an immense range of literature, mostly in German, and from contemporary comment. The book has 800 footnotes and almost as many references in the text.

It was necessary at an early stage to decide upon a method of transposing Marc Lienhard's use of this rich variety of reference into a form that would be consistent and useful for the reader. There is little doubt that this book will become a reference work for all who seek to study the christology of Luther in the historical setting of his developing thought.

Wherever quotations or references to Luther occur, the references are given to the Weimar Edition of his works: *Luthers Werke. Kritische Gesamtausgabe.* Weimar: 1883 onward. The references are given as *WA (Weimarer Ausgabe).* The American Edition *(AE)* of *Luther's Works,* edited by Jaroslav Pelikan and Helmut T. Lehmann, has most frequently been used, though not in every case.

With due attention to the French version which Marc Lienhard

has used and the occasions when he makes his own translation from
WA, I have sometimes taken the liberty of making a direct translation or using another translation. The Middleton Text has proven
helpful in the chapter on Luther's *Commentary on the Epistle to the
Galatians* (Chap. 6). Reference to the Middleton Text *(MT)* is made
at the opening of that chapter and elsewhere.

Inevitably, most quotations are from German writers. I have been
greatly helped by the typescript of the German translation of Marc
Lienhard's book, which Vandenhoeck & Ruprecht, Göttingen, so
kindly made available to me. This enabled me to translate all German quotations from the original. Where possible, I have used the
standard translations into English, and appropriate references are
given. Occasionally, the argument in Lienhard's text depends upon
the way in which the original has been translated. On a few occasions, the standard translation has not made the point clear, and I
have used my own translation.

In his preface to the original French edition, Marc Lienhard
writes: "The present book is both the fruit of personal research and
of that valuable aid given to me by many collaborators. To all those
who have contributed to the origin and completion of this book I
would express here my profound gratitude."

Those to whom he is indebted are referred to in the course of the
book and their writings appear in the bibliography. Marc Lienhard
does, however, single out certain writers who have been of special
help to him. They should be noted here: Charles Hauter, of the
Protestant Faculty of Theology at Strasbourg; Karl Barth, who led
him to explore a theology of revelation based upon christology and
the Word; Gerard Siegwalt who directed his attention to Regin Prenter of Aarhus; Peter Brunner of Heidelberg and Theobald Süss of
Paris; but primarily Francois Wendel of the Protestant Faculty of
Strasbourg, who carefully read the manuscript before publication
and brought his rigorous intellect and critical mind to bear upon the
material; Vilmos Vajta of the Center for Ecumenical Studies at Strasbourg of the Lutheran World Federation, and Etienne Jung, presi-
dent of the Church of the Augsburg Confession in Alsace-Lorraine.

Just as Marc Lienhard thanked all those who prepared the manuscript for the press, I should also like to thank the staff of Augsburg
Publishing House for their patience and constant encouragement.

Edwin Robertson

INTRODUCTION

"For in my heart there rules this one doctrine, namely, faith in Christ [*fides Christi*]. From it, through it, and to it all my theological thought flows and returns day and night; yet I am aware that all I have grasped of this wisdom in its height, width, and depth are a few poor and insignificant first fruits and fragments." [1]

That is what Luther wrote in the 1535 preface to his *Lectures on the Epistle to the Galatians* of 1531. Some years earlier he wrote, "To have Christ is to have all: if Christ remains to me, all remains to me and can be found." [2] He never ceased to direct his hearers and his readers toward Jesus Christ, by whom God was revealed to human beings and who achieved for them salvation.

But although innumerable studies have already discussed the soteriology of the reformer, his concept of justification by faith and his controversies on this subject, far less attention has been given to his christology proper, i.e., to Luther's understanding of the mystery of the person of Christ and to Luther's place in the christological tradition of the church. In all, only three monographs of any significance have tackled the question, and it is important for us at the outset to locate our research with respect to these works.

The first of these three studies is by a theologian of the last century, Theodosius Harnack. His second volume, *Theology of Luther,* is devoted to christology. [3] It is conceived dogmatically and tackles

the christology of Luther by systematizing his thought. It is a method
which I view critically. Even if the unity of the reformer's thought is
greater than many are willing to recognize, it seems to us preferable
to present it more historically, following its course through different
situations and through the different literary forms in which he expressed it.

It is precisely that which is the merit of the second work, which is
by Erich Seeberg.[4] He presents the christology of Luther in three
distinct stages. But for many reasons, which will appear in the course
of this work, his study does not satisfy us completely. The principal
reason is that instead of coordinating the christology and soteriology
of Luther, he is interested primarily in the philosophy of the reformer, whether implicit or explicit. We do not deny him the right
to do this, but for our part we shall deal with his christology by cen-
tering our attention on the subject itself.

The third study was published in 1970. It is the work of an Aus-
tralian theologian, Ian Kingston Siggins.[5] We have particularly appreciated the author's care in taking into account all periods of
Luther's activities and his different literary forms, while concentrating especially on Luther's commentaries and sermons on the gospel
of John. By these means, Siggins rightly emphasizes the Johannine
character of Luther's christology. One must also acknowledge his
effort to identify the themes and expressions typical of the reformer,
while not applying to him a dogmatic framework taken from christologies earlier than, or later than, Luther's own. We have also shared
Siggins' desire to locate Luther especially in relation to the early
church and the Council of Chalcedon, and we have appreciated his
critical spirit in analyzing the thought of the reformer.

However, the work of Siggins, according to our view, must be received with some caution. He seems to have neglected or badly interpreted certain aspects of Luther's christology. For our part we wish
to emphasize, more than Siggins has done, the real humanity of
Christ, his sufferings and his temptations. Furthermore, we do not
share Siggins' reservations with regard to the "technical" side of
Luther's christology. The *communicatio idiomatum* (communication
of attributes) and the trinitarian background, for example, require
a careful study which so far has been lacking.

In addition, we have some reservations about the method followed
by Siggins. Once again, it is a presentation of the thought of Luther
which does not follow faithfully enough the course of the reformer's

ideas used at different periods, in confronting different adversaries, and in different literary forms. Despite the unity of Luther's thought it is necessary to differentiate more. Also one may ask whether the presentation of Luther's thought with the help of typical expressions, often synonymous, takes one beyond a mosaic of themes, which scarcely encompasses the logic of Luther's mind. At this point, Siggins is not systematic enough. In effect it seems to us necessary first of all to examine the reformer's thought both from a point of view which is strictly speaking historical (influences, different situations and forms of expressing his thought) and from a point of view which is more systematic (questions about the logic of his thought).

Apart from the three studies that we have already mentioned, Luther's christology has hardly been the subject of much significant work. Of course, there are a number of smaller studies, often very interesting, from which we have been able to benefit. We shall refer to these in the course of our presentation. The studies that have been done tend either to give a total view of Luther's christology (and these of necessity are too general or too systematic) or they present some particular aspect of his christology, or limit their field of investigation to one period of activity, or to one piece of writing by the reformer. These studies have been a great help to us. But it was necessary to try to go farther and to give a more comprehensive view, following the method which we shall describe later.

Is it necessary to insist here upon the importance of christology, i.e., a reflection upon the subject of Christ, for a Christian theologian? Certainly, according to Holl and the researchers who follow him, Christ played only a secondary role in Luther's thought. But that is a thesis which our work wishes to invalidate. It has equally been asked whether Luther had really worked out a christology, that is to say a well thought-out reflection on the person of Jesus Christ, his two natures and his being as the second person of the Trinity, or whether he was not content to speak only of the work of Christ in winning human salvation. Our study must answer this question.

It is necessary also to draw attention to the ecumenical range of a study on the christology of Luther. It was this consideration which was the origin of our work. In fact, one of the comprehensive studies of the christology of Luther is by Yves Congar.[6] He believes that he can find characteristic differences between the christology of Luther and traditional christology. According to him, the reformer thought of Christ in such a way that God alone accomplished the work of salvation. Congar speaks of the *Alleinwirksamkeit* (monergism) of God which would reduce the humanity of Christ to the level of a mere location where the drama of salvation was unfolded, while in the Thomist tradition, for example, "the source of salvation, although secondary and totally dependent upon God, is in his humanity." [7]

Congar thinks that he can find one of the characteristic differences between the Reformation and Catholicism precisely in the way in which the cooperation of human nature in the work of salvation is conceived. It is not a new thesis and was expressed many times in connection with justification by faith. What is interesting about Congar's study is that he poses the question in connection with the christology of the reformer, reproaching him for moving away from the traditional interpretation of the dogma of the two natures. He reproaches him further for the insufficiency of his doctrine of the Trinity.

One sees the interest that a fully developed study of the christology of Luther can offer on the ecumenical level. Such a study would be likely to correct the analysis of Congar and show that Luther is closer to traditional christology. It will in any case be necessary to give particular attention to Luther's thinking about the humanity of Jesus Christ and the part it plays in the accomplishment of salvation.

It is necessary for us to explain briefly at this point the method that we intend to follow. It will not be dogmatic, in the sense that we shall not apply a christological theory to the thought of the reformer as a whole, but we will attempt to derive it from his historical development. It did not, for example, appear to us to be sensible to cite, without further comment, a passage from Luther's *Commentary on the Psalms* (1513) side by side with a text taken from the *Disputations* of 1539. It is necessary to take into account the period, the kind of literature, the listeners (or readers), and also Luther's opponents at the time. There is no doubt that the thought of the reformer remained fundamentally the same—we shall have to prove this with regard to his christology—but it must be recognized that this thought took on certain emphases according to the opponents he met; thus, for example, one will ascertain some incidental changes in the course of the Eucharistic Controversy.

For this reason we shall approach our subject in nine fairly long chapters, each corresponding both to a particular period in Luther's life, and where possible also to a specific literary genre. The justification for this plan cannot be demonstrated here, but it will emerge.

in the course of the work itself. The method presents certain major difficulties, because it will not be possible to avoid some repetition. But such difficulties are compensated for by the fact that in this way the continuity of Luther's thought will appear more clearly.

In expounding the thought of an author one must try to present this thinking as faithfully and as objectively as possible. It is also desirable to situate it with respect to the whole of the Christian tradition, to discern its possible sources and to determine, if possible, the originality of the thought studied. It seems to us that this belongs to the field of the historian of dogma. That is why there are some digressions comparing Luther's thought on christology with that of certain authors of the early church, of the Middle Ages, or even of the present time.

In analyzing Luther's texts themselves, we shall be concerned to present his thought in the way in which he conceived it and to discern its fundamental themes. Such a procedure seems legitimate to us, because it does not introduce into the study of an author's thought criteria foreign to it. Criticism of Luther's thought will remain in the background. It will only draw attention to inaccuracies or omissions in the thought or point out where Luther has stopped short of the theological task that he intended to carry out.

Any study of the whole of Luther's thought is faced with one major problem inherent in such research—the sheer magnitude of his work. Which writings must be studied? Which can be left to one side? The answers will obviously depend on the subject. And it is thus that we have determined our choice.

Another book on the thought of Luther! That is what some will say, perhaps with some skepticism in view of the countless number of those who have already studied this astonishing author. Their number in a way attests to the rich complexity of the reformer's thought. Our research has convinced us both of the number of studies as well as their limitations. When we are concerned with the thought of the reformer, there can only be approaches to it. At the most one can only be sure of being on the right road, by linking Christ intimately to human salvation, theology to soteriology. It is within these limits that our study will be set.

Notes

1   *WA* 40, 1, 33, 7-11; *AE* 27, 145. Quotations from Luther's works are from the *Weimarer Ausgabe (WA)*. References to English trans-

lations are usually to the *American Edition (AE)*, though sometimes
to the Middleton translation of 1575 *(MT)*.

2   *WA* 23, 207, 27.

3   Theodosius Harnack, *Luthers Theologie mit besonderer Beziehung
auf seine Versöhnungs–und Erlösungslehre*, vol. 2 (first edition, Erlangen: Blaesing, 1862-1886; second edition, Munich: Kaiser, 1927).

4   Erich Seeberg, *Luthers Theologie*, vol. 2: "Christus: Wirklichkeit und
Urbild" (Berlin: 1937; Darmstadt, 1969).

5   Ian Kingston Siggins, *Martin Luther's Doctrine of Christ*, Yale Publications in Religion 14 (New Haven and London: 1970).

6   Yves Congar, "Regards et réflexions sur la christologie de Luther,"
an important study that first appeared in *Das Konzil von Chalkedon:
Geschichte und Gegenwart*, vol. 3 (Würzburg: 1954), pp. 457-487.
The unchanged text (though completed with additional comments)
was newly published in *Chrétiens en dialogue* (Paris: Cerf, 1964),
pp. 453-489. We quote from this edition, but refer to it as "La christologie de Luther."

7   "La christologie de Luther," p. 472.

1

The Christology of Luther to 1517

THE SOURCES

Luther elaborated his own thought on the subject of Christ as he meditated on the Scriptures and the Fathers of the church, and as he interpreted traditional christology. The piety prevalent at the end of the Middle Ages, determined by mysticism and the *Imitation of Christ,* must also be taken into account. All these influences constitute what can be called the sources of Luther's christology. And it is in this broad sense that we use the word *sources.*

Here we can give only general indications. In fact, the problem of the sources of Luther's christology, although it has been the preoccupation of researchers, remains obscure at many important points, despite the progress that has been made over the past 50 years. For example, Luther's relationship to certain of the church Fathers, such as Augustine, Athanasius, and Irenaeus, still requires more precise study.

On the other hand, the object of our work is not to research the sources of Luther or to compare his thought with that of other theologians. Such research should be the object of some special study, but it is not within the compass of our work.

Finally, our presentation of the sources of Luther will be brief for quite another reason. The remarks which we now make at the beginning will be added to in the course of our study. In fact, any aspect of the thought of Luther is clarified when seen in relationship to its sources.

One additional general remark must be made here. According to our view, to speak of the sources of an author does not necessarily mean to impugn the originality of his thought. Originality is shown sometimes in agreement, sometimes in disagreement, in a new synthesis or in the selection of points for emphasis. This is true in Luther's case. One must also point out the dialectic method of the reformer. He took up certain ideas that he found in the course of his reading and at the same time opposed them on certain points. There we have two aspects of his theological journeying which must be clarified.

In any case, the question of an author's sources must be treated with great care. Identical formulations do not necessarily mean the direct dependence of one author on another. Even when there is explicit reference, the agreement can prove to be illusory. The context of a statement can change its meaning and its scope significantly.

We shall examine successively three kinds of sources for Luther: traditional christology, medieval spirituality, and the Holy Scriptures. We shall have occasion to return to the order that we intend to follow in the exposition of these three themes.

Traditional Christology

The Christology of the Early Church: St. Augustine

The Christian message on the subject of Christ rests on a solid foundation: the Holy Scriptures. It is there that the Christian church finds the testimony which forms the basis of all that it affirms on the subject of Christ. It very soon became necessary to express the scriptural message in the form of confessions of faith—particularly in view of the many heresies on the subject of Christ. Thus were born the confessions of the early church. One knows that their great preoccupation was to affirm the reality of the incarnation. Quite early, Christian thought defined the divinity of Christ in this way and then elaborated the doctrine of the Trinity. Attention was then directed toward the person of Christ, who was at one and the same time God and a human being, issuing eventually in the Chalcedonian Definition of 451, which proclaimed that Christ has two natures, that he is truly God and truly human and that these two natures coexist in him, neither separable nor confused.

One can say that the first five centuries of the church, with their doctrinal experience (that is to say their trinitarian doctrine and their christology), form part of the common heritage of all the churches. For his part, Luther consciously reaffirmed them. One may certainly discuss his manner of interpreting the christology of the early church, but one cannot question his desire, expressed and often affirmed, to be associated with it. In this matter he was a great deal more conservative than one usually thinks. Despite his criticism on occasion of certain accepted traditional formulations, he never questioned the tradition itself, except when it was, in his view, opposed to the witness of Scripture.

It is possible, of course, to ask if Luther has paid sufficient attention to all aspects of traditional christology. Thus concerning the incarnation: does it play an important role in the reformer's christology? Is he not more concerned with the cross, the saving work of Christ? It seems to us that historians have often assumed a conflict here, with regard to Luther, which does not exist for him. It is the whole of the Christ event which holds his attention, i.e. the incarnation as well as the cross and the resurrection. It is one of the merits of Erich Seeberg [1] and of Wilhelm Maurer [2] that they have made this fact clear. They have rightly, it seems to us, insisted on the importance of the incarnation in the thought of Martin Luther.[3] Without sharing all their conclusions, we are indebted to them on this point.

But does the study of Luther's writings show that he placed sufficient importance on the incarnation? We think so. We shall have occasion to return to this point, particularly when we analyze a passage in his *Epistle to the Romans*. But for the present, we should like to support our thesis with the help of some examples taken from the earliest of his great commentaries, *Readings from the Psalms* of 1513 *(Dictata super Psalterium)*.[4]

First, it can be said that he speaks quite naturally of Christ as "God incarnate" (WA 4, 53, 22; 4,7,12). It is in Christ that God is present to the highest degree: *praesentissimus* (WA 3,93,12). The Lord Jesus Christ is our God. He brings grace to us by the incarnation (WA 4,125,10). Further, Luther also mentions the threefold coming of Christ (WA 4,147; 4,261,25; 4,305). He comes for the first time in the incarnation; for the second time, under a different form, in the resurrection and the preaching of the word; finally, he will come at the end of time, when we shall see him face to face.

The most important developments appear when Luther is speaking of the "indwelling" of God and particularly of his secret indwelling. When commenting on Ps. 18:11,[5] "He makes darkness his covering around him," Luther uses the translation, "The hiding place of God is darkness" and comments: "In the first place, because he dwells in the riddle (enigma) and in the darkness of faith. Second, because he dwells in an unapproachable light (1 Tim. 6:16), so that no mind (intellectus) can penetrate to him. Third, this can be understood as referring to the mystery of the incarnation. For he is concealed in humanity (absconditus latet), which is his darkness. Here, he cannot be seen, but only heard. Fourth, this refers to the church or the blessed Virgin, for he was concealed in both. Fifth, it refers to the sacrament of the Eucharist, where he is most completely concealed (occultissimus). For that reason, this can also be understood as referring to Christ's incarnation" (WA 3,124,29ff; AE 10,119-120).[6]

Sometimes this passage has been interpreted in a Neoplatonic sense. Under the influence of St. Augustine, as we shall show later, Luther learned his Neoplatonism largely from Dionysius the Areopagite. This was a negative type of theology. Dionysius saw his goal as being raised from the finite to the distant hidden God, with whom he would be united in ecstasy. Traces of Neoplatonic terminology can certainly be found in Luther's writings, particularly in his *Commentary on the Psalms*. But this does not mean that he followed Neoplatonism fundamentally. What is fundamental to Luther is that the inaccessible God is present—hidden certainly—but real, in the humanity of Christ.[7] That is where God would be found, not in speculation or in ecstasy.

Let us take one further passage which emphasizes the hidden presence of God in Christ.

Commenting on Psalm 68, Luther frequently refers to the incarnation as an explanation of the statement: "God is in his holy habitation" (v.5).[8] The heaven where God would be found is the humanity which he assumed in the incarnation (WA 3,385,6). As in the passage which we quoted above, Luther writes here that the secret dwelling places of God are the church, faith, and the humanity of Christ. Examining the list of places where God is present, albeit hidden, one can say that the humanity of Christ here comes at the head of the list (*WA* 3,403,38). "The light inaccessible" of which the list in Psalm 18 speaks does not appear here.

The exposition of this psalm is interesting on yet another point. It is here that Luther shows how the appearances of God reported in the Old Testament prefigure the incarnation. In this way he takes up the current allegorical interpretation and concentrates it upon the incarnation. Thus "Sinai which quakes at the presence of God" (v.8) is the incarnate Christ. The burning bush which Moses saw signifies the humanity of Christ "in which the fire of divinity was present in bodily form and who was born of the desert earth, i.e., the Virgin Mary" (*WA* 3,385,38).[9]

One could quote other passages where Luther concentrates attention upon the incarnation, but they would add nothing to what we have already seen.[10]

We must content ourselves here with these brief comments intended to underline the importance of the theme of the incarnation for the thought of Martin Luther. But one fundamental question must be raised. While recognizing the importance of the incarnation for Luther, can we truly say that there is in his work a christology, i.e., a "science of Christ," a systematic reflection on the person of Christ, and on the mystery of the hypostatic union? In addition, it is not only necessary to ask if Luther has a christology, but also if he interprets the christology of the early church correctly. In fact, is he clear that it is the Son who is incarnate and not the trinitarian God as such? Is it sufficient and in fact is it correct to confine oneself to seeing "the incarnation as God hidden and acting in and under the humanity of Christ"?[11] Does not Luther tend to consider the humanity of Christ as a place, certainly a special place, but nevertheless a place among other places (the church, faith, the Eucharist, the Virgin) where God hides himself? Would that not impugn the specific character of Christ, who is God and a human being in a unique sense? Such are some of the questions that must be posed about Luther's christology.

We are not yet able to reply definitively to these questions. That is the object of our study as a whole. However, some indications must be provided at this point, because we are dealing here with the christology of the early church as a source for the thought of Luther.

It is important first of all to emphasize the following points. The passages that we have quoted so far are extracts from a biblical commentary and not from a treatise on christology. Luther did not write any treatise of this kind. At the most one can classify certain essays under this rubric. It would be useless to expect a biblical commentary to furnish a complete exposition of christology. One could make the same remark about most of Luther's works.

In the second place, it must be noted that the early church itself left many questions open. The Councils of Nicea and Chalcedon laid the foundation: Christ is God and a human being. He is God in the person of the Son. More precise details were desired, and, in effect, these were added in the course of later centuries. Reading Luther one sometimes has the impression that he goes back directly to the early church. As Congar has written, "Luther has left aside, or freely discarded, certain developments of Scholastic theology in the matter of christology" (p. 488). Thus what a St. Thomas can say about the two natures of Christ and the cooperation of the humanity and the divinity does not appear in the *Commentary on the Psalms* from which we have quoted. Luther hardly considers the way in which the Occamist theologians debated the hypostatic union, even though he knew that debate very well. The link to the early church was direct.

When we later expound the christological themes in the *Commentary on the Psalms* at length, we shall modify slightly our impression that Luther was content to speak of the presence of God in the humanity of Christ. However—and this will be our third remark—Luther directs attention not so much to christological questions as to the importance of the incarnation for the salvation of human beings and for the knowledge that we have of God. The incarnation is so important because in it God offers himself to human beings. God becomes present in order to save us. Luther's passionate interest is in the presence of God. He cannot conceive salvation apart from this presence. The idea of the incarnation affirms precisely this presence of God become human.

Also, Luther discovered in the incarnation the dialectic of God hidden and revealed. God does not hide himself by remaining far from human beings, he hides himself *in* the humanity of Christ. But he hides himself there in order to be revealed to faith. If he were not there, there would be no assurance; if he were not hidden there, there would be no faith.

Placing the incarnation in the thought of Luther in this way and explaining the emphasis that he has put upon it does not in our view imply that he did not accept the traditional doctrine of christology.

But the question which above all preoccupied him is that of salvation and of faith. Where to find God? How to participate in the saving reality which is Jesus Christ? These are the questions that move him to reflection. To answer them, he had to insist upon the incarnation as such. Little by little, notably in the debate with Zwingli, Luther was pushed to a more precise definition of how he thought of the doctrine of christology. This was not in question, according to Luther, in his debate with Rome. That is why he speaks little about it. In the early years of his activity he is content to speak of the incarnation in general terms, as we have demonstrated above. And for reasons that it will be necessary for us to look at more closely, he concentrates his attention first on the suffering humanity of Christ, and then on the faith which unites human beings to Christ.

We have seen so far the extent to which the christology of the ancient church can be considered as a source of the thought of Martin Luther. We have spoken of the christology of the first centuries in a general way, thinking particularly of the incarnation and the official definitions formulated by the church on this subject. Another approach to the question, both possible and desirable, would be to show how the thought of one of the Fathers of the church influenced Luther. He affirms that he had read the Fathers already before his struggle against the Pope.[12] According to the common practice of his time, he quotes the principal Fathers in his works. This fact is important and should be emphasized. As Wilhelm Maurer has noted, Luther's christology has not often been fully seen in its relation to that of the early church, because the patristic quotations of Luther have been judged unimportant and a distinction has been made between Luther's own thought and that of the authors that he quoted.[13] But Luther quotes them because they have inspired him. In the same way he praises equally the *Sentences* of Peter Lombard, that classical manual of medieval theology, which is largely an anthology of patristic quotations.[14]

A detailed study of the patristic quotations used by Luther has not yet been undertaken. It would be extremely useful. It would, of course, be beyond the range of our work. We will have to limit ourselves to showing, in the course of our exposition, such patristic sources as are relevant, without being able to undertake a detailed comparison between the thought of Luther and that of the Fathers.

But there is one Father whose influence on Luther we must underline here: Saint Augustine.

Luther was an Augustinian monk and he read much of St. Augustine during his studies and throughout his theological activity.[15] It is not necessary here to deal with the question of Luther's connection with Augustine in any broad sense. The subject has often been treated. But to what extent is it possible to detect an influence of Augustine in his christology? It seems to us necessary to speak of this at two levels. At the one level it is possible to ask whether Luther is Augustinian with respect to certain structures of his thought.[16] The reformer insists, as does Saint Augustine, that the action of the grace of God is all-powerful. On this point Saint Augustine is opposed to the Pelagians, and Luther to the School of Occam.[17] We shall not deal with the difference which separates Luther from Augustine in their understanding of grace. For Augustine, grace was a created gift and became a quality infused in human beings. "For Luther, on the contrary, grace is none other than God himself." [18]

What interests us here is that Luther, like Augustine, seems to be unaware of, or rather reject, what the Scholastics called "secondary causes." [19] There is only one cause of our salvation, and that is God himself. For a theologian familiar with Scholastic thought, the question arises: From this point of view, what is the role of the humanity of Christ? Thus Congar remarks that Saint Augustine is unaware of "the instrumental causality of the humanity of Christ in providing grace . . . His Platonic categories have led him to the position where he holds that every spiritual gift comes from 'God,' while the Christ in his humanity is only able to cause physical effects." [20] According to Congar, one could make the same comment about Luther. On this point, he speaks of the "religious monism" of the reformer and at the center of his remarkable study of Luther, he develops the idea of the *Alleinwirksamkeit Gottes.*[21]

We are not able to discuss here Congar's interpretation of Luther's christology. But on the level at which he discusses it, that of the unique activity of God, it seems possible to speak of an influence of Saint Augustine, or at least of the convergence between him and Luther. But is it the "Augustinianism" of Luther which prevented him from having a "correct" christology, in the sense in which Congar understands it? And again, is Luther's stress on the *Alleinwirksamkeit Gottes* irreconcilable with the christological tradition of the church? These are questions that we shall have to take up again.

But there is another level at which these questions may be posed.

It is possible to ask whether there are christological themes typical of the thought of Saint Augustine which can be found in Luther.

One notes that in his *Commentary on the Psalms,* Luther frequently refers to Saint Augustine, that he quotes him 270 times, as Held has pointed out.[22] Both interpret the Psalms christologically. That means that the Psalms are considered not only as the words of an Old Testament believer, but as prayers said by Christ. And as Held [23] has also pointed out, Luther shows his agreement with Saint Augustine when he attributes a particular psalm to Christ, and it is from him also that he draws in order to resolve certain difficulties that arise in connection with christological interpretations.[24]

But he departs from him on one important point. Saint Augustine did not think he could apply the more somber psalms of penitence to Christ *in persona sua,*[25] i.e., those passages where the psalmist considers himself abandoned and punished by God. Luther, on the other hand, does not hesitate to place them in the mouth of Christ himself. He thus separates himself from the method (current in his day and followed also by Saint Augustine) of applying the passages of distress to Christ *"in persona ecclesiae,"* and toning down the meaning. Affirmations which underline the abandonment, the suffering, and the punishment of Christ are too shocking for theologians still stamped with the idea of the impassibility of God! Luther, on the other hand, does not recoil from this position.

Apart from this important reservation, it is right according to Luther to emphasize the inseparable unity of Christ the head with his body the church. In order to express this unity Luther refers, at several points, to Saint Augustine's Commentary on the Psalms.[26] Christ and the church speak *una voce* (WA 4, 275, 30; 4, 127).[27]

Apart from the christological interpretation of the Psalms, which Luther did not only find in Saint Augustine, there are several themes typical of Augustine which are to be found in his writings. Thus he follows the Father of the church in speaking of Christ as *"sacramentum et exemplum,"* which is a distinction found in Saint Augustine's *Treatise on the Trinity.* By taking up this theme, Luther wishes to affirm one of his fundamental ideas, that Christ can only be an example for human beings on the condition that he is, also and above all, sacramental, i.e., that his death must be realized in me and that I must die in him before I am able to imitate him. In the study already mentioned, Iserloh has shown that this Augustinian theme appears at every period of Luther's activity, and particularly in the works of his youth. We shall have occasion again to refer to this.

According to Hamel, a convergence can also be traced between the Augustinian theme of the humility of Christ and Luther's thought on this subject.[28] He writes, "The humiliated Christ has frequently been referred to in the *Enarrationes*. It is an essential part of Augustinian christology and soteriology . . . (p. 197). Luther also has spoken of the humility of Christ which is manifest already in the incarnation of Christ, notably in his Jewish descent and also in the cross. Christ demanded humility of his disciples" (p. 199). In much the same range of concepts one may find in Luther the idea, common in Augustine, of the divinity hidden under the humanity (p. 200).[29]

But these influences of Saint Augustine could be very indirect and in any case were found in the piety of the cloister which is stamped upon Luther. The reformer did not need to read Augustine to discover the theme of humility! In any case, it is useful to note these convergences, and useful also to see that Luther, like Augustine, does not see the humiliated Christ only from the point of view of a spirituality of the imitation of Christ, but also in the perspective of a theology of revelation, the revelation of God hidden in weakness. One could complete this list of christological themes of Saint Augustine which could have influenced Luther. Thus, as a working hypothesis. Congar speaks of the "way in which Luther conceives of the unity of the 'person' of Jesus Christ as constituted of two natures," and Congar speaks of the themes:

1) of Christ taking our weakness in order that he may communicate to us the riches of God,

2) of Christ and us forming *una persona*.[30]

One could perhaps, according to Congar, find on these points a dependence of Luther upon Saint Augustine. We simply note this hypothesis without discussing it here. One thing seems certain: Luther took up these themes from the early church. But can one single out Saint Augustine for the privilege of being the source of Luther's thought?

Medieval Christology

Christological considerations which followed the Council of Chalcedon in 451 had, as their main objective, a sharpening and clarification of the definitions.[31] The council had spoken of "one and the same Christ, made known in two natures, without confusion, without conversion, without division, never to be separated, the distinction of natures having been in no way abolished through the union, but rather the property of each nature being preserved and meeting in one person and one unique hypostasis." [32]

The Alexandrian theologians feared that the "one being" of the incarnate Christ would be put in question by the Chalcedonian Definition. It is known that the head of this school, Cyril of Alexandria, had even spoken of the unique nature of the incarnate Christ. The christological discussions which followed upon Chalcedon sharpened the meaning of the hypostatic union, in the sense of admitting that at no moment did the human nature of Christ exist separately from the divine hypostasis (John the Grammarian) post-Chalcedonian christology emphasized equally the unity of the divine-human when speaking of the suffering of the Word *(unus ex trinitate passus est in carne)*, which gave rise to the controversy called Patripassianism. Following Cyril and formulating the doctrine of the *enhypostasis* of the human nature in the person of the Logos,[33] Leontius of Byzantium contributed and had recognized an Alexandrian interpretation of the Chalcedonian Definition at the Council of Constantinople in 553.

Finally it is necessary to discuss the dispute over the two energies or wills of Christ. Do the two natures signify that there are also two wills in Christ (Maxentius the Confessor)? Or must one emphasize the unity of the acts of Jesus and of the Father to the extent of speaking of only one will (Monotheletism)? It may be asked to what degree the idea of *substance* made possible a resolution of such a problem. In any case the Council of Constantinople (680) proclaimed the two wills of Christ: a divine will and a human will, the latter, in fact, being inserted into the former (Duotheletism).

All this post-Chalcedonian evolution was systematized by John of Damascus, who also developed the older concept of a communication of attributes, in the sense of a true participation of each of the two natures in the properties of the other *(perichoresis)*.

We have deliberately given a glimpse of the post-Chalcedonian development of christology because the themes discussed are found again in the christology of Luther.

He also speaks of the communication of attributes in the sense of John of Damascus [34] and equally of the suffering of God. Concerned about the unity of the person of Christ, he seems to have been largely sympathetic to the Monothelites.

To what extent did Luther know and consciously take over certain themes of post-Chalcedonian christology? The question is still poorly understood. In his *Treatise on the Councils and the Churches*, Luther stopped at Chalcedon.

But even if the question of dependence is left in suspense, it is necessary to look again at the convergences. In any case, Chalcedon required an interpretation. All this took Luther in the direction of the theology of Alexandria and also toward its post-Chalcedonian representatives, that is to say toward that theology which strongly affirms the unity of God and humanity in Jesus Christ.

This way of thinking developed above all in the East. The West took a less active part in the formulation of christology, properly understood—that is to say in the elaboration of definitions concerning the person of Christ. One should note however that since Tertullian there had existed in the West a certain tendency to emphasize the independence of the man Jesus in relation to God.

Little by little, however, post-Chalcedonianism was imposed everywhere and most notably in the Adoptionist controversy of the eighth and ninth centuries. During the Middle Ages the discussion of the person of Christ slipped into the background. The great achievement of medieval christology was to have described in a rigorous and systematic way the *work* of Christ. This was the great merit of Saint Anselm. However, theologians continued to meditate upon the mystery of the person of Christ and to clarify one or another point.[35]

It is necessary to note in particular one christological concept which to a certain extent prefigures the thought of Luther. It is connected with the thought of two German theologians of the twelfth century, Gerhoh and Arno de Reichenberg.[36] Without knowing of Cyril and without being great systematizers, they nevertheless linked themselves to the christology of Alexandria. But their ideas are peculiar to themselves. By struggling against the dialectic common in other Scholastic theologians, who separated the humanity too much from the divinity, these two theologians insisted upon the divinity of the man Christ to the point of falling into a certain amount of Monophysitism. One should also note that this christology led them to elaborate a doctrine of the ubiquity of Christ which prefigures somewhat some of the ideas of Luther on this subject. We shall content ourselves here with noting a certain parallelism between

Luther and these two theologians, leaving the question of any dependence open.

Other Scholastic theologians of the twelfth century sought rather to establish some kind of independence of the humanity of Christ within the hypostatic union. According to them, this was a necessary condition in order to conceive of the work of Christ as a cooperation between divinity and humanity.

It appears that Luther knew very little of what has been called high Scholasticism. For example, to what extent has Luther read the writings of Saint Thomas? He does not appear to have been very familiar with his thought. It is not for us to analyze the reasons given for this lack of familiarity, which may be surprising to us. But the opinion of Congar is certainly worth quoting: "It is apparent to us that Luther has left to one side or deliberately discarded certain developments of Scholastic theology in matters concerning christology." [37] In any case, Luther knew the *Sentences* of Peter Lombard, that classical Scholastic manual of the twelfth century on which he has commented. And he read deeply in the writings of theologians who came after Saint Thomas and who often opposed Thomas: Duns Scotus, Occam, Gerson, Pierre d'Ailly, and above all Gabriel Biel. The current of thought represented by these authors was dominant toward the end of the Middle Ages and it constitutes the theological climate in which Luther grew up.[38]

Concerning the christological opinions of these theologians whom we shall call Occamists, we shall confine ourselves here to a few remarks,[39] depending much upon the works of Heiko Oberman [40] and R. Schwarz.[41]

Peter Lombard has listed three ways of understanding the union between the two natures of Christ. According to the first, Christ was a complete man assumed by the Logos and not uniquely a human nature. According to the second, each nature subsists normally in itself (that is, has its own supporting structure). But in the incarnation the human nature subsists in the divine nature. Only one and the same *hypostasis,* namely the divine Logos, supports the two natures, i.e., the human nature, composed of body and soul, and the divine nature. The third way of understanding this union considers, above all, the immutability of the divine. God cannot change and he did not change in the incarnation. He put on a human nature, taking off at the same time certain fundamental attributes, like a cloak.[42]

Since Saint Thomas, it has in fact been the second way of understanding this union which expresses the official doctrine of the church. As for the Occamist theologians, they were preoccupied with preserving the true humanity of Christ and thus avoiding an overly strong union of humanity and divinity. Duns Scotus strove to show that the human existence of Christ does not end with the hypostatic union. Although subsisting in the divine *persona*, it had its own way of existence; otherwise Christ would not have been able to die on the cross. There is here an obvious effort to emphasize the true humanity of Christ.

Occam, d'Ailly, and Biel set themselves against any way of understanding the union in which the human nature constituted with the divine *persona* only one *persona*. In its union with the Logos the humanity of Christ does not become *persona* in the sense of the Logos being the *persona*. That would be an illicit divinization of humanity. It must rather be said, according to Occam, that "the human nature is supported by the divine person *(sustentificatur)*." According to this conception, the human nature does not become itself a *persona*, but in the union with the Logos it is realized in a concrete and individual existence—even if it had been able by itself to manifest itself as an individual being. The human nature has not then received a personal being. It has lost its subsistence in itself and exists in unique dependence upon its support, which is the Logos.

In this christology one can observe that there is from the start a distinction which is strongly felt between the two natures. The uncreated being of the Logos must be radically distinguished from the created being. That is why the humanity of Christ does not become a *persona* in the union with the Logos. Thus the Occamist theologians have in certain respects been able to preserve the true humanity of Christ without thereby falling into Nestorianism. It was a middle way between the concept of the man assumed on the one hand, and the personification of Christ in the union with the Logos on the other hand.

But to return to Luther. What was his reaction to the christology of the Occamists? To what extent can one discern an influence of the Occamists in the elaboration of his thought about Christ? One knows the severity of his judgments on the Scholastics.[43] According to him the Thomists (whom he knew less), as much as the Scotists, lack respect when they pronounce the name of God (WA 3, 382). They had all been led into error by Aristotle and philosophy. And Luther's concept of justification by faith was elaborated to a large extent in reaction against the Scholastic thought that he knew. Protestant authors have treated this subject sufficiently fully for us to pass over it rapidly.

But it must be noted that in certain passages, Luther also praises his masters, notably Peter Lombard, Duns Scotus, and Occam. He much prefers them to Thomas and the Thomists. Besides, he evidently took up a traditional view and questions which were being debated in the theology of his time. That appears in his commentaries and above all his *Disputations*.

This is where we must situate the question of christology. A certain influence of Occamist christology is difficult to deny, even though Luther appears to have reacted little by little against the theses of Occam and Biel which we have discussed earlier. This reaction is felt particularly after the Eucharistic Controversy. In his *Disputations* of 1539 he is consciously opposed to Occamist christology.

It is in Luther's commentary on the *Sentences* of Peter Lombard that we trace most clearly a christology which might be termed Occamist. R. Schwarz has recognized there two characteristic traits.[44] For Luther, as for Occamist christology, it is clearly understood that one cannot attribute to the humanity of Christ that which properly belongs only to the divine nature.[45] Later, in contradiction to this, Luther will not hesitate to say that ubiquity, which is a property of the divine, is attributed to the human nature. There is another point in his commentary on the *Sentences* in which Luther follows Occam.[46] One says in christology, both that "this man is the Son of God" *and* "this man is not composed of a divine nature and a human nature, but of one body and one soul." One thus employs the word "man" in two different senses. The Occamists spoke of *aequivocatio*. In each of these two cases they explained that the subject, i.e. man, supports *(supponit)* a different thing. When we say, "This man is the Son of God," we are concerned with an affirmation of identity—"man" here means Son of God. When we say, "The man is not composed of a divine nature and a human nature, but of one body and one soul," we mean by "man" that human nature assumed by the Logos.

In this discussion, which may appear overly subtle, is shown again the care to distinguish the human nature that is assumed from the Logos which assumes it. When Luther comments on Peter Lombard, he still shares this preoccupation fully.[47] Later he will insist upon the identity, in the personal existence, between he who is assumed and he who assumes.[48]

We will not go more deeply here into the question of the influence of Occamist christology on Luther. It can suffice to show traces of this influence on the early Luther. We shall come back later to this when we consider the disputations that Luther devoted to the questions of christology between 1539 and 1545. But one interesting and astonishing fact must be noted. The christological questions debated by the Occamists began over the years to pass into the background of Luther's thought. One finds very few indications of this before the Eucharistic Controversy and even there these indications are of little importance. Luther is preoccupied above all with the following questions: How does Christ act in a saving way in human life—and how do human beings have access in a saving way to the reality of Christ? At the same time he highlights the human image of Christ.[49] Such an orientation is certainly due to Luther's concentration upon the Scriptures. But before we look at this fundamental source of Luther's christology, it will be necessary to examine yet one more source; we shall give it the general title of *medieval spirituality*.

Medieval Spirituality

It would be wrong to place Luther only in relation to a theological and dogmatic tradition. The man also lived in the environment of a certain kind of spirituality. Of course, this can be in accord with the dogma. In the best of cases, there is a constant correlation between the dogma and the spirituality of the church. That seems to have been the case in high Scholasticism, with Bonaventura for example. But there can also be a hiatus between theology and spirituality. The evolution of medieval theology in the direction of Occamism and Nominalism seems to have produced such a split.

Whatever the situation, it is important to place Luther and his christology in relation to the principal currents of spirituality which he knew. We shall do that briefly here because we shall have occasion to return to this when we examine Luther's sermons devoted to the correct way of considering the passion of Christ.

There is a current of mystical thought, properly so-called, which has always been manifest in the Christian church under most forms.[50] We shall cite here above all Saint Bernard and Tauler.[51] But it is also necessary to speak of the great influence exercised on medieval piety by the mysticism of Neoplatonism, mediated through the writings of Saint Augustine, and even more through those of Dionysius the Areopagite.

Without wishing or being able to encompass the diversity of mystical currents in one formula, one can say that the object of all the mystics is to realize union with God here and now. What interests us in this study is first of all the place of Christ in mysticism. The different currents in mysticism separate on this point. For Dionysius, it is necessary to be raised from the finite to the infinite, to go toward the hidden and incomprehensible God. Christ has little place in this system. It is the uncreated Logos, that is to say, God outside of the incarnation, who matters most. But union with God can consist also of union with Christ. With Saint Bernard, Saint Gertrude, and Saint Mechthilde, as well as with Thomas a Kempis, the place of Christ is very much more important. This mystical current insists upon consideration of the sufferings of Christ which leads to repentance (mysticism of the cross), on the gift of the soul to the crucified (the nuptial theme) and on the imitation of Christ. This current continued to be represented in the 16th century with Saint Teresa of Avila and Saint John of the Cross.

It seems to us that Luther turned from Neoplatonic mysticism, but that one can nevertheless find in his work a certain influence of Saint Bernard, whom he quotes often in his *Commentary on the Psalms.* Certainly the reformer knew Neoplatonic mysticism by way of both Saint Augustine and Dionysius the Areopagite. And in his first *Commentary on the Psalms* he declares himself partial to a *"theologia negativa,"* a theology which takes account of God as hidden and incomprehensible.[52] But for Luther, God is hidden in the humanity of Christ. He never slights Christ as the Neoplatonic mystic did.[53] On the other hand, there could never be for the reformer any question of rising to God from the finite and joining in ecstatic union with him. Relationships to God are established by the Word and by faith. It is by this way that human beings have access to God hidden in Christ.[54]

But on the other hand, a mystic who placed emphasis on Christ crucified, on the contemplation and imitation of his humanity, was sympathetic to the reformer. The idea of an intimate union between the believer and Christ was very close to his heart. There seems to be an influence of the mystics there which has not always been acknowledged. Too often Luther's teaching of salvation *propter Chris-*

tum has been interpreted in juridical and concrete terms. Thus persons are said to be justified by an act of God, who would not impute to them their sins because of Christ and his work. This legal concept is certainly not false in itself, but it is incomplete. It does not sufficiently take into account the fact that Christ is present and that the believer is united to him in an indissoluble way. As the apostle says, "It is no longer I who live, but Christ who lives in me" (Gal. 2:20). Luther rediscovered this emphasis in a more emphatic way in certain of the mystics. One will thus encounter in his writings certain themes current among the mystics who tried to describe the union of Christ with human beings. One rediscovers, for example, the marriage theme, according to which the soul is united to Christ as a bride is united to the bridegroom.

Certainly there are characteristic differences between Luther and the mystics, even those who are christocentric. Thus he is quite unable to minimize, as most of them did, the ontological difference which separates God from human beings. On the other hand, the union with Christ does not signify an absorption of the believer by Christ or a kind of identification between the two. Christ is simultaneously exterior to persons, to whom he offers himself through the Word, and interior in the framework of faith, until there is a very real communion of life and destiny between Christ and the believer.[55]

One may ask whether Luther's christology owes much to the mystical current represented by Eckhart, Tauler, and Suso. In 1515, the reformer discovered Tauler with enthusiasm. According to his own account, he discovered in Tauler "a theology more solid and more sane than in all the scholastic doctors of all the universities" (WA, 1, 557). One knows that he refers here to intellectual mystics, for whom speculation has a dominant role, far more than to Saint Bernard or the mystics associated with him. We cannot deny a certain spiritual affinity here with Dionysius the Areopagite. It is not necessary for us to dig out, in a general way, the question of the direct influences of this mystical current on the thought of Luther. Luther certainly did not follow its speculative orientation, even if we do find in his writings certain expressions current in Tauler's writings, for example. As for the bond of the believer with Christ, one can find some parallels. Luther too can speak, somewhat like Meister Eckhart, of the birth of Christ in the believer, but without sharing Eckhart's views on the divinization of the soul.

Meditation on the life and passion of Christ was a preoccupation found among certain mystics, as it was with Saint Bernard, but it is found also among spiritualities which we might hesitate to call mystical. We think of two writings which Luther quotes many times and which concentrate upon this meditation. They are *Meditationes vitae Christi* [56] and *Rosetum*.[57] The latter is an edifying discourse which dates from the end of the 15th century.[58] It is characteristic of that spirituality which is designated *devotio moderna*. This "new piety" stressed both a personal experience of the believer with God and the study and meditation of the Scriptures; it strove to renew the church within the framework of the existing institution.

It was concerned above all with meditation on the life of Christ and particularly on his humility. Great attention was paid to the passion, where the humility of Christ reaches its peak. The believer is invited to follow Christ along this way. Martin Elze points out particularly the fact that "the author of the *Meditationes* speaks constantly of the Lord Jesus and underplays the idea of his divine majesty which is signified by the title *Christ*" (p. 386). In the same way, he points out that "all is concentrated upon Jesus, while the mysteries of the trinity appear only on the periphery in this context" (p. 392). What can we conclude from a comparison between Luther and the spirituality we have just mentioned?

It seems, as Martin Elze has shown, that Luther followed the invitation contained in these writings, as also in the sermons of Saint Bernard, to concentrate on the humanity of Christ. In Luther there is also a definite concentration on the cross and on Christ's suffering humanity. That appears as early as his *Commentary on the Psalms,* and is particularly striking during the period 1517-1521. There is a definite dependence there. Luther was a man of his time. Particularly in the later Middle Ages, attachment to the cross was one of the dominant themes of current piety.

But three essential differences separate the reformer from this spirituality:

1. This spirituality insists less on the Christ of dogma than on the man Jesus and his imitation. For Luther, this man is, in a hidden way, the Lord. He speaks not only of the Lord Jesus, but of Christ. His concentration on the humanity of Christ certainly seems to overshadow at times the trinitarian questions, but as we shall have occasion to show later, the trinitarian basis is certainly there. And it is in

full conformity with the traditional dogma. Luther goes far beyond the piety and theology of the imitation of Jesus. He returns to the theology of the incarnation of the early church.[59]

2. Before he is the model to be imitated, Christ is, for Luther, the Savior to whom human beings must be united by faith. Following the terminology which Augustine used and which Luther has adopted, "Christ the sacrament precedes Christ the example." [60]

3. Another difference which must be pointed out and which again shows in a typical way how closely Luther is attached to the early church, is the relationship between the cross and the resurrection. These two are, in fact, bound together by a fundamental unity. Certainly it seems that Luther concentrated his attention essentially on the cross and on sin. But a fundamental *simul* unites the cross and the resurrection. The cross is never given preeminence over the resurrection. When Christ suffered and died, the resurrection and victory had already been given (WA 3, 63, 1; 432, 84; AE 10, 372).[61]

The Holy Scriptures

The essential source for any Christian theologian reflecting on the subject of Christ is evidently the Holy Scripture. It may therefore appear to be surprising that we have left it until now. But there are several reasons for this. First, Luther, like the rest of us, knew the Scriptures by means of tradition. We shall content ourselves simply to state this without being able to go deeply into the questions which it raises.

On the other hand, it was the reading of the Holy Scripture which pushed Luther to criticize the forms of traditional doctrine and contemporary piety. This is perceptible also in the area of christology. It is of the greatest importance for the understanding of Luther that we note that his first considerable works were biblical commentaries. It was by working on biblical texts that he became the reformer, not by commenting on the *Sentences* of Peter Lombard, which he had done a few years earlier.

If we place Holy Scripture as a source for the thought of Luther after tradition, it is for reasons of biographical chronology, not dogma. In addition, it seems to us that Luther familiarized himself simultaneously with the christological tradition and the Holy Scripture. It is only little by little that the Bible emerged and played that important role that we now consider characteristic of the Reformation and of Protestantism in general.

In any case, one must not conclude from this, as certain theologians and historians who belong to "liberal" Protestantism have done, that there is in Luther an opposition in principle between a biblical christology, designated as living and dynamic, and the traditional christology of the church, designated as Scholastic or speculative. It is an opposition which one is able to find more readily in Ritschl or Harnack than in Luther. The Bible certainly played a decisive role in Luther's thinking. But the reformer was far from putting in question the received doctrinal tradition on the subject of Christ. It can be affirmed, on the contrary, that he renewed that tradition from within. That is to say, he made evident, on the basis of the Bible, the theme of salvation with which all christology must be coordinated if it is not to become a mere abstraction. At the same time, he discovered (or rather rediscovered) in the light of the biblical witness certain aspects of christology which had been often neglected. We think, for example, of the humanity of Christ or of the correlation between the Christ, the Word, and faith. We shall have to come back to these points in the course of our study.

We shall not go, in any detailed way, into the relationship of Luther to the Bible, nor into the theme of justification by faith which he rediscovered, nor into his work as translator and interpreter. These questions have been dealt with often enough. But we must attempt to show how the Bible determined his christology. It seems to us that that can be considered from two levels.

We must, on the one hand, point out the passages of Scripture which particularly influenced the reformer, those that one finds constantly flowing from his pen. They are in some way key texts which oriented his christology in a completely typical way. We shall limit ourselves here to general indications, for we shall have occasion to return to this subject.

As Congar has rightly pointed out, those biblical texts speaking of the presence of God in Christ have acquired a particular significance for Luther.[62] Above all, one must quote Col. 2:9, "For in him the whole fulness of deity dwells bodily"; and John 14:9, "He who has seen me has seen the Father." [63] One could add other verses to these where the idea of the incarnation is expressed, such as John 1:14. It is striking, moreover, to note the particular importance that the gospel of John acquired for his christology,[64] even if one can wonder, as Walther von Loewenich does, whether Luther has interpreted the gospel of John in all its fulness. It seems to us that this gospel conveyed to Luther both the theme of the incarnation and the vision of Christ in glory, which goes some way to explain his insistence on the real humanity of Christ during the Eucharistic controversy. According to Karl Barth, Luther's christology is more closely linked to the gospel of John and the teaching of Calvin more to the synoptic gospels.[65] Without wishing to put that distinction in question, we must however define its implications. We shall show in our analysis of the sermons of Luther that he also used those biblical affirmations which bring out the real humanity of Christ.

Luther is also evidently indebted to Pauline thought on the subject of Christ. Here we need only mention the importance for his christology of the great christological passage in Philippians (2:5-11). We shall have occasion to come back to this, but there are two Pauline verses that must give us pause for thought now. One is 2 Cor. 5:21: "For our sake he made him to be sin who knew no sin, so that in him we might become the righteousness of God"; the other is Gal. 3:13: "Christ redeemed us from the curse of the law, having become a curse for us." These texts are in some way the source of Luther's soteriological concepts. The reformer derives from them the idea that Christ has not only become human, but that he has in some measure become identified with our sin.[66] On this point he passes beyond the theology of the incarnation as it is found in the early church. He also found in 2 Cor. 5:21 an exchange between Christ and his righteousness and human beings and their sin. We shall see that we are here concerned with a very important element of his thought. That is as far as we will go here in the exposition of the biblical sources of Luther's christology. It would still be necessary to speak of the influence of the epistle to the Hebrews, of the christological interpretation of the Psalms, or of certain particular biblical texts (e.g., 1 Peter 1:18-19; 2:24). But the essentials have been indicated, and we shall have occasion to return to all these questions. We must also leave to one side the question raised by the Catholic historian J. Lortz as to whether Luther was a *Vollhörer* (totally attentive to the whole) of the Holy Scriptures. In matters concerning christology, did he adopt the witness of the Bible in its fulness? We can only give here and there a few brief indications of an answer to that question.

It is not enough simply to indicate, as we have just done, the key biblical passages used by Luther in developing his christology; we must raise the question of his interpretation of the Scriptures. The Scriptures have, in fact, nourished christologies of very different kinds. And almost all the heretics have appealed to Scripture as their authority. One cannot therefore pass by the principles of hermeneutics, the rules by which a text is interpreted. One soon discovers that the hermeneutics of Luther had clear consequences for his christology, while his christology has born fruit in his hermeneutics.[67] We shall begin by dealing with the manner in which Luther made use of the traditional fourfold method of exegesis at the beginning of his work in order that we might go on to examine in the next section the way in which his hermeneutic developed.

In his series of lectures on the Psalms, Luther made use of the fourfold method of exegesis current in his time.[68] He explained the principles of this method himself in the preface to the special edition of the text of the lectures written for his students.[69] According to this method, a biblical text can be interpreted in four ways. First, literally. That means (for Nicholas of Lyra, for example) making a historical exegesis, questioning the reported facts. But for others, *literal* was synonymous with *prophetic* or *christological*. These latter would say that when dealing with the Psalms, for example, one should not question the piety of David, but should put the prayers into the mouth of Christ. Besides the literal meaning there was the allegorical, the tropological, and the anagogical. In the framework of this fourfold exegesis, the allegorical interpretation refers to the church. It would then perhaps be more accurate to refer to this as the *ecclesiological* meaning. There is then the *tropological,* which is the way one applies a text to the believing individual. Finally, one applies the *anagogical* method, which shows things to come, the eschatological.

We have already seen that Luther adopted the traditional christological interpretation of the Psalms and that, at least in the beginning, he used the fourfold exegesis. That needs to be emphasized. By taking over the christological interpretation, he places himself beside Faber Stapulensis and the early church and is opposed to the strictly historical interpretation of certain Humanists.[70] If the christological interpretation was not new, we must point out the energy and the exclusive way in which Luther employed it, not hesitating, as we shall see a little later, to put into the mouth of Christ himself some of the most dolorous exclamations of the Psalms.[71]

But while Faber Stapulensis had for his part renounced the fourfold exegesis, which had often become forced and arbitrary, in order to concentrate on the literal historic sense and the literal prophetic sense (the christological),[72] Luther nevertheless begins to use the fourfold exegesis. The literal sense, which for him is always the christological, comes to be the starting point for the fourfold exegesis. For Luther it is, *"fundamentum ceterorum, magister et lux et author et fons atque origo"* (*WA* 4, 305, 3ff.). "The foundation of the rest, the master and light, the author and fountain and origin" (*AE* 11, 414).

It is possible to make three principal remarks about the way in which Luther uses the fourfold exegesis. One must note first of all that he attributes even the most realistic of the Psalms to Christ. In the second place, one must point out the concentration of his attention on the tropological. Finally one needs to look at the original way in which he ties together the literal (i.e., christological) and the tropological senses. Let us examine these three aspects of his hermeneutics one by one.

We had already remarked in relation to Saint Augustine that one of the difficulties of traditional exegesis arose in connection with the penitential Psalms. Could one really put them into the mouth of Christ? Could one realistically speak of him being abandoned on the cross and being crushed by sin? In a system of thought where the impassibility of God, a Platonic heritage, was not in doubt, there was need for a solution to such a problem. One could overcome the difficulty by saying that Christ spoke *in persona ecclesiae* in these passages. That is the origin of the allegorical meaning given to these psalms. "Thus a certain arbitrariness is introduced into the interpretation, since it is left to the good will of the individual interpreter to know which verses of the Psalm to apply to Christ and which to the church." [73]

For his part Luther does not hesitate to apply the most realistic passages to Christ *in persona sua*. Thus the cross of Christ, his true humanity, will be vigorously affirmed in the *Commentary on the Psalms*. All his interpretation of Scripture in any case is a commentary on the cross. "For the cross of Christ occurs everywhere in the Scriptures" (*Crux enim Christi ubique in Scripturis occurrit* (*WA* 3, 63, 1). To the theology of the incarnation which he inherited from the early church he adds the theology of the cross.[74] It is Christ crucified who stands at the center of his reading of the Scriptures. It is to Christ that humility is attributed in the first place. He is the man of sorrows.[75] He is abandoned by God in the presence of sinners (*WA* 3, 623, 2; *AE* 11, 14). He weeps in torment (*WA* 3, 70, 28; *AE* 10, 78). He suffers the pains of hell (*WA* 3, 121, 32; *AE* 10, 115). Saint Augustine had seen the suffering only from the point of view of the physical crucifixion.

In the second place we must emphasize how Luther concentrates attention on the tropological sense. In the comment on Psalm 77 he speaks of the tropological sense as being the principal meaning *(primarius)* of Scripture. It would be wrong to conclude from this that Luther would sacrifice or neglect the literal (or christological) sense, or that he no longer concerns himself with Christ, but only with the believer. The tropological sense is *'primarius'* in relation to the remaining two senses of the fourfold exegesis, the allegorical and anagogical.[76] We have already seen that, unlike the method of Saint Augustine, the allegorical meaning which referred to the church had slipped somewhat into the background in Luther's thinking. In any case, it no longer appears as the connecting link between the literal (christological) and tropological meaning. If Luther insists then on the tropological sense, it is only in relation to the *two* others. Luther also seems to emphasize the tropological sense as a reaction against an exegesis (such as that of Faber) which was limited to the literal sense. The reality of Christ demands to be applied to the life of the believer. Christ calls forth faith. There is no christology without soteriology.[77]

But the literal interpretation is not devalued. Insofar as it is christological, it is the basis of all the other interpretations. Luther reproached those interpreters who had preceded him (including Saint Augustine) precisely because their interpretations did not always have their bases in Christ.[78] "Even where the tropological interpretation is completely indicated, it can be communicated within only by the christological sense." [79]

Our third comment concerns the intimate bond between the literal (christological) and the tropological sense. The two together form an organic unity. All that is said of Christ concerns the believer, and conversely, there is nothing in the life of the believer that is not based on Christ. As such, this affirmation was certainly not new. But the tropological interpretation had little by little resulted in a certain moralism. The believer was invited to follow Christ, to imitate his example. With Luther, on the contrary, the tropological interpretation consisted of revealing Christ as the one who justifies believers. To interpret a text in a tropological fashion means, according to Luther, appealing to faith and announcing to believers what is given to them by the present Christ. This will be to present Christ as the only justifier of believers before God and will by the same token cause believers to renounce their own justification and to confess their sins.

Thus we are able to assess the importance of this hermeneutical method for Luther's christology. On the one hand, it allowed him to emphasize in a radical way the humanity of Christ. On the other hand, it makes clear the indissoluble bond between the events of redemption, as reported in the Gospels, and faith between Christ and believers. And it becomes clear that the primary connection that human beings have with Christ is not of the order of imitation, but of faith.

Once he had established the close relation between the christological and the tropological interpretation, between Christ and faith, Luther was able to abandon the fourfold method of exegesis which he had inherited from the Middle Ages. It is scarcely found again in the commentaries later than the Psalms. But one principle remains: all that believers find in the Scriptures must be interpreted in terms of Christ and his significance for salvation. This christocentric interpretation characterizes Luther's exegesis to the end. At the same time, Luther never ceases to pose the question: What does a passage mean, when interpreted in this christocentric way, for the life of a Christian? [80]

THE FIRST BIBLICAL COMMENTARIES AND THEIR CHRISTOLOGICAL THEMES

The Commentary on the Psalms (Dictata)

We speak deliberately of "christological themes" and not of "christology." For in this way we want to express the fact that these commentaries of Luther do not constitute a treatise on christology. Whatever be the place that Christ holds in them, they do not give us a truly worked out christology. There is rather a general orientation to be noted and several themes to be made clear. The christology of the *Commentary on the Psalms* has already been made the subject

of a work by Erich Vogelsang, but the alert reader will have no difficulty in noticing the points at which we differ from this study. We
shall speak in turn of the following themes: the central place of
Christ in the commentary and in the history of the world as seen by
Luther; Christ as the reality of revelation; the person and work of
Christ; Christ as the *cause* of salvation and as a *figure* of the Christian life; the reign of Christ.

It is necessary first of all to emphasize the central place which
Christ occupies in this commentary. We have already seen the principal reason for this: Luther practices the christological exegesis of
the Psalms. The importance of Christ in Luther's thought is repeatedly manifest when he emphasizes that Jesus Christ is not only the
center toward which the prophets and the whole history of salvation
point, but quite simply that toward which the history of the world
points—or to use Platonic terms, he is the central idea which gives
meaning to reality; he is what reality means.[81]

It is in him that all the opposites find their unity. The Commentary teems with dualism and paradox: [82] spiritual/carnal; hidden/
manifest; invisible/visible; heavenly/terrestrial; interior/exterior.[83]
All these paradoxes and tensions find their unity, and, from the point
of view of eschatology, their solution in Jesus Christ: *"Fere omnis
contradictio hic conciliatur in Christo"* (WA 3, 52, 24). Christ is the
simul who unites all contradictions: God and humanity, judgment
and grace, etc. And he is that, not only as an image or figure of an
ultimate unity that lies beyond him. But he is in truth that place
where all these things and contradictions have found their unity!

But how is it possible to know the mystery of Jesus Christ? This
question held the attention of Luther to a considerable extent, as
we have already shown. In fact, God is hidden in Christ. The humanity hides the divinity, it is the other side of God. A revelation is then
necessary in order to acquaint us with this hidden presence. The
instrument of this revelation is the Word, which reveals the presence of God to faith.[84] From this perspective it becomes necessary to emphasize that the christology of Luther is centered on the
resurrection, on the work of the Holy Spirit, and on the Word. Because God is hidden in the incarnation, the *clarificatio* is needed,
which is the work of the Holy Spirit by means of the Word. Now
the Holy Spirit is given only with the resurrection of Christ. So long
as Christ is not risen we are unable to grasp what he is. All the
mystery of his earthly life is directed toward the future, first toward

the resurrection, then toward the preaching of the Word, and ultimately toward the final glorification when we shall see him face to face.[85]

In the same way as God is hidden in Christ, he is also hidden in faith, in the church, in the Eucharist, in the Word.[86] In this regard, Christ is the prototype of all the outward activities of God. God is always present, and he always acts in ways that are hidden. In this connection Luther frequently uses the term *mysterium*.[87]

However, Christ is not just one place among many where God dwells. The presence of God in Christ is particular and unique. We must examine Luther's thought on this point and deal with the manner in which he speaks of the person of Jesus Christ in the Commentary.

It appears that Luther took over the traditional trinitarian doctrine [88] without any elaboration. It is the Son who is incarnate. Luther speaks of the preexistence of the Son (WA 3, 200, 12), of his eternal birth (WA 3, 364, 12). The Son has part in the rule of the Father, he is creator with him (WA 3, 261, 24). The Son is at the right hand of God (WA 3, 557, 35). He is himself in the bosom of the Father (WA 3, 502, 34; 595, 14). Luther emphasizes on the other hand the equality of persons (WA 3, 233, 20; 461, 6) and yet he takes over the explanation of Peter Lombard, according to which the incarnation is only a continuation of a subordination which already existed in the heart of the Trinity (WA 3, 37, 21).

In the explanation of his text Luther evidently speaks less of intertrinitarian relationships than of the relation of the incarnate Son to his Father, as it is manifest in the prayers of the Son. Luther is concerned with relationships that we know of from revelation. There is one passage, picked out by Father Congar, where Luther seems to make little of the case for trinitarian dogma.[89] In fact it is not the trinitarian dogma that Luther puts in question. But this dogma, according to him, is mere "flesh," without any link to the spiritual, when there is no faith. Luther says that of all dogmas! This certainly does not mean that he dropped the trinitarian dogma.[90] About the same period, he explained himself at some length on this subject in a Christmas sermon.[91] We shall have occasion again to study the question at greater depth when we come to the text of the sermons of 1522. Certainly Luther does not go deeply into the trinitarian problem in the *Commentary on the Psalms*. But he is roused against those who speak of the Trinity with disrespect.[92] It is not the Trinity as such that is in question, but rather a certain manner, too speculative and irreverent, of speaking about it.

So far we have seen what Luther says on the subject of the person of Christ in his relationships within the Trinity. We must now ask how he describes the incarnate Christ. He is "God incarnate," that is the fundamental statement which we have already emphasized.[93] "God has been seen by the Jews, and he appeared in the flesh" (*WA* 3, 545, 13; *AE* 11, 31). Christ is God, hidden under the weakness of the flesh (*WA* 3, 547, 24; 548, 8; *AE* 11). He was "like unto us in our humanity" (*WA* 3, 625, 15). In Christ, God participated in our flesh (*WA* 3, 265; 6, 16, 18, 23). Christ is God and human (*WA* 3, 134, 28; 319, 22ff.; 364, 19; 373, 20; 467, 19; 4, 408). The incarnation can express itself by the image of the Word transmitted by the voice (*WA* 3, 157, 30). This is another traditional means of expression. The incarnation carries with it the mystery of the virgin birth to which Luther frequently refers (*WA* 3, 459, 10; 136). At several points, he specifies the particular character of the incarnation: the divinity dwells in Jesus bodily *(corporaliter)* (*WA* 3, 162, 5; 484, 27). He uses both terms *corporaliter* and *hypostatice* (*WA* 3, 387, 6; 388, 1).[94] (These references can all be found in *AE* vols. 10 and 11).

There are very few concrete details about the man Jesus. Luther hesitates to speak of the faith of Christ, but he attributes to him hope (*WA* 4, 267, 1). He speaks of the active obedience of Christ. God does not desire a passive victim (*WA* 3, 225, 11). Christ is the first to have accomplished the law *hylari et libera voluntate* (by a beautiful and free will) (*WA* 3, 17, 3). As a balance to this, there are many statements made by Luther that prove he saw the incarnate Christ above all as a suffering man. He highlights the weakness of the flesh (*WA* 4, 82, 32ff.), the forsaking on the cross (*WA* 3, 450, 18). We have already noted this orientation of Luther's thought. The weakness of Christ has a precise meaning. The incarnation has service as its goal. Christ became a servant in order that he might serve and fight for us.[95] He was made sin for us.[96] We are thus led to speak of the work of Christ.

How does Luther see this? In fact, one finds in him diverse ideas from the tradition which he inherited. He speaks of the struggle against the devil (*WA* 3, 562, 22; 565, 2). Christ saves us from our sins and from the power of the devil (*WA* 3, 604, 15). He has destroyed sin and carried off the victory over death (*WA* 3, 613; 19; 393, 2). Without going into details, Luther speaks of propitiatory suffering (*WA* 3, 207, 5; 27; 607, 14). He speaks of the sacrifice of Christ "for us" (*WA* 3, 157, 13; 225; 613). There is an interesting explanation in his writings, that Christ has in some way inserted us into his sacrifice on the cross. Thus he can write: "His cross was the altar on which He was Himself given for us, offering us up in Himself" (*AE* 11, 141; *WA* 3, 646, 13). He suffered according to the will of God, for the sins of human beings (*WA* 3, 171, 11; 288, 2; 304, 12; 316, 6). Our sins constitute his punishment (*WA* 3, 418, 27). He appeased God (*WA* 3, 276, 11-15) and saves us from his wrath (*WA* 3, 174). He is our mediator (*WA* 3, 211; 229, 11; 238, 15; 337, 39). Luther speaks, still in accordance with tradition, of the *meritum Christi*, the legal right that Christ has before God, to the title of "meritorious" (*WA* 3, 106, 4ff.). In numerous passages Luther is content to state the fact that Christ is our salvation, without going into any details of *how* he is that. Christ is righteousness (*WA* 3, 621, 13). He is himself the beginning of salvation (*WA* 3, 53, 39). He is *salvatio*. The Father acts only "in Christ and by Christ" (*WA* 3, 132, 33).[97]

Luther's primary interest bears on two matters: on the one hand, to affirm that Christ is the source of our salvation, that he is our righteousness and our redemption; on the other hand, on the basis of this, to move the faithful to confess their sins, which is the best way to believe in Christ and in his work for us.

But a very important question is raised here. After what we have said so far it might seem that Luther had taken up an entirely traditional view of Christ, as the cause or the author of our salvation. Christ's life and his death, in a way yet to be worked out in detail, had established and effected redemption. Now, if we are to follow certain authors, Luther would not in fact have seen things in this way. On the basis of the fourfold exegesis which we have described above, he would first of all have stressed the role of Christ as example in the moral sense. Christ would be in his life and in his death a kind of figure or type. He would prefigure what was going to happen in the life of the believer. But he would not in any true sense of the word be the cause of the salvation of the believer. The believer would be saved by the all-powerful God to the extent that he or she conformed to the life, death, and resurrection of Christ.

It must certainly be recognized that there is nothing in the life and death of Christ which is *not* an example, in the sense indicated, for the faithful.[98] From the incarnation to the ascension, all appears as a figure, types of what the believer will experience. The incarnation and the ascension prefigure the humiliation of human beings and then their knowledge of God (*WA* 3, 124, 11). The divinity hidden in the flesh signifies the obedience of faith hidden in works. The incarnation is a figure of the birth of the faithful *nullo opere humano sola gratia dei* (*WA* 4, 463, 18). The crucifixion and resurrection of Christ are types of the Christian life (*WA* 4, 390, 21). To preach Christ crucified is to preach *mala nostra crucifigenda et arguendos nos* (*WA* 4, 122, 126). Again, Luther can say, what Christ has suffered as head of the body prefigures (*significant spiritualiter*) what he will do and suffer in the faithful (*WA* 4, 264, 29).

Must one then conclude from all this that Christ is only a rather timeless figure? His life, his death, and his resurrection, were they no more than a preview? Is his presence in faith destined only to show the believer where God will lead him or her? Such a view certainly does reflect one of the biblical perspectives on the subject of Christ. He is the firstborn raised from the dead. He is the "image" (Rom. 8:29). But according to the Scriptures, Christ is not only a figure who illustrates or makes known what God is going to do with the believer. He is also the cause of salvation. The believer is saved by being united with that saving reality which is Jesus Christ. How does Luther present those ideas? Does he have this double perspective: Christ the *cause* of salvation and Christ the *type*?

We have already indicated above how Luther took up the traditional ideas about the work of Christ. Would he really have done that if they had had no importance for him? Could he possibly have thought of Christ apart from this salvation which he gives? Of course, with Luther one must point out something to which we shall return in the next chapter: Christ is not only the cause of salvation because of his work in the past. He is the cause also by his actual presence in faith.[99] We shall leave to one side for the moment the question of whether the young Luther insisted on Christ present in faith to such an extent that he neglected his work accomplished "once for all" on the cross (Heb. 9:28). What must be emphasized here is this: Christ signifies two things for Luther. First he is the righteousness which is given to me by God. It is the incarnate Christ, dead and risen, announced by the Word, which I present to God as my only righteousness. One also finds this theme already in the writings of the young Luther, although it may be less in evidence than the second theme, which is that of Christ as figure.

It is important now to show how these two themes are bound

together. At the foundation is the idea of Christ present in faith. Here the concept which is fundamental to Luther must be made quite clear, that of the *fides Christi*. Innumerable passages in the *Commentary on the Psalms* and in his later works put this forward.[100] It is at one and the same time faith in Christ and the Christ present in faith. One may remark in passing that Luther gave preference to the personalist aspect of faith. Faith is not primarily acceptance of supernatural truths, but union with a person, union with the present Christ.

The present Christ signifies two things for the believer. On the one hand, he is the righteousness which the believer presents to God. On the other hand, the *fides Christi* comprises a communion in life and in death between the believer and Christ. Where this communion is absent, the union with Christ is not real, and consequently Christ cannot be the justification of the believer. The communion of life between Christ and the believer, according to the tropological interpretation, means that the believer is transformed to the image of Christ present in him or her, or that the path of Christ going from the incarnation to the ascension is repeated in some way in the life of the Christian. It is necessary to die with Christ, descend into hell with him (*WA* 3, 432, 16), to be crucified and to be exalted with him (*WA* 3, 63, 32). Nevertheless, it remains clearly understood that it is not this conformity which saves me, but Christ who alone is my justification and my salvation. One can say also that the cross of Christ always has a double meaning. It is his cross, unique because it is propitiatory; and it is ours because we participate in it. In the *fides Christi* Christ is, on the one hand, the reality and cause of salvation, and, on the other, the image and type. It is by the *fides Christi* that we receive forgiveness of sins (*WA* 3, 175, 8). Again Luther can say, "We preach the crucified Christ, the power and wisdom of God, Christ or more precisely *fidem Christi*. For it is this faith which effects these great things."[101] And on the other hand it is by the *fides Christi* that we become "new people," people transformed to the image of Christ. We see that the young Luther has concentrated on the second theme. However, in our view while he has not made it depend on the first, he has related it to it.

There remains one last, but important christological theme in Luther's commentary to be looked at. It is his concept of the rule of Christ.[102] Luther obviously accepts the traditional view that Christ rules over the church. One can even say that the sovereignty of

Christ over the church will be more and more emphasized. While one finds still in the commentary the idea of a certain identity between Christ and the church (this in some way continues his incarnation), it is the aspect of his sovereignty which more and more takes preeminence.[103]

How does Christ reign? By the Word. Holl has already pointed out the importance that the Word assumes in the *Commentary on the Psalms*.[104] "*Rod of iron* is the holy Gospel, which is Christ's royal scepter in His church and kingdom." [105] The church is the royal throne of Christ, there Christ rules by his Word.[106] Besides, Luther speaks repeatedly, and already in the commentary on the *Sentences* of Peter Lombard of 1509, of the rule of Christ according to his humanity, a rule that he exercises by means of faith *(in quo ipse regnat per fidem)*.[107] One finds this idea taken up at several points in the *Commentary on the Psalms*. He speaks of the church *in qua Christus homo regnat* (WA 4, 399, 32), of the rule of Christ which he exercises now "as man and by means of the faith (of men) in the humanity which he derives from David" (WA 406, 4, 24ff.; AE 11, 548).

At first sight these passages are somewhat difficult to understand. Does Luther mean by them that Christ rules only as a human being now over the church? Of course not. Christ, who is in us in order to rule there, is not only the man Christ, but the Christ who is God (WA 4, 406, 26). But Christ rules now, "enveloped" in his humanity *(in nobis involutus et incarnatus in humanitate* (WA 4, 406, 31). This humanity is not only his historical humanity, but it is the church *(domus David propter humanitatem Christi [WA 4, 406, 22])*, the Word and all these outward things that Christ uses to rule over us and in us. But one day, Christ will rule in us *clare sine involucro humanitatis* (WA 4, 406, 29). The rule of Christ as a human being, such as we experience it now, concerns therefore the form of his rule. And because he rules in a hidden way, one must believe, that is comprehend, his hidden presence and reign both hidden under the terms of his humanity. That is why Luther can speak, rather improperly it is true, of *fides humanitatis suae* (WA 4, 406, 24).

But there is another perspective which must be brought out. In the comment on Psalm 123 which we have cited several times, there appears also the idea of a certain subordination of the Son to the Father. Luther quotes 1 Cor. 15:28: "When all things are subjected to him, then the Son himself will also be subjected to him who put all things under him, that God may be everything to every one." That signifies, according to Luther, that the rule of Christ, as a human being, by the Word and by the church, will come to an end one day. Then only the rule of the Father will continue, in which the Son will of course participate as God, but his humanity will no longer be associated with his rule.

The rule of Christ is manifest in the fact that he leads persons to confess their sins.[108] The Word of God strikes the saints (WA 4, 437, 30). The judgments of God are accomplished through the gospel (WA 4, 462, 34). This rule of Christ is unique. Only to him can one attribute a "causality" for the Christian life. He alone exercises this rule in which persons are called to faith and receive the new life. On this point, Christ is not a type or an image of the Christian life. Here a tropological interpretation is excluded.[109]

The Commentary on the Epistle to the Romans [110]

The second great commentary by the young Luther was on the epistle to the Romans. We know how important this close contact with Pauline thought was for the development of his own thinking. It is from the apostle Paul that he will learn what is to become the great affirmation of the Reformation: justification by faith. The epistle to the Romans is concerned with human justification before God and with the Christian life in general. It is precisely this which catches the attention of the commentator Martin Luther. If it is necessary to examine his christology, it is necessary to note the indissoluble link between Christ and the Christian life, between christology and soteriology. Neither in Paul nor in Luther do we find reflections on the person of Christ taken by themselves, detached from human beings and their salvation. Explicit christological texts are moreover rare, both in the apostle's and in the reformer's writings. With Luther it is a question of *fides Christi*—of Christ as *exemplar* and as *exemplum*—of justification by Christ, that is to say, always Christ in relation to human beings.

A christological passage of importance is the commentary on Rom. 1:3-4.[111] This passage deals with the questions of the incarnation, the two natures, the resurrection of Christ, as well as the problem of the revelation of the hidden divinity of Christ effected by means of the proclamation of the Word. We find in this text the importance of the incarnation in Luther's thought. We have already drawn attention to that. It is important to note that the theme of the incarnation never ceases to recur in his works. If in the *Commentary on the Epistle to the Romans* he is going to be concerned primarily with justification by Christ, he will also insist on the fact that the Christ who is the justifier of the believer is the same as the one who was made flesh. Justification is given to human beings in the person of a man who truly lived in the world. This justification is then no idea or dream, but a reality, as real as the body and blood of Jesus Christ.

The repeated appearance of the theme of the incarnation is important also for another reason. One often tends, when dealing with Luther, to insist one-sidedly on the theme of the cross. Of course it is right that one should point out his insistence on the passion of Christ and on the work that he accomplished on the cross. But it is equally necessary to note that the cross is not emphasized at the expense of the incarnation. It is better to emphasize the unity of the two themes when dealing with Luther.[112] By the incarnation Christ entered into flesh and by that same act, according to Luther, his suffering already began. But at the same time, as we have already noted, it is necessary to emphasize the incarnation as such, that is to say, this concrete existence of the man Jesus in the flesh, this union between God and humanity in Jesus Christ.

We shall examine, then, in the first place, the commentary of Luther on Rom. 1:3-4 in order to extract from it his affirmations on the incarnation, the resurrection, and the rule of Christ. In the second place we shall study how Christ brings salvation to human beings.

The Incarnation, the Resurrection, and the Rule of Christ

The Way of the Son of God

In the passage which we shall study here, Luther makes clear which Christ it is that he wishes to speak of—or rather which Christ the gospel speaks of. Not the Son of God considered in his eternity *(absolute)*, but the Son of God become flesh and born of the race of David. The reformer does not thereby wish to reject all consideration of the eternal Son of God, but it is necessary to start from the Son *in the flesh*. We can talk of the eternal Son and of his way toward humanity only because we know the point of arrival, that is to say Christ in the flesh, and only because the mystery of this Christ in the flesh is revealed to us by the Holy Spirit.

Luther contents himself here to describe the way of the Son of

God, on the basis of revelation, i.e., Christ incarnate revealed by the Holy Spirit, in such a way that he goes from preexistence to incarnation. *Qui ante omnia fuit et omnia fecit, ipse nunc cepit et factus est* (*WA* 56, 167, 12). (He who was before all things and by whom all things were made, himself now has a beginning and was made.) That is a classical christological affirmation. But Luther's interpretation goes off in a typical direction when he points out the weakening which the incarnation represents for the Son of God. He continues, *se exinanivit et infirmus factus* (he emptied himself and became weak), and further, *in carnis inanitatem nascendo inmundum* (emptied himself into the nothingness of the flesh by being born in the world (*WA* 56, 167, 20). Luther is not content to speak of the human and historical existence of Christ. What holds his attention is the word *flesh* with its associations of weakness. We find here once again the *theologia crucis* in its central place, such as we have already shown it to be in the *Commentary on the Psalms: "per humilitatem et exinanitionem sui factus est filius David in carnis infirmitate"* (it is by humility and by emptying himself that he is made the son of David in the weakness of the flesh [*WA* 56, 167, 16]).

The incarnation as *kenosis* [113] certainly does not mean that Christ by becoming incarnate abandoned his divinity or even part of it as some curious kenotic theories of the 19th century suggested. Everything collapses for Luther if Jesus Christ is not substantially God. The humiliation for the Son consisted in taking the condition of a servant, i.e., not presenting himself as God. He goes to attract to himself humiliation and suffering. The figure of Christ humiliated is going to be invoked at several points in the course of the commentary. [114]

But the way of the Son leads to the resurrection and glorification. A certain parallelism appears between the humiliation which leads him to the condition of a servant and the glorification which leads him from the condition of a slave to that of divinity. *"Ita secundum formam servi se implevit, usque in plenitudinem divinitatis ascendendo in celum"* (So, according to the form of a servant, he fulfilled himself to the fulness of God by ascending into heaven [*WA* 56, 167, 20]).

The Mystery of Christ in the Flesh

This manner of considering the Son of God is translated by Luther into the terminology and way of thinking of the doctrine of the two

natures. It is a remark of an exegetical kind that drives him to reflect
on the mystery of Christ in the flesh. He observes that Paul says of
the Son that he has been "created from David according to the flesh,"
but he does not say that the Son was created Son of God with power.
On the contrary, one reads in v. 4, "declared Son of God with power."
Why this difference? Jesus did not become Son of God only at the
time of the resurrection; from the incarnation, the Son is Jesus and
Jesus is the Son.[115] Thus there is no progressive union between the
eternal Son and the man Jesus. Already as an infant Jesus is the Son.

But what, according to our text, does this union of the two natures
signify for the divinity and for the humanity? For the divinity this
union means that it is hidden and that it must suffer; for the humanity it means an accomplishment and a transposition into divinity.
"Impleta est humanitas et in divinitatem traducta" (humanity is fulfilled and translated into divinity) he writes (*WA* 56, 168, 3).

It is rather difficult to know what Luther means exactly by this
"transposition of humanity into divinity." Is it only a traditional
concept which will later disappear? The question is basically this:
Did Luther envisage, on the basis of the communication of properties, a divinization of the human Jesus, and of human beings in him?
Do the premises of his thinking really permit him to draw that conclusion? Could one then link this somewhat to the Greek Fathers,
to Athanasius, for example, and to all that he meant by the term
divinization (theopoiesis)? Does the expression *traducta in divinitatem* suffice to give a reply to these questions, especially since the
expression seems rather isolated in the thought of Luther? It seems
after all to be rather weak when one compares it with the terminology of Athanasius, for example. *Traducta in divinitatem* seems to
suggest less of a transformation than an insertion into divinity.[116]
It is in being placed in the divinity, surrounded and supported by it,
that the humanity is made perfect. But is it not also a certain participation in the divine life? One is not able to exclude entirely the idea
that the theme of divinization was present to a certain extent in the
mind of Luther. The contrary would have been astonishing when one
remembers how familiar he was with the patristic writings. However,
it is certain that this theme takes a new turn with him. We see it in
another passage in the lectures on the epistle to the Romans.

In connection with Rom. 6:17, Luther writes, "Thus the Word
became flesh and assumed the form of a servant, so that the flesh
might become Word and man might assume the form of the Word;

then man becomes just, true, wise, good, gentle, chaste like the Word
itself, to which he conforms himself in faith" (*WA* 56, 330, 1ff.).
From this point of view, one can effectively speak of man's becoming
the Word. But for Luther it is less a question of envisaging a communication of the divine life than it is of seeing conformity of human
beings with God on the ethical plane. It is a question of the condition of God. What is important to Luther is less a participation in
the divine life than the personification of human beings, their hu-
manization when they again become the image of God by faith.

Has Luther concentrated on the unity of the two natures at the
risk of confusing them? This is a criticism often leveled against him.
We shall have occasion to return to this in connection with the controversy over the Eucharist. How can one reply on the basis of his
Commentary on the Epistle to the Romans? To the passage that we
are analyzing here, there must be added another passage in which
the concept of the communication of attributes appears. We have
already drawn attention to the role played by this concept in post-
Chalcedonian christology to emphasize the union between the two
natures. The concept has sometimes led to the Monophysite position. But the way in which Luther makes use of it in these lectures
maintains the distinction between the two natures quite clearly. Thus
we read in the notes on Rom. 7:18 where Luther compares the individual person, composed of realities as opposed as are flesh and
spirit, with the person of Christ, which he characterizes also as a
fundamental dualism: "The same and unique person of Christ is at
the same time both living and dead, suffering and blessed, active and
quiet, and so forth because of the *communicatio idiomatum,* although nothing that is proper to one of the natures is allowed to mix
with the other, but they are differentiated from each other in the
strongest possible way" (*WA* 56, 343, 20ff.).

Thus by affirming a communion of properties in order to emphasize the unity of the person, Luther maintains the distinction between the two natures very well. The divine nature is hidden in the
human nature, the cross hides the resurrection, weakness hides the
power of God. This conception does not confuse the natures, but is
turned toward the future, toward the time when, by the resurrection
and the proclamation of the gospel, God himself will unveil the
hidden realities in the incarnation and in the cross. This passage
shows that the concept of the communication of attributes does not

necessarily lead to the suppression of the distinction between the two natures of Christ.

The Resurrection and the Holy Spirit

As he comments on the text, Luther comes to the theme of the resurrection and the Holy Spirit. To speak truly, it is not so much the resurrection as such which is important for him, but the work of the Holy Spirit or once again the rule of Christ. We find again this concept whose importance we underlined in the last section. The entire passage he comments on here is oriented toward the rule of Christ; that gives Luther's christology a dynamic orientation.

Christ in the flesh is God hidden and not recognized as such. After the resurrection, his rule begins in the sense that the Holy Spirit glorifies him and makes him known for what he is, the Son of God in the flesh of the son of David. This rule is exercised through the apostolic Word. The real source of it is the Holy Spirit. By the public proclamation of the apostolic gospel, mediated by the action of the Holy Spirit, Christ is instituted in his rule. Thus he becomes the Son of God with power.

One is tempted to ask the following question: Is the resurrection of Christ identified in his rule, or is Christ raised in the preaching *(kerygma)*? According to our view, this would be to force Luther's thought. It is necessary to note carefully that in fact he places the Holy Spirit's work of revelation through preaching in a chronological relationship with the resurrection. "The Holy Spirit is able to do it only after the resurrection" (WA 56, 168,18). One is not therefore able to say that the resurrection and the glorification by the Word are identical. According to our text, the resurrection is both the end of Christ's passion and the condition necessary for the Holy Spirit to be able to do his work. But Luther does not linger over this problem. He does not question the fact of the resurrection at all. What is important above all for him is the work of the Holy Spirit, i.e., the glorification of Christ by preaching, the manifestation of what he has been since the incarnation, the proclamation of the divinity of this man who suffered. That is the true elevation of Christ.[117]

One finds in Luther the distinction between what Christ is and the fact of being recognized for what he is, which fact is linked to preaching. In itself preaching adds nothing to the being of Christ, and yet the mystery of Christ is not completed without the work of the Holy Spirit. The incarnation requires the preaching. Thus the

power of Christ as such calls his kingdom into being, which is none
other than the manifestation of the mystery of Christ for me today.
It is thus that christology is directed toward the Word and soteriology, without, however, being absorbed by them.

The theme of the rule of Christ will appear and reappear in the
commentary like a filigree, while there will scarcely be any mention
of Christ as the head of the body. It is the rule of Christ which is
important, and this rule is exercised by the Word. In the commentary on Rom. 4:17, Luther writes: "He is King and Lord of the people, over whom he has obtained a better victory than the Jews once
did over the peoples of Canaan. For he slew them spiritually by the
sword of the Word, making the impious pious. Thus he rules in
them, both in their lands and in their possessions" (WA 56, 294, 31–
295, 3). While he thus reigns in the hearts of the believers he is "the
king of the Jews, that is to say, of those who confess their sins (WA
56, 259, 20). This last affirmation does not so much portray Christ
the prototype as Christ the Lord acting through his Word.

Christ and Salvation

There are in the Bible a certain number of passages which try to
describe how the death and resurrection of Christ are the origin of
human salvation. Theological tradition has explained these passages
by speaking of the work of Christ as a reconciliation between God
and human beings and as a redemption, that is to say, a liberation
of human beings from their enslavement to sin, death, and the devil.

One finds very few remarks about this in Luther's commentary.
Of course, the text on which he comments only rarely lends itself
to such discussion, but even where that is the case, Luther passes
rather quickly over those Pauline passages which approach the death
and resurrection of Christ as the cause of salvation. Thus he hardly
pauses to comment on Rom. 3:21-26, which is strange because this is
the principal passage in the epistle devoted to the reconciliation
effected on the cross between God and human beings.

It would be wrong, of course, to think that Luther had abandoned
in one way or another the biblical and dogmatic concepts of the work
of Christ. He has a marginal gloss on Rom. 3:21-26, but he designates
the passage as "obscure" and "confused" (WA 56, 38, 13). That gloss
reads, "He did not wish to become this propitiatory victim for us,
except in first making satisfaction for us by his blood." It is thus
that he has become by his blood a propitiatory victim for believers.

If then Christ is the source of salvation for believers, it is because there is at the root his death on the cross and the gift of his blood.

Forgiveness of sins rests on the sacrifice of Christ. Thus Luther remarks in relation to Rom. 3:24 that the *gratis* concerns human beings. They receive salvation *sine meritis*. But from God's side a price has been paid.[118] However, Luther does not construct a system of reconciliation. He is content to note that the death of Christ is *satisfactio sufficientissima* (WA 56, 296, 20). But why was the cross necessary? Luther does not reflect on this here. Or rather he leaves it to the mystery of God. There are two points at which this becomes apparent.

In his comment on Rom. 1:24 he is led to criticize that line of thought which accuses God of condemning persons unjustly when they are not capable of doing good. Luther leaves the problem to the inexplicable will of God and remarks that this problem is analogous to that of the meaning of the death of Christ. The elect are saved only by means of this death and by means of salvation instituted by God. Such is the plan of God.

The same reasoning is found again in the marginal comment on Rom. 3:25. Christ agreed to die on the cross. His will corresponds to an eternal decision of God. Luther is able to say, as does Saint Anselm and the theological tradition in general, that the Son has thus acquired merit. The expressions, *meritum Christi* and *meritum mortis* occur here and there (WA 56, 75, 6; 290, 16; 359, 26), but they are used above all in a negative sense, in order to reduce our merit to nothing and to show the worth of the *propter Christum.*

The reserve with which Luther approaches the death and resurrection of Christ as the cause of salvation calls for some comment. Of course, one must observe that this reserve corresponds to that of the text on which he comments. But this is not enough, because there is more in Paul on this subject than there is in Luther. We must rather underline the importance for Luther of predestination and the all-powerful action of God at this point when he is commenting on the epistle to the Romans. God would also have been able to save human beings independently of the cross of Christ. Luther is a Nominalist on this point. It is not possible for him, as it was for Saint Anselm, to construct a system wherein the work of Christ appears as a rigorous necessity logically established.

Is this to say that the death and resurrection of Christ are in the last resort only figures signifying what is going to happen to Chris-

tians by the all-powerful action of God? We have already met this
problem in connection with the *Commentary on the Psalms*. In the
commentary that we study here, the concept of Christ as *exemplar*
in fact acquires a considerable importance, as we shall show later.
But it does not seem to us that we are justified in reducing the death
and resurrection of Christ in history to the level of a Platonic idea,
on the basis of Luther's silence—or rather relative silence—on the
subject. Luther insists on the present Christ as fundamental to salvation. He does not question so much the meaning of the historical
death and resurrection of Christ, but he affirms very clearly, it seems
to us, that the only righteousness that human beings are able to present before God is Christ.

The righteousness of Christ over against human unrighteousness—
that, in effect, is the theme that dominates the commentary throughout. It appears in many variations. Sometimes it is the righteousness
of Christ,[119] the righteousness which is his alone,[120] sometimes it is
the righteousness of God which is in his person,[121] which he gives,[122]
which is given in him,[123] or which God gives by him.[124] At yet other
times, Luther speaks of the righteousness of which Christ is the orig-
inator,[125] or again of his righteousness by which we are justified before God, because it is the only righteousness which is not judged
by God.[126] Moreover, the expression "righteousness of Christ" can be
associated with other terms and even replaced by another expression,
such as "grace." [127]

It is because of Christ and his righteousness that the believer can
be presented before God. Luther shows this in different ways. To
those whom he describes as "presumptuous," he emphasizes very
strongly that righteousness is not an idea or an objective situation
between God and human beings which would exist independently
of Christ (comments on Rom. 3:22 and 5:2). The "presumptuous,"
of course, recognize Christ, but they wish to be justified without him
and to obtain righteousness by their prayers and by their confession
of sins.[128] To that Luther replies in his comment on Rom. 5:2 that it
is Christ who is *protectio et adjutor*. He is *sol justitiae et salus* (WA
56, 299). The reformer had already expressed very clearly in his
comment on Rom. 2:5 that link between the righteousness of God
given to believers and Christ. When a believer is accused by his or
her own heart, he or she "takes refuge in Christ and says, 'He has
made satisfaction (to the righteousness of God), it is he who is justi-

fied, it is he who is my defense, it is he who has died for me, he has made his righteousness mine and my sins his' " (*WA* 56, 204, 17-19).

In his comment on Rom. 4:7, Luther develops his concept of justification with the aid of the term *propter Christum.* Sin is covered by the Christ (*WA* 56, 278, 5) living in us (*WA* 56, 278, 1-2). The righteousness of Christ covers the sin. Or again, on account of *(propter)* Christ, sin is covered and not imputed (*WA* 56, 280, 2). On account of Christ, God forgives us. Thus the righteousness of Christ does not become a quality of human beings. True, Christ lives in us, but it is by faith. Also, his righteousness does not in itself belong to us, but is outside of us. *"Tota justitia hominis ad salutem pendet ex verbo per fidem et non opere per scientiam"* (All human righteousness depends on the Word, coming by faith and not by words coming by knowledge *[WA* 56, 415, 22]).

Christ comes to us by the Word. "He is found entirely in each word" *(In omni Verbo totus est Christus et in singulis totus [WA* 56, 252, 11]).* Faith consists of renouncing the wisdom of the flesh, allowing oneself to be led, listening to the Word which comes to us not only directly from heaven, but which is addressed to us "by any just person, particularly through the mouth of a superior" (*WA* 56, 416, 5-14). One must be attached above all to the Word,[129] for it is evident that this Word, insofar as it is a proclamation of the gospel, presents Christ to us and also the acts of salvation.[130] The outward character of our righteousness then stems from the fact that it is bound to Christ, who comes to us in the Word. "All the benefits that we have in Christ come to us from the outside" (*WA* 56, 279, 22; 280, 3). We turn to him by faith and by hope. Apart from faith we have no access to Christ or salvation. Faith acquires a great importance in this commentary. In his glosses, Luther often adds to the text of Paul such words as *per fidem* or simply *fide.*[131] Thus two realities are important to obtain salvation. First, *Christ,* i.e., the presence of Christ, thanks to the proclamation of the Word; then *faith.* The union of these two realities, *fides Christi,* constitutes one of the dominant themes in Luther's thought.

When Christ is thus present in the *fides Christi* to save human beings, he takes upon himself the sin of believers and gives to them his righteousness. A kind of exchange is effected between Christ and the believer—what the reformer calls the "the joyous exchange." This theme, which is fundamental in the treatise of 1520 on *The Freedom of a Christian* (AE 31), is already present in the *Commentary on the Epistle to the Romans*.[132]

This theme appears in the Fathers, particularly in Athanasius and Augustine.[133] It came to Luther by way of the Christmas liturgy. But while in the Fathers it appears to us to be concerned principally with the incarnation in general (Christ becomes human in order that we might become "divine"), Luther limited the exchange to sin and justification. He adopted the Pauline interpretation of this ancient theme.

One will note in any case how often this theme underlines the active role of Christ in our salvation. He comes to us by the Word, gives us a righteousness which permits us to appear before God, takes from us the sin which separated us from God.

So far we have emphasized the role of mediator played by Christ and his work as Lord and Savior. But there are two terms in the commentary which present Christ from a slightly different point of view. These terms are *exemplar* and *exemplum*. They show Christ rather as the place where God is revealed. They put the accent on the model to which Christians must conform or the example which they must follow.[134]

One will note first of all the relative frequency of these two terms. It is astonishing that certain scholars have tried to make one or the other of these concepts the key concept of Luther's christology in this period when he was writing the *Commentary on the Epistle to the Romans*. Some have insisted on the term *exemplar;* others on *exemplum*.[135] For example, in a very notable study of the theology of the young Luther,[136] Ernst Bizer several years ago maintained the thesis that the concept of *exemplum* must be considered to be of prime importance. Until 1519 Luther would not have taught justification by faith in the sense that we have explained above, but rather a justification by humility. Christ would be the Savior in the sense that he reveals the way that we ourselves must follow, that is to say, the way of humility.[137] It is however understood that we cannot do it by our own strength.[138] Humility is not a work that we would be able to realize ourselves. It is God who realizes it in us. But in any case, Christ is then only the model. He is not the cause of salvation as he is in the perspective of justification by faith.

The use of the term *exemplar* belongs to what Luther, in his *Commentary on the Letter to the Hebrews*, calls the "theology of the cross." This theology tries to make clear the action and presence of

God in the light of the cross. God appears there as the one who constructs by destroying and who makes alive by killing. Calling often on 1 Cor. 1:18ff. and on the theme of the power of God being "hidden in weakness," Luther develops his "theology of the cross" in relation to the crucified and weak Christ, after whose image the Christian life is to be formed.

When he says that Christ is the *exemplar* for the Christian, he takes his stand on Rom. 8:29, where it speaks of Christ as an image of what God wants to make of us. And Luther remarks (*WA* 56, 83, 27-29) that merit is excluded since it is the action of God which enables believers to conform to the image of the Son. Christ is *"opus suum proprium et examplar omnium operum suorum"* (his own work and the example of all their works [comment on Rom. 8:26]).

Like Christ, believers live by dying, they are raised up by being rejected. Thus in his comment on Rom. 6:5, the reformer is able to say concerning a person's being buried with Christ, that the latter had prefigured the life of the Christian. In his turn, Christ appears dead and buried to the eyes of others.

In the comment on Rom. 7:18 Luther explains the anthropological *simul* (justified and a sinner) by the christological *simul* (God and a man, living and dead). Christ appears as the prototype of the action of God *sub contraria specie*. In effect, in Christ the most astonishing opposites are reunited: life and death, suffering and joy, activity and passivity (*WA* 56, 343, 18). This conjunction of opposites in Christ helps us to understand an analogous conjunction, equally astonishing, which one finds in Christians. Each is both spiritual and carnal, both justified and a sinner.

But Luther uses the term *exemplum* as well. He often uses *exemplar* and *exemplum* as synonyms to speak of Christ as an illustration of the road along which the action of God leads us or the way of salvation on which we must go. A certain difference can appear in this. When it is a question of the concept of Christ as *exemplar*, then what is envisaged principally is the all-powerful and mysterious action of the God of the "theology of the cross." Christ as *exemplum* is he who accepts this action in humility, and we follow him, with the help of God, as Ernst Bizer has judiciously noted. One should understand that, as distinct as they are, the two terms *exemplar* and *exemplum* are very often linked.

Thus in the comment on Rom. 1:16, Luther shows first of all that the power of God manifested itself in the weakness of the crucified;

as such, one could say that Christ is *exemplar* for believers. At the same time, he is *example*, model, in this sense that believers must hide (in the sense of destroy) their power and recognize their weakness, according to the image of Christ and in imitation of him (*WA* 56, 171, 5).

In the comment already mentioned on Rom. 6:4, Luther shows at once that the buried Christ represents the path along which God leads believers. One could talk here of Christ as *exemplar* by explaining the thought of the reformer. Looked at again, Luther invites believers to accept willingly this path by following the example of Christ.

In the comment on Rom. 9:3 (*WA* 56, 392, 7ff.), Luther evokes the figure of "Christ damned more than all the saints," then raised because of his love for God in his suffering. Believers are invited to follow this attitude. In effect, they too are going to be led to suffer, "some more, some less" (*WA* 56, 392, 12). May they be ready to follow Christ in his faithfulness.

We are not surprised to find several examples of Christ as example in the section covering chapters 12-15 (e.g., *WA* 56, 131, 22). It seems to us that Luther does not there fall back into a spirituality of the imitation of Christ, where faith and humility are identified, but, like the apostle, he wishes to discard all consideration of Christ which does not draw the believer after Christ, along the path of love and service. Thus in a particularly interesting passage (the comment on Rom. 15:3-4) Luther admits that one could object to the Christ as an example, under the pretext that what is said of him is said only of him *ad litteram*. But again following the apostle he observed, "What is said of Christ is also said for us, for our instruction, in order that we may imitate him. Thus we must not only understand it as a speculative affirmation about Christ, but (and note this) that what is said is given to us for an example."

We are not able to enter here into the details of the debate raised by the interpretation of Ernst Bizer. It is certain that one cannot fail to be struck by Luther's insistence in this commentary on the humility and necessary conformity of the believer with the *kenosis* (humiliation) of Christ. The fact that this course of lectures was addressed to monks does not sufficiently explain this orientation of his thought. Without wishing to deny *a priori* that the commentary could still contain some traces of pre-Reformation thought, we think all the same that the concepts of *exemplar* and *exemplum* could have inserted themselves into the concept of *fides Christi,* as we have explained so far.

Christ present in faith constitutes for believers the righteousness which they are able to present before God. But the Word by which he is thus offered to human beings equally transforms believers to the very image of Christ by making them pass through the way of the cross. There is no justification which is not at the same time accompanied by a destruction of the old person. God makes alive by putting to death, he raises up by humbling. It is the very principle of the theology of the cross. In other words, forgiveness and confession of sins, faith and humility, are bound up in an inseparable manner; without doubt they are as distinct as the two natures of Christ, but like those two natures, like the suffering and the glory of Christ, they cannot be separated until the last day.[139]

To the extent that he is the new human being accepting this path which passes through the cross in order to go to glory, Christ is effectively *exemplum* for believers. But how could he follow this example if he were not moved by the Word and united to the Christ in the *fides Christi?* We shall find the same problem in the next chapter with regard to the two terms, *sacramentum et exemplum.* And in the period 1517 to 1521 we shall again find the theme of the conformity of the believer to the humiliated Christ. The connection with justification by faith will appear very clearly there.

The Commentary on the Epistle to the Hebrews [140]

Luther commented on the epistle to the Hebrews in the years 1517-1518. That means that this commentary belongs partly to the period we shall be dealing with in the next chapter, that is to say the period of his struggle on the matter of indulgences. One cannot deny that this commentary is close to the "Propositions" which Luther wrote on the subject of the 95 Theses—particularly in his concentration on the cross and the theme of the "theology of the cross."

At the same time, however, this commentary is closely connected, by its form and by most of the christological themes which it treats, to the biblical commentaries we have already studied. It must be noted, however, that the text we have of this *Commentary on the Epistle to the Hebrews* does not come from Luther himself. It is derived from the lecture notes of one who heard them.[141] In spite of that, a solid continuity of thought appears when it is compared with the preceding commentaries.

Christ Seen in the Light of the Old Testament

It is necessary first of all to bring out the way in which Luther enters into the atmosphere of the epistle to the Hebrews which places Christ in the perspective of the Old Testament.

In this commentary we find again the christological interpretation of the Psalms. In connection with Psalm 8, for example, Luther takes the alternative interpretation to that of Augustine, Ambrose, and Chrysostom when he says that it is not necessary to attribute this psalm to humanity in general (WA 57, 2, 116, 10), but to Christ.[142] In the interpretation of this psalm one should also note that Luther holds to the Hebrew text when he is explaining the verb rendered in the Vulgate at v. 6 by *minuisti*.[143] In Luther's view Christ was not only "humiliated" by God, but "abandoned" by him. God failed him. God withdrew himself from him.

Let us also note the importance of the promises of God made in the Old Testament for understanding, according to Luther, the fact of Christ. It is within the perspective of these promises that the incarnation and the death of Christ are explained. In commenting on Heb. 9:10ff. he says, in connection with the covenant which God had made, that this term and the concept of promise already indicate that God is going to take flesh in order to die. In fact a covenant or will only becomes effective when he who made it dies. "*Cum (deus) enim non possit, et moriturum esse promittat, necesse fuit, ut homo fieret et sic impleret, quod promiserat*" (As God is not able to die, but announces that he will die, it was necessary for him to become human and thus accomplish what he had promised [WA 57, 2, 211, 20]).

Note once again the concern to place the incarnate Christ at the center. It is to Christ, come in the flesh, that the figures in the Old Testament refer, like the sacrifice of Isaac, the Ark of the Covenant, as well as the various promises. That is why Luther dissociates himself from speculative christological interpretations of the Old Testament texts. In commenting on Heb. 1:5 (Ps. 2:7), for example, he does not, of course, reject the interpretation of Saint Augustine and Peter Lombard, who found in the verse some indications of the eternal birth of the preexistent Son, but Luther preferred to relate the text to the historical birth of the Son by the Virgin Mary.

God Hidden and Revealed in the Humanity of Christ

The Theme of the Theology of the Cross

Once again we find in this commentary the theme of God both hidden and revealed in Jesus Christ.

We are not able to know God directly as the mystics or the speculative theologians think; it is necessary for us to go through the incarnate Christ. "The humanity of Christ is for us the holy ladder by which we ascend to knowledge of God. . . . Whoever would rise wholesomely *(salubriter)* to the love and knowledge of God, must abandon human and speculative rules for knowing the divine and must first exercise himself in the humanity of Christ. When God humbled himself in order to become knowable, it would be proof of the most impious blindness if human beings were to seek to find another way in accordance with their own inclination and their own designs" (*WA* 57, 2, 99, 1ff.).

The fact that God has thus bound himself to the suffering and humiliated humanity of the man Jesus in order to reveal himself to human beings is not self-evident. It is a mystery which Luther designates for the first time in the *Commentary on the Epistle to the Hebrews* by the expression *theologia crucis* (theology of the cross). The thought had earlier attracted the attention of Luther as a means of explaining the way in which the presence and action of God are manifest: God is present in weakness; he makes alive by death; he judges in order to be gracious. At the center of this *theologia crucis* is the suffering humanity of Jesus Christ. God hides himself there in order to reveal himself there. But he can reveal himself only to those who agree to abandon all preconceived ideas about God and who equally accept humiliation in their own existence. That is why the knowledge of God through the humanity of Jesus Christ requires of persons a kind of exercise in which they agree to be corrected in their ideas about God and their own lives.

The theme of *theologia crucis* will be in the forefront of our study of the years 1517-1521, and we shall have opportunity to give attention to it then. But one can say here, with Walther von Loewenich, that this theme is a basic principle of Luther's theology in general.[144] In fact, the key concepts of his thought are all linked to it: the role of the Word, faith, and the eschatological orientation of his thought. It is in fact the Word which calls on human beings to discover God under the abandoned humanity of Jesus Christ, at the same time as it sets in motion this exercise whereby persons confess their weaknesses as sinners. Only the gospel can transform persons *per fidem Christi* (*WA* 57, 2, 109, 18). Again we find in the commentary the idea of the rule of Christ, which is exercised through the Word (*WA* 57, 2, 108, 17; 109, 9). Because God is hidden under the humanity of Christ, it is necessary to have faith, i.e., this attitude which trusts the Word and accepts the presence of God in the weakness of Christ (*WA* 57, 2, 202, 15).

Finally, the eschatological orientation appears particularly clearly in this commentary. Now, God is hidden under the weakness; now, Christ rules as a man (*WA* 57, 2, 104, 17)—in the sense that we have already seen in the *Commentary on the Psalms*. But one day the veil will be lifted and "Christ will appear in his glory" (*WA* 57, 2, 202, 13).

The Person of Jesus Christ, God and Man

We must now see how Luther describes the person of Jesus Christ. The angels adore him, that is to say, that he is God. He is the God who has promised the testament and who comes as a man to die and thus to grant unto us the legacy. Luther repeats the classic affirmation that Christ as God created the world (*WA* 57, 2, 98, 14). In commenting on Heb. 1:1ff., Luther emphasizes the difference between the saints, the prophets, and the angels on the one hand, and Christ on the other. He alone is God. The reformer insists on the uniqueness of the Son as the reflection of the glory of God.[145] God is recognized in Christ, but not in us. For our part, we recognize God only through his image which we find in ourselves (*WA* 57, 2, 101,1). Elsewhere Luther discards all trinitarian reflections about this passage. Not that he questions it on principle, but he reckons that the text does not require it and can be understood without such reflections (*WA* 57, 2, 100, 2ff.).

Concerning the humanity of Christ, Luther emphasizes that he not only had a body identical with ours (differing only in his individuality, as we differ one from another), but that he was tempted like us, although without sin.[146] Therefore he can be high priest quite differently from those who must first offer sacrifices for themselves (*WA* 57, 2, 27, 16). Thus Luther does not wonder about the psychological being of Jesus Christ nor the general conditions of his humanity. He contents himself with stating, with the epistle, the reality of his flesh and of his temptations.

On the contrary, he insists at several points on the suffering of Christ. In his interpretation of Psalm 8 he speaks of him as of Enos, of the man abandoned, forgotten by God. He has suffered in the flesh, *"a patre derelictus"* (abandoned by the Father [WA 57, 2, 28, 12]). We notice, however, that Luther is not among those who isolate the cross from Easter and remain in the sentimental sadness of the cult of suffering. In fact, the epistle to the Hebrews leads him to think of the suffering of Christ as the passage of the high priest into the holy of holies. In other words, suffering is his way to glory, it gives him access to the Father. We find this idea clearly expressed in the comment on Heb. 10:19ff.: the rending of the veil is the flesh of Christ which dies on the cross. But this death is already the victory.[147]

The link between the cross and the resurrection is given by the mystery of the person of Christ. Christ, being not only a man, but also God, could not remain subject to death. "In his person, Christ was at the same time mortal and immortal, subject to death by his humanity, but in his whole person not able to die" (WA 57, 2, 129, 9). "Through his union with the immortal divinity, when he died, he vanquished death" (WA 57, 2, 129, 22). And it will be noted how many times Luther underlines Paul's triumphal assurance in order to proclaim the resurrection (WA 57, 2, 130, 8).

How did Luther envisage the two natures? The distinction and the union of the two natures appear at several points and under different forms. At times, Luther distinguishes the Christ as Son of man and as Son of God, at times he speaks of two sorts of times in which he sees Christ according to his two natures (WA 57, 2, 173). But it is in his death and in his resurrection that the union and the distinction of the two natures are manifest in a characteristic way, as we have already seen.[148] Christ can die as a man, but he is invincible as God. The union of the two natures assures that the humanity will not remain in death.

Christ and Salvation

Scholastic theology had questioned the way in which the human nature cooperated with the divine nature in Christ. Yves Congar summarizes the conclusion which his master Saint Thomas reached in the following words: "By his incarnation, the person of the Word assumed a second level of activities, those of a humanity like ours; he took the character of a concrete human subject (even though this subject was metaphysically not autonomous); so much so Saint Thomas speaks of a "composite person," i.e., subsisting in two natures and playing the roles of two concrete subjects of activity. Thus Christ was not only the place where God would vanquish the devil and exercise a rigorous justification, according to the triumph of his love; he was also, in his holy humanity, a secondary but real source of salvation.[149]

How does this matter stand with Luther? Is it possible for him to see things as did Saint Thomas and all the tradition of the Scholastics; i.e., to consider the divinity of Christ as the first cause and his humanity as the second cause of our salvation?

In the commentary that we are studying here, two passages give us some clarification on this subject. In the comment on Heb. 5:9 (Vulgate text reads, "obtemperantibus sibi causa salutis factus est"), Luther recalls the statement by Gabriel Biel [150] in which he says, "the man Christ is the mediated cause of salvation" (causa salutis mediata [WA 57, 2, 178, 2]). How did Luther understand this causality? The comment continues: "He is usually a sign, i.e., a cause to make us understand and to make us love."

This is not evidently what Saint Thomas or even Biel meant when they spoke of the humanity of Christ as a second cause of salvation.

With Luther these things are on the level of knowledge and example. As he reveals the love of God, the human Christ collaborates in salvation, but does not enter into the drama of reconciliation in a constitutive or meritorious way.

The idea of Luther appears more clearly still in the comment on Heb. 2:10. The Vulgate text speaks of Christ as "auctorem salutis eorum." [151] Luther makes the observation that he would prefer to follow Saint Ambrose and read, "leader, prince, or head of our salvation." In this he is keeping closer to the original Greek word archegos ("pioneer").

Five principal ideas come from this comment:

1. It is the Father who is the author of salvation, the Son as a human being obeys.[152]

2. But by the will of the Father,[153] the Son is an instrument of salvation, not by cooperation, but because he is idea et exemplar or signum et idea.

3. We are transformed to the image of this *exemplar,* but only in a relationship of faith with Christ.[154]

4. By Christ, God leads his children to glory.[155]

5. But Christ can be this instrument only by being himself made perfect by suffering (*WA* 57, 2, 126, 3).

Luther had thus not taken up the Scholastic ideas on the subject of a cooperation of the humanity of Christ as a free instrument or as a second cause. This thought and this concept are foreign to him. According to the texts that we have just looked at, Christ appears as the *exemplar,* the image to which God alone brings us into conformity. But we have already seen elsewhere that the concept of *exemplar* must not be considered a privileged term with Luther. We will see elsewhere that the reformer clearly describes Christ as a man who stands before the Father in the liberty of faith and hope. The concept of an "inanimate instrument" or the figure of a glove cannot be applied to him. However, Luther does not speak of *cooperation.* This concept seems to hold no place in his thought; or rather, he rarely employs it in his christology.[156]

Now for a second look, we shall examine how Luther describes the saving work of Christ as such. He approaches it from two viewpoints. He speaks from one viewpoint of the priestly office and from the other of his struggle against the powers.

The Priestly Office

The epistle to the Hebrews presents Christ as the supreme sacrificer who has reconciled God and human beings by offering up himself. One cannot say that Luther has plumbed the depths of this matter in the commentary. However, one finds a number of indications which we must present here. He observes that the image of the supreme sacrificer who takes away sin is characteristic of the work of Christ. In contrast to Moses, he not only makes us aware of sin, but he takes it away (*WA* 57, 2, 165, 23). In the comment on Hebrews 9:26 we read: "Christ is not announced to us as chastising sinners or as judge, but first of all as supreme sacrificer, destroyer of sin, and author of justice and salvation; and, an even greater consolation yet for afflicted consciences, he is not described as present with us, but present before God, there where he is most needed and where we are most accused and most guilty" (*WA* 57, 2, 54, 13-17). This supreme sacrificer is acceptable to God. He is himself without sin, and he is our only assurance.

It will be noticed that Luther does not engage in reflection concerning the sacrifice of Christ and the meaning of the cross. It is not a question of *meritum Christi*. Attention is focused on the fact that Christ has truly taken our sins on himself.[157] In this context the theme of joyful exchange also reappears: Christ has taken our sins, and he has given us his righteousness (WA 57, 2, 136).

The Struggle Against the Powers

The priestly aspect of the work of Christ is closely bound up with this other aspect, which is the struggle against the powers. With the help of Chrysostom, cited 39 times, this theme of the early church surfaces here in Luther. How are the two aspects related to each other? The supreme sacrificer not only carries sin, but he destroys it as he destroys death and the fear of death (WA 57, 2, 133, 10). The passage most explicit on this subject is the comment on Heb. 2:14. There he takes up again the image of deceiving "the devil deceived," which is already found in the Fathers, notably Gregory the Great. The devil is the author of death, also of the death of Christ. But in this latter case he is deceived. Christ does not remain dead. By putting him to death, the devil made his life appear. Thus he is defeated by his own weapons.[158]

However, Luther does not simply reassume the perspective of the early church. A shift has taken place. The reformer insists in a characteristic fashion on a reality which the early church only glimpsed—namely, the anger of God. To this anger, according to Luther, there is on the human side, a corresponding uneasiness of conscience, accused by God and confronted by the anger of God. It is what he calls *Anfechtung*.

For the early church (Athanasius, for example) the evil to be destroyed was death, sin, and the devil. In our commentary, Luther adds to that the anger of God (and later the law). One can never insist enough on this aspect of Luther's theology. The work of Christ stands out against this background. The terrible uneasiness of human beings does not come from the fear of death as a physical reality, but from the fact that after death comes the anger of God, the last judgment, the rejection. In such a perspective, Christ appears as the only salutary reality, in which believers may wrap themselves as in a garment or where they can shelter as in a safe hiding place.[159]

According to Luther a true understanding of Christ is only possible in the existential perspective of human beings overwhelmed by their sin and confronted by the holy God. It is in such a situation that the saving role of Christ can truly be seen.[160] "It is true that only the consciousness of sin makes death horrible, because 'the sting of death is sin,' nothing takes away the consciousness of sin if it is not faith in Christ *(fides Christi),* for 'it is Christ who gives us the victory.' That is why, in order to manifest the power of faith in Christ, God made clear the fact of death, judgment, and hell in order that the Christian might surmount them by faith" (*WA* 57, 2, 131, 22).

"Fides Christi." The Sacrifice of Christ, Unique and Repeated

The passage which we have quoted leads us to that other concept that we have already raised in the preceding chapters: the theme of the *fides Christi. Per fidem, fidei in Christo, fides Christi.* At three points, faith is underlined in this text where Luther has again taken up the theme of the struggle against the powers. The redemptive work of Christ on the cross is actualized in some way in the *fides Christi;* the battle continues there. It is not uniquely a cognitive phenomenon—faith becoming aware of that which took place in the past on the cross and applying that to itself. In a certain measure one can say that faith is a part of the redemptive work or again that Christ, the victor on the cross, wins the same victory in the life of believers. "Just as it is impossible that Christ, victor over death, should die again, so it is impossible also that those who believe in him should die . . . for just as by union with the immortal divinity, Christ in dying has surmounted death, so also by union with Christ immortal (which union comes through faith in him), the Christian equally in dying surmounts death" (*WA* 57, 2, 129, 16ff.).

At the same time, the text of the epistle furnishes him with the opportunity to approach an inevitable question, left a little in suspense until now—that of the uniqueness of the sacrifice of Christ. It is evidently in connection with Heb. 9:24-28 that this question is raised.

In the comments on chapter 8 (*WA* 57, 2, 44) he had spoken of an *oblatio caelestis* (heavenly sacrifice) offered by Christ, without being precise as to whether it is a continuing sacrifice or how it is linked to the sacrifice on the cross. In commenting on chapter 9 he repeats the affirmation of the text and is a bit more precise: "Christ has been offered only once" (*WA* 57, 2, 217, 29). How then can it

be a "repeated" sacrifice? Luther continues, "Why then has our sacrifice not ceased, since by the grace of Baptism and repentance we
are justified and perfect? Each day in fact Christ is offered for us
[here taking up the explanation of Chrysostom] . . . what is offered
for us each day is not so much the sacrifice as the memory of his
sacrifice" (*WA* 57, 2, 217, 25ff.). Luther explains himself again on
this subject when he points out the difference between the sacrifice of the head of the church (Christ) which is completed and the
spiritual sacrifice of the body (the church) which continues to be
offered. This sacrifice is the putting to death of evil tendencies, the
passage toward the world of the glory to come. And Luther concludes, "The sacrifice which is pleasing to God is faith in Christ
(*fides Christi*)" (*WA* 57, 2, 221, 15). In fact, it is Christ who is the
real subject of this sacrifice of faith.

Sacramentum et Exemplum

In order to understand clearly the christology which Luther develops in his lectures on the epistle to the Hebrews, it is important
finally to examine a phrase which appears several times: *sacramentum exemplum*.[161] The reformer found the association of these two
terms in Saint Augustine [162] whom he quotes on this subject in his
lectures on the epistle to the Romans.[163] The two terms appear already five times in these lectures, "to express the significance *pro
nobis* of the death and resurrection of Christ."[164] That is to say, to
show that Christ has not only died and been raised for himself, but
for us. He is the cause of the death of the old person and of the
new life of the Christian. He leads believers there. That is the
meaning of the word *sacrament* for Luther.[165] At the same time as
Christ is thus the cause of salvation—i.e., sacrament—he is also the
example. Thus the believer, dead and raised with Christ, must also
imitate him.

The association of the two terms in question, already present in
the earlier works,[166] is put into high relief in the lectures on the epistle to the Hebrews. Take first the comment on Heb. 2:3 (*WA* 57, 3,
114). There Luther distinguishes between the gospel and the law.
In other words what concerns him is to distinguish faith, and the
righteousness hidden in God which is given by it, from works, whose
righteousness is realized by the works themselves. Faith is characterized by the active presence of Christ in it. Works are derived

spontaneously from it. That is a concept which Luther will not cease to maintain.

It is into this perspective of a faith which abounds in works that the schema of *sacramentum—exemplum* is inserted. It is not necessary, according to Luther, to limit ourselves to considering what Christ has done for us (there is the sacrament), but rather to see that he has equally left us an *exemplum*. From this point of view, the suffering of Christ is a *sacramentum* to the extent that the death of the old person and forgiveness of sins are given by it. It is an *exemplum* in the sense that believers must imitate Christ and suffer in their turn.

To forget the order of the two terms, to want to commence by the imitation of Christ and forget the *sacramentum*—that is the danger Luther distrusts most. That, according to him, would be to confuse the law and the gospel, to wish to accomplish works apart from faith.

We find the two terms again in the comment on Heb. 10:19ff. (*WA* 57, 3, 222ff.). Applying the rent "curtain" of which v. 20 speaks to Christ and to his passage to the Father, the reformer remarks that one must not only think here of Christ *corporaliter,* but also of Christians. In this light the death and suffering of Christ are the sacrament—one could say they are the sign—of our repentance, or of the death of the old person. His entry into the heavens then becomes the sacrament of our new life.

It is proper to ask at this point how the death and life of Christ are a sacrament of the death and new life of the Christian. Does it mean—as we thought we saw in the preceding passage—that there is a true action of Christ present (by the Word and by the sacrament) on the person to whom he is united by faith? Or is it—and this question had already been posed in relation to earlier works—for Luther, only a matter of speaking of Christ as the type to whose image the Christian is transformed or must be transformed?

In the latter case, the term *sacramentum* would be applied to the interior person who must die according to the image of Christ, and the term *exemplum* would be applied to the outer person who must outwardly imitate Christ. It is in this way that Ernst Bizer wished to interpret the thought of Luther when he employed the schema *sacramentum et exemplum.*[167]

It is our view, in common with Erwin Iserloh, that Luther wished above all to distinguish Christ as *sacramentum* from Christ as *exem-*

plum in the sense that we have already indicated.[168] And when he speaks of Christ as a *sacramentum,* he does not think only of a figure—he is that too—but of Christ present who brings death and life to the believer—precisely of Christ who prefigures not only the Christian life or is only the model of our passage toward the new life, but also he who supports the believer who depends on him.[169] United to him, believers become capable of following him. United to him, believers, in their turn, take up their cross, suffering, and pain as punishment for his sin. But the one "who is outside Christ is not able to repent" (*WA* 57, 3, 226, 1).

A GENERAL OVERVIEW OF THE THEMES STUDIED

The Christological themes of the commentaries on the Psalms, the epistle to the Romans, and the epistle to the Hebrews have been expounded. A brief overview of the results of our study will bring to an end this first chapter devoted to the christology of Luther up to 1517.

One remark at the beginning is necessary. The texts studied do not constitute christological treatises properly so-called, like the treatise of Saint Athanasius, *De Incarnatione* or Saint Anselm's *Cur Deus Homo.* They are biblical commentaries. Luther approaches the questions of christology when and where, according to him, the text lends itself to it. When selecting Luther's christological affirmations, it is necessary to take account of the text on which he is commenting. Thus the *Commentary on the Psalms* insists particularly on the incarnation. And Luther's christology is there elaborated in the framework of a hermeneutic which is absolutely characteristic. The four traditional senses are taken up. The christological exegesis is practiced in a radical way, since even the Psalms of distress are put into the mouth of Christ. At the same time, the tropological sense is placed in the foreground, i.e., according to Luther, the importance of the work of Christ for the Christian life.

The lectures on the epistle to the Romans put forward, as of special importance, the righteousness of Christ opposed to the unrighteousness of human beings. It is this righteousness which saves us. At the same time, the theme of Christ as example, as type of the Christian life, occupies an important place. The lectures on the epistle to the Hebrews places the mystery of Christ against the background of the Old Testament and pays particular attention to the question of the sacrifice of Christ.

These are all themes or specific orientations which are explained by the text which is commented on. But one also finds in the three commentaries a collection of common themes. There is an indisputable consistency in the thought. Here we will review the constant christological themes during the period in question.

We have seen first of all that the incarnation, the cross, and the resurrection are dealt with equally. The cross is not preferred to the incarnation or the resurrection, as is too often alleged about the reformer. The theme of God, known and hidden in the flesh, is central in the thought of Luther. It receives a particular emphasis when Luther concerns himself with the suffering flesh. Thus the incarnation and the cross are bound together. But even when his attention is concentrated on the cross and on the "theology of the cross," Luther does not lose sight of the resurrection. The incarnation and the cross call up the resurrection, which reveals their meaning. On the other hand, the reformer stressed the joyful theme of the victory of Christ over the powers. In this perspective, inherited from the early church, the resurrection as victory over death holds a place of first importance.

Our study has shown that the traditional doctrine of the two natures is accepted by the reformer, but that he has made scarcely any mention of the refinements of the Occamists on this subject after his commentary on the *Sentences* of Peter Lombard in 1509. We have emphasized the insistence of Luther on the *vere homo*. Christ truly became human like us. He was human to the point of solidarity with the sin of others. He was human to the point of suffering abandonment on the cross. To the physical suffering is added, according to Luther, the moral suffering characterized by the experience of God's wrath. For Luther, as for traditional theology, Christ is at one and the same time God who turns toward human beings and the Son, become human, who turns toward the Father. On the one hand, Christ is the hidden and saving God come among humankind. He reveals the love of God in submitting to his wrath. It is that mystery which the theology of the cross mediates: God loving through his anger, making alive through death, present in weakness. We have noted on the other hand that Luther was far from neglecting the confrontation between Jesus and God. The Son become human and the Father are face to face. This perspective is translated, for example, in the *Commentary on the Psalms* by putting the prayers into the mouth of Jesus. In the lectures on the epistle to the Romans, Christ is the example of the believer also in his attitude before God. Finally, the lectures on the epistle to the Hebrews treat of the sacrifice whereby the Son offers himself to the Father.

But for Luther this confrontation of the Son with the Father is different from what it is for Saint Anselm. In the thought of the reformer, Jesus is not a human representative, acting outwardly upon God, in order to render him the honor which is due him and acquire merit by which he could benefit other human beings. It is the Son, sign of the Father's love, who offers himself in the place of sinners. Thus love triumphs over the wrath of God.

We have pointed out that Luther did not reflect on the cooperation between the divinity and the humanity in Christ—apart from the two passages in the *Commentary on Hebrews*. With traditional theology and according to the texts which he is interpreting, Luther speaks of the work of Christ simultaneously from the point of view of reconciliation with God and from the point of view of redemption, i.e., the struggle against the powers.

The principal interest of the reformer rests on the relationship between the believing individual and Christ. How is Christ the reality of salvation for human beings? That is the fundamental question. Luther answers it by placing at the center of his thought the concept of *fides Christi*—which signifies at one and the same time, Christ present in faith and faith in Christ. Christ is present both as the righteousness foreign to human beings, that they can present to God for their justification, and as the example, the reality to whose image believers are transformed. This last view is considerably developed, as we have shown. And one cannot help from finding here or there some traces of Neoplatonism, at least in the terminology. Can we say that Christ is salvation for the young Luther, in that he is the model indicating the way that a person must follow in order to be saved? Luther is attracted to a spirituality of the imitation of Christ. He often adopts certain expressions from it, but he separates himself from its fundamental principles. We think that the young Luther has already taught justification by faith. And the faith discussed here is not humility, even if it is not without humility, understood as confession of sins.

While noting the importance of *fides Christi* for Luther, we have also pointed out the importance of the Word for the reformer's christology. The link between the believer and Christ, designated by the phrase *fides Christi,* is not the fruit of a mystical union between Christ and the faithful. It is by the Word that Christ is presented and revealed to human beings as saving reality. This does not exclude an intimate union between Christ and the faithful, a union without which the theme of "joyous exchange" would be unthinkable, but the role of the Word is essential to maintain the liberty of God and the personal character of the relationship between the faithful and Christ.

From now on the role of the Word will be underlined more and more. That will be very plain in the "Resolutions," Luther's commentary on the 95 Theses, which will be the subject of our next chapter. At the same time it will appear more and more clearly that before being example, Christ is sacrament, i.e., he gives salvation before he is the model to be imitated. Luther affirms this, from this period on, notably with the help of the Augustinian schema *sacramentum et exemplum.* But if one or another passage should still be ambiguous, that ambiguity will definitely be lifted in the period that we will now study.

Notes

1 Erich Seeberg, *Luthers Theologie; Luthers Theologie in ihren Grundzügen,* 2nd ed. (Stuttgart: 1950).

2 Wilhelm Maurer, *Von der Freiheit eines Christenmenschen,* Zwei Untersuchungen zu Luthers Reformationschriften 1520/21 (Göttingen: 1949); "Die Einheit von Luthers Theologie," *Theologische Literaturzeitung* 75 (1950):245-252; "Die Anfänge von Luthers Theologie," *Theologische Literaturzeitung* 77 (1952):1-12, reprinted in *Kirche und Geschichte,* Gesammelte Aufsätze, vol. 1 (Göttingen: 1970), pp. 11-21, 22-37.

3 Seeberg, *Luthers Theologie,* p. 22: "In that which concerns the person of Christ, Luther emphasizes primarily the incarnation. In Christ, God has *de facto* appeared in the flesh, an appearance which is prefigured in the Old Testament appearances"; *Luthers Theologie in ihren Grundzügen,* p. 82: "His theology is constructed on the foundations of the doctrine of the early church, even in its ultimate ramifications, we shall find in it the traces of the glorious idea of the incarnation of God in Christ, the key idea of his theology." Also, Maurer, "Die Anfänge von Luthers Theologie," p. 4: "The doctrine of justification by faith is not the root, but the fruit, not the fundamental principle, but the ultimate consequence of the

young Martin Luther's theology. It has grown out of a new understanding of the great early church doctrines of the Trinity and christology. It is a result of a return to the roots, which the young Martin Luther has undertaken, getting beneath the surface of Scholasticism, down to the theology of the Fathers of the church."

4   *WA* 3 and 4. We shall also refer to these lectures as *Dictata*.

5   *WA* uses the numbering of the Psalms as found in the Vulgate (here Psalm 17).

6   Cf. the analysis of this passage by Maurer, "Die Einheit von Luthers Theologie," pp. 249-251.

7   Maurer, "Die Einheit von Luthers Theologie," p. 249: "If the text we have quoted (*AE* 10, 119-120) seems to distinguish between the hiddenness of God in himself from that of his hiddenness in humanity, we must not for all that suppose that even though Dionysius the Areopagite is specifically mentioned, there must be Neoplatonic influences at work, as Seeberg does. We must rather consider the paradoxical reality of the God hidden by nature in an inaccessible light, and who hid *for us* in his humanity, i.e., the human nature of Christ. It is the christology of the early church, which was elaborated partly under the influence of Neoplatonism, which accounts for echoes of Neoplatonism in young Luther, and not mysticism tinted with Neoplatonism."

8   *WA* 3, 385ff.; *AE* 10, 324ff. (but incomplete in the *AE*). A more complete commentary on Psalm 68 is found in *AE* 13, 3-37, which is a translation of *WA* 8, 4-35.

9   *WA* 3, 387, 1-11; 388, 1; *AE* 10, 324 (but fragmentary). See K. O. Nilsson, *Simul: Das Miteinander von Göttlichem und Menschlichem in Luthers Theologie* (Göttingen: 1966), p. 158.

10   E.g., Luther's commentaries on Psalms 74 and 85 (*AE* 11).

11   This is how Father Congar characterizes Luther's views on the incarnation. See his "La christologie de Luther," p. 468.

12   "I, too, read the fathers, even before I opposed the pope so decisively. I also read them with greater diligence than those who now quote them so defiantly and haughtily against me; for I know that none of them attempted to read a book of Holy Scripture in school, or to use the writings of the fathers as an aid, as I did. Let them take a book of Holy Scripture and seek out the glosses of the fathers; then they will share the experience I had when I worked on the letter to the Hebrews with St. Chrysostom's glosses, the letter to Titus and the letter to the Galatians wih the help of St. Jerome, Genesis with the help of St. Ambrose and St. Augustine, the Psalter with all the writers available, and so on" (*WA* 50, 519, 18-27; *AE* 41, 19).

13   Maurer, "Die Anfänge von Luthers Theologie," p. 5.

14   *Ibid.*, p. 6: In his treatise *On the Church and the Councils* (1539), Luther praises Peter Lombard because he collected the sayings of the Fathers and compared them, and he writes, "In my opinion, he did it better than we would, and you will find in no one council,

nor in all of the councils, and in none of the fathers, as much as in the book *Sentences*. The councils and fathers deal with several points of Christian doctrine, but none of them deals with them all as this man does" (*WA* 50, 543, 17-21; *AE* 41, 48). Nonetheless he issues a rebuke to Peter Lombard: "And yet, about the real articles, such as faith and justification, he speaks too undecidedly and weakly, even though he gives high enough praise to the grace of God" (*WA* 50, 543, 21ff.; *AE* 41, 48-49).

15 See particularly: Freidrich Held, *Augustins Enarrationes in Psalmos als exegetische Vorlage für Luthers erste Psalmenvorlesung* (Kiel: 1929); Adolf Hamel, *Der junge Luther und Augustin* (Gütersloh: 1934); Erwin Iserloh, "Sacramentum et exemplum," in *Reformata reformanda*, Festschrift für H. Jedin (Münster: 1965), pp. 247-264.

16 Both owe a great deal to Platonic or rather Neoplatonic philosophy. For the Platonism of Luther, see Theodore Süss, *Luther* (Paris: P.U.F., 1969), pp. 55-72.

17 Occam also taught the absolute sovereignty and the infinite, almighty power of God. And yet Luther opposed him on this point. As Theodore Süss writes: "For both, God's almighty power is identical to his absolute freedom, his unlimited sovereignty, his independence from all determinism. But, according to Occam, this freedom of God has the effect of endowing human beings, his most excellent creation, also with some measure of free will" (*Luther*, p. 53). Luther comes to the opposite conclusion.

18 H. Strohl, *Luther jusqu'en 1520*, 2nd ed. (Paris: P.U.F., 1962), p. 181.

19 Cf. Süss, *Luther*, p. 68.

20 Congar, "La christologie de Luther," p. 488.

21 Luther is monist in his affirmation of salvation as the act of God . . . in this he has *monoergism, monopraxis*, or, if you like, economic *monophysism*. In the economy of salvation, God alone acts. In a word, Luther has the christology of the *Alleinwirksamkeit* of God," pp. 485-586.

22 *Augustins Enarrationes*, p. 17.

23 *Augustins Enarrationes*, p. 17.

24 Christ speaks *in persona patris* or *prophetae* (*WA* 3, 316, 33; *Enarrationes* 713, 1) or more often *in persona ecclesiae*. See Held, *Augustins Enarrationes*, p. 17.

25 Erich Vogelsang, *Die Anfänge von Luthers Christologie* (Berlin: 1929), pp. 18-19.

26 Held, *Augustins Enarrationes*, p. 23.

27 The question of knowing what role the Augustinian doctrine of the mystical body still plays for the Luther of the *Dictata* cannot be fully discussed here. According to Seeberg (*Luthers Theologie*, p. 11), "It is the concept of the mystical body which makes possible, at the religious level, a *tropological* interpretation" (a passage is interpreted tropologically if it is related to the individual Christian). Erwin Iserloh ("Existentiale Interpretation in Luthers erster

Psalmenvorlesung?" *Theologische Revue* 59:76) admits the same: "The tropological method of Luther is sustained by the idea of the mystical body." Nevertheless, it seems to us obvious that the relation between the christological and tropological interpretations is direct in the *Dictata* and is not replaced by the allegorical interpretation (a passage is interpreted allegorically if it is related to the church). Iserloh himself recognizes this in his study of 1965, *Sacramentum et exemplum*, p. 248: "In the Dictata, the accent is placed on the identification of the individual Christian with Christ, i.e., on the tropological interpretation. Luther often omits the intermediate link, i.e., the church, and concerns himself only with the relationship between Christ and the Christian." It must be recognized very clearly that, as Regin Prenter in his *Der barmherziger Richter* (Copenhagen: 1961) says (p. 126), that "the church is not the medium which links the literal to the tropological interpretation." The comments on Psalms 30 and 70 show quite clearly that the two interpretations are directly linked to each other. Luther does not need to pass through the church in order to go from Christ to the individual Christian. Thus we have here a position which goes beyond that of Saint Augustine. This is a good illustration of the fact that it is not sufficient to place Luther in relation only to the early church. He must also be understood in the light of the development of his hermeneutical methods, which are both traditional and original.

28   *Der junge Luther und Augustin*, pp. 197, 199.

29   Hamel, *Der junge Luther und Augustin*, p. 200: "The works of Christ are hidden under the infirmities of the passion, the divinity under the humanity."

30   "La christologie de Luther," pp. 488-489.

31   For the evolution of christology after Chalcedon, see: Werner Elert, *Der Ausgang der altkirchlichen Christologie: Eine Untersuchung über Theodor von Pharan und seine Zeit als Einführung in die alte Dogmengeschichte* (Berlin: 1957); J. Meyendorff, *Le Christ dans la théologie byzantine* (Paris: Cerf, 1969).

32   Based on Meyendorff's translation in *Le Christ dans la théologie byzantine*, p. 28.

33   According to this doctrine, the human nature of Christ can only be receptive, it does not possess a *hypostasis* of its own (i.e., it cannot subsist alone). Its reality is based on the *hypostasis* of the *Logos*. From this point of view, one speaks of the *enhypostasis* of the human nature in the divine nature. One will also speak of *anhypostasis*, in order to express the fact that the human nature has no *hypostasis* of its own. On this subject see Wolfhart Pannenberg, *Grundzüge der Christologie* (Gütersloh: 1964), pp. 349ff.

34   "Let us remember that by this he [Luther] meant the attribution to Christ's humanity of certain properties of his divine nature and, conversely, the attribution of certain properties of his human na-

ture to his divine nature," Francois Wendel, *Calvin* (London: Collins, 1963), p. 221.

35 See Reinhold Seeberg, *Dogmengeschichte*, 6th ed., vol. 3 (Stuttgart: 1960), pp. 250ff.
36 See R. Seeberg, *Dogmengeschichte*, pp. 263-265.
37 "La christologie de Luther," p. 488. See also M. Sorley, *Luthers Lehre vom unfreien Willen* (Munich: 1967), pp. 137ff. on "Hat Luther Thomas gekannt?"
38 Cf. R. Seeberg, *Dogmengeschichte*, vol. 4, part 1, p. 76, n. 2.
39 On this subject, see Philipp Katiser, *Die Gott-menschliche Einigung als Problem der spekulativen Theologie seit der Scholastik* (Munich: 1968).
40 Heiko Oberman, *Spätscholastik und Reformation—Der Herbst der mittelalterlichen Theologie* (Zurich: 1965), pp. 235-250.
41 R. Schwarz, "Gott ist Mensch—Zur Lehre von der Person Christi bei den Ockhamisten und bei Luther," *Zeitschrift für Theologie und Kirche* 63 (1966):289-351.
42 For medieval christology before Occam, see A. M. Landgraf, *Dogmengeschichte der Frühscholastik*, part 2: Die Lehre von Christus, I-II (Regensburg: 1953).
43 R. Seeberg, *Dogmengeschichte*, vol. 4, part 1, pp. 75-78.
44 See the article "Gott ist Mensch," pp. 345-348. Schwartz rightly leaves open the question of knowing to what extent all the affirmations on christology in this commentary on the *Sentences* are inspired by Occam. What R. Seeberg says about the relation of Luther to Nominalism must also be noted (*Dogmengeschichte*, p. 71): "Certain passages in the commentary can be explained as part of what Luther had been taught about Nominalism. But that in no way means that Luther must, at this period, be considered to be a representative of all the theological doctrines of Nominalism. Moreover, at this period adherence to Nominalism is essentially concerned with philosophy."
45 *WA* 9, 88, 28ff.
46 Schwartz, "Gott ist Mensch," p. 346.
47 *WA* 9, 85, 36ff.
48 Schwartz, "Gott ist Mensch," p. 347.
49 R. Seeberg, *Dogmengeschichte*, p. 74: "Anyone who studies these lectures [the *Dictata*] of Luther which have been preserved is astonished that the young theologian, fresh from the reading of the *Sentences* of Peter Lombard, could plunge himself so completely into subjective piety. Likewise his systematic techniques only play a subordinate role. The Nominalist theology and philosophy, of course, make up the scientific background, but without intervening in any significant way in the formation of his thought." One can, of course, dispute Seeberg's objection that Luther seems to divide his subjective piety from his theology (or dogma), but the opinion expressed is right, to the extent that it empha-

sizes the degree to which Occamist speculations passed into the background from the lectures on the Psalms on.

50   Strohl, "Luther jusqu'en 1520," pp. 111-115; 187-210; Heiko Oberman, "Simul gemitus et raptus: Luther und die Mystik"; Erwin Iserloh, "Luther und die Mystik"; Bengt Hägglund, "Luther und die Mystik"; in *Kirche, Mystik, Heiligung und das Natürliche bei Luther* (Göttingen: 1967). Walther von Loewenich, *Luther's Theology of the Cross* (Minneapolis: Augsburg, 1976), pp. 147-166.

51   For a full treatment see Martin Grabmann, *Mittelalterliches Geistesleben*, vols. 1-3 (Munich: 1926); Dom Besse, *Mystiques bénédictins des origens au* 13e *siècle* (Paris: 1922); Etienne Gilson, *La théologie mystique de s. Bernard* (Paris: Vrin, 1934).

52   WA 3, 124, 32ff.; AE 10, 119-120: "Therefore blessed Dionysius teaches that one must enter into anagogical darkness [the mystical shadows] and ascend by way of denials. For thus God is hidden and beyond understanding." See also WA 3, 372, 13ff.; AE 10, 313.

53   Iserloh, "Luther und die Mystik," p. 61: "Luther rejects all speculation that would attain to union with God without passing through the incarnate God, or which bypasses him."

54   More and more, Luther will warn his readers against speculative mysticism which minimizes Christ crucified. Examples of this are in WA 9, 98, 33; 5, 163, 17-29; WA Tischreden 1, 302, 30ff. We shall also refer to other passages in the course of our study. See also Iserloh, "Luther und die Mystik," pp. 62-68. Iserloh speaks of "Luther criticizing speculative mysticism and negative theology, to the advantage of a communion with Christ, as communion with God *sub contraria.*"

55   Iserloh, "Luther und die Mystik," p. 60: "This refers to a real presence of the risen Christ in the believer, as Luther says most emphatically in opposition to the Enthusiasts (WA 40, 1, 546, 8), a presence which is in some way spiritual, passing beyond intellect and consciousness. It is concerned with a communion of life and destiny, and not communion based only on similar views and kindred feelings."

56   This is a writing attributed to St. Bonaventura, but which dates back to the first third of the 14th century. Luther quotes from it in his *Commentary on the Psalms* (WA 3, 358, 31ff.; AE 10, 302-303).

57   Likewise quoted in the *Commentary on the Psalms* (WA 3, 387, 27ff.; 3, 381, 14; AE 10, 320 [cited there as "Rosegarden"]).

58   On this subject see Martin Elze, "Züge spätmittelalterlicher Frömmigkeit in Luthers Theologie," *Zeitschrift für Theologie und Kirche* 62 (1965):381-402; "Das Verständnis der Passion Jesu im ausgehenden Mittelalter und bei Luther," in *Geist und Geschichte der Reformation,* Festgabe Hanns Rückert zum 65. Geburtstag (Berlin: 1966), pp. 127-151. We would agree with Elze when he empha-

sizes the importance of the theme of meditation on the life and passion of Christ for Luther. However, in our view, and in opposition to Elze, one does not find any theology based on an imitation of Christ in Luther. Moreover, it does appear to us that Luther was more of what Strohl calls "the friend of the mystics" than Elze is willing to admit.

59   It is in this sense that we understand the statement by E. Seeberg, *Luthers Theologie,* p. 14: "It is not what one calls the 'historic Christ' whom Luther emphasizes; it is the Christ of dogma, the incarnate Christ, who died and rose. This Christ is the foundation and origin of his theological thought."

60   Iserloh, "Luther und die Mystik," p. 61: "It must be said with decisive emphasis that Luther is not content to plunge into a meditation on the sufferings of Christ and then draw conclusions from that experience on the ethical level, as regards a moral imitation of Jesus Christ. This imitation is moreover impossible without preexisting union in every action with Christ at a very personal level, an experience which is normally not accessible to us. Thus Luther fights on two fronts—on the one, against a speculative mysticism, which passes over in silence the incarnate Word; on the other, against a late medieval piety based on suffering, which, confined to the psychological and moral domain, seeks to imitate Christ without first having been conformed to him, a piety which wishes to follow Christ as an example before he has become a sacrament."

61   Maurer, "Die Einheit von Luthers Theologie," p. 249: "The cross and the resurrection are, for Luther, as for the early Church, indissolubly bound up one with another." See also Ulrich Asendorf, *Gekreuzigt und Auferstanden: Luthers Herausforderung an die moderne Christologie* (Berlin-Hamburg: 1971).

62   "La christologie de Luther," p. 469.

63   Regin Prenter, *Spiritus Creator* (Munich: 1954), p. 265: "It can be said that the formula for Luther's christology can be found, already given, in Col. 2:9 and John 14:9. These two scriptural texts completely express the christology of Luther."

64   On this subject see the following studies: Walther von Loewenich, *Luther und das johanneische Christentum* (Munich: 1935); Carl Stange, *Der johanneische Typus der Heilslehre Luthers im Verhältnis zur paulinischen Rechtfertigungslehre* (Gütersloh: 1949); J. Atkinson, "Luthers Einschätzung des Johannesevangeliums," in *Lutherforschung Heute,* Vilmos Vajta, ed. (Berlin: 1958), pp. 49-56; E. Ellwein, *Summus Evangelista: Die Botschaft des Johannesevangeliums in der Auslegung Luthers* (Munich: 1960); "Die Christusverkündigung in Luthers Auslegung des Johannesevangeliums," *Kerygma und Dogma* 6 (1960):31-68; the study by Siggins, *Martin Luther's Doctrine of Christ,* which interprets the christology of Luther from an essentially Johannine point of view.

65   Karl Barth, *Church Dogmatics,* vol. 1, part 2 (Edinburgh: T. & T. Clark), p. 24.

66   In this perspective it is also necessary to emphasize the importance of Isaiah 53 for Luther's christology.

67   Concerning Luther's hermeneutics, see: Erich Vogelsang, *Die Anfänge von Luthers Christologie*, pp. 16-30; Gerhard Ebeling, *Evangelische Evangelienauslegung* (Munich: 1942; Darmstadt: 1962); "Die Anfänge von Luthers Hermeneutik," *Zeitschrift für Theologie und Kirche* 48 (1951):172-229; A. Brandenburg, *Gericht und Evangelium: Zur Worttheologie in Luthers erster Psalmenvorlesung* (Paderborn: 1960); Erwin Iserloh, "Existentiale Interpretation . . .?" pp. 73-84.

68   On this subject see Henri de Lubac, *Exégèse médiévale: Les quatre sens de l'Ecriture*, vol. 1 (Paris: Aubier, 1959); vol. 2 (1961).

69   *WA* 3, 12-13; *AE* 10, 3-5

70   Vogelsang, "Die Anfänge von Luthers Christologie," p. 23: "In a period when humanism was growing, it is surprising that Luther should attach himself to an older tradition."

71   Ebeling, *Evangelische Evangelienauslegung*, pp. 280-283; "Die Anfänge von Luthers Hermeneutik," pp. 219-226.

72   Ebeling, "Die Anfänge von Luthers Hermeneutik," p. 222.

73   Vogelsang, *Die Anfänge von Luthers Christologie*, p. 19.

74   Vogelsang, *Die Anfänge von Luthers Christologie*, pp. 91-95.

75   *WA* 3, 113, 33 (omitted from *AE*): "Christ in fact sustained in his passion, bore with a divine courage many wounds *[dolores]*, of which any one could have brought about his death, according to the doctors." Cf. also *WA* 3, 121, 37; 3, 410ff.

76   "But since we have often said that the tropological is the primary sense of Scripture, and, when this has been expressed, the allegorical and anagogical and particular applications of contingent events follow easily and of their own accord *[sponte]*" (*WA* 3, 531, 33; *AE* 11, 12).

77   Ebeling, "Die Anfänge von Luthers Hermeneutik," p. 223. (Going beyond Faber) Luther asks, "What now is the relationship between the christological sense and the actuality? Does a statement, even when it concerns the word of a psalm, interpreted christologically, also have in itself a spiritual meaning?"

78   Vogelsang, *Die Anfänge von Luthers Christologie*, p. 26.

79   Vogelsang, *Die Anfänge von Luthers Christologie*, p. 26.

80   G. Gloege, *Mythologie und Luthertum*, 3rd ed. (Gottingen: 1963), p. 72: "Luther's basic contribution to the art of interpretation consisted of raising the christological sense of the word to the level of a hermeneutical axiom and at the same time relating it directly to the tropological sense of existence. Apart from the books already mentioned, we also recommend the following: Karl Bauer, *Die Wittenberger Universitätstheologie und die Anfänge der Deutschen Reformation* (Tübingen: 1928); Paul Schempp, *Luthers Stellung zur heiligen Schrift* (Munich: 1929); R. Josefson, "Christus und die heilige Schrift," in *Lutherforschung heute*, pp. 57-63.

81   *WA* 3, 368, 18; *AE* 10, 311: "Therefore Christ is the end and cen-

ter of them all. To Him they all look and point, as if they were saying: 'Look, He is the One who is in reality, but we are not; we are only signs.'" *WA* 3, 341, 1; *AE* 10, 285: "This sign is faith in Christ, the mark they are signed because of the truth." *WA* 3, 375, 29: "The creation of the whole world and all the symbols *[figuralia]* of the ancient law are works that signify, but the acts realized are the accomplishment of those same symbols: that which begins to be accomplished in Christ and which now is being accomplished, will be completely accomplished at the end" (the passage is omitted from *AE*, but see the commentary on Psalm 66, *AE* 10, 317-318.

82   We leave to one side the question as to whether there are traces of Neoplatonism in Luther.

83   Ebeling, "Die Anfänge von Luthers Hermeneutik," pp. 187ff.

84   *WA* 3, 564, 37; *AE* 11, 44-45
      WA 4, 450, 39; *AE* takes the *Commentary on the Psalms* only up to Psalm 126:4, which is *WA* 4, 414.

85   *WA* 3, 55, 2; *AE* 10, 65
      WA 3, 79, 31ff.; *AE* 10, 86 (in part only)
      WA 3, 564, 37; *AE* 11, 44-45
      WA 3, 565ff.; *AE* 11, 45ff.
      WA 4, 450, 39; *AE* does not go beyond 414.

86   *WA* 3, 89, 2; *AE* 10, 92-93
      WA 3, 124, 29; *AE* 10, 119-120
      WA 3, 367, 28; *AE* 10, 310
      WA 3, 387, 21; *AE* 10, 328
      WA 3, 495, 32; *AE* apparently omitted
      WA 3, 547, 5ff.; *AE* 11, 33ff.

87   *WA* 3, 188, 13; *AE* 10, 338
      WA 3, 201, 29; *AE* apparently omitted

88   Vogelsang, *Die Anfänge von Luthers Christologie*, p. 159. The author points out the difference from St. Augustine in relation to the christology of the Logos: "The point of departure and the aim of Augustine's christology is the non-historical *(geschichtslos) verbum aeterna,* which does not participate in the act of becoming historical and has always remained the basically Neoplatonic foundation of Augustine's theology. The *verbum incarnatum,* the humiliated Christ, are for him only the means whereby access is obtained to the contemplation of the *verbum aeternum.* Luther completely restructures this speculation on the *verbum* from within. At the heart of his theology is the Word of the gospel, as is the word from the cross. It is this clear, bright *Word* whose rays can shine on the preexistence and on eschatology. But the other way round would be quite impossible" (p. 165).

89   "La christologie de Luther," p. 455.

90   Prenter, *Spiritus Creator,* p. 177: "Particularly with the young Martin Luther, it is difficult to find any deviations from orthodoxy in matters that concern the doctrine of the Trinity, such as we do find in St. Augustine and the Scholastics. Wherever his activity as a

teacher or preacher gave him the opportunity, he treated the traditional dogma of the Trinity to which he adhered as a premise not
lending itself to any discussion."

91   *WA* 1, 20, 1ff.
92   *WA* 3, 382, 10; *AE* 10, 322: ". . . their three names are exceedingly
formidable *[tremenda]* and should never be uttered without a
trembling of the heart."
93   *WA* 3, 385, 38; 3, 547, 11; 4, 7, 12; 4, 53, 22; *AE* 10 and 11
94   *WA* 3, 80; *AE* 10, 88: "Thou visitest Him, namely by taking on His
nature *[visitas eum hypostatice]* through the Son."
95   *WA* 3, 390, 21; *AE* 10, 324
96   *WA* 3, 236, 33; *AE* 10, 195: "Christ was made sin, curse, excom-
munication, and anathema for us." Cf. *WA* 3, 215, 1; 3, 220, 11;
AE 10, 177-179, 183.
97   See again: *WA* 3, 316, 8; *AE* 10, 262
98   Vogelsang, *Die Anfänge von Luthers Christologie*, pp. 64ff., 99ff.,
129ff.; Bernhard Lohse, *Lutherdeutung heute* (Göttingen: 1968),
p. 43: "Keeping within the limits of traditional christology, it is
practically impossible to find a single article of christological dogma
which has not been interpreted tropologically."
99   *WA* 4, 34, 28ff.; *AE* 11, 187, 182: Luther speaks of the risen Christ
as "the first cause of all those who are raised." See also *WA* 4, 243,
14; *AE* 11, 378.
100 *WA* 3, 224, 22; 3, 231, 28; 3, 244, 1; 3, 388, 15; 3, 441, 22; 3, 458,
11; 3, 469, 20; 3, 473, 38; 3, 523, 27; 3, 529, 2; 3, 601, 37; 3, 607,
22, etc. (All these references may be found in *AE* 10 and 11.)
101 This emphasizes the fact that Christ acts in the salvation of humanity only in faith. In different ways, it is Christ and faith who save
human beings.
102 For a general treatment of the relationships between Christ and
the church, see Wilhelm Maurer, "Kirche und Geschichte nach
Luthers Dictata super Psalterium," in *Lutherforschung heute*, pp.
85-101. For the theme of the church in the *Dictata* see Johannes
Vercruysse, *Fidelis populus* (Wiesbaden: 1968).
103 *WA* 4, 264, 29
104 *Gesammelte Aufsätze*, 3rd ed. (Tübingen: 1923), pp. 291-293.
105 *WA* 3, 32, 2; *AE* 10, 35
106 *WA* 3, 371, 12; 3, 372; 3, 374; 3, 463, 22; 4, 368ff.; *AE* 10 and 11
107 *WA* 9, 23, 31ff.; 9, 39, 31ff.: "He reigns in the faith of his humanity and under his veil of flesh." See Maurer, *Kirche und Geschichte*,
p. 87; Lohse, *Lutherdeutung heute*, p. 43.
108 *WA* 3, 541, 26: "It is from Christ and the gospel that a very great
number of the faithful are born." "Christ is the Head of all saints,
the Fountain of all, the Source of all . . . of whom all partake"
(*AE* 10, 52; *WA* 3, 46, 17). And in this way, Luther notes again
the difference between Christ and the saints (*WA* 3, 461, 8): "He
alone does marvellous things by himself, but the saints and the angels do not, and only act in God and by the grace of God."

109 Lohse, *Lutherdeutung heute,* pp. 43-44.

110 Our quotations refer to *WA* 56. For the christology of Luther's *Commentary on the Epistle to the Romans* see Hanns Hübner: *Rechtfertigung und Heiligung in Luthers Römerbriefvorlesung* (Witten: 1965); Hanns Iwand, *Rechtfertigungslehre und Christusglaube* (Leipzig: 1930); Marc Lienhard, "*Christologie et humilité* dans la Theologia crucis du commentaire de l'Epitre aux Romans de Luther," *Revue d'histoire et de philosophie religieuses* 42 (1962):304-315; E. Seeberg, *Luthers Theologie,* pp. 103-173; Hanns Thimme, *Christi Bedeutung für Luthers Glauben* (Gütersloh: 1933).

111 Marc Lienhard, "Notes sur un texte christologique de jeune Luther," *Revue d'histoire et de philosophie religieuses* 49 (1969):331-340.

112 The two themes of incarnation and cross are clearly presented by Johannes Ratzinger, *Einführung in das Christentum* (Munich: 1968), pp 184-186, "Inkarnationstheologie und Kreuzestheologie." It is our view that incarnation is more important for Luther than Ratzinger appears ready to admit. Dietrich Löfgren *(Die Theologie der Schöpfung bei Luther* [Göttingen: 1960]) rightly insists on the unity of the two themes (pp. 256-257, n. 5). See also Nilsson, *Simul,* pp. 190-192, 211ff.

113 The term *kenosis* is a transliteration of the Greek word *kenosis,* meaning degraded to nothingness. Christian theology uses it, following the apostle Paul, who writes of Christ that he was despoiled or emptied himself (Phil. 2:7). A question which is discussed by the theologians concerns the subject of this despoiling. The question asked is how to know if it is the Christ who was incarnate, or Christ according to the flesh, or both.

114 *WA* 56, 139, 21; 56, 329, 26; 56, 392, 7

115 *WA* 56, 167, 24: "For from the very moment of Christ's conception, it was correct to say, because of the two natures united in one person, that this God is the son of David, and that this man is the Son of God" (*WA* 56, 167, 24).

116 The translations of the expression vary. E. Seeberg, *Luthers Theologie,* p. 108: "The humanity is carried over *[überführt]* into the divinity." E. Ellwein translates more freely: "The humanity is transposed into the divine nature [in göttliches Wesen versetzt]" *(Martin Luthers Vorlesung über den Römerbrief),* 4th ed. (Munich: 1957), p. 21.

117 Cf. *WA* 3, 36, 22; 4, 216

118 *WA* 56, 37, 26: "He does not give grace freely to the point of requiring no satisfaction, but for us he gave Christ who satisfied [his righteousness] in order to give freely, nonetheless, grace to those who satisfy [his righteousness] through another." "It is Jesus Christ alone who has redeemed our sins by satisfying [his righteousness] and by paying for us" (*WA* 56, 37, 14).

119 *WA* 56, 3, 11, 13; 56, 18, 18; 56, 97, 24; 56, 159, 7; 56, 204, 20; 56, 267, 6; 56, 347, 9

120   WA 56, 49, 22; 56, 117, 17; 56, 252, 31
121   WA 56, 274, 24
122   WA 56, 51, 15; 56, 318, 28
123   WA 56, 62, 3; 56, 234, 16
124   WA 56, 255, 25
125   WA 56, 55, 9; 56, 127, 11—"by his death and resurrection";
       WA 56, 296, 22; 56, 101, 21
126   WA 56, 247, 1
127   WA 56, 63, 12; 56, 184, 14; 56, 202, 26
128   WA 56, 235, 25: "But we do not want Christ, God can give us his
       righteousness without Christ"; WA 56, 298: "They believe that one
       can approach God without Christ, as if it were sufficient to have
       had faith. . . . They believe that they can approach him by their
       faith alone, and not by the intermediacy of Christ."
129   WA 56, 417, 9: "That is why it is necessary for us to listen with
       simplicity to the Word and to do it with all our zeal, with all our
       powers, modestly closing our eyes and with all possible prudence."
130   WA 56, 114, 27: "The word that must be believed is no other
       than this: Christ died and is risen."
131   Let us quote some examples. In his glosses on Romans 6 (WA 57),
       he qualifies "baptized into Jesus Christ" by the words "by faith."
       Or again, when commenting on Rom. 4:25, which speaks of Jesus
       Christ "raised for our justification," he adds, "if we believe." Or
       again, commenting on Rom. 7:25, "Thanks be to God through
       Jesus Christ our Lord," Luther inserts after "Christ," the words
       "by faith in him." It is possible to multiply such examples.
132   WA 56, 204, 18ff.: "Here, he has made his righteousness mine,
       and my sin his. I have that sin no more and I am free. But if he
       has made his righteousness mine, I am already justified by the
       same righteousness as he is. Of course, he cannot make my sin dis-
       appear, but it does disappear in the infinite abyss of his righteous-
       ness." See also: WA 56, 267, 5-7; 56, 329, 30; 56, 330, 5.
133   See Martin Herz, Sacrum commercium (Munich: 1958).
134   We make a distinction between the term exemplum, which con-
       siders Christ as a model which must be imitated, and that of
       exemplar, which designates Christ as the image to which God en-
       ables us to conform.
135   Erich Seeberg, "Die Anfänge der Theologie Luthers," Zeitschrift
       für Kirchengeschichte 53 (1934):232ff.: "Thus it is in Christ that
       Luther reads the fundamental law which holds for all of life: he
       is at one and the same time cursed and blessed, at one and the
       same time living and dead. . . . It is in him that we find the model
       for the great idea of 'one and the same time,' which constitutes
       the basis for the doctrine of justification: at one and the same time,
       righteous and sinner. . . . It is in Christ that one sees how God
       acts all the time." In this connection Seeberg uses the term Urbild
       ("original") frequently. See also Thimme, Christi Bedeutung für
       den Glauben, pp. 18ff., 73ff., etc. A good critique of these inter-

pretations is found in W. Joest, *Ontologie bei Luther* (Göttingen: 1967): 355-365; 382-386.

136 Ernst Bizer, *Fides ex auditu*, Eine Untersuchung über die Entdeck-ung der Gerechtigkeit Gottes durch Martin Luther, 1st ed. (Neu-kirchen: 1958). We quote from the 2nd ed. of 1961. A 3rd ed. was published in 1966. Bizer's thesis was disputed by O. H. Pesch, "Zur Frage nach Luthers reformatorischer Wende: Ergebnisse und Probleme der Diskussion um Ernst Bizer, *Fides ex auditu*," *Catho-lica* 20 (1966), nos. 3-4, pp. 216-243; 264-280. A collection of studies relating to the date and the nature of the emergence of Reformation thought in Luther is to be found in *Der Durchbruch der reformatorischen Erkenntnis bei Luther*, Bernhard Lohse, ed. (Darmstadt: 1968).

137 Bizer, *Fides ex auditu*, p. 19: "Christ is raised to the heights by his humility. This is therefore the revelation of God, by which human beings come to God." P. 25: "Christ is our Savior, in that he is our example." P. 27: "Luther points out the way that Christ has taken, as the way of salvation, along which we are all sent and which we all must take" (p. 27).

138 Bizer, *Fides ex auditu*, p. 20: "God himself must effect the true humility." P. 22: "If it is a consequence of our humiliation by God, this humility is not our own work." Bizer is in accord with Holl when he notes, "This cuts out any idea of humility as a work" (p. 24). But that does not imply justification by faith. P. 39: "Humil-ity is not a work, of course, but must it therefore be faith?" We would refer here to our study, "Christologie et humilité . . . Ro-mains."

139 *WA* 56, 343, 9ff.

140 We would refer to the second part of *WA* 57. Bibliography: E. See-berg, "Der Anfänge der Theologie Luthers," pp. 174-205; Thimme, *Christi Bedeutung für den Glauben*, pp. 40-57.

141 E. Seeberg, *Luthers Theologie*, p. 175: "We have to deal with notes of the lectures. But often the attentive reader will note the auda-cious formulations of Luther himself appearing through what the listener has written. Nonetheless, this is not pure Luther."

142 *WA* 57, 116, 3: "That is intelligible only in relation to Christ him-self." *WA* 57, 117, 2: "However, that can only be understood prop-erly in relation to Christ."

143 Erich Vogelsang, *Luthers Hebräerbriefvorlesung von 1517/18* (Berlin-Leipzig: 1930), p. 22, n. 2.

144 Von Loewenich, *Luther's Theology of the Cross*, p. 13: "The the-ology of the cross is a principle of Luther's entire theology, and it may not be confined to a special period in his theological develop-ment. On the contrary, as in the case of Paul, this formula offers a characteristic of Luther's entire theological thinking." See also H. O. Kadai, "Luther's Theology of the Cross," in *Accents in Lu-ther's Theology* (St. Louis and London: 1967), pp. 230-272.

145 *WA* 57, 100

146   Cf. *WA* 57, 126, 25ff.
147   See also *WA* 57, 118, 17: "In fact, the passion itself was a 'passage,' that is to say, a transition to the supreme glory."
148   See also *WA* 57, 66, 22: "Hence, the Son of God, being mortal and immortal in the same person, was certainly offered up in sacrifice, but only his flesh, i.e., his humility, died."
149   "La christologie de Luther," p. 472. In *Le Christ, Marie et l'Eglise* (Paris: 1952), Congar writes: "The humanity of Christ is an instrument for the divine operations which God will accomplish through it, an instrument which is not only joined to God, but animated by him. The humanity of Christ is not like a glove which the divinity puts on, but it is itself animated, it carries the spiritual faculties of intelligence and of free will, really free" (p. 472).
150   Sent. IV, dist. 16, qu. 2
151   Cf. Congar, *Le Christ, Marie et l'Eglise*, pp. 470-471.
152   *WA* 57, 2, 124, 5: "Concerning the man Christ, it must be understood that, in order to save the children, the authority of the Father has made of him a guide. In fact, authority is rather with the Father, but obedience is more with the man Christ."
153   Here Seeberg rightly emphasizes "the idea of the status of God, by which Christ is and effects what he is and acts, an idea which demands that God—the Father—be also superior to Christ" (p. 193).
154   *WA* 57, 2, 124, 7: "Those who are attached to him by faith are transformed according to the same image."
155   *WA* 57, 2, 125, 7: "One could say colloquially that Christ is the instrument, the intermediary, by which God leads his children to himself."
156   For the use of the concept of "cooperation" by Luther, see Martin Seils, "Der Gedanke vom Zusammenwirken Gottes und des Menschen," in *Luthers Theologie* (Gütersloh: 1962).
157   *WA* 57, 2, 166, 8; 57, 2, 133, 10ff.
158   *WA* 57, 2, 129, 8: "In Christ, our head *[caput]*, death is destroyed, with all the works of the devil."
159   Comment on Heb. 4:14: "For those in fact who fear the terror of his eternal judgment and the horror of a separation and a division, there remains no refuge but this unique asylum, which is Christ, our high priest, whose humanity alone protects us and saves us from a judgment of this kind" (*WA* 57, 2, 164, 14).
160   Regin Prenter, *Schöpfung und Erlösung* (Göttingen: 1960), p. 363: "When there is a question in Luther of reconciliation, it is always in relation to justification. If sin, death, and the devil are vanquished, it is not outside of us, it is in us, in our conscience, where they appear under the form of legalism and wrath."
161   *WA* 57, 3, 114, 4-9, 13-19; *WA* 57, 3, 124, 6ff., 122ff.
162   *De trinitate* IV, 3
163   *WA* 56, 321
164   Erwin Iserloh, "Sacramentum et exemplum—Ein augustinisches Thema lutherischer Theologie," *Reformata reformanda*, p. 254.

165 *WA* 56, 51, 20ff.: "The resurrection and the life of Christ are not only a sacrament, but also the cause, that is to say the effective sacrament of our resurrection and our spiritual life, because by this sacrament those who believe in it are made to live and rise again."

166 See Iserloh, "Sacramentum et exemplum," pp. 247-254.

167 Bizer, *Fides et auditu*, p. 77: "When he asks that contemplation of the death of Christ be considered *sacramentum*, then he is asking that persons die spiritually, so that they completely renounce themselves and that they put their hope in God. Earlier, he called that *humilitas*. If he now calls it 'faith,' this faith must be understood as a spiritual death, i.e., as a spiritual, interior work." Pp. 78-79: "*Exemplum* is related to the flesh, *sacramentum* to the inner person, whose death is the way to life. Not even the *sacramentum* can raise itself above the level of the law, even if 'mortification' can be realized in us only by the work of God."

168 "Sacramentum et exemplum," pp. 257-258.

169 *WA* 57, 3, 224, 3ff. Joest, *Ontologie der Person bei Luther*, p. 383: "Luther's central affirmations about the relationship to Christ in faith spoke not only of 'like Christ,' but 'by means of Christ.' Christ as *sacramentum* must therefore be understood in a way that is fundamentally 'demonstrative' *[exhibitiv]*: the action of God, who saves, who justifies, who recreates, it is God himself in his being who is united to humanity. It is God himself who, when he takes on himself the subjectivity of our spiritual life, forms us according to himself and becomes our *exemplar*."

2

The Beginnings of the Struggle
and the Spread of Luther's Thought
(1517-1521)

The Struggle Against Indulgences (1517-1518)

The year 1517 marks the beginning of the Reformation. It was in fact the affair of the indulgences which launched it by provoking Luther to draft and post 95 theses devoted to this subject.[1] By "indulgences" one understood the remission of temporal punishment for sins already forgiven. This remission was granted by the ecclesiastical authorities on the basis of the treasure possessed by the church, which consisted of the superabundant merits of Christ and the saints. The living received it by absolution, the dead by intercession. The indulgences, fruit of a long history of penitential piety,[2] gave place in Luther's time to abuses which are today admitted as such by the majority of Catholic historians.[3] However, it seems to us that Luther not only criticized the abuses, but the principle of indulgences itself.

We do not propose to describe once again the events of the struggle against indulgences and compare it with other tentative approaches of the same kind (Wycliffe, for example), but try to show that Luther's position is based on a certain understanding of Christ and his significance for the Christian life.[4] He would not have engaged in the struggle with such ardour and tenacity if the indulgences had not, according to him, called in question the gospel itself: the uniqueness of Christ as Savior and Lord of the Christian life. The texts of Luther concerned with indulgences show, on the one hand, that it is christology, in the larger sense that we have just indicated, which is the critical principle by which the reformer leads the attack.[5] On the other hand, this affair and the struggles which it entailed pressed Luther to clarify and emphasize certain points of his christology. Thus it is possible to observe that in these years, 1517-1518, the theology of the cross comes to the forefront.[6]

We shall examine successively four aspects of the reformer's thought: 1) the uniqueness of Jesus Christ as source of salvation and assurance; 2) Christ, the church, and the Word; 3) faith and the conformity of the believer to Christ; 4) the theology of the cross (theologia crucis).

The Uniqueness of Jesus Christ
as Source of Salvation and Assurance

Luther thinks that the very way in which the indulgences are presented invites confusion. In fact, people can come to believe that the indulgences are necessary for their reconciliation with God. Thus Luther writes in Thesis 33: "We should be most carefully on our guard against those who say that the papal indulgences are the inestimable divine gift, through which a person is reconciled with God." Luther thinks it necessary to distinguish two levels: that of God and that of the church. To be reconciled with God is one thing; to be reconciled with the church is another. "It is possible to ask one who is reconciled with the church whether he or she is also reconciled with God" (WA 1, 539, 26).

That is not to say that the action of the church is to be deprived of significance—we shall see that later. But it makes sense only in connection with salvation offered freely by God in Christ. It is Jesus Christ who is the foundation of assurance: "There is for us no other certainty fiducia of salvation than Jesus Christ alone" (WA 1, 587, 19). "Christ alone is the light, justice, truth, wisdom, all our good" (WA 1, 612, 3). Compared with Christ, all human practices are valueless. "Indulgences are not to be compared with the grace of God and the piety of the cross" (Thesis 68). "The indulgence is not able to remove the least venial of sins" (Thesis 76).

The same insistence on the uniqueness of Christ as Savior and on the distance which separates him from the practices of the church appears also in the use Luther makes of the phrase, meritum Christi.[7] One knows how strongly this concept was rooted in tradition. It is also at the root of the doctrine of indulgences. In fact, the "treasury of the saints," from which the church drew its right and possibility to grant indulgences consists partly of the infinite satisfaction brought by Christ, i.e., by his merit, and partly (and in dependence on him) of the "superfluous" merits which the saints had acquired by their works.

Luther will first of all concentrate his attention on the *meritum Christi*, i.e., on the work of Jesus Christ, and underline its unique and sufficient character. The works of the saints are thus relegated to another level. Even if one admits the idea of merit, which the reformer rejects, he denies that the saints have superfluous merit.[8] It can be noted that the problem of indulgences will lead Luther to describe the work of Jesus Christ, much more now than earlier, with the help of the concept of categories of "satisfaction" both in christology and in soteriology, where the work of Christ is envisaged as a "satisfaction" brought to God for the sake of human salvation.[9] Thus a displacement is operative, with respect to the earlier writings, where we had noted the predominance, although by no means exclusively, of the theme of the example of Christ.

But although the reformer speaks well of the merit of Christ and thereby emphasizes that fact that Jesus Christ is the exclusive source of salvation, he does not ask, as did a "satisfaction" christology, how such merit works. Is it accomplished by the purely human obedience of Jesus, the satisfactory work taking the place of and benefiting humanity? He contents himself with setting Christ and his merit over against us sinners, his justice over against our injustice. In fact with Luther, the term "merit" includes simply all that Jesus Christ is for us in our salvation: "All things, that means justice, power, patience, humility, all the merits of Christ" (*WA* 1, 593, 19).

The decisive question which places the discussion at the proper level is that of participation in this saving reality constituted by the merits of Christ. In other words, what connection is there between the church and these merits and how is the individual Christian able to benefit from them?

Christ, the Church, and the Word

When Luther speaks of the church, he recognizes that its true treasure is the *meritum Christi*. That is to say, that it has nothing else to give or to announce to the world than Jesus Christ, Lord and

Savior. If Christ is really the Redeemer, the price paid for the salvation of the world, he is also truly the only and unique treasure of the church (*WA* 1, 608, 19).

But it must be emphasized that the church does not possess this treasure as a thing which can be disposed of at will. That is why Luther can deny that this treasure belongs to the church: "The merits are a treasure, not of the church, but of God the Father, because Christ through his efficacious intercession before the Father obtains forgiveness of sins for us" (*WA* 1, 613, 6).

Then we must clarify what the treasure of the church consists of and place it in relation to the work of Jesus Christ. And Luther writes: "We do not speak rashly in saying that the treasure of the church consists of the power of the keys of the church (given by the merit of Christ)" (Thesis 60). What does that mean? First, that the church has a role of intercession to play; then, that it must bear witness to the forgiveness given by Christ (*WA* 1, 593, 36). Luther's considerations here come to an affirmation of the decisive importance of the Word. The word of the pope, as of any priest, is necessary to give a person assurance of salvation. It is difficult to believe that that means "to be sure that one participates in the benefits of Christ, i.e., such ineffable benefits as participation in the divine nature" (*WA* 1, 594, 25). The word addressed to believers from outside themselves is a great help to them. However, it is not the pope or the priest who matters, but the Word (*WA* 1, 594, 33): not because of the priest, nor his power, but because of the Word.

What is it that Luther understands by the Word? It is the gospel, the promise which proclaims Jesus Christ to me: "It is preaching on the subject of the Son of God incarnate, who is given for us who are without merit, for our salvation and our peace. It is a word of salvation, a word of grace, a word of joy, the voice of the bridegroom and of the bride, a good word, a word of peace" (*WA* 1, 616, 20).

The gospel is presented by Luther against the background of a distinction which is going to become fundamental for him. It is that of law and gospel. The law accuses. The gospel, on the contrary, presents Christ as our salvation. Christ is thus not to be seen from the point of view of the law, as if he were requiring that some work be accomplished. He is that one who has accomplished everything and who is given to us by God for our righteousness (*WA* 1, 616, 32).

The Word as promise calls forth faith. Thus Luther separates himself from certain sacramental, traditional concepts. A system according to which the church disposes of the *merita Christi* and distributes them by means of the sacraments is called into question in the name of a christology in which Christ himself distributes salvation by means of the promise, to which the church can only bear witness, and by calling persons to faith. We come thus to the problem of knowing how the individual Christian can benefit from the merits of Christ.

Faith and the Conformity of the Believer to Christ

In this matter Luther's great contribution will be to underline the importance of faith. And when Luther speaks of faith he does not mean in the first place assenting to a dogma or a faith founded simply on the affirmation and conviction of the historical truth of certain facts attested by Holy Scripture. He is concerned with that personal relationship which the believer has with Christ, and which we have already noted in earlier chapters when dealing with the idea of *fides Christi*.

To an exaggeration of the role of the church, Luther opposes the *fides Christi*. In Thesis 37, he writes: "Any true Christian whatsoever, living or dead, participates in all the benefits of Christ and the church; and this participation is granted to him or her by God even without letters of indulgence." And in the "Resolutions," he comments on Thesis 37, "It is impossible to be Christian if one does not have Christ. But if one has Christ, one has all that belongs to Christ" (*WA* 1, 593, 7).

In this comment on Thesis 37 the theme of "joyous exchange," which we have already met, reappears. The union of believers with Christ, given by the *fides Christi*, is so close that it allows believers access to all the benefits of Christ.[10] There is an exchange in the sense that believers give to Christ their sins and receive, on their part, righteousness.[11]

The communion with Christ does not only include this exchange, but also the "conformity" of the believer with Christ.[12] The *bona Christi* are not things that could be given to persons without changing them—that is precisely one of the complaints Luther makes against indulgences. On the contrary, the communion in which a believer receives the *bona* or *merita Christi* carries with it equally for him or her a participation in the sufferings of Christ. This is what Luther deals with in Thesis 58: "The merits of Christ and the saints, even apart from the Pope, always produce grace in the inner person, as the cross, death, and hell do in the outer person" (cf. *WA* 1, 605-615).[13]

Luther can also say: the greatest treasure for a Christian is to be transformed into the image of the Son of God, which is only done by the cross.[14] To take away the cross would be to deprive human beings of being God's children. The conformity of the Christian to Jesus Christ thus continues to be strongly affirmed. But Bernhard Lohse has rightly noted [15] that the term *exemplar* now passes into the background. Seeberg and Thimme, among others, had placed the accent strongly on this idea, thinking that it continued to be central for Luther's christology, at least up to the struggle with the spiritualists (Seeberg) or even beyond (Thimme).

But even if the term appears far less frequently, the biblical theme of human beings conformed to the image of Christ remains and acquires a new clarity in the texts we are studying. Christ is the image of God. Human beings, created in the image of God, lost this state by sin and find it again in judgment and grace, in conformity to Jesus Christ, image of God.[16] That comes out of the text that we have just quoted. The expression *exemplar* will not disappear from Luther's pen, but from now on it is quite clear that it must be understood in the sense of Pauline thought about the only-begotten Son, the image of God, and our transfiguration into conformity with this image.

The "Theologia Crucis"

Our remarks on the participation of the Christian in the suffering of Christ lead us finally to a point of view very important for the relationship between Luther's christology and his struggle against indulgences: the *theologia crucis*. We found this expression for the first time in the *Commentary on the Epistle to the Hebrews,* but the reality envisaged is much earlier.

In the Heidelberg Disputation, we find the *theologia crucis* raised to the level of a theological program. God acts and reveals himself in a different way *(sub contraria specie)* also in Christ, where he is God hidden in the sufferings *(deus absconditus in passionibus* [Thesis 20; *WA* 1, 362, 9]), as in the Christian life and in the church. God is always strong in weakness, he brings life by destroying, he grants grace by his judgments. It is in the cross and in the weakness of

Christ crucified that he would be found. There he is totally present with the very ground of his being, which is love.

The cross is thus found at the center of the thought of Luther. But this does not mean that he simply takes over a certain type of spirituality which is traditional in the church, by which believers had simply to follow Christ and take up their cross. Luther's perspective is markedly *theo*centric. It is God who imposes suffering in order to give salvation. That begins in Christ and continues in the life of the believer. One is not able to believe in Christ, i.e., in this God hidden in suffering, without taking up one's own cross (Heidelberg Disputation, Thesis 21). Luther believed that this entire theology and this spirituality were compromised by the traffic in indulgences. While for him salvation followed the path of suffering and restlessness, indulgences promised rest. While the Christian life is unthinkable without the cross, indulgences wished to avoid it.

The Reformer, for his part, sees the *meritum Christi* or rather the *thesaurus Christi* (WA 1, 614, 3) in the light of his theology of the cross. Henceforth he can no longer envisage it as a remission of punishments. That would be to construct what he calls here, as in the Heidelberg Disputation, a theology of glory (WA 1, 614, 3). For the theologian of the cross, on the contrary, "The treasure of Christ is the imposition of punishments and the obligation to undergo them, things which are best and most worthy of being loved and most desirable" (WA 1, 614, 24). We have earlier given great prominence to the idea that for a Christian, the greatest treasure consists of being transformed into the image of the Son of God, which is precisely what is accomplished through the cross.

Of course, the cross is not an end in itself. As we shall one day see God face to face, so the cross is a stage, never surpassed here below, a stage of the Christian life toward our glorification. Luther defines the place of the cross in the Christian life by means of a dialectic which will acquire more and more prominence in his thought. He distinguishes the work proper to God from that which is not proper to him, but alien. The work proper of God is "to create grace, righteousness, truth, patience in the spirit of a person because the righteousness of Christ and his merit justify and remit sins" (WA 1, 612, 42). The alien work, on the contrary, brought about by the merit of Christ is "the cross, labor, punishments of all kinds, finally death and hell in the flesh, in order that the body of sin may be destroyed" (WA 1, 613, 11).

If then the theology of the cross moved Luther to fight against indulgences, it was not because he thought that there is no pardon nor remission of punishments. But he did not wish to have cheap grace—to the detriment of a true faith which, in the human condition here below, necessarily includes suffering.

The Sermons of 1518-1519

The works that we have studied up to now were biblical commentaries or theses, drafted in Latin and intended for specialists; the sermons which we are now about to turn to are written for the most part in German and intended for the general public. The difference is considerable. The literary form, the intended audience, and the language have their importance as much for the elaboration of thought as for its expression. And one is able to affirm from the outset that the sermons of Luther constitute a source of prime importance for the understanding of his thought. This thought is in fact much less speculative than kerygmatic. It brings out unceasingly the soteriological point of the mysteries of the faith and thus directs theology toward human beings and salvation, toward faith and the Christian life.

The sermons of the years 1518-1519 are from the hand of Luther himself and were published by him; they are instruments deliberately chosen for the purpose of making known his views on the subject of the gospel to a vast audience, views which were set in motion by the affair of the indulgences. One can admire their tough and direct style. While the commentaries include many essays and digressions, references to the Fathers of the church and fundamental discussions with theologians, the sermons in question treat their subject step by step without digression, going straight to the essential point. However, these are not sermons in the classic sense of the word. There is no biblical passage commented on for the faithful, but a devotional theme: meditation on the passion of Christ, a general human concern, how to prepare for death, or this or that aspect of life in the church. Thus in these sermons the celebration of the Eucharist, marriage, Baptism, and penitence are all dealt with.

A study of the sermons of the years 1518-1519 shows how concerned Luther was with the passion of Jesus Christ and the proper manner of meditating on it. This point will be the subject of our first part. Elsewhere the sermons give us a number of indications of the way in which, at this time, Luther envisaged the relationship between the Father and the Son, the incarnation seen from the point of view of *kenosis,* and the relationship between Jesus Christ and the saints. These questions will be the subject of our second part.

The Passion of Jesus Christ
and the Right to Meditate on It

In the years of these sermons that we are studying, Luther accorded special importance to the cross. Of course, this theme will be at the center of his reflections for the whole of his life.[17] But in the period which concerns us here, this theme dominates in a striking way. Several reasons explain this fact. First, there was nothing new in the theme. The spirituality of the Middle Ages was nourished on works such as the *Meditationes vitae Christi* and the *Rosetum exercitorium spiritualium et sacrarum meditationum,* which Luther evidently knew and from which he quoted.[18] This spirituality is characterized by its concentration on the man Jesus. One clings to the figure of the crucified, to his humility. One tries to accept suffering as he did.

In other ways, the years 1517-1518 and those that followed would place the reformer himself under the cross, in a very personal way. The attacks of which he is going to be the object, the great disappointment which came to him in Rome, uncertainty about the future of the church and about his own future—these all are so many crosses to bear which would help him to discover the cross of Christ, both in its human reality and in its saving reality for the believer.

But there are not only these two historical and biographical reasons. The cross became for Luther the key to his whole theology. We have confirmed that, in the preceding chapter, by reference to the *Resolutiones* and the Heidelberg Disputation. When Luther speaks of *theologia crucis,* he is not only concerned with a theme of spirituality such as it was understood in current piety, but as an entirely precise way of thinking about the revelation of God in Christ and the Christian life, as a theological theme. And it is in the name of this fundamental theological theme, the elaboration of which we have followed from his earlier works, that the struggle over the indulgences raged. The traffic in indulgences was in fact for Luther, like the speculative theology of the Scholastics, a blow to the theology of the cross, an emptying of the meaning of the cross, the presumptuous human attempt to find God independently of the cross and suffering.

All these reasons can explain the attention that Luther directed toward the cross, which is both the cross of Christ and the cross of the Christian.

The sermons which we shall study particularly in this connection are: two Latin sermons of 1518 (*WA* 1, 335-345); the sermon "Contemplation of the Sufferings of Christ" (*WA* 2, 131-142); and finally the sermon "Preparation for Death" (*WA* 2, 685-697).

Wrong Ways of Contemplating the Passion of Jesus Christ

Since the meditation on the passion of Christ was an integral part of the spirituality of the time of Luther, one should not be surprised at the success of his "Sermon on the Meditations of the Holy Sufferings of Christ." That popularity was probably also due to the fact that it was written in German and thus made accessible to the larger public. Therefore it was reissued more than 20 times. The two sermons of 1518 on the passion of Christ, still written in Latin, were less known, but they are no less important.

It is good to meditate on the passion of Christ, Luther thinks,[19] and at the beginning of the German sermon (Point 4), he opposes those who are content for their salvation with the ritual enactment of the mass, *opere operato non opere operantis*. Of course, one of the most solemn moments of the mass is the actualization of the suffering of Christ in the elevation of the host. But that is also precisely the point at which the danger had arisen. One was tempted to ascribe a magical meaning to the elevation. Those who had seen the Christ present in the host at the moment of elevation thought themselves thereby to be protected from all misfortune for the rest of the day. That explains the multiplication of masses.

Luther accepts the idea of participation. The mass makes one truly participate in the sacrificed body of Christ. At the same time, however, he distinguishes between a participation which is purely exterior and an interior participation. This places him in line with Bonaventura and the German mystics. They too had insisted on a participation in the passion of Christ which was not only intellectual, but also emotional. Nevertheless, Luther goes further in his critique by emphasizing the participation under the sign of faith.[20] In effect, even when a person is thus "touched" inwardly by the cross of Christ, there is still the possibility of a false usage of the passion of Christ.

Luther denounces this false usage in the first three points of his sermon of 1519. He criticizes those who allow themselves to be carried away by anger against the Jews and rise up against "poor Judas" (WA 2, 136, 5). "That is not meditating on the suffering of Christ, but upon the wickedness of the Jews and Judas" (WA 2, 136, 8). There is on the other hand a sentimental way of considering the passion of Christ. This nourishes an emotive piety, which is dominated by pity for the crucified. That is to repeat what the women of Jerusalem did, whose tears Jesus wanted to stop (Luke 23:27ff.).[21] Luther places this emotive participation on the same level as the strictly external participation in the mass. In both cases, one is not confronted with the *pro me* of the cross, nor is one personally challenged to the very depth of his or her being by the passion of Christ. Compassion alone does not reach the human heart and does not transform it.

The Right Way to Contemplate the Passion of Jesus Christ and the Fruits Which Grow from That

Luther does not confine himself to criticizing the ways, false according to him, by which many of his contemporaries meditated on the passion of Jesus Christ. He opposes to them his own idea and shows how great are the benefits that in life and in death, a person is able to draw from meditation on the cross.

We shall follow in detail here the unfolding of his thought in the sermon of 1519: "Contemplation of the Sufferings of Christ" (Points 4–15), occasionally also referring to the two sermons of 1518, as well as that in which Luther dealt with "Preparation for Death" in 1519. The benefit which is derived from a good contemplation of the passion of Jesus Christ can be presented under three aspects:

1) knowledge of sin; 2) the cross, human salvation, and the love of God; 3) Christ as example.

1. Knowledge of Sin

"The total value of the suffering of Christ consists in this, that human beings come to a knowledge *(Erkenntnis)* of themselves, are terrified at what they learn of themselves, and are cast down" (WA

2, 138, 15).[22] "This shock must come to the point that you see the strong and inflexible anger of God against sin and the sinner, so that he was not willing to remit sins even to his only beloved Son, except by means of so dire a punishment" (WA 2, 137, 12). Such passages recall the thought of Saint Bernard of Clairvaux. But we shall develop further what Luther means here.

The passion of Christ is an accusation against human beings. Their sin is unveiled. If the only-begotten Son had to suffer this punishment in order to save us, how great must be the anger of God and the weight of sin! [23] Persons arrive at this knowledge of themselves, that is of the situation *coram Deo* (as seen by God), only by considering Christ,[24] and not by considering themselves in mere introspection, which despises the passion of Christ on the cross. But when they consider Christ on the cross and through him God, in his holiness and love, human beings also discover themselves.[25] Seen thus, knowledge of God and knowledge of self coincide.[26]

It is also necessary to note that knowledge of sin, for the ones confronted by the cross, is an existential knowledge. They do not have to deduce their own from a general condition of sin in which all persons are found. But it is each individual, each person in particular who has contributed toward the crucifixion of Christ. They are my own sins that he bears.[27] I cannot rid myself of sin by accusing the Jews, "for the malefactors, the Jews, as God judged and punished them, are nonetheless servants of your sin, and it is truly you who by your sin, have killed the Son of God and crucified him" (WA 2, 138, 29).

It is striking to note, especially in the sermons of 1518, how much Luther underlines the necessity for persons to be touched in their heart (*affectus*) by the cross of Christ.[28] The knowledge of Christ and of my sin cannot be limited to the *intellectus* but must reach me and move me in my heart, which includes also my emotions.[29] This is not sentimentalism, which has been denounced above, but terror of conscience. The absence of this terror indicates also the absence of Christ. It is a sign of the death of the soul which Christ has left and of which therefore the devil has taken possession.[30]

But the decisive question is to know how all that is possible. How then can a person be personally touched by the cross of Christ—moved in the heart? How to go beyond compassion and imitation? It is a work which God alone can accomplish. Luther writes thus: "That is why you must pray to God that he touch your heart and allow you to consider the suffering of Christ in a fruitful manner, for it is not possible for you to consider the suffering of Christ well unless God has made it penetrate into your heart" (*WA* 2, 139, 1). "This work is not in our hands" (*WA* 2, 139, 12). Without the Holy Spirit, Christ is a dead letter—able to be grasped by the intellect, but not penetrating into the conscience of people or touching them personally.

There is another aspect of our question which is generally not considered enough (G. Heintze, for example, has neglected it). That is the union of the believer with Christ, effected by the Holy Spirit. It is within the framework of this union, and not outside of it, that the Holy Spirit touches the human conscience. Luther is able to say it in this way: "If Christ dwells in a person, he or she weeps when Christ weeps, suffers when Christ suffers" (*WA* 1, 336, 19). This union with Christ is not only a communion in spirit, a sympathy in the sense that we use the word today. It produces a kind of identification between Christ and the believer. Even the death of Christ does not stay outside of the believer, nor the sins of the believer outside Christ. "In his suffering Christ has taken our form" (*WA* 1, 336, 24); "In his suffering he has assumed (*suscepit*) the form of our sins" (*WA* 1, 339, 31); "In Christ and with him, we suffer his suffering" (*WA* 1, 339, 23).

What is Christ for the believer in this spiritual exchange? He is first and foremost sacrament and mystery (*WA* 1, 339, 19).[31] Christ to whom the believer is mysteriously united is at one and the same time he who prefigures (*significat*) "our spiritual death by his corporal death" (*WA* 1, 337, 14) and also he who effects it—that is to say, "makes us die and live" (*WA* 1, 337, 16). He makes the old person die and the new person live.

All that we have said so far about the acknowledgment of sin and the terror of conscience must be seen in the light of union with Christ. United to Christ, Christians acknowledge their sin. They agree to be before God what Christ has agreed to be before human beings, that is, despoiled and poor (*WA* 1, 336, 24; 339, 3). Therefore confession of sins is nothing other than conformity to Christ. "It is necessary that you become conformed to the image and to the suffering of Christ, in life or in hell; you must at least fall into fear, into death, into purgatory, and feel again all that Christ suffered on the cross" (*WA* 1, 138, 35). "The proper work of the suffering of Christ consists in his conforming [32] human beings to himself, in order that as Christ was miserably tortured in his body and his soul by our sins, we must be tortured as his disciples in the consciousness of our sins" (*WA* 1, 138, 19).

It is not a question here of an imitation of Jesus Christ considered as an exterior model. The cross is no longer a work realized in the past by Christ, whose fruits one could distribute today. At the center is the real union between Christ and the faithful, where the past joins the present and where the present becomes clear and is realized as a function of the past.

2. The Cross, the Salvation of Human Beings, and the Love of God

The cross does not only reveal my sin, it also takes it away. Knowledge of sin is one thing, liberation from it another. And Luther knew the despair of a man who saw only the anger of God and his own sin and could not believe in forgiveness.

Christ is not only Judge, as Luther often emphasized, but also Savior. Therefore Luther also invites us to cast our sins anew on Christ, those sins which the believer united with Christ has acknowledged as his or her own. That evidently presupposes that union with Christ of which we have just spoken. The reformer writes thus: "When believers have taken cognizance of their sins and have totally become afraid, they must be careful that the sins do not thus remain on their conscience. For all that would come of them would be sheer despair. But just as they have flowed from Christ and been made known, so it is necessary to cast them on him anew and to liberate the conscience" (*WA* 2, 139, 34).

But that evidently requires faith. "It is then that you cast your sins again on Christ, when you believe firmly that his wounds and his suffering are your sins, and that he bears them and pays for them" (Isaiah 53; 1 Peter 2:24; 2 Cor. 5:21 [*WA* 2, 140, 6]). This faith is born by the Word which those verses bring to me: "It is to these verses and others like them that you must entrust yourself again and again, in proportion to the severity with which your conscience tortures you" (*WA* 2, 140, 11).

Thus the passion of Christ is truly a consolation for those confronted by their sins: "Let the consideration of Christ suffering all things innocently and without deserving it be your one consolation" (*WA* 1, 340, 13). "For a single drop of blood, even a part of a drop, is sufficient for all my sins, and how much more so his whole passion!

I do not despair because of my sins, says Saint Augustine, because I remember the wounds of the Lord" (*WA* 1, 334, 21).

However, redemptive suffering is not the only theme taken up by Luther. Christ, to whom the believer is united, does not keep the sins; he destroys them. Here the theme of combat and victory reappears. "They [the sins] are not able to remain on Christ. They are swallowed up by his resurrection and you see no more the wounds and the sufferings, the traces of sin no longer cling to him" (*WA* 2, 140, 20).

The sins have then really disappeared—and disappeared also for the believer united to Christ. But it is certain—and Luther underlines this once again—that this is not true for human beings apart from faith. "When we see that they [our sins] rest on Christ and that he surmounts them by his resurrection and that we have the audacity to believe it, then they are dead and annihilated" (*WA* 2, 140, 18). This faith is also a gift of God for which we must ask (*WA* 2, 140, 27).

In this work of Christ, who has taken on himself the cross and suffering in order to save human beings, all the love of God is revealed. Luther is consistent in repeating often that we must rise from Christ to the Father, that is to say to possess in him all the good intentions of God toward us. From the work of the Son, from which the believer benefits, he rises to the heart of God and receives the certainty of God's love. "The Scripture urges us above all to attend to love in this passion. The incarnation and the suffering of Christ are offered to us above all to enable us to contemplate the love of God" (*WA* 1, 341, 36).

Luther insists on this particularly in the sermon which he devotes to "Preparation for Death." In the face of the despairing images which constitute death,[33] sin, and damnation, Jesus Christ is the saving image which believers must contemplate and have before them. This image is the mirror of the heart of God. Thus the dying person can hold to Jesus Christ when troubled by the thought of predestination and hell. A ruse of the devil is to disturb the believer with the problem of predestination. "Hell becomes great and grows as one contemplates it too much and raises untimely thoughts, hard to bear . . . . the devil leads persons beyond God, so that they long for another god, and imagine that God's love has been extinguished by the storm and his hate has grown" (*WA* 2, 688, 1). And Luther warns against every attempt to seek for God beyond Jesus Christ. This would be to lose sight of the love of God and fall into "hatred of God, and into cursing him" (*WA* 2, 688, 13). As the reformer was already indicating in his lectures on the epistle to the Romans, it is only the sufferings of Christ that give assurance to the one anguished by the problem of predestination.

3. Christ As Example

In the sermons devoted to the contemplation of the suffering of Christ, Luther pays little attention to this point. In fact, he thinks that if the spiritual movement of the Christian which leads to the confession of sins is realized, that is to say if the Christian is joined to Christ, as in the sacrament of his death and of his new life, all the rest will follow easily. The Christian will then have no difficulty in being humble and following the example of the passion of Christ (*WA* 1, 337, 9; 1, 340, 3).

The question of the imitation of Christ is made the subject of the last point in the sermon of 1519 where Luther writes thus: "When your heart is thus fixed on Christ and that for love, and not for fear of punishment, you have become the enemy of sins, the suffering of Christ will henceforth also be for you an example for your whole life, and you will think of it in a quite different way. Until now, we have thought of it as a sacrament which works on us and to which we submit. Now we shall consider it as something which we also can realize" (*WA* 2, 141, 8). And he lists a number of trials that we must endure: sickness, contradictions, mockeries, struggle against all kinds of temptations.

In the sermon devoted to the "Preparation for Death," the theme of *exemplum* is developed more fully. Luther here emphasizes the way of Christ suffering the sorrows of death. To the one tempted to despair is presented the image of Christ who was forsaken and tempted more than us all. "Behold the heavenly image of Christ, who for you has descended into hell and has been forsaken by God, as one who is damned eternally" (*WA* 2, 690, 17).

That is at one and the same time both a consolation (election and grace do not do away with temptation) and a challenge to share the same faith. At Point 14 in particular Luther develops this aspect. Christ, he says, has been confronted with the same despairing images as we have (*WA* 2, 691, 23). But he did not murmur. He remained faithful in the struggle and in the temptation. He has won the victory by saying yes to the Father. "Thus we also, we must let go those same images . . . and we must concern ourselves only with being joined to the will of God who wishes us to be united with Christ and to believe that we rise above our death, our sin and our hell, in him, and that these things are no longer able to do us harm" (*WA* 2, 692, 16).

It is striking to see in this sermon how Luther considers the double aspect of the way of Christ, his humiliation and his exaltation. As Christ humiliated, he is the prototype of human beings in submission to the wrath of God and yet reaching God across death, sin, and hell. As Christ exalted, he is with the saints the one who intercedes for us and he is my way to the Father because in him all that separates us from God is surmounted.

Other Christological Themes in the Sermons of 1518-1519
Jesus Christ and God, the Son and the Father

It is above all in the sermon on the "Preparation for Death" that Luther describes the relationship which unites the crucified Jesus Christ to the Father.

It insists on the abandonment of the Son. He is abandoned by God "as one who is damned eternally" (*WA* 2, 690, 18).[34] It is that which explains his cry of dereliction: "My God, my God, why hast thou forsaken me?" Between the Father and the Son there lies the abyss of human sins. The anger of God breaks over the Son and drives him down even to hell. No pains that we endure in our conscience are alien to him (*WA* 2, 691,22).

How did Christ behave in this situation? "He overcame the sin which he had taken on himself through invincible obedience" (*WA* 2, 691, 18). Even abandoned by God, he did not cease to love him, bearing witness thereby that he was truly the well–beloved Son (*WA* 2, 691, 19). When the mockeries of the Jews reached him on the cross, he kept silent in order "to attend only to the beloved will of his Father, to the extent of forgetting his death, his sins, and his hell, to the extent of praying for those who mocked him, in their death, their sin and their hell" (*WA* 2, 692, 13).

You will notice that Luther does not here attempt a theory of reconciliation such as we find in Anselm. With Anselm, the suffering of the man Jesus, united with the Son of God, had acquired a meritorious character for all persons, being the work of a just person, because of his union with the Son of God, of a person representing other persons. With Luther also, as we shall see again several times, the face to face encounter between the Father and Jesus is important. But it is not a question of the person Jesus acquiring merit. It is rather a matter of Jesus Christ, God and a man, interposing himself between sinful human beings and the wrath of God, bearing the punishment and thus dissipating the wrath of God. Such a work is not the achievement of the man Jesus considered in isolation, but of the Son become human, so that he is "the happening of divine love among human beings living under the wrath of God." [35] Thus there is no contradiction between Luther's two great affirmations on the subject of the relationship between the Son become human and the Father:

- the Son surmounts the anger of the Father
- the Son expresses the love of the Father

It is precisely in bearing the anger of the Father, as he does, that Jesus reveals the love of God in all its depth. That is why Luther is so insistent that one must not stop at the man Jesus, but rise from him to the Father.[36] Before looking more closely at this affirmation and discarding possible false interpretations of it, it is necessary to emphasize here that the attitude of Jesus Christ before God is an active one. He does not passively suffer the abandonment by the Father, but continues to love him, to offer himself to him. And it is thus that the anger of God is disarmed, not simply by the juridical effect of a punishment or by a satisfactory work accomplished in perfect fashion, but because the love of the Son for the Father, a reflection of the love of the Father for the Son and for all human beings remained active even in the night of anger.[37]

We have already drawn attention to Luther's expression, "rise from the Son to the Father," and other synonymous expressions. Some further explanation is needed here, because these expressions have often given rise to false interpretations.

From the basis of traditional, dogmatic christology, does one not run the risk of devaluing Jesus Christ in relation to God, by turning the attention of believers away from him in order to direct it toward God? Is that not to lay oneself open to a kind of subordinationism? Karl Holl, the leading figure in the revival of Luther studies, has spoken of a "subordination of the Son to the Father." [38] In fact, Luther's repeated affirmation that it is necessary to rise above the Son to the Father has no trace of "subordinationism." It simply expresses in the trinitarian concept the idea that the love manifest by

Jesus Christ toward us, contrary to our experience of the wrath of God or our anguish over predestination, is the very love of the eternal God. In other words, it would be necessary to make perfectly clear that the entire Godhead—Father, Son, and Holy Spirit—is revealed even while hiding itself in the man Jesus. However, the persons of the Father and the Son are not to be confused. Otherwise a doubt could arise in the heart of a believer who might imagine two divine wills, one which would be revealed in Jesus Christ and another which would remain hidden. It is to avoid this dualism that the reformer invites us to go from Jesus Christ, the God revealed, to the hidden God who from this point of view is revealed to be the Father.

But here an interpretation could arise which would bring Luther close to *modalism*. This is a heresy condemned by the early church for not distinguishing sufficiently between the three persons of the Trinity. The exposition of Luther's christology by Althaus goes a little in this direction, particularly when he wants to highlight the truly original element in this christology (pp. 161-171). He rightly emphasizes the Johannine verse, "He who has seen me has seen the Father" (John 14:9) as one of the keys to Luther's thought. And he expounds well the insistence of Luther on the Son as the revelation of the love of the Father. But certain of his statements take a modalistic turn: "Luther finds in Jesus Christ, God himself, the Father in person" (p. 162). In this context, Althaus does not insist sufficiently on the distinction of the persons.[39] This distinction does not exclude —and we have shown this—the revelation by the Son of the love of the Father, but it places this revelation in the framework of a history unfolding itself between the Father and the Son, that is to say of a series of dramatic events which reach their climax on the cross.

In conclusion, it must be remembered that Luther invited the believer to go beyond Jesus Christ in order to avoid all "Jesus worship," which would limit itself to the consideration of Christ in a way that was emotional or merely historical. One must go beyond an imitation of Christ or a mysticism striving for union between Christ and the believer. The real importance of Christ is the salvation which he has realized according to the eternal plan of God. In the light of this work the heart of God is open. Of course, God and his ways remain hidden, but from now on we know that the ground of his being is love.

The Humiliation of the Son in His Incarnation
The Interpretation of Philippians 2 by Luther [40]

We have already noted references to the christological passage in Philippians 2 here and there in the commentaries of Luther. But the first full commentary on this text is found in the sermon on the "Double Judgment" (*WA* 2, 145-152), which according to *WA* goes back to 1519, or according to more recent research, to 1518.[41]

The subject of *kenosis* is not the preexistent Christ, but the incarnate Christ. Here Luther is to be distinguished from the Patristic writers. He must be distinguished also from certain kenotic theologians of the 19th century. For Luther, Christ does not abandon a part of his divinity when he becomes incarnate. Christ incarnate is substantially God and he remains so. Luther takes care to distinguish the "form of God" from the "divine substance of which Christ is never despoiled" (*WA* 2, 147, 38). What does the abandonment of the *forma dei* mean? Christ did not show himself as God. The man Jesus would have been able to show himself in the *forma dei,* but he renounced that. That is to say, that he renounced his liberty, his power, his righteousness, and his goodness. "He emptied himself, not wishing to use those titles against us, not wishing to be different from us. He made himself one among us for our sakes and took the condition of a slave (the slave of all our sins). . . . He took upon him our sins and our punishments . . . even though he was of such a rank as to be our God and our master, he refused it, preferring to become our slave" (*WA* 2, 148, 14).

Luther has noted clearly that the *forma servi* is not humanity as such. The humanity was assumed in the incarnation, the *forma servi* was freely chosen by the Christ man. Luther sets this attitude of the Christ man against that of the Pharisee. The Pharisee does not let go what he has; he renders it neither to God in worship, nor to his brothers in service. Jesus in contrast attributes all to the Father and is in solidarity with human beings.

As Althaus has noted: "This concept of *kenosis* reveals all the depth of Luther's christology. The plan by which he has become human crosses all his life with an incessant actualization. One can say: the incarnation is a continuous event, an act of Christ constantly renewed . . . the *kenosis* is realized anew without ceasing in the actuality of the gift to sinful human beings, in that Christ, wishing to be similar to persons, placed himself under the misery which weighed on humanity and assumed it, he who was free from all that in the *forma dei*. The incarnation is accomplished in the cross of Christ" (p. 172).

Thus understood, *kenosis* becomes, quite naturally, as Paul has shown, the basis for a new ethics. The Christian life is also a *kenosis*. "The apostle desired that every single Christian, following the example of Christ, should become the slave of others. All wisdom, righteousness, or power which would permit one to prevail over others must be referred to God: one must leave it all out of account so as to become as one who had not" (*WA* 2, 148, 32).

Christ and the Saints [42]

We do not propose here to study the problem of the saints in Luther from an anthropological point of view.[43] In any case, it is not the ecclesiological *(communio)* or properly sacramental aspect of the union with Christ and his saints which interests us here.

But from the point of view of christology we pose the question: What does the expression "Christ and his saints," which comes frequently from Luther's pen, particularly in the sermon on the "Preparation for Death" and that on "The Body of Christ and His Brethren," really mean? One might also ask the question in this form: Why are the saints associated with Christ to give assurance of salvation to the believer?

They are, with Christ, images of the grace of God. Believers are not invited to consider the damned and to be moved at their plight for fear of their own fate, but to contemplate those whom God has elected, i.e., Christ and his saints (*WA* 2, 689, 8, 28). Considering their election and thus discovering the grace of God, is to be already elected oneself (*WA* 2, 690, 26). At the same time, they are examples in the faith (*WA* 2, 690, 37). On these two grounds, Christ and his saints are on the same level. They are images of the grace of God and examples of a victorious faith. However, Luther also notes the difference between the saints and Christ. Compared with him, they are on the same level as us. They have cast their sins on him and are thus members of his body.

Let us note moreover that Luther uses the term "saints" in a rather vague manner. In the majority of cases it signifies the holy dead, but it can also encompass "the holy angels and devout men on earth" (*WA* 2, 745, 13). It is in this direction that his thought will tend more and more: the saints are the believers, i.e., the living.[44] In the sermons that we are studying, Luther insists on the invisible character of the communion of saints (*WA* 2, 752, 36). It is a matter of faith—and it evidently does not exclude the living. In another passage (*WA* 2, 745, 23) Luther speaks of the saints on earth whose misfortunes affect the saints in heaven. But the accent is not yet placed on the saints as living members of the body of Christ. Communion with Christ and with the saints is realized by the sacrament and by faith. Luther affirms this constantly (*WA* 2, 692, 33; 2, 694, 23; 2, 695, 16; 2, 743, 7; 2, 748, 14). The dimension of *synaxis*, of communion, is the principal theme of the eucharistic sermon of 1519.[45]

But what Luther develops further is that of which the communion with Christ and the saints consists. It signifies that the angels and the saints "love me, concern themselves with me, intercede for me and suffer with me, that they carry my sin and overcome hell" (*WA* 2, 694, 24),[46] but Luther says a little later on that the assurance of the dying Christian rests on two things: first, on God himself; and then partly on Christ and partly on the angels and the saints (*WA* 2, 695, 16). "If God looks upon you, all the angels, all the saints and all creatures follow his gaze, and if you remain in the faith, you are in their hands" (*WA* 2, 695, 16). "For God gives orders to his angels, to all his saints and to all creatures to take care of human beings" (*WA* 2, 697, 22).

Luther sees communion with the saints as an exchange. In Christ and with him, the saints bear the sins of believers and struggle with them and for them. As for the believer, he or she has part in the sufferings of Christ and the saints. With Christ then the saints struggle against sin. In effect Luther writes: "We have need not only of the community and of Christ so that they may struggle against temptation, but it is also necessary that Christ and his saints place themselves before us, in order that sin may not be imputed to us according to the severe judgment of God" (WA 2, 744, 22).[47] From this point of view and at this point, Luther even counselled invocation of the saints (*WA* 2, 696, 24; 2, 697, 5-24), a thing which he expressly discouraged in 1528.[48]

As for believers, united to Christ and to the saints, he or she becomes conformed to them (*WA* 2, 748, 33). In communion with them the vexations which they suffer touch the believer also. Of course, Christ and the saints are in heaven. But the vexations and sufferings which they endure are the injury done to the truth and to the Word of God or to the saints who are on earth, and in a more general way to what Luther calls "the needy" of Christ (*WA* 2, 745, 21). The communion is thus oriented toward a perspective which is entirely ethical and concrete.

Placing ourselves on a christological plane, we do not think that this bringing together of Christ and the saints is another form of *subordinationism,* as Holl indicates. If in his humanity, Christ seems to be a human being among others, he remains the head of the body, the source from which the saints as believers live. It is this aspect which Luther will from now on bring to the fore. To the extent that the church, the body of Christ, is truly a community of the living and the dead—which it was for Luther—it is difficult to see how a concept of the saints envisaged as believers could restrict his thought.

The Commentary on the Psalms
 (Operationes in Psalmos) 1519-1521 [49]

With this commentary written in Latin we return to Luther's strictly academic and exegetical work. But the spiritual climate is the same as that we have found in the writings against indulgences and in the sermons that we have just analyzed. It is the cross—of Christ and of the Christian—which is at the center of his thought. "*Crux sola est nostra Theologia*" (the cross alone is our theology).[50]

The Cross of Jesus Christ—
 Jesus Christ Made Sin for Us—a Tempted Man

It was when commenting on Psalm 22, whose opening verse New Testament tradition puts into the mouth of the crucified Jesus (Matt. 27:46), that Luther developed in the most explicit and profound fashion his conception of the passion of Christ.

Christ really suffered on the cross. And his suffering was not only physical, but moral. The depth of his sorrow came from the fact that he felt himself abandoned by God. It is thus in his conscience that the drama reaches its paroxysm. And Luther protests against the interpretation according to which Jesus was not abandoned by God (whom he would have continued to see), but only deprived of his help (*WA* 5, 601, 19). At several places he criticizes the Fathers of the church, who hesitated to apply to Christ certain verses like, "Why art thou so far from me?" (v. 1b). No, says the reformer, this is an exclamation of Christ himself and not only of his people (*WA* 5, 607, 11). And Luther opposes Saint Augustine who applies v. 2 not to Christ as head, but to Christ as body, i.e., to Christians (*WA* 608, 31). 'I will not admit that any part of this Psalm has been said by Christ only in the person of his members, as many Fathers affirm, but I wish to apply everything in the context [*quadrare*] of his own person" (*WA* 5, 610, 20).

In interpreting this psalm, Luther is not preoccupied with the natures of Christ, nor with the theology of the incarnation as such. His preoccupation is to make clear the suffering of the man Jesus. That is the *scopos* (or aim) of the whole psalm. Here Christ does not indicate the mode of his birth nor of his nature, but of his passion as a human being (*WA* 5, 614, 8).

We have already said that the suffering of Christ is not only physical. Of course this aspect of his passion is not negligible, but the true source of his suffering is the troubled conscience, the terrible agony of a person who feels cut off from God, abandoned by him. "The blows with which God strikes because of sins are not only the pain of death, but also the fear and the terror of a troubled conscience, which feels the eternal anger and behaves as though it were eternally abandoned and rejected from the face of God (*WA* 5, 603, 14).[51] It is really the pains of the damned that he suffered.[52] And in the *Operationes in Psalmos*, Luther interprets the descent into hell in the existential sense of a conscience confronted with the eternal anger of God.[53] Commenting on Psalm 16:10 he writes: "Hell is the fear of death, that is to say the taste of death by which the damned are terrified of death without being able to escape it" (*WA* 5, 463, 23).

The way in which Luther describes the suffering of Christ on the cross certainly constitutes a break with tradition.[54] Even those who, like Gerson and Tauler, for example, paid great attention to the temptations (*Anfechtungen*) to which human beings are exposed, have not dared to attribute them to Christ. For the Fathers of the church and for all the medieval theologians, the suffering of Christ was of the physical order, while his soul remained in possession of the beatific vision, that is to say a blessed and uninterrupted contemplation of God. The Scholastic theologians and the mystics attribute suffering to Christ in the less noble inclinations of his soul. But the upper levels had remained firmly anchored in the assurance of eternal salvation.

Luther, on the contrary, envisages in a radical fashion the feeling of abandonment and damnation in the consciousness of Jesus Christ.[55] Luther set out in this direction by understanding the humanity of Jesus Christ, no longer only in the categories of nature, but also in the perspective of his consciousness. And he has comprehended the humanity of Jesus Christ, thus characterized, beginning with his own struggles of conscience, as one confronted by the anger of God.[56] On this matter, the *Commentary on the Psalms* of 1519-1521 contains some particularly penetrating passages.[57] It is thus right to emphasize, as does for example Ernst Wolf, the importance of temptation in Luther's view of a proper knowledge of Jesus Christ.[58]

We have spoken of the link which exists between the temptation of Jesus Christ and that of Christians. We must now show that this link must be understood dialectically. One part of the dialectic is that the understanding of the cross of Jesus, in the way that it has been developed here, is rooted existentially in the experience of the sinful human being—and of Luther in particular—confronted by the wrath of God. And Luther can say: If the saints are thus abandoned by God, what must be the abandonment of Christ, the chief of saints, who has carried all our weaknesses in himself! (*WA* 5, 603, 2). In his interpretation of Psalm 22, particularly from *WA* 5, 619, 25, Luther gives a penetrating description of what this temptation is, that belongs simultaneously to Christians and to Jesus: "Thus they have also shaken the Christ, their head, i.e., God, so that like a person who wavers he cried out: My God, my God . . ." (*WA* 5, 621, 40).[59]

As the second part of the dialectic, Luther shows the difference between the temptations of Jesus Christ and ours.[60] His are infinitely more profound. But there is not only a difference of degree (*multo ergo magis*, *WA* 5, 603, 2) due to the fact that Jesus carries the sins of all, but two qualitative differences separate us from Christ. For one, his suffering is propitiatory. Secondly, in his suffering Christ commits no sin; he does not curse God. We will return later to these two aspects.

The cross of Christ is explained from ours. At the same time his cross casts a special illumination on our suffering. It reveals, in effect, the dimension of judgment which we are tempted to forget and which Christ assumed. On the other hand, the cross is consolation for us since the punishment has effectively been assumed in our place and for our sake.

One may well ask how the fear of abandonment and the feeling of the misery of the damned can be attributed to Christ who is innocent. Luther himself poses the question (*WA* 5, 603, 36). He replies to that by showing that the reality of sin appears in human beings in two ways. On the one hand, there is sin which has been done, but not consciously. This is precisely the most serious state of sin, because the sinner is not conscious of himself or herself as a sinner (WA 5, 604, 3). Then comes the law which makes sin evident, that is to say, conscious.

Then the conscience is disturbed. It is this confusion which the damned feel that is the descent into hell. This is the way in which Christ had assumed the suffering of sin (WA 5, 604, 8). Because Luther introduced a new dimension, that of conscience, he could go beyond Saint Anselm, for whom the idea that Christ had become sin for us would have been inconceivable. In contrast, Luther will be able to say: "He felt in his conscience that he was cursed by God" (WA 5, 603, 34), and to speak of "sin which he had felt in himself without blasphemy, without cursing" (WA 5, 605, 8).

At the same time, however, Luther does not cease to insist on the innocence of the actions of Christ. If he felt sin in his conscience, like a condemned person, it was not his own, but that of others with which he identified himself. He is himself innocent by nature. Luther establishes this innocence in the traditional way, explaining it by the virgin birth of Jesus (WA 5, 605, 5).

But the innocence of Christ, or the absence of sin in him, is not only a question of nature, it is also one of acts. Christ proves and preserves his innocence when on the cross he is confronted with the eternal anger of God. He did not blaspheme God on the cross and did not curse him (WA 5, 604, 32; 5, 605, 9). Certainly the temptation to blaspheme was there for him (WA 5, 611, 33; 5, 612, 19).

But he rose above the temptation. Therefore, for Luther, his cry of dereliction is no more than the "creaking of the timbers" (WA 5, 604, 23; 5, 605, 3-26), while in our mouth it would be an accusation against God and proof of our lack of faith. In our case, in fact, "the tree is not good" (WA 5, 605, 1). In spite of the similarity between Christ and us, in which he suffers as we do, and is found submitting to the wrath of God, there is then a great difference. We continue to sin, carrying in our conscience the weight of sin; while he accepts the judgment of God and undergoes, without sinning, the anger as well as temptation (WA 5, 604, 12ff.). While the damned hate God, Christ, who suffers the same pains, continues to love the Father with all his might (WA 5, 605, 25).

According to Luther, the mystery of Christ crucified can only be expressed paradoxically. One must affirm that two contraries coexist in him: "In Christ there coexisted both the highest joy and the deepest sorrow, the most abject weakness and the greatest strength, the highest glory and the lowest shame, the greatest peace and the deepest trouble, the most exalted life and the most miserable death" (*WA* 5, 602, 22).

He was abandoned by God, not partially, but totally, although God was entirely present in this suffering man. Sin and righteousness are not divided in Christ; but on the one hand he bore in himself all the sins of human beings and assumed the anger of God even unto damnation, while on the other hand he did not cease to be righteous and to translate into his life the righteousness and love of God. He was truly, as we have seen in the sermons and from the point of view of the *theologia crucis,* the love of God present in his anger.

This fundamental *simul* is manifest, according to Luther, in the attitude of Christ on the cross—particularly by this word which the crucified cries out when he is abandoned by God: "My God!" Now no one expresses himself thus when he is entirely abandoned by God (*WA* 5, 602, 27). Here it is necessary to affirm the *simul* which we have just developed. Thus the *theologia crucis* has plumbed the depths and pushed the *simul* between the human and the divine nature as it was given in the incarnation to its mysterious and most paradoxical point.

The *simul* of the *theologia crucis* points toward Easter. It was necessary to reveal to the world that this man, apparently abandoned by God, remained present with God and that God remained present with him. This eschatological perspective appears notably in the comment on Psalm 8: "Christ became for us a human being everywhere and in every respect without hope and afflicted. Now he has the lordship over all things and his rule will be praised, commended, and worshiped" (*WA* 5, 277, 11ff.). The cross is not the last word from God, it points toward glorification. The rule of Christ now reveals that this man, abandoned by God, was at the same time God, but that is revealed only to the eyes of faith, to believers who accept that their own humanity must be conformed, as we shall see later, to the humiliated humanity of Jesus Christ.

It remains for us to show that the suffering of Christ belongs in the context of soteriology, which dominates all Luther's thought. In fact, "Christ has not assumed this evil for himself, but for us (*WA* 5, 606, 16 and 21).[61] He has done it from grace (i.e., love which is spontaneously granted), while we are immersed in it from birth (*WA* 5, 606, 17). By suffering, he has destroyed sin, vanquished death, and made possible the renewal of all things (*WA* 5, 600, 24). Having disarmed the wrath of God by his love and being, by his resurrection, the image of the victory of love over wrath, he is the greatest consolation possible for believers who are accused by their sin and confronted by the eternal wrath (*WA* 5, 274, 10). In this distress, therefore, believers can call on him with confidence (*WA* 5, 606, 22).

Luther's thought leads ultimately to the theme of "joyous exchange." Christ is not only my Savior, "out there," but in close communion with believers he takes their sins and gives them his righteousness. That is what Luther shows in a very beautiful passage (*WA* 5, 608, 6-22). The theme of "joyous exchange" will occupy our attention again when we come to study the tract, *The Freedom of a Christian*, 1520.

The Reign of the Cross and the Reign of Glory

In the preceding pages we have considered the cross of Jesus Christ and the reality of his suffering. We emphasized how Luther described the humanity of Jesus Christ in a quite new way, when compared with the traditions. But this description is not at the expense of the divinity of Christ. He who has thus suffered is in fact God, although hidden. He is both: on the same level as we are, he submitted to the wrath of God, and he is also the one who saves us. The Lord is the crucified one, and the cross is the place where the saving power of God acts and where his solidarity with sinners is shown.

We must now place the cross of Jesus Christ in its total context. We must show how it is oriented toward the glory to come. We must also show that human beings have access to that glory and to the knowledge of God in Jesus Christ only if they first allow themselves to be humiliated by considering this man who is abandoned. In him the preaching of the Word invites us to an encounter with God, and, by becoming conformed to this humanity, our humanity truly finds itself restored. There is a particularly significant passage in relation to this subject in Luther's commentary on Ps. 5:2. There he writes: "Christ is our King when he turns us from ourselves and leads us to him; he is our God when he receives us, we who come to him, and he fills us from himself, i.e., with the divine goodness. The first condition is the cross, the passion, the crossing, the renunciation of the world, of its attractions, and, in general, our mortification. Only there is the possession and our glorification. By his human rule, or as the apostle says, by his rule in the flesh, which he exercises by faith, he conforms us to himself and crucifies us. He transforms our arrogant and miserable divinities into true humanity, i.e., into persons who are pitiable and sinful. Because in Adam we aspired unto likeness with God, so he descended to our likeness, to bring us back to a knowledge of ourselves. That took place in the mystery of the incarnation. That is the rule of faith, where the cross of Christ dominates, that cross which overthrows divinity perversely sought, but which brings back the humanity and the feebleness of the flesh, perversely abandoned. But on the other hand, by the rule of his glory and his divinity, he imprints on us the form of his glorified body, wherein we shall be like him. We shall no longer be either sinners or weak, no longer persons who must be led and corrected, but we shall be kings and children of God, like the angels" (WA 5, 128, 31– 129, 6).

It is necessary to place this text against the background of the confrontation of the two Adams. Christ is the new Adam. The first Adam —and we in him—tried to raise himself up to God, to be like him, to snatch deification as a prize. That is the perverse way of seeking divinity *(divinitatem perverse petitam)* (WA 5, 129, 2). That is the very essence of sin. In Christ, the new Adam appears, the true human being. Whoever discovers him, discovers himself at the same time to be a sinner. But to be conformed to him is also to become a child of God. That is the background to this text and the thread of its argument.

Now let us look more closely at the different aspects of Luther's thought.

The reasoning is based on the idea of the rule of Christ, such as we noted already in the *Dictata*. He rules now by his Word and by his sacraments;[62] this rule is exercised in faith and is dominated by the cross (WA 5, 129, 1). Of what does it consist? In turning us away from ourselves and in leading us to him (WA 5, 128, 31), that is to say, in turning us away from our presumption, from our false way of wishing to be gods. We are led by Christ, that is to say, by his Word, to his humanity, weak and crucified. And we are invited to believe that this is the true human being—the one who does not seek to raise himself up, but who refers everything to God and accepts his weakness. To believe that this Jesus is the true human being is to acknowledge oneself as a sinner, since our humanity is different from his. This confession of sins, springing from faith in the Word which invites us to consider the humanity of Jesus, gives a true understanding of the self. It is thus that we are led to knowledge of ourselves (WA 5, 128, 40).

To accept the humanity of Jesus Christ as being our true humanity is not possible without the cross, since our tendency to self-deification must be shattered. In order to "transform our arrogant and miserable divinities into true persons, i.e., into human beings who are pitiable and sinful" (who acknowledge their sin) (WA 5, 128, 38), Christ must make us pass through the cross. And I recognize the humanity of Jesus Christ as true humanity only by accepting also the cross of my own feebleness. By thus confessing my sin, by accepting a humanity dependent in every respect on God, I am conformed to Christ in his humanity.[63]

And thus, in this way, I shall have part in the divine life of Christ. That is the other aspect of the rule of Christ. He reigns and exercises his lordship as God, by which he "fills us with himself, i.e., with the divine goodness" (WA 5, 128, 32). Further on in our passage, Luther uses the future tense to describe this "deification" of human beings. He is concerned, in effect, with an eschatological perspective. Certainly, the rule is exercised here below already, to the extent that being conformed to Christ, we acknowledge our sins and accept our humanity. But it is a rule or reign which will be completed only at the end of time. It is then that he will fully "imprint on us the form of his glorified body so that we shall be like him. [Then] we shall no longer be sinners or weak, no longer persons who must be led and corrected, but we shall be kings and children of God, like the angels" (WA 5, 129, 4).

At this point, we should like to clarify the thought of Luther with four remarks:

First. One here clearly understands the place of the cross of Christ and that of the Christian in the thought of Luther. There is a definite order to be followed by human beings toward God, leading ultimately to recognition of God and participation in his life. One must first pass through the cross.[64] That means that one must not begin with the divinity of Christ and construct a theology *from above* (for this Luther condemned the Scholastics), but one must consider Christ in his humanity. The word by which Christ rules in the Holy Spirit will thus lead us quite naturally to God or will bring us near to God (*WA* 5, 129, 11).

But the knowledge of Christ as God can never be an isolated part of human existence. His cross is also mine. It is by accepting it in faith that I am led to God and have my part in the divine life. There is no direct access to God. It is necessary to go by way of humiliation, by confession of sins, by the humanity of the crucified, and by my own cross. This idea is at the center of Luther's affirmation.[65]

Second. Christians are persons in the image of Christ. That does not mean simply that they must imitate him or be made like him, but that the christological dualism is also found on the anthropological level. What does that mean? In the *Unbekannten Fragmenten* (Anonymous Fragments), we read: "By the cross each disciple of Christ becomes a double person *(gemellus)*; stupid *(stultus)* in the flesh, wise in the spirit; outwardly abject, inwardly glorified . . . as in Christ, the double person and type *(forma)* of all double persons, who by his weak humanity renders persons weak, anxious, captives, slaves, but by his powerful divinity makes them powerful children of God and like gods, free lords" (Vogelsang, 45, 19).[66]

Hence the anthropological *simul* derives its origin from the christological *simul*. In the same way that Christ is both weak human being and all-powerful God, so the Christian is both acknowledged sinner and also the righteous and new person.

Third. It seems to us that the concept of "deification," dear to the ancient church of the East, reappears here in an original variation. We have already compared Luther with Athanasius in reference to his commentary on Rom. 1:3-4.

Certainly, if one conceives of "deification" as a full ontological transformation of human beings, as a change from humanity to divinity, as the leveling of the difference between the Creator and the creature, then evidently it is not possible to find "deification" in Luther. But if one conceives of it as human beings participating in the righteousness and liberty of God, like filial participation in the divine existence, without the creatures confusing themselves with the Creator, then one can speak of "deification" in the thought of Luther, in the sense of a restoration of the image of God.

Naturally, Luther insists particularly on the cross. It is this which distinguishes him from Athanasius. He has rediscovered the thought of the apostle Paul, the weight of sin, the human tendency toward self-deification. But he also emphasizes that to become children again, we must pass through the cross, through suffering and through the confession of sins.

Fourth. Our text makes quite clear the strong eschatological orientation of Luther's thought. In order to know God now, it is necessary to pass through the Word, the cross, the humanity of Christ, but one day we shall see him face to face. Surely that is not to say that God has been transformed into a human being. Thus all *Monophysitism* is excluded. That means also that the relationships between God and human beings are of faith and not of sight. All christological theory must take account of the relativity given by this eschatological orientation.

Luther's Eucharistic Teaching in 1520 and Its Christology [67]

Every idea about Christian worship and particularly the Holy Supper, which is the essence of the mass, implies a christology. In fact, the work of Christ, the manner of his presence in the church, his relations with human beings—all these questions arise when one talks of worship. That is why it is indispensable to examine Luther's most important writings on the Eucharist. In 1520 a treatise appeared which was devoted entirely to the Lord's Supper: *Ein Sermon von dem neuen Testament, das ist von der heyligen Messe.*[68] In addition, the treatise on *The Babylonian Captivity of the Church* contains a long exposition devoted to the same question.[69] Luther had actually already expressed himself on the subject of the Eucharist as early as the sermon of 1519, *"Von dem Hochwürdigen Sacrament des Heiligen Waren Leychnams Christi, und von den Bruderschaften"* to which we have already referred. We showed that the central theme was "the communion and the incorporation [of the believer] in Christ and in all the saints." [70] Luther shows there how believers find an aid for their faith in this sacrament and in the communion with Christ and the saints, but he scarcely mentions the means whereby Christ is present, the importance of the words of institution or why the Eucharist is sacrament and not sacrifice!

It is in 1520 that all these themes come to the fore. The application of justification by faith to the understanding of the Eucharist and the opposition to Rome now begin to appear with force: "When I published my sermon on the Eucharist, I did as everybody did, and I did not trouble myself about the pope, whether he was right or wrong. But now that I am provoked and dragged into this arena by force, I am going to say freely what I think."[71]

We shall first expound Luther's ideas about the Eucharist before we separate out the christological elements implicit in them.

It is of fundamental importance for Luther that the mass should be placed under the sign of the promise and not under the sign of a work to be accomplished. It is neither work nor sacrifice, but there we receive a gift, we benefit from a testament which Christ, on the eve of his death, has bequeathed to his disciples and to all those who believe. The content of this testament is the forgiveness of sins. This testament comes into effect with the death of Christ. At the same time, it is attested by a seal and a sign: "his own true flesh and blood under the bread and wine." [72]

And Luther shows further how since the time of Adam, God has blessed sinful persons with promises of grace.[73] But "the Old Testament did not promise remission of sins, i.e., eternal benefits, but only temporal benefits."[74] In the New Testament, on the contrary, on the basis of the death of Christ, "by his blood and by means of the Spirit, grace is promised for the remission of sins, in order that you may grasp the inheritance.[75] Almost always in the Old Testament, God joined a sign to the promise.[76] It is much the same in the New. To the quality of the gift—pardon and eternal life—the quality of the seal and the sign correspond: the body and blood of Christ united to the bread and wine.

In these two treatises, Luther protests against a number of practices and doctrines which, according to him, deform the sense of the Eucharist. It is in this connection that he criticizes the doctrine of transubstantiation.[77] According to this doctrine, only the accidents of the bread and wine remain at the moment of consecration, while their substance is replaced by the body and blood of Christ. No, the reformer replies. "It is real bread and real wine in which the true flesh and true blood of Christ are found, not less than as those people think who describe them as their accidents." The doctrine of transubstantiation is "without foundation in Scripture and in reason." [78] "One must never do violence to the divine words, whether of human beings or of angels. But as far as possible they should be kept in their plainest meaning . . . so also here: since the evangelists say clearly that Christ took bread and blessed it, and when in turn the book of Acts and the apostle Paul speak also of bread, it must be understood [that it concerns] real bread and real wine." [79] Besides, transubstantiation was not taught "until the pseudo-philosophy of Aristotle undertook to invade the church, i.e., only during the past three hundred years." [80]

"But why could Christ not have made his body remain in the substance as well as in the accidents?" [81] And Luther recalls the image of iron and fire to illustrate his statement. He refuses to make Aristotle and his fellow human teachers into judges of such elevated and divine things. Why, he asks, do we not refrain from being curious in order to attach ourselves simply to the words of Christ, accepting that we do not know all that takes place in this act, happy to know that Christ's true body is present by virtue of his Word.[82]

And a little further on he continues, "As for me, then, if I do not manage to grasp the manner by which the body of Christ is in the bread, I will shut up my soul, captive in obedience to Christ. And attaching myself simply to his words, I believe firmly not only that the body of Christ is in the bread, but that the bread is the body of Christ." [83] The reasoning of the reformer concludes by a comparison between the mystery of the sacramental union and that of the two natures of Christ. In the hypostatic union these two natures continue in their integrity. The divinity is not contained in the accidents of the human nature. "Similarly, in order that the true body and the true blood be found in the sacrament, it is not necessary that the bread and the wine be transubstantiated, changed into another substance, so that Christ be contained under the accidents" (WA 6, 511, 39).

Another deformation criticized by the reformer lies in the practical sphere; it was customary to pronounce the words of institution in a very low voice, so that they are "hidden" (WA 6, 362, 14). A grave abuse, he observes, for the words must be heard, at all cost, by everybody. They are a summary of the gospel. Preaching is only a way of explaining the content of the words of institution.

Besides, "without these words, the sacrament would be nothing, a body without a soul, a barrel without wine, a pocket without money, a sheath without a sword" (WA 6, 363, 13ff.). The Word being more important than the sign, the church is party to a culpable ritualism when it is content to make the liturgical gestures before the people without causing them to hear the words of institution. In fact, it is to abolish faith and transform the mass into a good work. But according to Luther, the mass does not consist of doing a good work, the occasion to give something to God, but rather of receiving

the promise of forgiveness.[84] The only legitimate attitude then is
that of faith.

Putting the accent on faith raises the question of the very meaning of the mass. Would it not be possible to have faith without celebrating the mass in church as is usually done? (*WA* 6, 372, 15ff.).
This is a singularly modern question which prefigures already the
consequences which certain followers of Luther will draw from the
attitudes taken by the reformer. Here is Luther's reply to this objection: of course, he says, what is essential is faith, but how could
we acquire faith in relation to the sacrament, that is the promise of
grace, if there were no sacrament and no call to faith in those very
places set apart for this, which are the churches? (*WA* 6, 372, 22ff.).
The mass is instituted precisely "because of God's Word, which no
one can ignore" (*WA* 6, 373, 10), "so that faith, furnished with the
divine words and signs, and strengthened by them, is able to stand
against all sin, suffering, death, and hell" (*WA* 6, 373, 29). Again, Luther gives two other replies to this question. He notes that on the one
hand, because the mass is instituted by God, it should be used with
gratitude" (*WA* 6, 372, 28). On the other hand, "We live still in the
flesh . . . we do not yet reign in the spirit. Therefore it is necessary
that we come together in a bodily fashion, in order to exhort one
another by example to prayer, praise, and thanksgiving, with an eye
toward faith" (*WA* 6, 372, 34).

We shall be returning to Luther's criticism of the concept of the
mass as a sacrifice. The mass is according to him "a sacrament and a
testament, and these are not and cannot be a sacrifice, any more
than the other sacraments, Baptism, absolution, penitence, unction,
etc., can be, without loss of the gospel, Christ, consolation, and all
the grace of God" (*WA* 6, 367, 16). Is this to say that the words of
the lesser and the greater canon, where the mass is treated as a sacrifice, are from now on no longer to be used? No! says Luther in reply
to this, but it does mean that these words are no longer applied to
the sacrament as such, "but either to the bread and wine which are
going to be consecrated or to the prayers. For the bread and the wine
are offered beforehand to be blessed, that they might be sanctified
by the Word and the prayer. But after having been blessed and consecrated, they are no longer offered, but received as a gift of God"
(*WA* 6, 524, 39ff.). On the other hand, Luther recalls the "collec-
tions" made for the poor, to which reference is made in the Acts of

the Apostles. It is from these that, according to him, the idea of the sacrifice in the mass has come.[85]

The theme of sacrifice is not, however, devalued in the thought of the reformer, but it is seen from a different perspective. In a fairly long passage, he develops the idea that it is necessary for us to sacrifice ourselves and all that we have, praying that the will of God be accomplished and thanking him.[86] But he insists that we do not have to present directly these prayers through which we sacrifice ourselves, but that we do have to go through Christ. He is our priest, that is to say, our intercessor before the Father. He is the mediator who transmits our prayers to God and makes us acceptable to the Father. In this perspective, it is not we who sacrifice Christ, an idea which Luther thought he could discern among those who made the mass a sacrifice accomplished by the priest. Luther affirms that it is Christ who sacrifices us. It is he who is the author of the action— and not human beings. If one then wishes to call the mass a sacrifice, "it cannot be in itself, but only that we sacrifice ourselves with Christ, that is to say that we rest on Christ with a firm faith in his testament and that we appear before God wih our prayer, our praise, and our sacrifice, only through him and his intermediacy. . . . It would be right to call the mass a sacrifice, not that we sacrifice the sacrament, but by our praise, our prayer, and our sacrifice, we urge Christ and give him a reason *(Ursach)* to sacrifice himself in heaven for us and to sacrifice us with him." [87]

Thus Luther is far from abandoning the idea of sacrifice. The theme of the Christ who stands before the Father appears constantly in his writings. What he objects to is the claim that Christ is at our disposal, to be made into an object that can be presented to God in order to gain his favors. It is that which damages both the sovereignty of Christ and the complete character of his work on the cross. In prayer, a person can do no more than remind God of the work of Christ and urge Christ to intercede for the believer before the Father. But what would this prayer be if it were not carried by faith? It presupposes the sacrament, that is, the promise of grace. And yet such a prayer can also be said outside the mass. In fact, Christ is "an eternal priest, for he is priest in every moment and sacrifices without ceasing to God." [88] That is why the sacrifice of Christians is not limited to the mass. Luther can even say, "There are many who celebrate the mass rightly and sacrifice without knowing, or even without noticing that they themselves are priests and are celebrating the mass." [89] However, because of our weakness, we are encouraged "to join together and in community to hold such a sacrifice." [90]

The idea of the sacrifice that we have outlined here leads directly to the priesthood of all believers. The privileged position of the priest who sacrifices the mass to God is abolished. "It becomes clear that it is not the priest alone who offers the mass, but the faith of each believer. It is this faith which constitutes true priestly office by which Christ is sacrificed before God, an office which the priest expresses by his outward gestures in the mass. We are then all spiritual priests before God." [91]

Our exposition had as its object the eucharistic ideas of Luther as such. It could not yet take into account the implicit christology. But we must now deal more explicitly with this christology. The first question to examine has to do with the connection between the mass and the saving work of Jesus Christ. At the center of the eucharistic teaching of Luther, as we have shown, lies the concept of testament. This is in fact the promise of forgiveness of sins and of eternal life. The validity of this promise, attested by the seal and sign that are the body and blood of Christ united to the bread and the wine, is dependent on the saving work of Jesus Christ, realized by his life and death. In a way, it is on this work that the gift promised by the Word is founded, namely the forgiveness of sins. In the passages on the Eucharist which we have just analyzed the reformer does not say precisely how he understands the saving work of Jesus Christ. But we have already seen in connection with other texts that it is not a question of a sacrifice which Christ brings to God the Father in order to merit salvation for human beings. Luther does not follow Anselm on this point. Undoubtedly the reformer can speak of the sacrifice of Jesus Christ on the cross—and we shall find several examples of this expression, notably in his great *Commentary on the Epistle to the Galatians.* But there he wants only to express the suffering of Christ, which freely and naturally assumes the sin of human beings and the wrath of God. This work has been accomplished. The mass can do no more than distribute its effects or its fruits. Luther will develop this theme some years later in his treatise of 1525, *Against the Heavenly Prophets* (WA 18, 203, 21ff.).

Luther's criticism of the mass does not bear in the first place on the idea of the repetition of the sacrifice of Christ. Of course he opposes that in the name of Heb. 9:28. But his criticism is above all against the sacrificial conception itself and the idea of merit hidden beneath. Salvation is realized in Jesus Christ by the victory of the love of God over his wrath. The mass will not then be a sacrifice brought by human beings to God—even if it is Christ that they think they are sacrificing, because God is already reconciled to them. The Father has sent the Son, the Son has satisfied the Father. The wrath of God has given way to love. That is why the mass must be placed under the sign of the promise, and not under that of a work or a sacrifice. The primary idea then is that of the gift offered to us in the mass. This gift is the forgiveness of sins and eternal life, but fundamentally it is Jesus Christ himself, to the extent that it is he who addresses to us the words of grace and testifies to them by his body and blood.

But salvation is not only offered to us by God by means of the person and work of Jesus Christ. We must also consider the other viewpoint in which Jesus Christ continues to stand before God as intercessor, permitting the believer to respond to grace and to approach God. In other words, faith is both the passive acceptance of Jesus Christ and the active response to the extent that the believer, incorporated in Jesus Christ, approaches the Father by prayer. We have seen above how the reformer describes the priestly office of Christ, in which he intercedes for human beings. Quoting Ps. 110:4, Luther can say, "Christ is a priest for ever." [92]

He continues to render us acceptable to God. The fact of insisting on the priestly office thus understood allows the reformer to safeguard the sovereignty of Christ. On the one hand, certainly, it is necessary to speak of the humiliation of Christ who gives himself to us under the categories of bread and wine. On the other hand, however, we do not have him at our disposal so that we can present him to God in sacrifice. On the contrary, it is he who presents us to God. United to him in faith, we are no longer masters of ourselves, but are incorporated into Christ the Lord, our Savior.

It is this priestly action of Christ in the faith of each believer which is basic to the universal priesthood. One would be wrong to conclude that Luther denied the sense of particular ministries in the church. But he would no longer base them on a sacrificial conception of the mass. He would see them in relation to the Word of grace which is to be proclaimed and which forms the essence of the sacrament.

The Treatise on *The Freedom of a Christian* [93]
and the Theme of "Joyous Exchange" [94]

We have already shown several times that faith was, for Luther, an intimate union of human beings with Jesus Christ. It is in this intimate union that we are saved. One of the most frequent and most striking images by which Luther, following a long tradition, describes the union of the believer with Christ is that of marriage. The believer is united with Christ as the bride with the bridegroom.

We shall first see how Luther understands the union, in order to examine the christology which this image implies, as well as the importance of this union with Christ in the life of the believer. Here we shall principally use the Latin version of the text. This text is certainly less condensed, but more detailed and precise.

Here is what Luther writes: "Faith unites the soul to Christ as the bride is united to her husband. By this mystery, says the apostle, Christ and the soul become one flesh. . . . Marriages between humans are only pale reflections of this supreme example: from now on, all that belongs to the couple constitutes a common possession, both the good and the bad. Thus all that Christ possesses, the soul can avail itself of and can boast of, as its own, and all that belongs to the soul, Christ abrogates to himself and makes his own." [95]

The marriage theme thus evoked in connection with the union between Christ and the believer is familiar to the mystics. Must we, therefore, compare Luther with them on this point? A certain parallelism, even a measure of influence, is undeniable. But by looking at it more closely, characteristic differences are discovered.

There is no question in this passage, or in any following text, of an effort by human beings, who would seek to be united with Christ. It is Christ who comes to them. He becomes incarnate and enters into union with us. The union between the believer and Christ is made by faith. Now Luther explained more precisely (a little before the passage we have quoted) what he means by faith by correlating it with the Word. Faith is defined as an attachment, that is a confidence accorded to the Word. At the same time, it is an attachment to Christ announced by this Word. This attachment is envisaged by the reformer as a union, but one which does not do away with the difference between the two partners. After having expounded the theme of "joyous exchange" he writes: "Thus it is that Christ takes a glorious bride, without spot or blemish; he purifies her, in the bath of his Word of life, that is to say, by faith in his Word, in his life, in his righteousness, and in his salvation." [96] The role of faith is thus fundamental. The juridical terminology used by the reformer draws us away from the mystical perspective. There is no question of the fusion of the persons, but of the community of their possessions and the exchange of these goods.

The theme of exchange, however, does not owe its origin to the mystics. It is found in the Christmas liturgy, in which Christianity from the early church on has sung of the mystery of the incarnation, thanks to which, as expressed by Saint Athanasius, "God became human in order that human beings might become God." Luther did not use this formula, but he also envisages an exchange between God and human beings, or more precisely between the divine righteousness on the one hand and human sin on the other. We must now look more closely at that.

Let us examine first the action of Christ. "It is no longer a question only of communion," the reformer continues, "but of a saving batttle, of victory, salvation, and redemption. God and human at the same time and, as such, above sin, death, and damnation. Christ is invincible, eternal, and all-powerful, and so also are his righteousness, his life, and his power to save.[97] Now it is he who by virtue of the marriage of faith takes his part of the sin, death, and hell, which belong to the bride. What do I say? He makes them entirely his own, as if they were truly his and he had sinned. He suffers, he dies, he descends into hell: but it is in order to surmount all. For neither sin, nor death, nor hell could swallow him up, and it is he who in a prodigious combat was to annihilate them. For his righteousness is higher than the sins of the entire world, his life is more powerful than all death, and his salvation is victorious over the depths of hell." [98]

The saving work of Christ is accomplished because he is both God and human. The doctrine of the two natures is thus taken up again; it is the very foundation of soteriology.[99] Christ saves human beings because he is God and human.

But how does the reformer envisage the humanity of Christ?

In this passage we again find the idea which has also been developed in the *Operationes in Psalmos* and which associates the incarnation directly with the solidarity of Christ with sinful human beings. The humanity of Christ is not described only in general anthropological categories. It consists of solidarity with the sin of hu-

man beings, "as if they [the sins] were truly his and he had sinned."
And he bears the consequences: "he suffers, he dies, he descends into
hell." It is however this solidarity which makes Jesus Christ, the just
man, the true human being, the new Adam, to whom we are conformed, as we saw in the last text of the *Operationes* which we
studied earlier.

But Jesus Christ is not only human, he is also God. In this man,
humiliated, it is God himself who is present. It is because he is God
that the sin which has been loaded on his humanity, with the effects
that we have listed in the previous section, does not remain on him,
but is destroyed. Unlike the believer, Christ does not remain *simul
justus simul peccator* (at once righteous and sinner).

It is necessary to note that the unity between God and humanity
in Jesus Christ is strongly emphasized. The saving work is accomplished by Jesus Christ, God and human. The two natures cannot
be separated. In other words, the actions which Christ accomplishes
as a human being are of the all-powerful activity of God. By virtue
of his union with the divine nature, his human nature is invincible,
eternal, and all-powerful. When he takes on himself the sins of
humankind, it is truly God who acts. This man Jesus, who as a
human being has assumed our sins, is also God. Conversely, this God
who receives us in the man Jesus is also human. He manifests his love
and his divine power through the weakness and humiliation of a
crucified man.

It must also be noted that from Luther's point of view, the person
and work of Jesus Christ in fact overlap.[100] For Christ to be God and
human means to take on himself the sins of human beings. There
are not two stages: a first stage when he begins to become human
and, later, at the end of his life, a second stage, that of accomplishing
the redemptive work. From the beginning, the incarnation coincides
with the redemption. To become human is, for him, to accept being
in our situation and to take on himself our sins. And he can triumph
over these sins because he is God and human. The work of salvation
is thus transposed into the very person of Jesus Christ.

Finally, it must be noted that the work of Christ is both past and
present. In the texts that we have quoted, the action of Christ united
to the soul is described as in the present. For in faith his liberating
work becomes in some sense contemporary with human beings. But
we do not therefore think that the reformer has neglected what the
epistle to the Hebrews calls the *ephapax* (once for all) of the cross:

i.e., the act of reconciliation on the cross accomplished once for all at a precise moment in history. In *Eine kurze Form der zehn Gebote,* (A Short Form of the Ten Commandments), a text which dates from the same period, Luther certainly speaks in the past tense of the work of Christ, as it was realized, when he writes in explanation of the Second Article: "I believe that he bore his suffering and his cross for my sin and for that of all believers. I believe that he died and that he was buried in order to put my sins to death and bury them completely, my sins and those of all believers and that he has killed physical death and made it in every sense harmless, and even useful and healthy." [101]

But when Christ is present for the believer, he is present with all his work. From the standpoint of the believer, it is now that the work of Christ is accomplished, in the sense that it is now that sin is destroyed and now that Christ stands before God as high priest. "He stands continually under the eyes of God for his own, he offers himself for them and does all that a good priest should." [102]

Finally, we must see what is given to human beings united to to Jesus Christ—namely, the fruits of Christ's work of redemption. As for the soul, it possesses in Christ the righteousness that it can regard as its own, and despite all its sins it can meet death and hell with total assurance, saying, "If I have sinned, my Christ has not sinned; it is in him that I believe, everything which belongs to him is mine, and all that is mine is his." [103]

Christ thus takes over, to his own account, the condemnation and the wrong of human beings derived from sin. On his side, he attributes to human beings his righteousness before God. We must remark in passing that it is not strictly accurate to talk of "exchange" *(commercium)*. In fact an exchange would lead us to suppose that there are two partners who make a sort of deal in which each receives benefits from the other. In this present case, all the benefits come from one of the partners, from Christ.

The righteousness of Christ is attributed to the believer. This is what one traditionally calls the imputation of the righteousness of Christ to the account of the believer. It is on this that justification by faith is based. The believer benefits before God from an alien righteousness, and Christ draws on himself the sin and the punishment. From now on, believers live before God with Christ, the only just one, whom sin and punishment do not devalue in the eyes of God. To the extent that persons are thus justified before God, they are "sheltered from death and assured against hell." [104] United to Christ, who is their righteousness, they share equally in Christ's victory over death and sin. Does the righteousness remain only alien to believers, or can one speak also of an effective transformation of their being, of a justification which would not continue to be only "legal," i.e., bound up with the imputation of God? A parallel text in the *Operationes* in which Luther developed the theme of "joyous exchange" to an equivalent degree seems to go in the direction of an "effective" justification.[105]

Rightly, it seems to us, W. Joest has pointed out that there is here more than a concept of an alien justification.[106] The righteousness of Christ becomes ours not only "objectively," but "formally," just as our sins become those of Christ, not only "objectively," but also "formally." In the Scholastic language, which Luther uses here, *forma* designates the power which realizes and gives form. The *justitia formalis* (formal righteousness) suggests a righteousness which determines the attitude of the person, i.e., "essentially" or "in essence" (see note 105).

Thus the union of Christ with the believer includes for the believer a double aspect, both *legal* justification (the acceptance by God who imputes to the believer the righteousness of Christ), and *effective* justification (the transformation of the person submitted to the activity of Christ). Of course, persons do not receive justification as a quality at their disposal and which would become their own *forma*. As W. Joest comments, "The believer does not have his or her own *forma;* but their *forma* is their life with Christ; it is that which is and remains the real power which vitalizes their life." [107]

Christ gives to human beings his righteousness—that is the theme of justification by faith which we have found in the exposition of the subject of "joyous exchange." Justified by faith we enter into a new life. It is with the description of this new life that the rest of the treatise on Christian freedom will deal. We will only take up Points 14 and 16 here. In these it appears that the Christian life is a participation in the royalty of the priesthood of Christ. This royalty and this priesthood which—in the saving work of Jesus Christ accomplished for us—save us, also equally determine the dimension of Christian existence. By the royalty and priesthood of Jesus Christ and in his image, Christians are going to be kings i.e., free persons, and priests, "worthy to appear before God and to pray for others."

Thus Christ is in a unique and specific sense both the Lord and the new human being, the image of true humanity to which we are called.

General Summary

The different works that have been studied so far differ—as much in their literary form as in the manner in which they approach the mystery of Jesus Christ or set forth particular points of view about it. And yet what they say displays an incontestable unity of thought. Christology is placed under the sign of the cross. A certain number of implications and consequences are given which concern as much the knowledge of Jesus Christ as the Lutheran understanding of the two natures and the saving relationship of human beings with Jesus Christ. But before identifying these common perspectives it is necessary for us to recall and summarize the different approaches that we have observed.

The struggle against indulgences pushed Luther to emphasize the sovereignty of Jesus Christ over the church, to give special value to the role of the Word and personal faith, in order to show the benefits human beings receive from the salvation given in Jesus Christ. On their part, the sermons distinguish a good approach to the cross by human beings—i.e., in faith—from false approaches, such as the simple, outward form of imitation of Jesus or a purely sentimental consciousness of the sufferings of Christ. There is also to be found in the sermons a list of the different aspects of faith as it is understood by Luther: personal confession of sins, acceptance of salvation by the believer, and conformity to the humanity of Jesus—on the basis of an intimate union with Christ.

The *Commentary on the Psalms,* for its part, lays great stress on the sorrows of Jesus Christ lived out in the consciousness of the crucified and also on the sorrows of believers, i.e., their temptations. The close link between the cross of Jesus Christ and that of the believer appears again in the perspective of the two rules of Jesus Christ—the rule of the cross and the rule of glory. The believer is called to accompany Jesus Christ and like him travel from the cross to glory. It is, however, only at this price that he or she penetrates the very mystery of Christ crucified.

In those texts where the reformer develops his conception of the Eucharist, there reappears that insistence on the Word and faith, which we have emphasized many times, as a means of encountering the Christ and benefiting from the fruits of his redemptive work. The body of Christ united to the bread and wine bears witness to the truth of the promise which announces the forgiveness of sins. Luther thus stresses the gift made to the believer in the Eucharist. This gift rests on the sacrifice accomplished once for all on the cross by Christ, a sacrifice which we can remind God of and whose effects are distributed to us. At the same time, Luther underlines the eternal intercession of the Son before the Father. The believer approaches God, carried and presented by this unique high priest, who is Christ.

The treatise on *The Freedom of a Christian* is centered on the relationship between faith and ethics: one could also say, between justification by faith and works. The theme of the "joyous exchange," which stresses the intimate union between Christ and the believer, is here developed in a particularly successful way. At the same time appear the ethical preoccupations of Luther, those of a Luther desirous of describing concretely the life of Christians thus justified before God, a life lived out in the image of Christ.

Noting these different approaches, it is now possible for us to attempt to construct a synthesis of the christological elements so far discerned.

We repeat that the dominant theme is the cross. And when Luther says cross he means both—that of Jesus Christ, and ours. He has borrowed from the spirituality of the imitation the concern to unite Christ closely with the Christian life, the sufferings of Jesus Christ and ours. And it is always important to the reformer to show that there is no true knowledge of Jesus Christ where human beings refuse the cross in their own lives, that is, conformity to the suffering humanity of Jesus Christ. Knowledge of God and of salvation in Jesus Christ and new life are thus inseparable. For the reformer, an orthodoxy which is not also an *orthopraxis* would be inconceivable.

But it is important to emphasize that the cross of Jesus Christ, interpreted by Luther in this profound way, is not only the cross of the man Jesus Christ, but that of the Son of God. It is God who is present in this man humiliated and crucified. We have pointed out more than once that Luther took his stand on the doctrine of the two natures.

The reformer introduces an extraordinary tension into this doctrine. Of course, the content of this doctrine constitutes a paradox for logical thought: "Jesus Christ, God and man" is an intolerable proposition for natural thought (the thought of Plato, for example) which distinguishes and opposes in a radical way God and the human, the eternal and the temporal, the uncreated and the created. But the paradox is further accentuated when one insists, as Luther does in the light of certain biblical passages, on the suffering of the man Jesus feeling in his consciousness the accusation of sin and the wrath of God. The latent Platonism of traditional christology, with its talk of the impassibility of God, is thus radically put in question. The traditional doctrine has been deepened in the sense that the reformer is not content to say, "God and man," but "God and sin." That is not, of course, to eliminate the human (sin can be assumed at this point only because Christ is a man) but it is to go beyond a concept of the humanity of Jesus Christ which might be limited to general considerations of what it is to be human and would place its emphasis (as in the early church) on the body or (as in modern theology) on the personality of Jesus.

We have just spoken of the extraordinary tension introduced by the reformer into the doctrine of the two natures, God being present in suffering humanity and being identified with the sin of others. It is necessary to point out another important aspect of the reformer's thought. He insists in many ways that the presence of God in Jesus Christ is a hidden presence. The *vere deus* is an affirmation of faith and of faith alone. In fact, the man Jesus was not transformed into God, he is truly human, a man limited by the human condition as we are, a man tempted, fearing suffering, death, and the wrath of God. It is here necessary to underline both the place of the word and the eschatological orientation of the mystery of Jesus Christ. Because Jesus Christ is God in a way that is hidden, the word of witnesses is indispensable. It is, in effect, this word which must announce that in this suffering man, God is present to save us, that he is the Son entered into our situation of sin in order to set us free from it. The christology of Luther thus inserts itself into this fundamental process by which the Word preached engenders faith. In this thought, Monophysitism, which would tend to divinize the man Jesus, to insist on the miracles as visible signs of the divine, to play down his suffering, is discarded. God is really present in this man, in the person of the Son. But there is no confusion; it is precisely because the humanity hides the divinity that the Word and faith are necessary.

At the same time it is necessary to point out the eschatological perspective in which Luther placed the doctrine of the two natures as he understood it. The glory of Jesus Christ, his divinity, will be seen only at the moment of our own glorification, when, according to the apostle Paul, we shall see God face to face (1 Cor. 13:12). Let us recall the distinction made between the two realms that we noted in the *Operationes.* The present rule of Christ is effected through the human nature, which is here extended, one must say, by the announcements of the gospel, the Word and the sacraments.[108] One day the Christ God will reign directly, that is to say, without need either of the cross, of his own humiliated humanity or of ours, nor of the Word and the sacraments. That does not mean that in the thought of Luther Jesus Christ would not forever be God and human. But it does mean both that the humanity will not always hide the divinity, and also that the rule of God in eternity will no longer be affected by means of suffering humanity or by any exterior means.

To say that we shall see the glory of Jesus Christ, i.e., his divinity, only at his return, is not to deny that there is given even now to the eyes of faith the simultaneous revelation of God and human beings in Jesus Christ. God and humanity must be revealed to us in Jesus Christ. In fact, human beings not only have wrong ideas about God; they also have wrong ideas about themselves. Natural persons think that to be human is to be raised above others, that is, to be like God. That is why the image of the true human being, such as God wanted him to be, must be revealed to him.

But let us first examine the image of God as it is revealed in Jesus Christ. Our problem here is not to know how far Luther admitted knowledge of God apart from Jesus Christ, but to see how he is revealed in Jesus Christ.

In Jesus Christ, God reveals himself as love. The "divine nature" of Christ is this love, which wants to save human beings and struggles for them. This love operates through the wrath *sub contraria specie.* This is what constitutes holiness. The active love, characteristic of God in Christ, is very different from the caricature that Voltaire gives of love when he says that it is God's job to forgive. Love, powerful and creative, operates through judgment, suffering, sacrifice. And it is precisely in the struggle with suffering that it shines. It is in the weakness of the man Jesus that the saving love of God triumphs. In all that, it can be seen how Luther has a dynamic concept of the nature of God. The divine nature is not a thing

in itself or a collection of properties which must be defined in opposition to human beings—almighty, omniscient, etc. The divine
nature is first of all that mysterious, creative love, at work in a
journey through life in which human beings are involved.

The human nature also must not be defined from a static point of
view. It is not a collection of properties such as corporeality, finitude, and other limitations which in Luther's eyes might characterize human beings. Without denying all that, he shows that Jesus
Christ is truly human, the new Adam, both because he is the man
who in dependence upon God is set free to rule the world, and also
because he is the man who does not raise himself above others, as the
Pharisees do, but places himself at their service—in solidarity with
their sins before God. It is in this way that we must understand the
vere homo of the christological confession, according to Luther. It
is to this new humanity that the believer is conformed.

Another aspect of the christology must again occupy our attention. Luther has sometimes been reproached for neglecting the trinitarian distinctions. He is said to be content to talk of God in Jesus
Christ, failing to note that it is the second person of the Trinity who
has become flesh. This impression comes, we think, from the fact that
the passionate interest of Luther bore on the following point: for the
believer confronted with the problem of predestination and of the
hidden God of history, it is above all important for faith to know
that God is fully revealed in Jesus Christ; in other words, that in
Christ we truly encounter the fundamental intentions of God, his
concern for human salvation. This basic preoccupation explains the
modalistic turns of phrase which can be found in certain of his
writings. In fact, we have often been able to show that the trinitarian
distinctions were truly present, in the sense that Luther insists in
many ways on the confrontation between the Father and incarnate
Son. This confrontation remains, since Christ continues to be the
high priest who intercedes for us before God. This sacerdotal office
did not cease at Easter.

Another point must be brought out. The confrontation between
the Father and the Son permits Luther to emphasize that the human
activity of Jesus is exercised toward the Father. Jesus is not only the
instrument of God, but he is the Son become human, who prays
and who hopes, who suffers from the wrath of God and who offers
himself to the Father. Of course, the reformer never separates the
two natures in the accomplishment of his work. Jesus is also God

when he suffers, and, on the other hand, he is equally human when he triumphs over death. There is there a fundamental *simul*, without having to construct a system in which the divine nature and the human nature cooperate. One must say both, that the man Jesus is free to offer himself to the Father and to human beings, and that it is precisely such an attitude of the human nature which reveals the divine nature of the Son.

Finally we must stress the characteristic unity of Luther's christology, the unity of the person and the work of Christ. Of course, traditional theology never failed to emphasize that the work of Christ, the satisfaction offered to the Father (Anselm) or victory over the powers (early church), was able to be accomplished only because Jesus Christ was God and human. A bond is evident between the work and the person of Christ. But as a general rule, one distinguished the person of Jesus Christ defined by the two natures and the work realized essentially in the death and resurrection of Christ. For Luther, on the contrary, the work begins with the incarnation itself, for this consists not only of Christ becoming human, but becoming from the beginning one in solidarity with the sins of others, assuming them before God and bearing the consequences of them, the wrath of God and death. But the cross only crowns the incarnation, or again, the incarnation is already the cross. In the same way also, the resurrection, which is the victory over death, is already given by the presence of God in Jesus Christ and by the innocence of the man Jesus. And this victory is won unceasingly anew in the resistance to temptation of the man Jesus.

Thus there appears a profound unity between what Jesus Christ is and what he does. He saves us precisely because of what he is, that is to say, the Savior God acting through the humanity of a man who is one with other human beings and reaffirming this solidarity even to the cross.

Our review would evidently be incomplete if we passed over in silence all that the reformer wrote about the saving relationship of human beings with Jesus Christ. It is, as we have seen, that very thing which excites his thought and leads him to ask questions about Jesus Christ. The question of salvation, of the manner by which it is realized and given to human beings, is in effect at the very heart of Luther's theological concerns. One of the central affirmations of the reformer, at the time of the struggle against indulgences, is that

Christ offers himself to us by the Word, with salvation bound to his person. In the spirit of Luther that means a sure sovereignty of Christ over the church which thus does not dispose of salvation, but only bears witness to it. It also means that the reformer separates himself from all kinds of attempts at mystical union, which would get by without the Word as exterior means. It also means that he opposes all spirituality of the imitation of Christ which has the aim of receiving his gifts, but forgets that Christ is the gift before he is an example. Christ offers himself to human beings by the Word, we said; thus he appeals to faith. For the human side, it is faith which in effect corresponds to the Word. Faith is described by Luther as an attitude of accepting the Word of judgment and of grace, by which Christ comes to meet us. But he also describes it as an intimate union between Christ and the believer. In the period that we have studied, the theme of marriage and of joyous exchange is preeminent in his considerations and reaches its highest point. It is in the framework of this intimate union that Christ offers himself as our righteousness, thanks to which we are able to appear righteous before God. Thus the basic affirmation of justification by faith appears in the theme of joyous exchange. But the Christ present also acts on us by rendering us in conformity with this new humanity which Jesus Christ incarnates.

What is faith in such a perspective? United to Christ in his life and in his death believers confess that when they are faced with the true human being who has appeared in Jesus Christ, they are themselves sinful. Confronted by the sacrifice of the Son who has been struck by the wrath of God on account of human beings, they accept the accusation and confess their sin.

But faith consists equally in accepting that the sins (my sins) have really been borne and overcome by the Christ. And it is in this work, from which they benefit that believers discover the true heart of God. Tempted to the very end of their lives by the subject of predestination or death, believers take refuge in Christ, in his Word and in his work which express this decisive fact, that God is, at heart, love and that he wishes the salvation of human beings.

Finally, faith consists of accepting the cross, of accepting that Jesus Christ renders me in conformity to his suffering humanity, in order to lead me thus toward glorification, that is to say, the liberty of the children of God.

Notes

1 We leave to one side the controversial question today of whether the theses were nailed to the door or not!

2 On this subject see the article, "Ablass," in *Die Religion in Ge-schichte und Gegenwart,* 3rd ed., vol. 1, col. 64-67, by K. G. Steck. There is a valuable bibliography on the subject attached to this article.

3 For example: J. Lortz, *Die Reformation in Deutschland,* 4th ed. (Freiburg: 1962), vol. 1, pp. 194ff.

4 On this subject see also Bernhard Lohse, "Luthers Christologie im Ablasstreit," *Luther-Jahrbuch* 27 (1960):51-63.

5 The texts concerned are the theses *WA* 1, 229-238 (1517) and the "Resolutiones disputationum de indulgentiarum virtute" (*WA* 1, 525-628) of 1518. The difference of date between these two texts is of little importance here. The unity is provided by the subject and by Luther's thought.

6 We shall include in this study the theses for the Heidelberg Disputation (*WA* 1, 350-374) of the same period—1518—which constitute the classic document of the *theologia crucis.*

7 J. Köstlin, *Luthers Theologie,* vol. 1, p. 246; Vilmos Vajta, "Sine meritis: Zur kritischen Funktion der Rechtfertigungslehre," *Oecumenica* (1968):146-195.

8 Max Lackmann maintained the interesting thesis that the young Martin Luther, even at this period, bracketed together the merits of the saints with those of Christ and only gradually separated Christ from the rest of the body, namely the Christians, of which he was the head. *Thesaurus sanctorum,* Festgabe für J. Lortz (Baden-Baden: 1957), vol. 1, pp. 135-171. We cannot discuss this thesis here. Of course, one can observe—and we shall return to this—that the saints still play an important role in the thought of the young Martin Luther, but already at the time of the struggle against the indulgences, Luther appears to us to underline, vigorously and exclusively, the role of Christ as the only source of salvation.

9 On this subject see also Martin Kroeger, *Rechtfertigung und Gesetz* (Göttingen: 1968), p. 170, n. 7. Kroeger nevertheless emphasizes that the christology of the example is not abandoned—a point that we shall have occasion to make also.

10 *WA* 1, 593, 14: "It is by faith in Christ that the Christian becomes a single spirit and one *[unum]* with Christ." Cf. the Heidelberg Disputation, *WA* 1, 364, 23.

11 *WA* 1, 593, 19: "Hence, thanks to the inestimable riches of the compassionate God, the Father, it happens that Christians can glory and in Christ can attribute all with confidence to themselves, since righteousness, virtue, patience, humility, and all the merits of Christ are most certainly also theirs, thanks to the unity of spirit stemming from faith in Christ, and since, inversely, all their sins

are no longer theirs, but those of Christ, thanks to this same unity which also absorbs all things." See also WA 1, 593, 24.

12 The term "conformity" does not completely translate the thought of Luther. In fact, he means the action of God which renders us in conformity with Christ. The word "conformity" is a little too static. We use it, nonetheless, for want of a better one.

13 Vajta, "Sine meritis," p. 170: "The *meritum Christi* is not thus set forth in itself, but proclaimed in its soteriological movement toward human beings."

14 WA 1, 613, 18: "So we must become like the image of the Son of God; if someone does not take up their cross and follow him, that person is of no worth, even if they are full of indulgences!"

15 "Luthers Christologie im Ablassstreit," pp. 57-58.

16 *Ibid.*, p. 58.

17 G. Heintze, *Luthers Predigt von Gesetz und Evangelium* (Munich: 1958), p. 213: "The cross and passion of Christ are not one special theme among others for Luther, but the central theme of his preaching [of the gospel]." For an analysis of the sermons of 1518/1519, see pp. 212-256.

18 He does this in a sermon of 1518 on the passion of Christ (WA 1, 341, 36). On this subject see Elze, "Züge spätmittelalterlicher Frömmingkeit. . . ."

19 WA 1, 342, 16: "Meditation on his passion is a very laudable thing."

20 We find these affirmations in the sermon, "On the Sacrament of the Body of Christ," and "On the Confraternities," which stem from the same period (WA 2, 742-758). In Point 20, Luther attacks all usage of the mass which is content with the *opus operatum* (automatic effectiveness) and neglects the *opus operantis* (the need for faith). In these sermons which we are now studying, Luther develops what he understands by the use of the passion of Christ in faith. But it must be noted that, according to Luther, a criticism of purely exterior participation in the mass does not put this in doubt. Cf. Iserloh, "Sacramentum et exemplum," p. 261.

21 WA 1, 338, 12-24. This pity is a *carnalis affectus* (worldly sentiment). A "sentiment" within the framework of faith is not, however, ruled out. To consider the suffering of Christ *pro me* implies this sentiment. Within this *affectus* are to be found again themes dear to Saint Bernard.

22 Unless otherwise specified, we refer to vol. 2 of WA.

23 WA 2, 137, 17; 1, 338, 30; 1, 340, 6

24 WA 1, 337, 34

25 "But the disgrace and suffering which are in him are also ours and give us knowledge of ourselves" (WA 1, 343, 1).

26 See also his explanation of the Lord's Prayer (WA 2, 113, 5ff.).

27 "That you are deeply involved and that you do not doubt that it is you who have martyred Christ, for these are your sins which have surely done it" (WA 2, 137, 22). Cf. WA 1, 338, 35ff.

28 WA 1, 336, 14-19; 1, 339, 23; 1, 343, 28; 1, 344, 9

29 WA 1, 344, 9: "Therefore no understanding *[intellectus]* can comprehend it and no tongue say it and no writing describe it, only the heart [affectus] can understand what this means: Christ has suffered."

30 WA 1, 336, 17

31 Iserloh has devoted a serious study to this use which Luther makes of the Augustinian distinction between *sacramentum* and *exemplum*. He attempts, rightly, according to us, to refute the theses maintained by Bizer, Jetter, and Ebeling. According to them, *sacramentum* was used by the young Luther in a uniquely allegorical sense, but not in an efficacious sense. That is to say that Christ seen as *sacramentum* would only be the image or the type of what happens to the faithful. That *sacramentum* would neither cause nor provide salvation. According to this interpretation, Christ as *sacramentum* would signify the interior death of human beings, as *exemplum* signifies the exterior death. In contrast to this, Iserloh points out a number of passages where the role of Christ is affirmed as "effective" in the *sacramentum* (WA 9, 18, 29; 1, 337, 13). It is difficult to see, he writes, why Luther should insist so much on the distinction between *sacramentum* and *exemplum* if he uses them only in an allegorical sense. On the contrary, this distinction between the two concepts permits Luther to overcome the danger of a way to salvation which follows the moralism of humility. It is first necessary for us to die to sin and to have part in the life of Christ *(sacramentum)* before we can take on ourselves physical death with all its sufferings. That is where Christ as *exemplum* comes in. Hence the old person is punished and destroyed in us.

32 Cf. WA 2, 748, 38

33 Death occupies an important place in the thought of Luther. It is not a natural reality, but is always associated with the wrath of God. See also H. Bornkamm, *Luthers geistige Welt*, 3rd ed. (Lüneburg: 1959), pp. 114-129, "Leben und Sterben."

34 Cf. WA 2, 139, 18

35 Regin Prenter, *Connaitre Christ* (Neuchatel: 1966), p. 164.

36 WA 2, 140, 30: "But you can work yourself up no longer by contemplating the suffering of Christ (for it has done its work and has shocked you), but you must go on to contemplate his loving heart, full of love for you, love which so compels him to bear the heavy burden of your conscience and your sin. Thus your heart will feel sweetness for him and your faith in him will be strengthened. Then by means of the heart of Christ mount up to the heart of God, and you will see that Christ would not have been able to give proof of this love for you if God in his eternal love had not wished it thus, the God whom Christ in his love for you obeys." Paul Althaus, *Die Theologie Martin Luthers* (Gütersloh: 1962), pp. 163ff. quotes several passages which follow much the same line.

37 O. H. Pesch, *Die Theologie der Rechtfertigung bei Martin Luther und Thomas von Aquin* (Mainz: 1967), p. 129: "Precisely in this

unbroken relationship with God, which held even in the trial of
abandonment—an inner state in Christ which obviously escapes
all attempts at psychological analysis—God's anger loses its power,
the just holiness of God is satisfied, and we too, if we believe in
him, are judged righteous before God."

38   Karl Holl, *Ges. Aufsätze*, vol. 1: Luther, 2nd ed., pp. 69-72. On the
subject of Luther's "subordinationism," see also Prenter, *Spiritus
Creator*, pp. 183ff.; p. 356f., n. 25; Watson, *Um Gottes Gottheit*,
pp. 159ff.; Nilsson, *Simul*, p. 177, n. 10 These three authors reject
any subordinationist interpretation of Luther's thought.

39   Prenter levels a similar critique against the interpretation by
Althaus and writes: "It is fundamental for the christology of Luther
and for his doctrine of justification, that God *the Son* came to us in
the flesh and represented us in our flesh and blood before the
Father. Certainly, for us, according to Luther, Christ is the reflection *[Spiegel]* of the fatherly heart of God. But he is so because he
was the Son who was obedient to the Father" ("Martin Luther, der
Lehrer der Kirche," *Theologische Literaturzeitung* 91 (1966), no.
1, p. 8.

40   See Althaus, *Die Theologie Martin Luthers*, pp. 172-173; Harnack,
Luthers Theologie, vol. 2, p. 163.

41   On this subject see D. Olivier, "Les deux sermons sur la double et
triple justice," *Oecumenica* (1968), pp. 39-69. In this article Olivier also gives us an excellent French translation of the principal
passages.

42   See Lackmann, *Thesaurus sanctorum*, and the discussion of Lackmann's theses in A. Peters, *Glaube und Werk* (Berlin-Hamburg:
1962), pp. 94-99.

43   On this subject see: L Pinomaa, *Die Heiligen in Luthers Frühtheologie*, Studia theologica XIII/1 (Lund: 1959), pp. 1-50.

44   Althaus, *Die Theologie Martin Luthers*, pp. 256ff.

45   For an analysis of this sermon see Strohl, *Luther jusqu'en 1520*,
pp. 329-334.

46   Cf. WA 2, 692, 33

47   Cf. WA 2, 745, 13; 2, 748, 14

48   WA 26, 508, 13: "This matter of addressing the saints has been
criticized by others before me. I do it also, and I believe that we
must address Christ only as our mediator; that is what the Scripture says and it is certain. Nothing in the Scripture exhorts us to
address ourselves to the saints; it is therefore an uncertain thing
and not necessary to believe" (*WA* 26, 508, 13).

49   Unless otherwise specified, reference is made to vol. 5 of WA. Our
field of investigation will also take into account the "unknown
fragments" discovered by Vogelsang in the Vatican Library and
published by him in *Arbeiten zur Kirchengeschichte* 27 (Berlin:
1940). We shall quote them as "Vogelsang." According to this
researcher, we are dealing not only with the *Commentary on the
Psalms*, published in 1519, with which these fragments have many

points of contact, but with a copy of notes taken during a course of lectures held by Luther in 1518 and subsequently published as *Operationes in Psalmos* in March 1519 (*WA* 5). This information is in Vogelsang, p. 11. In these fragments there are several interesting passages for Luther's christology (Vogelsang 45, 19; 55, 18; 88, 28), and one is struck by his insistence on the cross of Christ and of the Christian.

50   *WA* 5, 176, 32

51   Commenting on Ps. 6:2, he writes: "The fearful conscience, overcome by its own guilt, feels nothing but the threat of eternal damnation" (*WA* 5, 203, 10). Psalm 8:5-6: "Christ abandoned by God" (*WA* 5, 273, 38). "He has been humiliated and abandoned by God in the midst of this power, subjected to infirmities and death also and even hell" (*WA* 5, 274, 4). "Bearing in himself the wrath of the Father against us" (*WA* 5, 271, 25).

52   *WA* 5, 605, 34; 5, 611, 20ff.

53   On this subject see Erich Vogelsang, *Der angefochtene Christus* (Berlin-Leipzig: 1932), pp. 45-52; Paul Althaus, "Niedergefaheren zur Hölle," *Zeitschrift für systematische Theologie* 19 (1942):365-384; Althaus, *Die Theologie Martin Luthers*, p. 182.

54   On this subject see Vogelsang, *Der angefochtene Christus*, pp. 22-23. Althaus, *Die Theologie Martin Luthers*, p. 183: "Luther's theology of the cross surpasses all theologies that went before him by the gravity with which he makes Christ suffer the total abandonment of God and hell." Friedrich Gogarten, *Luthers Theologie* (Tübingen: 1967), p. 63: "There is no theology before him, nor apart from Kierkegaard, any after him that so makes the tempted Christ into the object and ground of faith." A. Peters, "Luthers Christuszeugnis als Zusammenfassung der Christusbotschaft der Kirche," *Kerygma und Dogma* 13 (1967):96: "From the inner contemplation of an assailed faith, the reformer has realized the true humanity of Jesus more profoundly than all the theologians that were before him and apparently also those who have come after him, without sacrificing the divinity of Christ."

55   Peters, "Luthers Christuszeugnis . . . ," p. 91: "Jesus lived here on earth, not always in the untroubled joy of the contemplation of God. He had not risen above it all in the pinnacle of his spirit *[acumen mentis]* or the brilliance of his soul *[scintilla animae]*, like a Neoplatonic stoic (Origen), nor a medieval mystic nor even a cultured friend of God among the elite from the Moravians (Schleiermacher); he has not risen above the strife of this world already; he has not already passed through the last trial of death and the curse of God over our sins. Truly, we Christians confess that in death too he is in the hand of God, who has smitten him for our sins. He has done this, not beyond faith and hope, but in the deepest agony of prayer, not beyond the justified wrath of God, but through the thick of it."

56   On this subject see L. Pinomaa, "Der existentielle Charakter der

Theologie Luthers: Das Hervorbrechen der Theologie der Anfechtung und ihre Bedeutung für das Lutherverständnis," *Annales Academiae scientarum Fennicae*, series B, vol. 47, 3 (Helsinki: 1940);
P. Th. Bühler, *Die Anfechtung bei Martin Luther* (Zurich: 1942);
H. Beintker, *Die Ueberwindung der Anfechtung bei Luther* (Berlin: 1954); Peters, *Glaube und Werk*, pp. 40-48; Von Loewenich,
Luther's Theology of the Cross.

57   For example: *WA* 5, 79, 14; 5, 385, 23ff.; 5, 619, 25ff.; 5, 209, 8ff.;
5, 156-180. Luther reproaches the Scholastic theologians with ig-
noring the temptations and for this reason giving themselves over
to vain speculations on subjects such as purgatory (*WA* 5, 497,
22f.). He addresses the same criticism to the mystics, enamored
of union with God (*WA* 5, 163, 17-29).

58   "Die Christusverkündigung bei Luther," in *Jesus Christus im Zeugnis der Heiligen Schrift und der Kirche* (Munich: 1936), pp. 217-
222. P. 221: "To dogma and Scripture are thus added, in the third
place, the experience of temptation and deliverance: there we have
the triptych by which Luther preached Christ."

59   *WA* 5, 387, 27: "One must believe that he was subjected to all the
temptations, as a pure and true human being." *WA* 5, 607, 31:
"Christ has become sin for us, because without guilt he was forsaken by God, like the least of sinners in all things, he into whose
conscience nothing erupted and nothing was able to cause despair,
except the wrath of God."

60   *WA* 5, 634, 4; 5, 635, 27

61   *WA* 5, 271, 25: It is for us that "he carries in himself the anger of
God."

62   *WA* 5, 64, 35: "The staff is the most holy gospel of Christ, for this
is the scepter of his rule. . . . What is the staff of the mouth of
Christ if it is not the Word of God." See also *WA* 5, 505, 35;
5, 550, 23-36

63   See also *WA* 5, 272

64   *WA* 5, 129, 9: "Christ must be comprehended as human, before
he can be understood as God; one must seek first the cross of his
humanity, rather than the glory of his divinity."

65   *WA* 5, 108, 9: "To know Christ means to know the cross and to
perceive God hidden beneath the crucified flesh." "All the benefits are hidden in the cross and under the cross, so that one must
seek them and recognize them in no other place than under the
cross" (Vogelsang 88, 28). It is in this sense that the following
expression, typically mystical in tone, must be interpreted: "Therefore, the one who returns to God, returns to nothingness" (*WA* 5,
168, 4). The *nothingness* referred to here means the annihilation
of human beings by the cross and by the confession of sins. See
also *WA* 5, 166, 15; 5, 176, 27.

66   Cf. Vogelsang 56, 19; 70, 29; *WA* 5, 128, 36.

67   On this subject see: Vilmos Vajta, *Die Theologie des Gottesdienstes
bei Luther*, pp. 43-113; H. B. Meyer, *Luther und die Messe,* Eine

liturgie-wissenschaftliche Untersuchung über das Verhältnis Luthers zum Messwesen des späten Mittelalters (Paderborn: 1965). At the beginning of chap. 4 of this present work there is a note listing works devoted to Luther's doctrine of the Eucharist.

68 *WA* 6, 349-378: "A Sermon on the New Testament Understanding of the Holy Mass."

69 *WA* 6, 484-573

70 *WA* 2, 743, 21ff.

71 *WA* 6, 502

72 *WA* 6, 359, 5

73 *WA* 6, 356, 20ff.; *WA* 6, 514, 26ff.

74 *WA* 6, 518, 8

75 *WA* 6, 515, 14

76 *WA* 6, 558, 35ff.

77 On this subject see Strohl, *Luther jusqu'en 1520*, pp. 337-341; Vajta, *Die Theologie des Gottesdienstes bei Luther*, pp. 173-177. A certain tolerance on the part of Luther with regard to transubstantiation can be noticed at the beginning. He took it over very much as he did other traditional conceptions—expressing some doubts (*WA* 6, 508, 7), but not making these an article of faith (*WA* 6, 456, 34). He reproached it as a philosophical theory of *humanae ratiunculae* (human rationality) (*WA* 6, 512, 3). But if he had been forced to choose between Zwingli's conception and transubstantiation, there is no doubt that he would have chosen the latter. That continues to be true of Lutheranism in general! In *Bekenntnis vom Abendmahl Christi*, which appeared in 1528, he will write concerning the doctrine that we are discussing here: "That does not have very much importance for me, for as I have confessed often enough, that is not worth quarreling about: whether it remains wine or not, it is enough for me that Christ's blood is there; God will make of the wine what he will. And rather than be with the Enthusiasts who want only wine, I would be with the pope and prefer to have only blood" (*WA* 6, 462, 1-5).

78 *WA* 6, 508, 19

79 *WA* 6, 509, 8

80 *WA* 6, 509, 29

81 *WA* 6, 510, 4. Without mentioning it, this statement takes up the position of the theory of consubstantiation, maintained by Duns Scotus, Occam, and Pierre d'Ailly. But the expression *consubstantiation* never appears in Luther. The controversy with Zwingli compelled him, doubtless, against his will, to define the means whereby Christ is present in the Eucharist. But as Vajta has rightly remarked (p. 178), the decisive question for him was not the "how" but the "why" of this presence.

82 *WA* 6, 510, 31: "Why do we not reject such curious inquiries and remain simply with the words of Scripture, and why are we not ready, not to know what happened, but to content ourselves with

the fact that by the power of the word of Christ, the body is there"
(WA 6, 510, 31).

83 WA 6, 511, 18
84 WA 6, 364, 14ff.
85 WA 6, 365, 26
86 WA 6, 368-370
87 WA 6, 369, 5-15
88 WA 6, 369, 26
89 WA 6, 370, 12. Here the reformer is thinking of those who address
    their prayers to God, outside the mass itself. It is a way of cele-
    brating the mass, accessible to all those who have faith in Jesus
    Christ.
90 WA 6, 369, 28
91 WA 6, 370, 7; 371, 22ff.
92 WA 6, 368, 32
93 This treatise exists both in a Latin version (WA 7, 49-73) and a
    German version (WA 7, 20-38). Both are from Luther's pen. For
    a comparison of the two versions, see Maurer, Von der Freiheit
    eines Christenmenschen. Both versions are translated in the AE.
    An English translation of the text, made from WA 7, 12-19, 20-38,
    was prepared by Bertram Lee Woolf and first published in 1952 in
    the first volume of Reformation Writings of Martin Luther (Lon-
    don: Lutterworth, 1952).
94 See also: WA 56, 267, 5-7; 56, 329, 30; 56, 330, 5; WA 2, 145-
    146; 2, 504, 4; WA 5, 608, 6ff.; 5, 311; WA 6, 131; WA 9, 224, 10.
    Relating to this theme, see also: F. Th. Ruhland, Luther und die
    Brautmystik nach Luthers Schrifttum bis 1521 (Giessen: 1938);
    Maurer, Von der Freiheit . . . ;F. W. Kantzenbach, "Luthers Ge-
    danke vom fröhlichen Wechsel," Luther 35 (1964):34-45; Iserloh,
    Luther und die Mystik; Joest, Ontologie der Person bei Luther,
    pp. 371ff.
95 WA 7, 54, 33
96 WA 7, 55, 20
97 In the German version we read here: "Because Christ is God and
    human, and had never sinned, and because his sanctity is uncon-
    querable, eternal and all-mighty" (WA 7, 25, 34).
98 WA 7, 55, 7ff.
99 About this period Luther also wrote, "Eine kurze Form der zehn
    Gebote, eine kurze Form des Glaubens und des Vater unsers."
    There, he very clearly confesses the two natures of Christ: "I be-
    lieve not only that Jesus Christ is truly the only Son of the one true
    God, begotten from eternity in an eternal divine nature and sub-
    stance; but I believe also that the Father has put all things in sub-
    jection to him, according to his humanity which is mine" (WA 7,
    217, 6).
100 Maurer, Von der Freiheit . . . , p. 57: "There is no neat and precise
    distinction made between the person and the work of Christ, as
    there is in the christology of the early church. The necessity and

the possibility of the saving work do not derive either, as with Anselm, from the holy status of the divine nature, which the human nature serves merely as an obedient instrument. But person and work come together. What happens outwardly in his work is fulfilled in precisely the same way in his divine and human person: his work is the direct expression of this person."

101   *WA* 7, 217, 25

102   *WA* 7, 27, 12

103   *WA* 7, 55, 29

104   *WA* 7, 55, 19

105   *WA* 5, 608, 8ff. After announcing the mystery of the *admirabile commercium* (joyous exchange), Luther continues, "For he emptied himself *[exinanivit]* in order that he might pour his qualities into us *[indueret]*, and he filled himself of us *[our sins]* in order to empty us of ourselves, so that Christ's righteousness may be ours, not only what might be called "objectively," but also in essence [formaliter], just as our sins belong to Christ, not only objectively, but in essence. For as he suffers sin and shame for us, so we rejoice and glory in his righteousness, and he himself suffers truly and essentially for each one of us.

106   Joest, *Ontologie bei Luther*, pp. 373ff.

107   *Ibid.*, p. 374.

108   By that, we mean that God uses the preaching of the gospel and the administration of the sacrament, as he made use of the man Jesus. These are in some way the exterior means by which grace is given. That is why one can speak in some way of a prolonging of the humanity of Christ, by the Word and sacraments, without thereby neglecting the unique and specific quality of Jesus Christ.

3

The Unfolding of Christology
in the Postils and Sermons of 1522

Since the beginning of the debate that pitted him against the traditional church, Luther had produced a continuous flow of popular works: treatises, edifying works, biblical commentaries intended for the general public, and sermons, all preceded, accompanied, and followed by Luther's great work at Wartburg, namely the translation of the New Testament. Among all his edifying works, the sermons occupy first place, at least from the point of view of volume! But they merit attention for other reasons as well. As we have already noted, the genius of Luther expresses itself in a particular way in them. His sense of the concrete, the soteriological cast of his thought, his concentration on the essential, and his precise exposition of biblical texts drew him quite naturally to this kind of literature (or rhetoric). Besides, as has been noted, it was by means of these sermons that his ideas were spread so widely.[1]

The sermons which we shall study in this chapter differ from the sermons we have already looked at. In fact, they comment on given biblical texts, usually the Epistle and Gospel for the day. The sermons of 1518-19, on the other hand, were sermons on themes. Of course, the relation to the Bible was not completely absent, but the presentation of the theme took precedence over the exposition of any particular text. The sermons of 1522, gathered together in vol. 10 of the Weimar Edition, were not all preached. Certain of them were postils, expositions of the pericopes for the help of the preacher, a practice common since the 13th century. Readings or pericopes from the Gospels and the Epistles were assigned to each Sunday or Feast Day of the year. These were gathered together and a short explanation added to them in the vernacular. After the Latin text came the words, *post illa verba,* which mean simply, "after these words." Hence the name *postil.*[2]

During his compulsory stay at the Wartburg, Luther edited a collection of postils relating to the pericopes for Advent and Christmas. They are also known by the name of the *Wartburg Postils.* Even though these postils are not sermons that have been preached, they can be considered as such. Certainly the biblical commentary occupies a large place in them, but the kerygmatic intention is clearly shown in these texts. The sermons for Christmas in particular hold our attention.[3] In addition to the interest that these sermons hold for the subject that we are studying, they have the merit of being from the pen of Luther himself, while the majority of the later sermons are the work of editors, more or less faithful to the original, notably Rörer and Roth. We shall however also make use of a certain number of these sermons which corroborate and clarify Luther's thought in the *Wartburg Postils,* in particular some sermons of 1522 (WA 10, 3), certain sermons contained in vol. 12 of the Weimar Edition, as well as the sermon on Philippians 2 from the Postil for Lent 1525, the text of which is by Luther himself.[4]

The sermons and postils in question constitute, in our view, one of the most complete sources for the christology of Luther. It is in fact the first time that he speaks in such detail of the two natures of Christ and the doctrine of the Trinity, without of course neglecting that which lies at the heart of his thought, namely the work accomplished by Christ for us. Here it is that the divinity of Christ, its reality and the way in which we know it, its relation to our salvation, the place of Christ within the Trinity—all these questions which until now have been somewhat neglected, are developed at length. And one discovers that far from having abandoned the traditional doctrines, Luther has on the contrary presupposed them in his way of understanding the salvation of human beings realized by Jesus Christ.

These texts are also interesting from another point of view. They enable us to view the christology of Luther at a stage in which the discussion has not yet hardened. We shall have other occasions to show to what degree christology is at the center of the debate between Luther and Zwingli. It often happens that a certain hardening of positions occurs in controversies. This also happened with Luther. It is thus all the more interesting to discern his christological attitudes before the struggle, at a period when the christological questions were not yet so directly objects of controversy.

At the same time, the examination of Luther's christology before the controversy on the Eucharist helps us to understand this controversy better. In fact, it is the Christ whom he preached over the years that Luther saw menaced by Zwingli and the other adversaries who opposed him with regard to the Eucharist. Luther's christology is far from being a dogmatic construction which must establish Christ's real presence in the Eucharist. It was already elaborated before the controversy in its profoundest form, and in itself it explains the controversy. That did not prevent the hardening to which we have already referred above.

If we then concentrate, with a few exceptions, on the sermons of 1522, it is not only for the reasons of textual criticism to which we have referred above, but because it is important for us to grasp Luther's christology before the controversies which will later pit him against the "Enthusiasts" [5] and with Zwingli. A definite cleavage is produced in the years 1522-1523, when the Enthusiasts appear and question the importance of exterior means of salvation (the Word and sacraments), attack images, preach the imitation of Christ in order to receive his Spirit, and oppose the reformer by means of various spiritualistic and illuministic tendencies. For the moment, the principal antagonist is still Rome. This opponent appears in the background throughout the sermons that we are now about to study.

The Significance of the Incarnation

"God will, and may, be found only through and in this humanity" (*WA* 10, 1, 1, 208, 24). Often enough, Luther is content merely to state the fact of the incarnation without probing the why.[6] God would have it thus. On this point, Seeberg accuses Luther of Nominalism.[7] But if the reformer is Nominalist on this point, it is only because of his concern to respect the ways of God and the mystery of his will. What must be avoided is any attempt to deduce the incarnation from the properties or the being of God. No necessity obliged God to choose the way of the incarnation.

In any case, this reservation is not Luther's last word on the incarnation. The incarnation is too bound up with the very center of his
faith, with his conception of God and salvation, for him to refrain
from asking frequently about its meaning. This is a legitimate enter-
prise, since, according to him, it is precisely the incarnation and it
alone which permits us to do theology, that is, the attempt to comprehend God and his mystery.

We shall reflect on the meaning of the incarnation for Luther in
two stages: (1) What does it mean for human beings, for their
knowledge of God and for their salvation? (2) What does it signify
for God? What does it reveal to us about God?

The Incarnation Represents for Human Beings
a Sure Way of Approach to God

One must first of all emphasize its particularity and its exclusive-
ness. Because God is present in the flesh, the mystical or spiritual
ways by which human beings try to raise themselves to God are
excluded. And among these ways, Luther includes the religion of
works, wherein we try to climb to God by ceremonies or works
which will make us acceptable to God.[8] Thus the way of a knowledge of God "from above" is excluded, as Luther said in the Heidelberg Disputation. One must not begin "from above," that is, by
means of the properties of God established apart from the incarnation. It is necessary to begin "from below," by means of the man
Jesus, and thus ascend to God.[9] It is the same problem that will set
Luther in opposition to the Spiritualists. According to him, they too
neglect the incarnation, which includes the outward means, in order
to raise themselves directly to God. They contravene the order of
things fixed by the sovereign will of God and fall under the same
judgment as the Scholastics and the mystics.

In the incarnation, God is certainly hidden, but he truly wants
human beings to discover him there. He offers himself to persons in
the form closest to them, i.e., in a human existence.[10] What God
reveals above all in the incarnation is his heart, his love, his grace.
This becomes particularly clear when the reformer sets the incarnation as the background to the distinction between law and gospel.
In a sermon on Matt. 21:1-19, for example, he distinguishes two
comings of God: his coming on Sinai and his coming in the gentle-
ness and compassion of a human life.[11] The believer, confronted by
the God of Sinai, by the holiness and wrath of God, can thus take

shelter behind Christ. When we must tremble before the majesty of God, we have Christ as our mediator (*WA* 10, 3, 163). Hence the incarnation gives human beings a mediator who permits them to approach God.[12]

And it reveals to human beings that which they absolutely must know—the love of God. We shall come back to this later when we are considering our place in the plan of God and what has been revealed to us on this subject. Thus God uses the incarnation to reveal himself and, in particular, to reveal his love. But human salvation does not consist only of knowledge, even if it be the knowledge of the love of God. Salvation consists of being reconciled to God and being set free from sin, death, and the devil. It is in order to realize this saving work, which is achieved by the union of Christ with the believer, that he became human. So long as this soteriological aim has not been grasped, one has not truly penetrated the mystery of the incarnation.[13] The incarnation, then, issues in the saving work of Christ, to which we will later return.

What Does the Incarnation Reveal to Us About God?

It reveals first the majesty of God. He determines his way in full liberty—without being compelled in any way to act.[14] He could have saved human beings in another way.

The incarnation is also a reaction of God, it carries a judgment against certain ways by which people have sought to attain to God. The incarnation is, hence, for him a way of affirming himself in his freedom and in his transcendence, in the face of all those who wish to ascend to him by speculation or mysticism or by works. The incarnation allows God to save his honor. In fact, he is jealous of his honor. He does not want human beings to believe in anything other than him. That is why, taking into account human weakness so attached to the visible, he chose the way of the incarnation (*WA* 10, 1, 1, 354-355).

But the incarnation is not only a manifestation of the deity of God, free, holy, and jealous. It expresses primarily—and this must be emphasized again—the love of God for human beings. First, it reveals God's faithfulness to his promises. "For God has promised his grace to the seed of Abraham" (*WA* 10, 1, 1, 465, 8). Even if Christ were not God (an impossible hypothesis), he would nonetheless be the reality of salvation to the extent that he is of the seed of Abraham, to which the promise is attached. The God who operates in and through Christ is the God of the promise. Not to see that would be to miss God entirely.[15]

Christ protects us from the wrath of God. At the same time, he reveals to us the essence of God, that he is love. In fact, this love to which Jesus bears witness in his life and in his death is God's eternal love for sinful human beings. "When I recognize that [the death of Christ for me], I must love him in return, for one must respond in love to such a man. After that I ascend beyond the Son to the Father and I see that Christ is God and that he has plunged himself into my death, my sin, my misery, and also that he gives me his gracious favor. I recognize there the friendly will and supreme love of the Father, which no heart can feel, thus I comprehend God where he is most gentle and I think: ah! so that is God, such is God's good will and his plan, what Christ had done for me" (*WA* 10, 3, 154, 14).

This text calls for the following remarks: we should note Luther's insistence on human beings ascending from Christ Jesus to the Father. Where he got the idea from is of little importance.[16] By that he does not wish to depreciate the humanity of Jesus Christ. That would be contrary to all his thinking about the incarnation. But he is concerned to see the origin of this love. It is not only the love of the man Jesus. This love corresponds to the eternal love of God. It is for that reason that we must not stop at the humanity of Christ. We must not practice an idolatry of Jesus, glorifying this man as one would glorify any other saint.[17] The meaning and the deep dimension of this love is that it reflects the heart of God.

For a man like Luther, who experienced both the majesty and the wrath of God, there is in this a basic element. When the holy God accuses human beings, the man Jesus rises up. But it is not the man in himself who counts; it is the eternal love which he expresses. In a number of passages dealing with Christ and his work, Luther draws attention to the love of God which is revealed there.[18] Let us cite one of these texts in conclusion: "Love has presented God to us in Christ by making him become human for us and uniting him to human nature, that we might be able to trace and recognize his friendly will toward us" (*WA* 10, 3, 416).

True God

We find in the sermons on Heb. 1:1-12 and John 1:1-14 some important developments on the divinity of Christ, considered in con-

nection with its trinitarian background and with the humanity of
Christ. It is the first time that Luther deals to such an extent with the
trinitarian questions. What he has discovered is that the question of
salvation is intimately bound up with the person of Jesus Christ. To
neglect this or to distort it by false teaching would affect salvation.
The doctrine of Luther on the person of Christ is that of the early
church. Seeberg [19] draws attention to it, as does A. Peters.[20] For our
part and in this section devoted to the divinity, we shall insist
further on the biblical climate of Luther's affirmations.

Of What Does the Divinity of Christ Consist?

It is not enough for Luther—and in this he is very modern—to
establish the divinity of Christ. He also needs to know why this
divinity is so important, and first of all what one really means by
"the divinity of Christ."

What does it mean to say, "Jesus Christ is God?" What does it
mean to be God? Luther does not look for the answer to that question in a metaphysical statement, in the concept of a supreme being,
endowed with certain specific properties which can be determined
by reason. To be God, for Luther, means to be Creator. It is to give
life. That is the sense in which we must understand Christ's divinity.
It is in the light of the biblical account of creation, which Luther
finds in John 1 and Hebrews 1, that he defines the divinity of Christ.
Christ is God because he is the Word by which God has created and
sustains all things. "He creates all things as a God" (*WA* 10, 1, 1, 150,
15) writes Luther, commenting on Heb. 1:2. And he continues, "If
all things were made by him, he must himself not have been made.
It follows clearly that he is truly God" (*WA* 10, 1, 1, 151, 13). And
commenting on v. 3, he adds, "If he sustains all things, he himself
is not sustained and must be superior to all things, so he must necessarily be God alone" (*WA* 10, 1, 1, 158, 4). In fact, all things subsist
in him. The sustaining of the world is a function which belongs
uniquely to the divinity and which characterizes him as much as
does the creation. The fact of reigning over all things, which is expressed as being "seated at the right hand of God," makes clear in
still another way what is meant by his divinity.

In his commentary on John 1:1-14 Luther connects before all else
the concept of divinity with that of life. The divinity of Christ is that
of the eternal Word present in him. This Word makes us alive.
"Therefore it is not the humanity of Christ which gives us life, but

it is in the Word that there is life, the Word which is in the flesh and which, by means of the flesh, makes us alive" (WA 10, 1, 1, 199, 14) and further: "See, all is in 'Christ made human,' he has made all things, and in him is life, he is the Word by which all things were made" (WA 10, 1, 1, 202, 15).

There, too, it is the idea of creation which characterizes the divinity. It is the power to create which distinguishes God from human beings. Christ is creator—there is his divinity! Let us note that he is creator, as much in that which concerns the creation confessed in the First Article of the creed (his divinity implies then his preexistence [WA 10, 1, 1, 149, 2]) in that which concerns the work of redemption, confessed in the Second Article.

Who is it who gives us life, salvation, peace, righteousness, redemption, power, and wisdom, things which we do not have by ourselves? It is Christ—not Christ the man, but Christ the Son of God become a man (WA 10, 1, 1, 126). By thus developing the idea of divinity within the perspective of creation, Luther succeeds in preserving the unity of God. It is the same God who creates and who saves; the God of creation and the God of the gospel are not two gods. It is God who calls into life those who do not exist and brings to life again those who are dead in their sins. God creates and recreates his creatures, unhindered by any resistance.

One will notice that Luther does not discuss the essence of God. Divinity is demonstrated by a work, and not by abstract properties. The reformer has adopted the dynamic perspective of Holy Scripture, which also characterizes God's being by his work. But that in no way for Luther signifies denying God as he is in himself, nor absorbs ontology into act, nor reduces theology to soteriology. In fact, on the basis of the work of Christ, creator and giver of life and salvation, faith seeks to comprehend his being and to adore him in his mystery. Thus ontological affirmations occur quite naturally in the christological confession, whether Luther uses the language of the Bible to speak of the radiance and the glory of God and of Christ as the eternal light (WA 10, 1, 1, 57, 9) or whether he uses the language of the two natures.

On the other hand, Luther does not forget the trinitarian distinctions when he establishes the divinity of Christ by his work or when he characterizes it by the work of creation. God operates as Father, Son, and Holy Spirit. Even if the three persons are united in the work, as Luther in common with tradition affirms, they are no less than three persons, as we shall see later. And if it is true that we know God—Father, Son, and Holy Spirit—only by his work, that is not to say that the trinitarian distinctions are situated only at the level of work. Such a modalism does not reflect the thought of Luther. The trinitarian mystery lies in the very life of God, even if we recognize it only in his works for our good.

How Can the Divinity of Christ Be Proven?

There is evidently no question of proving the divinity of Christ by an argument placed outside of revelation and faith. In fact, according to Luther, there is no other argument for the divinity of Christ than the witness of Scripture. And this witness is not concentrated on the extraordinary works of Christ Jesus. It is not the miracles which establish the divinity of Christ, even though they are signs of it (*WA* 17, 2, 242, 12).

The witnesses of the Holy Scripture proclaim the divinity of Christ, and believers add to them their own faith. They announce Christ as the one by whom the world was made; they proclaim him as the unique image of God who sustains all things by his Word and whom God has placed at his right hand in his humanity. One must therefore conclude that he is God. That is the way Luther reasons. This reasoning is placed strictly at the very heart of the *kerygma*. Its only logic is that of the message itself and faith. "If he were not God, this glory of the great God would not be attributed to him" (*WA* 10, 1, 1, 57, 8).

Since the world was made by him, since he is the image of the Father, since all things are sustained by him and since he is seated at the right hand of God, he must of necessity be God (*WA* 10, 1, 1, 151-155). This is what we have called the logic of the *kerygma*. It is by proclaiming Christ creator that one proclaims his divinity. You can take it or leave it.

We find a particularly striking example of this logic in a sermon on Matt. 2:1-12. In reference to the prophecy of Micah (5:2): "But you, Bethlehem Ephrathah . . .," Luther keeps close to the ancients, i.e., the tradition, and writes: "If Christ is to be Lord of his own people, his lordship cannot be temporal or physical, but he must reign over all the people, past, present, and future; therefore he must be an eternal lord, which can only be accomplished spiritually. Since God gives him his own lordship, he could not be simply a man; for it is impossible that God should give his honor, his lordship, his own properties, his people, to another who is not truly God" (*WA* 10, 1, 1, 600, 3).

The *kerygma* is here a prophecy. The eternal kingdom of Christ is announced. It is in the logic of this proclamation that the divinity of Christ is inscribed. But that is only true for faith which believes the Word. That is what we must look at now.

How Is the Divinity of Christ Recognized?

Since the divinity of Christ is present only in preaching and is not open to sight or accessible to reason, faith is necessary to comprehend it. That evidently continues to be true after Easter, even though the certainty of faith is strengthened by the resurrection, which is the basis of the *kerygma*. We touch here on the fundamental correlation between the Word and faith. In the sermon already mentioned on Matt. 2:1-12, Luther writes further: "Both Word and faith are bound together in one, as God and a man in one Christ is one person" (*WA* 10, 1, 1, 618, 13).

But it is in the sermon on John 1:1-14 that the reformer dwells most on the question of recognizing the divinity of Christ (*WA* 10, 1, 1, 214ff.). Christ was physically present among the Jews, he writes. They saw only his humanity. Therefore it fell to the ministry of John the Baptist to reveal the eternal light present in this man (*WA* 10, 1, 1, 215, 13, 19; 243, 21). Christ is the light everywhere present and illuminating the darkness, but he needs to be "revealed by the Word and recognized by faith in the heart" (*WA* 10, 1, 1, 217, 12). Only faith can comprehend what the gospel announces: "The gospel only proclaims this light, the Christ-man; the darkness is not able to comprehend it by reason or sense perception *(Empfindung)*, but only by faith (*WA* 10, 1, 1, 217, 20). Luther calls this faith "suprarational" *(übervernunftig)* (*WA* 10, 1, 1, 218, 4).

Thus faith is opposed to reason *(Vernunft)*, to feeling, to experience *(Empfindung)*, to nature, and to sight.[21]

This knowledge of the mystery of Christ is placed beyond these other modes of knowledge.[22] It is an attitude which involves the whole person at the deepest level of one's self. "The one who hears it preached and believes it finds it in the heart; for faith can only be in the heart" (*WA* 10, 1, 1, 216, 8). By opposing the knowledge of Christ according to reason to that according to faith, Luther can say: reason knows Christ only as a holy man and as an example, but faith knows him as the Son of God, that is, as the source of salvation (*WA* 10, 3, 209).

Now, we know the divinity of Christ by faith; but one day we shall see it. Luther places all his christological affirmations in an eschatological perspective. There will come a moment in fact when we shall see the divinity of Christ directly (*WA* 10, 1, 1, 222, 21). Here below it is lit only by the light of faith (*WA* 10, 1, 1, 222, 18). Now the humanity of Christ is for faith like a mirror, or like a transparency through which the eternal light shines (*WA* 10, 1, 1, 223, 22). Taking up the thought of 1 Cor. 13:12, Luther insists that one day we shall see God face to face. The light of Christ incarnate will cease because it will be transformed into eternal brightness (*WA* 10, 1, 1, 223, 9). But note that the eternal light will not be different in itself from the light of faith: there are not two gods! God is really present in his true being in Jesus Christ. All that is needed is the removal of a veil: then we shall see God directly. "Not that there are two kinds of light, nor that there will be something else to see, but this same light, this same God whom we now see by faith, we shall see in another way. Today we see him hidden in faith; then we shall see him unveiled" (*WA* 10, 1, 1, 223, 13).

The Divinity of Christ and the Trinity

When explaining Heb. 1:1-12 and John 1:1-14, Luther always begins by establishing the divinity of Christ on the basis of scriptural evidence. Then he proceeds to distinguish among the persons of the Trinity; and he relies again on the Scriptures for this distinction. "Since he is the Son of God, he cannot be alone, he must have a Father: and since God made the world through him, this God who made the world through him cannot be he through whom he made it. The result then is that there must be two persons, the Father and the Son, both distinct persons" (*WA* 10, 1, 1, 151, 21).[23] And Luther criticizes Sabellius for confusing the persons (*WA* 10, 1, 1, 191, 6). It can be seen that here Luther uses the term "person" in the usual sense that this word had in trinitarian theology.

After having distinguished the persons, Luther is nevertheless quick to stress their unity: "And yet, because the divine nature is only one and there cannot be more than one God, the result is that Christ with the Father is one true God, in a single being, sole creator of the world; and there is no difference there, except that one is the Son and one is the Father (*WA* 10, 1, 1, 152, 2).[24] "The Father is another person from the Son, but he is not another God" (*WA* 10, 1, 1, 191, 12).

Luther succeeded in translating into the language of the people the trinitarian mystery, which until then had only been formulated in Greek or Latin.[25] It will be noted in the texts we quote that Luther uses two words for the nature of God. He sometimes uses the word *nature (Natur)* and sometimes the word *being (Wesen)*. Seeberg pointed out very perceptively that the concept of *Wesen* corresponds not to *essentia,* as in the early Latin writings of Luther, where *essentia* signifies *person* in the sense of the Augustinian doctrine, but rather to *substance* or *nature* (p. 247). We shall return to this point when we discuss Christ as the image of the Father.

The only difference between the Father and the Son, according to Luther at the end of the text we have cited, lies in the fact that the one is the Father and the other is the Son. And he makes that more precise with the words: the Son has his being from the Father, not the other way round (*WA* 10, 1, 1, 152, 8-20; 155, 3; 183, 27; 184, 16). "The Father is the first and original person in the Godhead" (*WA* 10, 1, 1, 152, 21).

How does the Son derive his nature from the Father? Here Luther simply takes over the idea of the eternal generation of the Son from the Father: "Christ is eternally born from the Father, ever proceeding from him like the sun in the morning, not as at noon or at eventide. And his person is not the person of the Father, as the rays of the sun are not the sun. And yet he is with the Father and in the Father, neither before nor after, but at the same time, eternally with him and in him, as the rays are at the same time with and in the sun" (*WA* 10, 1, 1, 154, 1). The image of the sun and its rays is traditional for expressing the trinitarian mystery.

According to Seeberg (p. 244), Luther would here stand very close to the Eastern tradition. In fact, since Saint Augustine, the Western tradition has stressed the *homoousios,* i.e., the unity between the Father and the Son, in contrast to the Greek theologians like Origen or Basil, who insisted on the primacy of the Father as *arche* or *pege theotetos*. We shall return to this question and deal with it in detail when we analyze the *Disputations*. For that reason we shall limit ourselves here to a few brief remarks.

Luther certainly affirms the original place of the Father who is not generated, but that is common to all trinitarian theology. In other respects, he stresses the equality of the Son with the Father, declaring the Son to be "in no way less than the Father, but equal to him in all respects, except that he was generated from the Father and that the Father was not generated from him" (*WA* 10, 1, 1, 152, 7). The Son is "fully and totally God, as and like the Father" (*WA* 10, 1, 1, 154, 15). "In Christ is the whole Godhead and to him belongs all glory as to a God, except that he has this not from himself, but from the Father" (*WA* 10, 1, 1, 155, 1). Strictly speaking, one can say that there is a balance in Luther between the Western tradition with its insistence on the *homoousios* and the Eastern tradition in its affirmations of the primacy of the Father.

A theme which the reformer develops specially, basing himself on Heb. 1:3, is that of the Son as the image of the Father. Thus he points out what a great difference there is between the images which human beings can make and the image of the Father which the Son is. "All the images that have been made have no other substance nor other nature than that of being images. But here the Son is an image of the substance *(Wesen)* of the Father, such that the substance of the Father is the image itself, and, if it is permissible to express it in this way, the image is made out of the Father's substance, so that it is not only like the Father, but also includes wholly within it his whole nature and substance totally" (*WA* 10, 1, 1, 155, 16).

To such an extent is the Son the image of the Father that he truly has the same being, the same nature, the same substance as he. All that is in fact found in the term *Wesen.* If the epistle to the Hebrews says that the Son is the "image of his substance, the reflection of his glory," that means that God is present in a unique way in the Son. The case of the saints is different. The Scripture does not use the same kind of language when speaking of the saints, who are without doubt also the glory of God, that is to say, made and created for his glory. But here when it says that Christ is the reflection of the glory of God, these words require us to admit that the glory of the Father resides in this reflection, otherwise it would not say that he is "the reflection of his glory" (*WA* 10, 1, 1, 154, 15).

Hence, God is present concretely and really in Christ. In him we meet the Father, fully and truly. But nonetheless only the Word was made flesh: "But it is a major article of faith that only the Word was made flesh, not the Father, although both are one God, complete, unique, and true" (*WA* 10, 1, 1, 239, 15).

Commenting on Heb. 1:2-3: "He sustains all things by the Word of his power," Luther asks the following question: Is it not improper to attribute this work to the Son? "If it were the person of the Father that was meant, then that would accord with the Scripture; for the Father made all things by his Word, by which he also sustains all things, as it says in Ps. 33:6" (*WA* 10, 1, 1, 158, 17). Luther replies to this objection, basing his answer on the traditional trinitarian principle, *opera ad extra sunt indivisa:* "What God has done," he writes, "each person has done. Thus God sustains all things by his Word, and this God is truly also the Christ, and this same Word" (*WA* 10, 1, 1, 159, 2).

Of course, the work of creation, redemption, and sanctification are respectively attributed to the Father, the Son, and the Holy Spirit. But the divine unity is the fundamental principle: thus in the Scriptures the appropriations are not always respected. "There are other quick transitions of this kind in the Scriptures from one person of the Trinity to another" (*WA* 10, 1, 1, 159, 3). Because the persons are united in the same divinity *(die person menge ynn eine Gottheit),* it is quite possible to attribute a work to one person while thinking of another (*WA* 10, 1, 1, 158, 3).

The Importance of the Divinity of Christ

It is impossible to overemphasize the fundamental importance in Luther's eyes of what he calls, "the major article of faith in the divinity of Christ" (*WA* 10, 1, 1, 143, 14). Everything would collapse for him if Christ were only human, one saint among many, and not God who saves us. "Whoever does not recognize and confess that Christ is true God, as I have described him up to this point, that he was the Word which was in the beginning with God and through whom all things were made, but holds him to be only a creature, who began in time and who had his existence only from his mother, as Cerinthus teaches, that one is eternally lost and cannot have life; for there is no life outside this Word and the Son of God, in whom alone is life. If the Christ-man were alone and without God, he would be no use to us" (*WA* 10, 1, 1, 198, 17). "The humanity would be no use if the divinity were not in it" (*WA* 10, 1, 1, 208, 22).

If he were only a man, there would be only imitation, i.e., only the law. But because he is God present in a human being, there is the gospel, the good news of our salvation, of a new life offered to sinners, without any merit on their part.

Truly Human

It is necessary for us "to let Christ be a natural man, in all points like as we are, and to separate him in nothing from nature, except in what concerns sin and grace" (*WA* 10, 1, 1, 67, 17).[26] Already at his birth, Christ arrived quite naturally. It was a true birth . . . it happened to her [Mary] as happens to other women, in full consciousness and with the collaboration of her body, as happens at any birth; she was a natural mother and he was a natural son" (*WA* 10, 1, 1, 67, 3). Like all people, Christ was born of a woman (*WA* 10, 1, 1, 355, 15). He came in time, in Bethlehem (*WA* 10, 1, 1, 600, 21). Against Apollinarius and Photin, Luther holds that Christ's humanity was composed of a body and a soul. Christ was "a human being like other human beings, who has flesh and blood, body and soul" (*WA* 10, 1, 1, 236, 11).

Commenting on Luke 2:40, Luther does battle against the legends of Christ's infancy (*WA* 10, 1, 1, 443-444). It is known that the imagination, more or less pious, of certain writers attributed to the infant Jesus a crowd of miracles, none of which was reported in the Gospels. The reformer is of the opinion that it is enough for us to know what Luke has told us about the infancy of Jesus. The infant grew up like other children, the miracles and signs began only later. "The time had not yet come for him to do signs and miracles *(wunderzeychen)*, he came and went and grew up like any other child; only this, that as there are some children cleverer than others, Christ was a particularly clever child" (*WA* 10, 1, 1, 445, 16).[27]

Luther also admits that there were certain things which Christ did not know. He writes thus: "The humanity of Christ, like that of any other holy and natural person, did not always think, say, wish, and notice all things, as certain people make of him an all-powerful being, mixing and confusing the two natures and their work. Even as he did not always see, hear, and feel all things, so he did not always consider all things in his heart, but, as God has led him and inspired him, he was full of grace and of wisdom, and was able to evaluate and to teach" (*WA* 10, 1, 1, 149, 13).[28]

The ignorance of Christ attested, for example, by Mark 13:32 (on the subject of the hour of judgment), was interpreted by the Fathers in general as a deliberate silence on Christ's part. He would not have been ignorant of this hour, even in his human nature, but in communion with the Father, he felt that it was not salutary for the disciples that he should tell it to them.

Luther's thought is not entirely clear on this point. On the one hand, he admits, in fact, in the text quoted, that Christ in his humanity knew only what it was useful for him to know and say, in communion with his Father. In that, he went beyond the early church, which admitted that Christ had here deceived his disciples. On the other hand, however, the text quoted ends a little further on with these words: "Thus Christ knew nothing of the last judgment, and yet knew it well" (WA 10, 1, 1, 151, 6). Here, Luther seems to return to the patristic exegesis.

Luther does not describe the humanity of Christ only by pointing out his limitations, but also by describing his submission to the law, which governs all human existence. It is in commenting on Gal. 4:1-7 that the reformer is led to develop this point of view.[29] To be submissive to the law means two things: first, to be submissive to the works of the law. "He allowed himself to be circumcised, to be presented and purified in the temple. He was obedient to his father and mother and did other acts of this kind." [30] He did these things freely, without being obliged to do so. "By his own will, he who is free and not under the law has submitted himself to the law by the works that he has freely accomplished." [31] Christ's submission to the law is the acceptance of daily and ordinary life, submission to the rules of life and to the authorities.

But there is another point of view: to be submissive in this way to the law, by doing its works, is not all. The law is bound up here below with suffering and punishment. To be human is to be accused by the law which can never be completely fulfilled. Without doubt, Christ fulfilled it perfectly, but in order to be entirely at one with us, he has like us submitted to the "punishment and the penalty of the law." [32] Hence Luther is not content, as we have already pointed out, to describe the humanity of Christ according to physical or general anthropological categories. To be human means for Christ to be submissive to the law and also to the accusation which this law addresses to us, with its consequent punishment. In this way, he has truly partaken of our human condition. "Thus we must allow Christ to be simply and entirely truly human (as we all are, except that he is without sin). Therefore he has suffered the pains of death." [33] "Christ must remain a simple man on whom have fallen death, hell, and sin with all their powers." [34]

The humanity of Christ is like ours, except in that which concerns sin. Luther evidently takes up this affirmation of the New Testament and in conformity with tradition confesses the virgin birth, which he links with the purity of Christ. "He derives from this birth chastity and purity, as can be seen as soon as one contemplates it and recognizes there the work of God" (*WA* 10, 1, 1, 69, 1).[35] However, the text of Gal. 4:1-7 leads him to ask about the meaning of the virginity of Mary. In fact, this is not mentioned in the passage. It is said only that Jesus is born of a woman. In fact, says Luther, what is important is not that she was a virgin, but the fact that "God's Son was born of a woman, i.e., not from a man, as all other children are born. Among all others, this man alone is born only of a woman. There is no emphasis on the fact that he was *born of a virgin*" (*WA* 10, 1, 1, 356, 19).

Here Luther introduces a distinction that is not easy to understand. Mary was a virginal woman, but not simply a virgin (according to the words of the apostle). The German is *jungferlich Weib* (*WA* 10, 1, 1, 357, 2). What Luther seems to mean is this: it was of very little importance whether Mary was or was not a virgin before the conception and birth of Christ. If she was, then that was only an additional adornment proper and personal to her. What matters about Mary is that she conceived Jesus Christ without the participation of a man. And Luther returns to the traditional line entirely when he writes, "That he had for a mother such a woman as made it possible for him to be born without sin, so that she could be a virginal woman (*jungferlich Weib*) who conceived and gave birth without the collaboration of a man" (*WA* 10, 1, 1, 357, 12).

The Union of the Two Natures

At several points, Luther insists that a clear distinction be made between the two natures, so that one does not attribute to the one that which belongs only to the other. "At times, the Scriptures and Jesus himself speak of him as a pure man, at times as a pure God" (*WA* 10, 1, 1, 149, 13). When he affirms his preexistence, Christ speaks as God; when he speaks of his ignorance on the subject of the hour or the last day, or when he speaks of the superiority of the Father, who alone has the right to place someone at his right hand or his left hand, he speaks as a human being" (*WA* 10, 1, 1, 149).[36] "He creates all things as God, but as a human being he creates nothing" (*WA* 10, 1, 1, 150, 15). On the other hand, "All that is said of the humiliation and exaltation of Christ must be attributed to the human being; for the divinity can neither be humiliated nor exalted" (*WA* 10, 1, 1, 150, 8).

It is the distinction between the natures which allows Luther to explain certain difficult passages in Scripture. Apart from those that we have already quoted (Matt. 20:23; John 14:28; Mark 13:23), there is also Matt. 23:37. Luther examines this text at greater length and then poses the following question: "Since no one can resist the will of God, why does he say, 'How often would I have gathered your children . . . and you would not?'" (*WA* 10, 1, 1, 278, 10). He rejects certain solutions, including one by Saint Augustine, and writes, "It would be very much easier to say that Christ spoke here as a man, who bears all the human characteristics; hence, he has endured all those things in his humanity which do not belong to his divinity, like eating, drinking, sleeping, walking, weeping, suffering, and dying. Thus he would be able to say what he said here, according to his human nature and emotions: 'I would and you would not'" (*WA* 10, 1, 1, 278, 19).

In any case, it is interesting to note what effort Luther makes in the postils and sermons of the years 1522-1525 to avoid confusing the two natures. Seeberg even speaks of a Nestorian tendency in this regard (p. 241). We shall see later how the decisive point which will separate Luther from Zwingli will be precisely this: To what extent must the two natures of Jesus Christ be united or separated? Zwingli for his part will insist—as will Calvin [37]—on the necessity of carefully distinguishing them. And he will reproach Luther for confusing the two natures and thus endangering the true humanity of Christ, to which he attributes divine properties.

Considering the conflict between the reformers on this point, it is well to remember that before the Eucharistic struggle, Luther criticized those who "made Christ an all-powerful man, mixing and confusing without consideration the two natures and their work" (*WA* 10, 1, 1, 150, 1), forgetting that "the humanity of Christ did not know all things" (*WA* 10, 1, 1, 149). They attributed to the divine nature that which belongs only to the human nature, and *vice versa*. Thus, "They blind themselves in the study of the Scriptures" (*WA* 10, 1, 1, 147, 10).

This effort by Luther to preserve the true humanity of Christ should be noted. We shall be obliged a little later to criticize Luther

with the help of his own writings! In fact, it is possible to think that
on this point there are certain contradictions in Luther's christology.
They are explicable on the grounds that his profound thought—for
example, on the subject of the real presence of Christ in the Eucharist—did not always find adequate conceptualization to express itself.
Therefore his christology will veer dangerously near to Docetism,
i.e., an illegitimate divinization of the humanity of Christ, during the
Eucharistic controversy.

But also in the period that we are now studying, Luther is primarily occupied with preserving the unity of the person of Jesus
Christ. "Although the two natures are distinct, it is yet only one person who does and suffers as Christ. Most certainly God has acted
and suffered, although only one nature has itself encountered these
things. A comparison: when I speak of the wounded leg of a man,
I say: this man is wounded, even though it is not his soul, nor the
entire man which is wounded, but only a part of his body, because
the body and the soul are one *(eyn ding)*" (*WA* 10, 1, 1, 150, 21).

In this text there appears an idea that is important for Luther's
understanding of Christ and salvation. In Christ, God also suffered,
not of course in his nature, but in the one person of Jesus Christ. It
is an idea which we shall meet again in the controversy with Zwingli.
This is how Luther describes the agony of Christ in Gethsemane as
a means of our liberation: "Now our God has suffered for us and
brought about a change in himself, so that the fear of death has lost
its force and power" (*WA* 10, 3, 73).

As Althaus has noted, this idea of a suffering of God does not
mean that Luther has become a Patripassian.[38] We know that Patripassianism was a modalistic heresy which refused to distinguish
between the Father and the Son, even to the point of admitting that
God the Father was crucified on the cross. It would be more accurate in Luther's case to speak of "Dei-passianism." But it is precisely
in the intimate communion between God and suffering humanity,
which allows us to talk of the suffering of God, that all the depth of
Luther's christology is revealed.

But to speak of the unity of the person does not mean only a
participation of the divinity in the humanity, but also the reverse.
That is the point at which those difficulties we have spoken of begin
for Luther. Once again it must be stressed that in the texts we are
studying here, Luther is very reserved on this subject. Of course, in
conformity with the tradition, he speaks of the participation of the

humanity of Christ in the reign of the Son: "For we must believe that it is not only according to his divinity that Christ is above all things, but also according to his humanity, so that all creatures are put in submission and subjection to the Christ man" (*WA* 10, 1, 1, 150, 12).

However, he scarcely stops at that aspect of christology. In the same way, the communication of attributes hardly appears in these texts. Luther avoids impairing the true humanity of Christ. But we find an interpretation of Philippians 2 in the postil for Lent 1525. Seeing how Luther understands the *kenosis* of Christ, we raise the question: Is he faithful at this point to the biblical image of the true humanity of Christ? That is what we must look at now.

The Different States of Christ: The Kenosis

One finds a double perspective in Luther on this subject. On the one hand, he insists on the simultaneity of the death and life of Christ—to the point where one may ask what purpose the resurrection serves. From the incarnation on, the passion and the resurrection coexist in Christ. By becoming incarnate, he is at the same time humiliated and exalted, and this double movement continues throughout the whole of his earthly existence.

But in a chronological perspective, Luther, in conformity with tradition, describes the way of Christ as a path whose different stages were the incarnation, passion, and glorification. There it is a question of a succession of states, of an exaltation succeeding upon a humiliation.

Let us look more closely at these two perspectives. Commenting on John 1:4, Luther writes: "Although he is really dead as a man, he has remained always alive, for life could and cannot die" (*WA* 10, 1, 1, 208, 8). Here it is the divinity of Christ which is meant. Consequently, Luther sees the whole of the incarnation from the perspective of this fundamental dualism in which humanity is sacrificed and dies, while at the same time divinity affirms itself as the source of life and salvation. Such is the mystery of the person of Christ: in this humiliated man is affirmed the life-creating divinity.

But one does not stop at this incessant struggle between life and death, this extreme dualism. In fact, the passage that we have just quoted continues: "Therefore, death, even in this life, is suppressed and conquered, so that the humanity also must soon become alive again, and this life is a light for human beings; for whoever recognizes and believes in such a life in Christ also passes through death and never dies again" (*WA* 10, 1, 1, 208, 10).

The confrontation between the life present in the humanity of Christ, and death, which attacked this humanity, has disarmed death. That is why the extreme humiliation of Christ in death and the descent into hell is followed by the resurrection and glorification. The resurrection puts an end to the *simul* of which we spoke earlier, in the sense that the humanity of Christ has also become immortal. He is the image of the new human being, who is no longer subject to death.

At the same time, the resurrection marks the beginning of a new state of Christ. In order to accomplish his redemptive work, he had been humiliated by his incarnation and his passion. He was despised and rejected, abandoned by God and human beings. Now he has ascended to the right hand of the Father. He is *exaltatus super omnia*.[39] He reigns by the Word—in the power of the Holy Spirit. Luther frequently speaks of the spiritual reign of Christ inaugurated by the ascension.[40]

When one studies the thought of an author on the subject of the different states of Christ, it is obviously essential to examine his interpretation of Philippians 2, which is a classic New Testament text describing the humiliation and exaltation of Christ. We have already seen that it is a basic christological text for Luther, together with Isaiah 53; Col. 2:9; John 1:14; 14:9; 2 Cor. 5:21; and Gal. 3:13. In the sermons we are studying here, the Philippians text is often quoted,[41] and it is the theme of a very beautiful sermon for Palm Sunday, when it is the Epistle for the day.[42] We shall examine the text of this sermon shortly.

First, a question arises about the interpretation of the text: Who is humiliated and despoiled? Is it the Word at the moment of its incarnation, or the Word become flesh, the God become human? Luther differs from the majority of earlier interpreters in attributing the *kenosis* to Christ in the flesh. We brought this out already in connection with the sermon on "double righteousness."

Everything rests entirely on the real and substantial presence of the divinity in the man Jesus.[43] By becoming incarnate, the Word of God comes to live in our very being, the humanity of Christ, but it does not renounce certain of its divine properties, as some Kenotic theologians of the 19th century, such as Thomasius and Franck, have taught. God in the person of the Son is present, albeit hidden, but really present in that which constitutes his very being. It is not outside of him. Otherwise that would lead to two gods, one God revealed, one God hidden.

Now we must ask of what Christ-in-the-flesh divests himself. We can answer that question only when we have examined what Luther says about the presence of God in the humanity of Christ and about his way of presenting himself to us. Christ did not have to search for his divinity. He had it from all eternity. Human beings in general search to find how they may comport themselves like gods and to snatch this condition as a prey which is not theirs by right because in essence they are not gods. Christ for his part "snatches at nothing . . . it is within him, this is his form . . . he has it by birth" (WA 17, 2, 242, 7). He possesses both the divine nature (göttliche Wesen) and the divine form (göttliche Gestalt). The essence is invisible, the form is visible.[44] The form of God—or the form of the servant—manifests itself by a series of acts (Gebärden).

Of what then does the kenosis of Christ consist? As we have already stressed, he does not renounce his divine essence. "He has not so laid aside the divine form to the point that one can no longer feel it, nor see it. If that were so, no divine form would remain. But he does not take it up nor use it to lord himself over us, rather he serves us with it" (WA 17, 2, 243, 4).[45]

The humiliation of Christ consists of his taking the form of a servant and placing himself at our service with all that he is by nature. One can say both, that he remains in the form of God and that he is humiliated. He remains in the form of God in the sense that the deeds he accomplishes express the love of God, while being realized as acts of the servant. "He took the form of a servant and yet remained God and in the form of God. That is to say that he was God and all the divine works and words which he accomplished, he did for our good and served us thereby as a servant" (WA 17, 2, 243, 19).

That of which Christ is stripped, one could say, is the divine form in itself, the deity proclaimed and visible, the glory and the honor, precisely that to which the Pharisees aspire.[46] It must be emphasized that this despoiling is not the result of the incarnation itself. Christ could have assumed a human nature without entering into the form of a servant. He assumed that freely—by a deliberate choice which shows the extent of his love.[47]

In offering himself to suffering and death, Christ laid aside not only those divine properties that we call metaphysical, such as omnipotence, but even those properties that we could call moral, in the sense that he places himself on the same level as sinners and allows himself to be judged as such. By this despoiling, he submits himself not only to human beings, but to the devil and to the consequences of sin.[48]

In this connection we find again the theme of joyous exchange. In fact, Christ is stripped, he makes himself a servant in order to assume our sin. Thus we become free. He snatches us from our slavery and makes us children of God.

The intentions that inspired Luther in his interpretation of Philippians 2 are the following:

On the one hand, he insists that the divinity was truly present in the man Jesus. That is a fundamental intention which recurs incessantly in his thought, to which the Kenotic theologians of the 19th century do not remain faithful. It is said, in effect, that Thomasius and others admitted a limitation of the divine in the human, freely accepted at the moment of incarnation. Luther would not have accepted this attempt to overcome certain difficulties of christological dogma.

On the other hand, it must be noted that he does not insist on a christological theory concerning the person of Christ and the relation between the two natures. He finds above all in Philippians 2 the affirmation of the love of Christ. This love drives Christ to the incarnation and animates him during the whole of his earthly life. It is from the point of view of this redemptive love that one must consider Christ, and not be preoccupied with the mystery of the person as such. The true miracle, he writes elsewhere, is not the incarnation, but the love of Christ (*WA* 10, 3, 432), and the quality of this love (which gives itself in sacrifice) is further underlined by the opposition between Christ and the Pharisees, whose human attitude is to seek at all costs to seize for itself the divine condition.

But the question which can hardly be avoided is: Has Luther not wrongly divinized the man Jesus? Is it not dangerously near to the teaching of Docetism to write, "The man [Jesus] was God and should have been able to comport himself in a divine manner, but he did not do so; he abstained and was despoiled, comporting himself like a simple man" (*WA* 17, 2, 242, 35) or again, "Like other human beings he ate, drank, slept, awoke, walked, stood, hungered, thirsted, was cold, was hot, became tired, clothed himself, prayed, living like any other person before God and the world. And all this he could have left and comported himself differently—as a God" (*WA* 17, 2, 244, 6)?

It is not always easy to grasp the exact and full significance of such affirmations. Luther has certainly often insisted on the unity of Christ. United to the divinity in a hypostatic union, the humanity knows a definite heightening. It disposes of a power which distinguishes it from other human beings. The hypostatic union does not remain without effect on the humanity of Jesus thus united to the divinity. This theme will acquire a great importance during the Eucharistic controversy, which broke out at the moment when Luther wrote the postils for Lent in 1525. One will also emphasize that from his earthly existence on, Christ already prefigures, in an eschatological fashion, glorified humanity.[49]

But an uneasiness remains. Do not these statements that we quote go a bit too far? If Christ had been able at any moment to stop being a man bound to the physical limitations of all human existence, then was he still of like nature with our humanity? Do we not have there a too one-sided Johannine Christ,[50] which takes account of the glory of Christ, but not of his true humanity, those human limitations to which the synoptics and Luther himself, in texts that we have looked at previously, bear witness about Christ?

We shall be content here simply to pose those questions, leaving the answers until we take up the Eucharistic controversy.

The Work of Christ [51]

To the degree that we have spoken of the person of Christ, we have actually already described his work. For Christ to be a human being signified not only leading a human existence, but living it for others, submitting himself to the law for others and being one with them in their sinful situation. As for the divinity of Christ, it is no longer described in abstract terms, but constantly in relation to the work of God the creator in creation and redemption.

Luther takes issue with all those who would consider Christ in himself, separating the person from the work. He writes thus: "The gospel reveals to us what Christ is, in order that we may learn to know him, that he is our Savior who takes away from us our sin and death, and saves us from all calamity, reconciles us with the Father, and makes us, without any work of ours, upright and blessed. He who does not know Christ in this way must fall into error. For even if you know that he is the Son of God, that he died and rose and is seated at the right hand of God, you have not rightly known Christ, and all your knowledge will not help you. It is necessary to believe and to know that he has done all that for you, to help you" (*WA* 12, 285, 9).

"For you, for you"—those are the key words which determine the preaching of Luther on the subject of Christ.[52] Constantly, the christological affirmations of the reformer lead to the work of Christ and the need to have a personal faith in order to be able to benefit from it. Christology and soteriology are inseparable one from the other. It is no less useful to examine more closely soteriology itself, that is to say, the way in which Luther conceived of the saving work of Jesus Christ, and to compare it point by point with traditional conceptions of this work. Let us recall very briefly those attitudes which, in the interpretation of the mystery of Christ the Savior, attested by Holy Scripture, have become evident in the course of time.

The early-church, particularly in its Eastern part, understood the work of Christ essentially as the liberation of human beings, enslaved by sin, death, and the devil. Guilt and the forgiveness of sins were less important than the victory over death and the devil. The reality of the wrath of God, in its personal dimension, was hidden behind those powers which can be called cosmic. The New Testament view of reconciliation with God passed into the background. The work of Christ was seen under the aspect of combat. The essential emphasis was placed on the resurrection as the victory of Christ. Both Irenaeus and Athanasius pointed in this direction.

But another tendency, equally present in the early church—with Tertullian for example—fixed on an understanding of the relationship between God and human beings, and hence the breaking of that relationship, from a juridical point of view.

For Tertullian, it is a matter of *reactus, culpa, poena, satisfactio, pretium compensatio*. In this perspective, which we find more fully developed in Anselm and even in Protestant orthodoxy, the work of Christ must reestablish justice by creating just relations between God and human beings.

The ideas presented by Anselm in his *Cur Deus Homo* dominated the medieval period. Anselm differs from the theologians of the early church, who placed their emphasis on the struggle between the powers, by placing his emphasis on the honor of God which has been impugned by the sin of human beings. Then humanity either accomplishes a work which reestablishes the honor of God, or else takes the punishment *(aut satisfactio aut poena)*. The necessary work—the satisfaction—is accomplished by the man-God who, by his innocent death, acquires a merit which can be attributed to other human beings. In relation to the early church, Anselm has deepened the concept of sin, as well as the vision of the holiness of God. But he interprets the work of Christ in terms of penitence *(satisfactio meritum)* and admits a system of compensation for the fault by the substitutive work of Christ. The miracle of reconciliation disappears in this rational system. On the other hand, he displaces the wrath of God from the present to the future. The Greek Fathers still envisaged a conflict by Christ against the hostile powers present in humanity, a conflict in which the wrath of God slipped into the background, behind the cosmic powers, but never entirely disappeared. In Anselm's system, Christ does not truly enter into the sinful situation of humanity; he does not experience the wrath of God and does not do battle, but pays the price necessary to safeguard the honor of God, so that God is able to pardon human beings on the basis of the superfluous merit acquired by Christ.

Another tendency showed itself in the Middle Ages with Abelard and was revived again in the 19th century with such theologians as Albrecht Ritschl. According to this tendency, it is not God who must be reconciled to human beings, but human beings who must be reconciled to God. They must be transformed, and in this way saved. They must surmount the hatred of God within them, and they can do this when, thanks to Christ, they acquire the confidence that God wants to forgive them. The work of Christ then consists of revealing the love of the Father and in response giving birth in human beings to the love of God.

We must, of course, be careful not to distinguish or oppose too rigorously the diverse tendencies that we have here described briefly, because between them there are many interconnections and variations. However, it is well to recognize the various characteristic tendencies which were known more or less to Luther.

There have been attempts to range the reformer on the side of one or another of these tendencies, but with no convincing success. It is striking, in fact, to note that the terminology and characteristic themes of these different tendencies can be found in Luther, but that he cannot be attached to any one of these systems. It is even necessary to avoid talking of a "system" or of a "theory" of atonement with Luther. He is content to follow the different ways by which the biblical witnesses attempted to translate the fall of human beings and the saving work of Jesus Christ, variations which must not be arbitrarily harmonized and which can have very different emphases.

We have already seen several times how he used, in conformity with Scripture, the titles that tradition attributed to Christ and which allow us to comprehend the work of Christ. He speaks of him as reconciler *(Versühner)* who renders us acceptable to God.[53] Christ is the mediator *(Mittler)* between us and the Father,[54] the mediator and intercessor.[55] He is the priest who takes the sinner's place before God.[56] He is our bishop, our mediator, our intercessor before God,[57] our Savior *(Heyland)* who helps us, delivers us, and makes us blessed.[58] When Luther speaks of Christ as Savior, it is often to oppose him to Christ as judge.[59]

It is not enough simply to repeat the titles that Luther ascribes to Christ. It is necessary to discern more closely the themes in his thought which he has derived from them. We shall try to describe them, but at the same time avoid systematizing his thought too much.

In accordance with tradition, Luther sets out the two fundamental premises of the saving work of Christ, which are the fall of humanity and the love of God.

How does he describe the fallen state? From what must human beings be saved? "Between God and human beings, there is only pure anger and enmity" (*WA* 10, 3, 127, 5). From birth, human beings are caught up in sin and in the fall and thus attract to themselves the wrath of God (*WA* 10, 3, 136, 4). The radical way in which the reformer understands the fall of humanity has been emphasized many times. This fallen state is more than humanity's slavery to death, which is only the consequence of a much greater fall, namely human sin and the wrath of God which follows it. And when Luther talks of sin, he is not only concerned with the failure to observe one of the Ten Commandments, but that movement inherent in human beings by which they assert themselves against God. Sin means to forget God and the fear of God. At the basis of all transgressions is to be found the transgression of the First Commandment. Sin is the revolt against God, the fact of no longer taking him seriously. Human beings do not sin against an impersonal code, but against the holy God. Sin and guilt are thus described in terms of personal relationships.

The wrath of God falls on guilty human beings. Whereas the early church talked mostly about the powers to which sinful persons were subject and Anselm insisted on the necessity of respecting and reestablishing a right, Luther placed his main emphasis on the wrath of God which must be appeased. Sinful human beings are subject to the wrath of God. Salvation can be nothing else but the appeasement of this anger and its effects and the reestablishment of normal relations, i.e., relations of love between God and human beings. With Luther, the point of departure from which one can and must understand the saving work of Christ is the conscience confronted by the wrath of God. It is sinful human beings, subject to death, the law, the devil, who are not only separated from God by the chasm of guilt, but know themselves pursued, accused, questioned, and indicted to the very depths of their being by the holy God, whose immense anger they feel.

Faced with the fallen state of humanity, thus described, the saving action consisting of the coming and sacrifice of Christ is set in motion. One of the dominant motifs in the thought of Luther sets out clearly the love of God which occasioned the work of the Son.[60] "Therefore God has given us in the first place a man who satisfied the divine righteousness for us all" (WA 10, 1, 1, 123).[61] In whatever way one describes the work of the Son, one must always see the love of the Father as the ground of this work.[62] This is a theme that we have already encountered many times.

Forgiveness and new life are given to us, without any merit on our part, but they cost Christ dearly.[63] "The grace which is without doubt given to us for nothing, so that it has cost us nothing, but it has cost another very dearly for us and is acquired with an immense, infinite treasure, namely by God's Son himself." [64]

Luther returns again and again to this matter of the price of this grace, which is Christ himself and his work. "It is only through Christ and his work that sins are pardoned, that God is reconciled, and that the conscience is set free and strengthened." [65]

How is the saving work of Christ accomplished? By the fact that "he has represented us in the fear of death, taken all our sins upon himself and has exterminated (ausgeleschet) them" (WA 10, 1, 2, 236, 28). "He has taken (geladen) my sins on himself, and has died because of them and has allowed himself to be slain because of these sins" (*WA* 10, 1, 2, 221, 24).

The relation of Christ to the law constitutes a particularly important aspect of his saving work. He must save us from this hostile power which does not cease to accuse the believer. On the one hand, he does this by fulfilling perfectly the requirements of the law. In my place, he thus "satisfies" the law entirely (*WA* 10, 1, 121, 19ff.; 10, 1, 2, 235, 29ff.; 10, 3, 127, 11ff.; 10, 1, 1, 471, 2). This perfect accomplishment is not shown only by the observance of all the requirements, but also by respect for the First Commandment. Christ loved God with all his heart; he remained obedient to him, even unto death.[66] On the other hand, he has thus fulfilled the law without being obliged to (*WA* 10, 1, 1, 366, 17), whereas we are grudgingly subject to it (*WA* 10, 1, 1, 365). As we have already indicated in the preceding chapter, Christ not only fulfilled the law in a perfect fashion, but he also accepted its accusation. The law is an instrument of the wrath of God by which he chastises human beings. It is to the law thus understood that Christ voluntarily submitted himself in order to save us (*WA* 10, 1, 1, 366, 3ff.).

When Luther describes the saving work of Christ, he sometimes places the emphasis on reconciliation with God, and sometimes on the victory achieved by Christ over the powers which enslave human beings. His exposition often links the two themes.

By taking our sins on himself, Christ has reconciled us with God.[67] Christ reconciles us with God by "satisfying" the justice of God, which means both perfect obedience to the law and the acceptance of punishment. It is thus that he is our mediator—our priest.[68] In conformity with tradition, Luther frequently uses the term *Genugtuung (satisfactio)*.[69] But as Althaus indicates, Luther found this term basically inadequate to express the work of Christ.[70] The term *satisfactio*, like that of *meritum*, belongs to a spirituality in which the sacrament of penance plays a dominant role. The work of Christ then risks appearing as a kind of restoration of a balance which has been upset in the moral order. Luther further insists on the personal dimension of reconciliation, making quite clear the obedience and sacrifice of Christ who offers himself to God, and bears his wrath in order to reconcile God with human beings.

But it is not at all necessary to oppose the ideas of Luther radically to those of Anselm, as some Scandinavian theologians have done.[71] The offense to the justice and the holiness of God which

characterizes Anselm's concept of sin is found again in Luther. As
with Anselm and in distinction to certain ideas of the early church,
Christ does not act only as God's representative with regard to the
powers that enslave human beings and with regard to human beings,
but his work is addressed as well to God in order to reconcile him
with humanity.

But one will also note that Luther emphasizes more than Anselm
that Christ does not work, as one might say, from outside upon God,
as though he were the qualified representative of humanity seeking
to reestablish an order destroyed by sin. We are dealing instead
with a struggle within God himself, a combat between the Father
and the Son become human, the Son offering himself to the wrath
of the Father in order to let love triumph and open the way to
forgiveness.

Luther does not describe the work of Christ only from the point
of view of reconciliation with God. Often he speaks of it in terms of
combat, making clear the victory of Christ over the powers that
enslave human beings.[72] This theme of combat is developed principally in the sermons and the catechisms, but also in other works. We
encounter it, for example, in the *Commentary on the Epistle to the
Galatians.*

Sin was not able to remain on Christ. "Christ was too strong for
my sins, they could not hold him. He breaks out from them and
throws them to the earth, ascends into heaven, and reigns there over
everything eternally" (*WA* 10, 1, 2, 221, 26). "On Christ, no sin can
remain" (*WA* 10, 3, 125, 31).[73]

Sin is not the only hostile power to be conquered. Luther adds
the devil and death, and, differing hereby from the early church,
also the law. These powers are often personified in astonishing ways.
In the same way as the law and the devil, death appears as one of
the tyrants with whom Christ enters into conflict. Thus, commenting
on Luke 2:21, Luther writes: "He has been placed under the law in
order to deliver those who were under the law. In fact, while on
the one hand death fell on him, killed him without having any rights
over him or the reasons for doing so, and, on the other hand, he
submitted freely to it and in all innocence allowed himself to be
killed. Thus death has become his debtor, has done him wrong,
and has sinned against him, has deprived itself of all things, so that
Christ has a just cause against it. Therefore the injustice of which
death was guilty with respect to Christ is now great. Death can

neither pay for it nor expiate it. So death must submit to Christ and be in his power eternally. Thus death has been overcome and slain in Christ" (*WA* 10, 1, 1, 516).

It will be noticed how much this text is in the climate of the early church. Certain Fathers had not hesitated to speak of death being tricked by Christ, since it attacked him without having the right to do so and without knowing it. That is why it is disarmed. Origen, Leontius of Byzantium, Gregory the Great, Gregory of Nyssa, and Saint Augustine all spoke of tricking the devil. The humanity of Christ was like the worm which the devil swallowed without seeing the hook, which was the divinity of Christ. Whereas Anselm and the Middle Ages in general had set aside such similes, often very mythological, in order to understand principally the reestablishment of relations between God and humanity in a juridical and penitential sense, Luther did not heistate to take up again such images.[74]

But far more than in the early church, the link with the wrath of God was evident. The powers that we are describing have no power over human beings except as instruments of the wrath of God. The link between the wrath of God, on the one hand, and the law, sin, death, and the devil, on the other, is characteristic of the thought of Luther. Sometimes he insists on reconciliation, sometimes on combat. Often, too, he describes both the reconciliation with God and the victory over the powers at the same time. In an interesting passage where he comments on Matt. 2:1-12, Luther establishes a difference between the reconciliation with God—his sacerdotal office —and his royal office, by which he reigns over the powers and creatures and preserves us from their attacks. This is what he writes: "By his sovereignty and lordship he preserves us from all things, but by his priesthood he preserves us from sins and from the wrath of God. He places himself before us and sacrifices himself in order to reconcile God, so that by him we may have confidence in God and our conscience not be afraid before his wrath and his judgment and fear them not. Now it is more important that he give us this certainty with regard to God and appease our consciences to the point that neither God nor we ourselves be hostile, than that his creatures be rendered inoffensive; for the guilt *(Schuld)* is more important than the pain *(Peyn)*, sin is more important than death. It is, in fact, sin which brings death, and without sin there would be no death, or else it would be inoffensive" (*WA* 10, 1, 1, 717-718).

One will observe to what extent Luther's description of the saving work of Christ includes the resurrection. This is obviously particularly clear when he speaks of the victory over the powers. They cannot overcome the Christ who is too strong for them. Thus the incarnation and the passion, as it were, call forth the resurrection, Christ not being able to remain in the death and sin of others which he has assumed. But the resurrection also manifests the reality of our reconciliation with God and thus holds a fundamental place in the thought of Luther. One can say that it has surpassed as well on this point a general tendency of medieval spirituality, which placed the accent on the cross and very often ended up plunging Christianity into despair. With Luther, on the other hand, the triumphalism so characteristic of the early church appears again, living in the joy of Easter.

The soteriological themes, which have just now sketched, call for the following remarks concerning the person of Jesus Christ, who realizes the saving work.

It is necessary to underline the fact that from the point of view of reconciliation and from that of combat, it is the Christ, God and a man, who accomplishes the work of salvation. That appears to be obvious. In fact, an examination of the different interpretations of Luther's thought shows that this basic principle has not always been sufficiently taken into account. Those who emphasize the theme of combat, such as Aulén, for example, tend to emphasize the role of the divine nature and describe redemption as a victorious combat of God against the powers—the humanity being reduced to the place where the combat occurs. On the other hand, those who insist on the priestly office of Christ tend rather to place the emphasis on the human nature of Christ. But what exactly is the attitude of the reformer?

When he describes the work of salvation from the point of view of reconciliation, he dwells extensively on the fact that he is concerned with a work in which God has taken the initiative and in which he accomplishes in the person of the Son—see 2 Cor. 5:18 ("God . . . through Christ reconciled us to himself"). He is not concerned with an activity accomplished by the God-man, working from outside in the name of humanity. It is the Son, become human, who by fulfilling the law and bearing the wrath of God, disarms this anger. But how could he do it if he had not become human? How could this work be accomplished without the truly human obedience of Christ to the law and without suffering in the flesh, and soul, of a person, because of the wrath of God? One will note well that in accomplishing such a work, Christ is not a *passive* object subject to the wrath of God, but from Luther's point of view, he offers himself actively in sacrifice to the Father and to human beings.

When the reformer describes the work of salvation as combat against the powers, he does occasionally put the emphasis on the divine nature. He adopts the old image of the humanity of Christ which, as the worm hides the hook, hides the divinity of Christ from the devil and thus leads the devil into error. The humanity appears to be passive in this view. In the same way also, when he says that in Christ, sin is swallowed up by divine power, he seems to limit the role of the humanity to becoming the place where sin is deposited in order to be destroyed by the divine power alone. In fact, it is necessary to note that the combat, undertaken by Christ as the God-man, consists for Luther in offering himself to the powers, in fulfilling the law, in becoming one with sinful human beings, and in accepting death. It is an intensive activity accomplished both as a human being and as God. There is no doubt that, unlike the medieval tradition, whether Thomist or Scotist, the reformer has hardly developed in the writings so far examined a concept by which it would be possible to be precise about the mode of cooperation between the two natures of Christ. Following the Alexandrine tradition, he is content to say that "Christ was the instrument and the house of divinity" (*WA* 10, 1, 1, 447). But while one must emphasize how much the realization of salvation remains for him in every respect a work of God, so one must take care to understand the work of God in a unique way. One must insist on the trinitarian dimension of the work of salvation. The Father sends the Son, who saves us by offering himself to the wrath of the Father and by triumphing over the powers. And he accomplishes this work in a truly human existence by a human obedience, a human faith, and a human love.

Christ, the Word, and Faith

Christ became incarnate. He accomplished the work of salvation. He reconciled us with God and triumphed over the powers which oppressed us. But how can we benefit from this work of salvation? How is the individual person integrated into this salvation thus obtained once for all? How do I recognize my Savior in this Christ, this man of the past, submissive in the ambiguity of the incarnation and the passion? Christ and his work must come to me in a certain way if they are to be present for me and convince me of their saving activity. That is done by the announcement of the Word. If the gospel, as a Word binding us to Christ,[75] is not preached, Christ does not exist for us.[76] The reformer emphasizes very often how much the incarnation of Christ points toward the resurrection and the ascension, which mark the beginning of the announcement of the gospel and the gift of the Holy Spirit. "Before Christ rose, it [the grace of God] was still hidden, and when Christ walked only in the land of the Jews, God's grace was not yet brought to light. But after his ascension he gave the Holy Spirit" (WA 10, 1, 1, 19, 16).

It is the Holy Spirit which makes us to know that Christ "did not walk on the earth only for himself, but for our good" (WA 10, 1, 1, 20, 1). The Holy Spirit alone gives faith in Christ. Thanks to him, the gospel preached is not only a discourse on Christ, but a Word which bears fruit (WA 10, 1, 1, 20, 5). It is when this faith is born and its fruits ripen that "Christ is made manifest in the hearts of all the believers in the world" (WA 10, 1, 1, 527, 1).

Here Luther takes up a theme of the mystics and can say that Christ is born a second time in faith.[77] The incarnation is so directed toward preaching, toward the here and now of faith which believes in the Word announcing Christ, that Luther can affirm that the Scripture says more about the transfiguration in the hearts of the believers than about the birth of Christ (WA 10, 1, 1, 527, 1; 10, 4, 2), or that the meaning of the incarnation is the preaching of the gospel (WA 10, 1, 1, 527, 3; 10, 1, 2, 7, 6).[78]

One would be wrong to conclude that the historical incarnation and the work on the cross were secondary for Luther. But "they would have been useless if there had not issued from them a gospel by which one recognized in the whole world why the Son had become human" (WA 10, 1, 2, 7, 8).

Again Luther can say on the subject of the actual coming of Christ: "Thus he comes to us through the gospel. Yet, it is much better that he comes through the gospel than if he were now the door to come through. He would enter your home and you would not know him. If you believe, you have [salvation], if you do not believe, you do not have it" (WA 10, 3, 92, 11).

You will have noticed that Luther says both that the Word announces Christ and that Christ comes by the Word, or again that

the Holy Spirit unites us to Christ or stirs up faith, to the extent that
he makes use of the preached Word. What does this mean? To talk
of Christ would not be sufficient to awaken faith, if after the resurrection, the Holy Spirit had not been given. On the other hand, the
proclamation of the gospel, by the power of the Holy Spirit, does
not elevate human beings to some distant past or to some transcendent location within which Christ is enclosed, but it renders
the Christ truly present. To be more precise, the Christ is rendered
present by the Word, given that he has taken the initiative, in the
power of the Holy Spirit. Those who preach are only his instruments. One can never emphasize enough the insistence of Luther on
the Word as the only saving way possible to Christ. "Christ would
not be recognized except by his Word . . . even if he came today"
(*WA* 10, 3, 210, 11).[79]

The gospel proclaimed is not information about Christ, but an
appeal for faith, a promise which one must accept personally. Luther
distinguishes two kinds of faith. Just as in the sermons of 1518-1519
he attacked false ways of considering the passion of Christ (senti-
mentality or hatred of the Jews), he now criticizes a false approach
to Christ which would consist of dwelling on "historical" details of
Christ, of believing in him in an impersonal way. There is an inadequate faith, he says, which is content to believe in the truth of the
facts in the Gospels. It is not a saving faith. The sinners and even
the damned can have it (*WA* 10, 1, 1, 71, 4). The saving faith (*der
recht gnadenreich glawb*) (*WA* 10, 1, 1, 71, 6) is, for the faithful, to
believe that Christ was born for them personally and has accomplished for them the work of salvation.

Luther is still more explicit in the postil for Advent, commenting
on Matt. 21:1-9: "I have often spoken of two kinds of faith," he
writes. "Here is the first: you believe it is true that Christ is the man
described and preached in the gospel; but you do not believe that
he is such a man for you, you doubt if you can receive that from
him, and you think: 'Yes, he is surely such a man for others, for
St. Peter and St. Paul and for pious and holy persons, but who
knows if he is also that for me, if I can expect with entire confidence
the same from him that these saints expect?' You see, this faith is
nothing, it neither receives, nor tastes anything of Christ. It cannot
feel joy nor love of him nor for him. This is a faith connected *with*
Christ, but not a faith *in* Christ: the devils have it also, as do all evil
persons. . . . The faith which alone deserves the name of Christian

is this: if you believe unflinchingly that it is not only for Saint Peter and the saints that Christ is such a person, but also for you yourself —for you more than for all the others. Your salvation does not reside in the fact that Christ is Christ for good persons, but that he is a Christ for you and that he is yours" (WA 10, 1, 2, 24-25).

If I believe this personally that Christ is my righteousness before God, then I am truly saved. No one can believe for me.[80]

Hence the saving faith is that by which believers discover themselves personally saved by Christ. We have already shown that the Christ to whom believers are attached makes himself present by the proclamation of the Word. He attributes the fruits of his work of salvation, but he does it by offering himself to believers in his own person.[81] Although he remains transcendent with respect to human beings, Christ gives himself to him in faith. That is what the expression *fides Christi*—which we have already used—includes.

By offering himself now with his work to believers, Christ has a double significance for them. He is on the one hand the "alien righteousness" imputed by God to believers. It is because of Christ present in faith that believers are justified. Here an indissoluble link appears between justification by faith and christology. And it is from this point of view that we can see Luther's urgent desire to distinguish between Christ the gift and Christ the example.[82] Before he is the example, Christ is this alien righteousness offered to faith and by which believers are justified before God.

On the other hand, Christ acts in faith. It is false to see in Luther only justification by faith from the forensic point of view. When Christ is present in faith, he is not only the mantle thrown over the nakedness of the sinner. He really takes the sin, destroys it, and gives righteousness to human beings. We have already stressed this in dealing with the theme of joyous exchange.[83]

In fact, by the *fides Christi* believers also rise above the powers. Constantly, sin is surmounted, death and the devil vanquished, the law disarmed. "Christ has overcome sin, death, hell, and the devil. Thus it happens that those who understand and believe this firmly and place their confidence in it become in Christ Jesus conquerors of sin, of death, of hell, and of the devil" (WA 10, 3, 356, 25).[84]

When one brings to light Luther's union of the believer with Christ, one discovers that the propitiatory work of Christ does not exclude the cross from human life, but includes it. By his gift, Christ brings to me the specific element of his work, which is the unique reconciliation realized on the cross by him. But at the same time he carries me along the way of the cross. United to him, I die and I rise again. The whole Christian life is thus by faith lived out in the image of Christ.

By associating Christ with a work in the past, one runs the risk of exaggerating the sacramental, and particularly the sacrificial, role of the church, and in this way developing a mystical spirituality seeking direct union with the eternal Christ, as well as a spirituality in which Christ was seen essentially as an example. By closely associating Christ and faith, Luther was able to avoid this danger.

Notes

1 Seeberg, *Luthers Theologie,* vol. 2, p. 227.
2 From the introduction to the French edition, *Oeuvres de Luther,* vol. 10, published by Labor et Fides.
3 The German text is found in the first half of *WA* 10. The Advent sermons are in the second half of that volume.
4 *WA* 17, 2, 237-245
5 We use this word to translate the German *Schwärmer.*
6 For example, *WA* 10, 1, 1, 202.
7 "Here, clear for all to see, the positivism of Nominalist theology shines through" (*Luthers Theologie,* p. 249).
8 "Therefore, no one must take it upon themselves to make their own way to God, by their own piety or works. . . . You must give up your own enterprises and be content with this seed, flesh and blood, or you are lost, you and all your cleverness and all you think you know about God" (*WA* 10, 1, 1, 335, 24).
9 "For the Scripture begins quite gently, leading us to Christ, as to a human person and then to a Lord, reigning over all things, and then to a God. Thus I came to recognize God. The philosophers and those versed in knowledge of the world, on the contrary, have tried to begin from above, and so they have been confounded. One must begin from below and then rise up" (*WA* 12, 585-591).
10 "The divine nature is too high and incomprehensible for us. That is why he came for us in the nature which we know best, our own. It is there that he wants to wait for us, there that he wants us to find him and nowhere else" (*WA* 10, 1, 1, 356, 9).
11 "The other coming of Christ, which is not fearful, but gentle, as the gospel says, not fearful like God in the Old Testament, but gentle, compassionate, like a human being" (*WA* 10, 67, 14).
12 It would be necessary again to show here that, in the incarnation, God reveals himself by hiding himself. That is why the Word and faith are necessary. We shall be speaking further of this later.
13 *WA* 10, 3, 364; 12, 285, 9

14 "God did not need to come and become human, but that was for us necessary and useful" (*WA* 10, 1, 1, 354, 22).

15 "That is why it does not help the Jews or the Turks that they believe in the God who created heaven and earth. The one who does not believe in Christ does not believe in God either" (*WA* 10, 1, 1, 465, 4).

16 According to Althaus (p. 163), Luther took it from St. Augustine.

17 Commenting on Rom. 15:4-13, Luther poses the following question: Why is it necessary to praise the Father of Jesus Christ, and not be content to praise only Christ? It is to combat the idolatry which places confidence in the saints and what they have done rather than in God. "For Christ also, in all the gospel, does nothing except show us the way to the Father, and he came in order that we might go to the Father by him" (*WA* 10, 1, 2, 83, 13). "And although Christ himself is truly God, whoever puts their trust in him will constantly be led to the Father, in order that one shall not remain attached to his humanity, as the disciples were before his passion, who, seeing only his humanity, thought not on his divinity. For Christ, according to his humanity, must be for us a way, a sign, a work of God, through which we go to God" (*WA* 10, 1, 2, 84).

18 See *WA* 10, 3, 109-161; 17, 1, 272; 17, 2, 244.

19 *Die Grundbegriffe der altkirchlichen Christologie*, pp. 241ff.

20 *Luthers Christuszeugnis*, pp. 2-11.

21 *WA* 10, 1, 2, 127, 8

22 When commenting on 1 Cor. 4:1-5, Luther used the term "mystery" to describe Christ (*WA* 10, 1, 2, 126ff.). For him, what is the *mysterium?* "I call him a mystery (Geheimnis)." What then are the mysteries of God? Nothing other than Christ himself, i.e., the faith and the gospel of Christ; for all that is preached in the gospel is beyond meaning, far from reason and hidden for all the world. One can only comprehend it by faith . . . a *mysterium*, because the fact that Christ was the Son of God, the way, the truth, and the life, and every good, was hidden.

23 One finds the same reasoning in connection with John 1. Since it is a Word of God, there must be two persons: "The Word and he who speaks it cannot be one person, for it is not possible that he who speaks can himself be the Word. . . . Hence Moses concludes that there are two persons in the Godhead from all eternity, before all creatures" (*WA* 10, 1, 1, 183, 13ff.). Again, when commenting on Gal. 4:1-7, he writes: "As he was sent from God and is his Son, he must be another person. Thus St. Paul teaches us here that there is one God and two persons, Father and Son. The same will be true of the Holy Spirit" (*WA* 10, 1, 1, 355, 10). See also *WA* 10, 1, 1, 57, 13.

24 It will be noted here that Luther takes up again the process of thought which led to an elaboration of the doctrine of the Trinity. And there is for him no other source than the statements of Scripture, of which the reformer says, in connection with the Trinity,

"See how the Scripture proceeds with easily comprehensible words, to teach such high things so clearly, that no one can deny them" (*WA* 10, 1, 1, 184, 3). "Hence this Scripture obliges us to conclude that these two persons are one perfect God, that each is truly God, one, perfect, divine by nature, who has created all things" (*WA* 10, 1, 1, 184, 13). It is because faith holds to Scripture that it does not err with respect to the mystery of the Trinity, which is so difficult for reason (*WA* 10, 1, 1, 191).

25 He takes up the classical terminology and translates it. There is an example of this in *WA* 10, 1, 1, 191, 11: "The truth of the Christian faith follows a middle path, teaching and confessing no confusion of the persons and no division of the nature."

26 See also *WA* 10, 1, 1, 355, 14ff.

27 "But it is in the nature of all human beings to grow in body, mind, spirit, and wisdom, and there are no exceptions. Luke agrees with Paul in saying that Christ, too, grew up in every respect and that he was a special child, who developed more than others; for his nature was more noble, and the gifts and graces of God were more rich in him than in others" (*WA* 10, 1, 1, 448, 9).

28 Concerning the ignorance of Christ, see also *WA* 9, 441, 11–442, 21 (sermons from 1519-21). "The cause of the wonder that he displays is his ignorance." "It must be admitted that he was a man who did not know certain things" (*WA* 9, 556, 30-32).

29 *WA* 10, 1, 1, 363ff.

30 *WA* 10, 1, 1, 365, 14

31 *WA* 10, 1, 1, 365, 23

32 *WA* 10, 1, 1, 366, 3

33 *WA* 10, 3, 73

34 *WA* 10, 3, 74

35 "Nature in him and in his mother was pure in all their members, in all the working of their members" (*WA* 10, 1, 1, 68, 2).

36 "Christ was presented in two different ways in Scripture, as a human being and as God. When the Scripture dictates how he was born, how he was suckled, then it shows him as a human being. In other places it shows that he is God" (*WA* 10, 3, 237).

37 See Françoise Wendel, *Calvin: Sources et évolution de sa pensée religieuse* (Paris: 1950).

38 *Die Theologie Martin Luthers*, p. 174.

39 "Exalted above all things" (*WA* 11, 191, 15-17).

40 *WA* 12, 546, 34–547, 4

41 *WA* 10, 1, 1, 163, 243, 448; 10, 1, 2, 16, 72; 10, 3, 217

42 *WA* 17, 2, 237ff.

43 "The humanity would be of no use if the divinity were not in it" (*WA* 10, 1, 1, 208, 22).

44 "Form of God means that someone has the appearance of a god, and conducts themselves as such, or that they adopt and arrogate the divine form" (*WA* 17, 2, 239, 5).

45 *WA* 17, 2, 243, 1-19

46   "Not that he could have divested himself of his divinity, putting it to one side, but he put aside the form of divine majesty and did not act like the God he truly was" (*WA* 17, 2, 243, 5).

47   "He was God and all the divine works and words of his divine nature were for our good, and thereby he served us as a servant and did not let himself be served as a Lord, to which he had the right. In doing this he sought neither honor nor profit, but our good and salvation only. It was voluntarily and for no gain that he did this, but for the good of others" (*WA* 17, 2, 243, 20).

48   "In which he submitted himself not only to human beings, but also to sin, death, and the devil and bore all this for us" (*WA* 17, 2, 244, 19).

49   J. K. Siggins, *Martin Luther's Doctrine of Christ*, p. 218.

50   A. Peters, *Luthers Christuszeugnis*, pp. 73-78.

51   For a general treatment of this subject, see: Th. Harnack, *Luthers Theologie*, vol. 2; J. Köstlin, *Luthers Theologie*, vol. 2, pp. 148-174; R. Seeberg, *Dogmengeschichte* IV, 1, pp. 237-253; R. Bring, *Dualismen hos Luther* (Lund: 1929); G. Aulén, *Den kristna försoningstanken: Huvudtyper och brytninger* (Stockholm: 1930); G. Aulén, *Christus Victor* (New York: Macmillan, 1969); G. Tiililä, *Das Strafleiden Christi* (Helsinki: 1941); P. Althaus, *Die Theologie Martin Luthers*, pp. 178-185; H. Alpers, *Die Versöhnung durch Christus: Zur Typologie der Schule von Lund* (Göttingen: 1964); A. Peters, *Luthers Christuszeugnis*, pp. 11-26; O. H. Pesch, *Die Theologie der Rechtfertigung*, pp. 123-141; J. K. Siggins, *Martin Luther's Doctrine of Christ*, pp. 108-143.

52   Siggins, *Martin Luther's Doctrine of Christ*, pp. 110-111.

53   WA 10, 3, 136, 3

54   WA 10, 3, 125, 29; 127, 6, 9; 159, 1; 161, 25ff.

55   WA 10, 3, 49

56   WA 10, 1, 1, 718, 18ff.; 720, 18

57   WA 10, 1, 2, 171, 25

58   WA 10, 1, 1, 518, 9

59   WA 10, 3, 163, 22–164, 2. For additional texts, see O. H. Pesch, *Theologie der Rechtfertigung*, p. 129, n. 24; Siggins, *Martin Luther's Doctrine of Christ*, pp. 113-143.

60   WA 10, 3, 162, 10-14; 10, 1, 2, 235, 27; 10, 1, 1, 471, 1

61   WA 12, 291. Commenting on 1 Peter 1:18, he writes: "See what price God paid for you and how great is the ransom through which you have been redeemed. The Father wanted to pour out his grace so richly upon us and was prepared to pay so much that he let his Son Jesus Christ pour out all his blood and has made over the whole treasure to us." See also WA 10, 1, 1, 470, 18ff.; 10, 3, 161, 19ff.; 162, 11ff.; 12, 544, 22.

62   Pesch, *Die Theologie der Rechtfertigung*, p. 132: "The fact that Christ took the place of me is not the cause of the love of God, but was already the consequence of a previous decision of the love of God."

63 *WA* 10, 1, 1, 470, 18: "If by a pure grace our sin is not imputed to us by God, he nonetheless refused to do that without his law and his righteousness being first satisfied. Such an imputation must first of all be paid for by a grace emanating from him and made available to us."

64 *WA* 10, 1, 1, 471, 3

65 *WA* 10, 1, 2, 171, 26; 10, 1, 1, 723, 21ff.

66 *WA* 17, 2, 291, 19

67 *WA* 10, 3, 125, 27; 127, 2; 136, 11

68 *WA* 10, 1, 1, 720, 18: "If he was to be priest and reconcile us with God according to his sacerdotal office, he had to satisfy for us God's righteousness."

69 *WA* 10, 1, 1, 121, 16; 720, 18; 10, 3, 49, 24

70 *Die Theologie Martin Luthers*, p. 178, n. 5.

71 On this subject see Aulén, *Christus Victor*.

72 On this subject see Harnack, *Luthers Theologie*, vol. 2, pp. 280-318; Bring, *Dualismen hos Luther*, pp. 103-132; 154-174.

73 See also *WA* 12, 515, 31; 17, 2, 291, 35.

74 *WA* 10, 3, 100, 24: "Here you can say that the devil attacked Christ, as the fish attacks the bait and is caught on the hook. . . . The worm on the hook was Christ as the world disdained him; when Satan tried to swallow this worm, he was stuck on the hook of the divinity and was pulled out." See also *WA* 17, 2, 292, 7.

75 *WA* 10, 1, 12, 13, 22: "For to preach the gospel is none other than this: Christ comes to us, or we are led to him."

76 *WA* 10, 1, 2, 154, 14

77 "The biblical birth of Christ means everywhere his spiritual birth, i.e., the way in which he is born in us and we in him" (*WA* 10, 1, 1, 619, 17; cf. 10, 1, 1, 72-73).

78 "God has taken more care over the gospel and its announcement by the Word than to the bodily birth and his coming among human beings. For it was a question of the gospel and our faith; that is why he wanted his Son to become human, in order that the gospel might be preached by him" (*WA* 10, 1, 2, 7, 12).

79 Again, see *WA* 10, 1, 1, 131, 19; 243, 21; 526ff.; 574, 5; 771, 14.

80 *WA* 10, 3, 306, 11: "Let no one think they can be saved by the faith or the works of another; that cannot happen even through the faith and works of Mary, or even of Christ, unless you yourself believe. For God will not permit Mary or even Christ to replace you, in order that you may be pious and just, unless you yourself believe and are pious." *WA* 10, 3, 306, 27: "No outside faith or work will help you, not even Christ, who is the Savior of the whole world; his benefits, his help will not serve you unless you believe and become enlightened."

81 "It is not enough that Christ has delivered us from the tyranny and lordship of sin, death, and hell over us, and become our king; but he gives himself to each one of us, so that all that he is and all that he has may be ours" (*WA* 10, 1, 2, 31, 4).

82   In the texts that we are studying, this distinction is found, for ex-
     ample in "Ein klein Unterricht was man in den Evangelien suchen
     und gewarten soll" (*WA* 10, 1, 1, 8ff.).

83   In the texts that we are studying,see: *WA* 10, 1, 1, 76; 319; 475ff.;
     10, 1, 2, 31; 10, 3, 98; 212ff.; 356ff.; 417ff.

84   There is a parallel between Christ and the believer. Just as the
     bodily life of Christ is destroyed and the divinity remains, whereby
     the humanity will equally be raised, so in the Christian life, Satan
     destroys the works and the life, but he must leave the faith, whereby
     both are restored (cf. *WA* 10, 1, 1, 419).

4

The Christology of Luther
and the Eucharistic Controversy
with His Protestant Adversaries
(1525-1528)

All eucharistic doctrine implies a christology. It is therefore necessary to examine with care the many writings in which Luther has
presented his views on the Eucharist.[1] Among these writings, the
treatises elaborated in opposition to Protestant opponents occupy
an important place. It is not only their number that gives them
importance, but also indications that one finds there relevant to the
subject of the reformer's christology. As Congar has justly observed,
"The most precise formulations are drawn from Luther in his encounter with Zwingli. The opposition of the two reformers on the
question of the eucharistic presence proves at once to be the opposition of two christologies."[2] For his part, Gennrich declares, "When
the attack was launched against his concept of the Eucharist, Luther
saw it as an attack on the principal article of his theology because
by it Jesus Christ himself was reduced to nonexistence. His christology must then be so linked to his doctrine of the Eucharist that
this doctrine necessarily derives from it.[3]

So it is obviously essential to see the relation between the christology of Luther and his ideas on the subject of the Eucharist. There
is no doubt that the christology of Luther was formulated to defend
a certain concept of the Eucharist. But at the same time, his doctrine
of the Eucharist derives from a christology which was already in

195

Luther's mind at the time when the Eucharistic controvery began. In the course of that controversy it underwent certain changes.

According to Luther, it is no less than Christ himself who is at stake when Carlstadt and others (Luther defines them as "Enthusiasts") call in question the necessity of "outward means" (the Word and sacraments) or the real presence of Christ in the Eucharist. "The Enthusiasts strangle Christ, my Lord" (*WA* 23, 83, 4), he writes. To lose Christ is to lose all. To have Christ is to have all. "There, where Christ remains for me, all remains and can be found" (*WA* 23, 207, 27).[4]

We shall see how, according to Luther, Christ is called in question by the Enthusiasts. Whether that is so or not, one can thus understand more easily Luther's relentlessness on this matter, because of his feeling that he is in an eschatological situation, exposed (he and Christ!) to the attacks of Satan,[5] while the last day is near at hand.[6] What he writes in the course of this struggle goes far beyond the limits of an academic controversy. He places himself in the eschatological perspective, to which we have just alluded. And what he says has for him the status of a confession. He proclaims his faith before Christ and expects his coming, in order that he might be faithful even until the last judgment: "I reckon to remain in this faith until death and with it (God helping me) to quit this world and come before the judgment seat of our Lord Jesus (*WA* 26, 499, 21). And again a little further on, "I know what I say, and understand well what that means for me, in view of the coming of the Lord Jesus Christ at the last judgment" (*WA* 26, 500, 21).

However, if it is true that the Eucharistic Controversy only arises out of different concepts of christology, this controversy has compelled Luther to clarify this or that point in his conception of Christ, and also pushed him in a certain direction. This is what we must now show.

Stages and Aspects of the Controversy
Before Zwingli
Honius and the Bohemian Brethren

When he expressed his thoughts about the Eucharist in 1520 in *Von dem Neuen Testament,* Luther had in mind those practical and theological deformations of the Eucharist in the heart of the traditional church. But from 1521, he will have to deal with Protestant ideas very different from his own. In a letter of 1521 from the Dutch-man, Honius, addressed to Luther, the former raises questions about the real presence. It is faith alone which constitutes the Eucharist. If it is absent, one does not receive the body of Christ. And Honius also opposes the adoration of the host, which he considers to be idolatry, because there is only bread there. This last question also troubled the Bohemian Brethren, who in order to express their opposition to the doctrine of transubstantiation, felt themselves unable to adore Christ in the elements of the Eucharist. Nevertheless, unlike Honius, they do not seem to have denied the presence of the body and blood of Christ in the Eucharist, although their affirmations on this subject were somewhat vague.

Luther thus felt obliged to take up a position. In 1523 he wrote a small treatise, *Vom Anbeten des Sakraments des heiligen Leichnams Christi.*[7] One finds there an insistence on the words of institution, "words of life and salvation, such that whoever believes in them will have all their sins forgiven by such faith" (*WA* 11, 432, 21). Luther affirms that these words are more important than the sacrament itself and that above all they must be honored by pronouncing them in a loud voice and believing them (as he had also said in the treatise written in 1520). He then opposes himself to the exegesis of Honius (without naming him), according to which the "is" of the words of institution should be read as "signifies." Honius refused to relate 1 Cor. 10:16 to the spiritual body of Christ, which would amount to saying, "that the sacrament would be none other than the com-munion in the body of Christ or rather an incorporation into his spiritual body" (*WA* 11, 437, 15), an opinion which Luther himself had maintained in his sermon of 1519, without ever denying the real presence. In 1523 he relates the passage 1 Cor. 10:16 to the body of Christ as such. And it is thus by the participation in the true body of Christ that Christians form his spiritual body.

By criticizing the doctrine of transubstantiation and the sacrificial concept of the mass, Luther only takes up again his old quarrels with Rome. It will be noted, however, that he seems now to have become more indulgent toward the doctrine of transubstantiation. He judges it less dangerous than other errors which he criticizes, "provided that the body and blood of Christ are left with the words" (*WA* 11, 441, 19). But, according to him, this doctrine contravenes no less the witness of the gospel, according to which the bread and the wine re-main what they are.

Must one then adore or not adore Christ in the sacrament? "But whoever believes . . . cannot, without sin, refrain from honoring the body and blood of Christ" (*WA* 11, 447, 7). However, the reformer comments that Christ is not present in the sacrament and in the heart of believers in order to be adored there, but "in order to work with us and help us, just as he came on earth in the flesh, not that he might be adored, but in order to serve us" (*WA* 11, 447, 22). We are allowed to adore him, but that is not demanded of us. Finally, Luther leaves his readers free to adore or not adore the body of Christ in the sacrament.

Carlstadt

In 1524, another man opposed Luther on the subject of the Eucharist: Carlstadt, one of his companions from the beginning. Truth to tell, the conflict was not confined to the Eucharist; the two men clashed more generally on the way in which the Christian life must be envisaged. According to Carlstadt, human beings must detach themselves from earthly things. This detachment, which following the mystics he called *Gelassenheit* or *Müssigkeit,* is accomplished with the aid of spiritual exercises in which meditation on Christ crucified played a large part. But it is a person acting by crucifying their own life in order to follow Christ as an example. In the framework of such a conception, the Eucharist cannot give an objective assurance on the subject of the forgiveness of sins. As external reality, it is, in effect, unable to touch the depth of the soul. It is celebrated so that Christians may be reminded of the body of Christ sacrificed by his death and might thus be transformed into the image of the death and life of Christ. As for the interpretation of the words of institution, Carlstadt provides an original exposition. When Christ said, "This is . . . ," he did not show the bread, but his own body. He meant to speak of his own body as it was present "the night on which he was betrayed."

Luther refuted the teaching of Carlstadt in a letter addressed to the Christians of Strasbourg and especially in his writing, *Wider die himmlischen Propheten von den Bildern und Sakrament.*[8]

His principal criticism of Carlstadt was this: "His theology does not go beyond giving information, which he dispenses to us, showing how we may become followers of Christ, and he makes of Christ only an example and one who gives us orders. He will teach us only to do works.

Carlstadt neither knows nor teaches Christ as our treasure and God's gift to us, from which faith flows. That is the most important article" (*WA* 18, 196, 34ff.). According to Luther, one must first hear the gospel and receive from it the corporal signs of Baptism and the sacrament. It is by these that God gives the Holy Spirit and faith. "After that comes mortification and the cross and the works of love" (*WA* 18, 139, 19). Before doing works mortifying oneself and imitating Christ, one must have received Christ and the forgiveness of sins. That is the heart of Luther's teaching as he expresses it in the concept of justification by faith.

We shall not stop to consider Luther's discussion about the meaning of the words of institution, except to note the firmness of his statements: "I see here words of God, precise, clear, powerful, which require me to confess that the body and blood of Christ are in the sacrament. . . . How Christ is introduced into the sacrament, I do not know. But I know well that God's Word cannot lie, which says to me that the body and blood of Christ are in the sacrament" (*WA* 18, 166, 8-13). One could separate the body and blood from the bread and wine only "by interpreting a clearly expressed article of faith differently or making other use of these words" (*WA* 18, 147, 25).

But how to express the bond between the body of Christ and the bread? Once again, Luther explains this by an analogy with the two natures and uses the image of iron and fire. In this context, he also uses a rhetorical figure which will later play an important role in the controversy with Zwingli—it concerns the *synecdoche,* a form of expression which names the whole, but refers only to a part (*WA* 18, 187, 16). Thus Paul uses this form when he calls the Corinthians and Galatians the church of God, although only a small number of them were children of God.

From the rest of this treatise, we retain both the way Luther clarifies the relationship between the sacrament and the historic passion of Christ and his important statements about the glorified existence of Christ and his coming in the sacrament.

He introduces a distinction between the accomplishment of salvation by Christ on the cross and its transmission by the sacrament (*WA* 18, 203, 27ff.). According to Carlstadt, Luther accorded too much importance to the sacrament; it is toward Christ himself and his passion that human beings should be directed. "When have we ever taught that a piece of bread pardoned sins?" (*WA* 18, 201, 16) Luther replied. It is true that salvation has been realized on the cross—once for all. But "one thing else is necessary. What then? The Word, the Word, the Word, listen, lying spirit, do you hear? The Word acts. For even if Christ gave himself for us a thousand times and were a thousand times crucified for us, all would be in vain if the Word of God did not come to distribute it and to offer it to me, saying: It is for you, take it, receive it. . . . If then I want my sins forgiven, I must not run to the cross, for there I do not find the forgiveness of sins attributed. Neither must I simply cling to the remembrance and knowledge of the suffering of Christ . . . but to the sacrament or the gospel; it is there that I find the Word which attributes it to me, offers it to me, presents it to me and gives me that pardon acquired on the cross" (WA 18, 203, 27-39). The salvation which the Word transmits has been realized on the cross, but it is bound here and now to the person of Jesus Christ. The Word does not inform me about a work in the past, but presents me Jesus Christ. It is as one united to Christ that the believer is justified, and this Christ is present with his work in the sacrament.[9]

But can one say that Christ is present in the sacrament? "Could we then snatch him from heaven? . . . Must he leave heaven to descend into the bread?" (WA 18, 206, 6) Luther asked, following Carlstadt. In fact, Christ does not leave heaven by descending into the bread, any more than he had abandoned it at the moment of the incarnation. "It is a childish thought to think that Christ goes up and down" (WA 18, 206, 18). According to Eph. 1:23, the kingdom of Christ is found everywhere. But can one in any way localize Christ in the host? Is not Matt. 24:23 opposed to that? Luther comments on this verse that it does not relate to Christ in the Eucharist, but refers to Christ in his totality and in his kingdom. This is not bound to a particular place, but according to Eph. 1:23, he is found everywhere and fills all things (WA 18, 211, 6ff.). The gospel, Baptism, the Eucharist, and Christians share in this liberty and must not be bound to a particular place or to a given institution, such as the Church of Rome, but they must be free. "But when he says, 'This is my body,' and not, 'This is the Christ,' that is in order that we might understand truly and corporeally that, in the sacrament, it is not Christ in his totality that is present, that is to say not in his kingdom, but in fact and clearly in his body, which makes up part of the kingdom and of Christ in his totality" (WA 18, 212, 17).

But how does the body of Christ come into the bread? That is to pose the question of the consecration which Carlstadt ridiculed. In fact, replies Luther, "We say the divine, all-powerful, holy, heavenly words, which Christ himself said at the Last Supper with his holy mouth and which he ordered us to speak" (WA 18, 202, 10). But he refrains from explaining the mystery of the sacramental union: "We are not commanded to research into how our bread becomes the body of Christ. The Word of God is there, which says it. We hold to that and believe it" (WA 18, 206, 20).

The Controversy with Zwingli [10]
The Beginnings (1524-1526)

Zwingli, the reformer of Zurich, like Honius and perhaps under his influence, also explained the "is" of the words of institution as "significance." That comes out in his letter to Matthaeus Alber (1524), one of the first writings in which he concerns himself with the question of the Eucharist. This was for him a memorial meal and also a confessional meal, because for the sake of the brethren, the believer confesses faith in the sacrifice of Christ.

Zwingli makes his views clear in his *Commentarius de vera et falsa religione* of 1525. Instead of speaking of the sacrament, a term which he rejects, as a means by which a grace is given to human beings or as a sign which would affirm the certainty of believers, Zwingli envisages it as a kind of initiation or a commitment, by which believers commit themselves to the service of the Lord. But the sacraments play no part in liberating consciences, for only God can liberate those. The material elements, such as water, cannot play a role in this process of purification in which God alone acts. Faith moreover has no need of external elements to affirm its certainty; it possesses that in itself. In connection with the Eucharist, Zwingli cites John 6:26ff. in order to say that Christ does not speak of a sacramental nourishment, but of faith. "To eat the bread" is a way of saying, "to believe in the gospel." To affirm that the body and blood of Christ might have, by the mediation of the sacrament, a particular importance would be wrongly to attribute privileges to human nature and to call in question the union of the two natures. Further, faith tends toward spiritual reality by its very nature; to bind it to the visible elements of the sacrament would be to attack faith itself. And the affirmation of a real presence leads ultimately to "cannibalism" (3, 789, 3; 794, 23).[11]

At the same time as Zwingli, Oecolampadius of Basel defined his attitude to the Eucharist, and his views are very close to those of

Zwingli without being identical with them at all points.[12] He introduces into the debate a criticism of ubiquity. It is impossible that a
person could be found at the same time in different places. That
would be to put in question the created character of Christ's humanity. Further, according to faith, Christ is seated at the right hand of
God. He is glorified, and it would be a great humiliation for him
now to become corporeal substance to be eaten. The contribution
of Oecolampadius is to have insisted on the christological side of
the debate. Thus in his criticism of *Sungramma suevicum,* a work
by the Lutheran, Brenz, he questions the Lutherans on the subject
of the nature of the body of Christ present in the Eucharist. Is it the
mortal body or the glorified body? In reality, Oecolampadius says,
the body of Christ is absent, it is localized in heaven. The Eucharist
is only a commemoration. However, he recognized that the body
and blood of Christ are attributed to the believer by faith, even
when they are in heaven. Despite his considerable agreement with
Zwingli, Oecolampadius prefigured certain positions diverging from
his, such as are found, for example, in Calvin.

In his treatise of 1526, *Klare Unterrichtung vom Nachtmal,*
Zwingli also entered more into the christological debate. He affirms
that Christ, in his divine nature, has never left the right hand of
the Father. According to John 3:13, he remained in heaven even
during his incarnation. Of course, he assumed a human nature in
which he suffered human limitations. He was crucified and ascended
into heaven. But the abandonment on the cross and the ascension
are related only to his human nature, even if the passage does not
expressly distinguish between the two natures. To talk of the suffering of God, according to Zwingli, is only a manner of speaking and
not a reality.

Luther counterattacks in a series of sermons preached to prepare
people for the Easter Communion. These are collected together in
the *Sermon von dem Sakrament des Leibs und Bluts Christi wider
die Schwarmgeister.*[13]

Luther's key argument for the defense of the real presence is
found in what he considers to be the scriptural witness: "He who
rightly believes in the words, believes this: that God gives Christ,
creeping *(krieche)* into the bread or into the cup or wherever he
wills; if I have the Word, I do not want to see or understand more"
(*WA* 19, 485, 6). "They are perfectly clear and distinct words: take
bread, give thanks, break, give, command to eat and drink; this is

my body, this is my blood" (*WA* 19, 485, 20). There again we have the fundamental theme of the *theologia crucis,* what Luther calls the folly of God (1 Cor. 1:18), acting contrary to human reason. This folly is in reality the wisdom of God, which we are only able to recognize by the Word.

The reformer tries to refute two objections: the first is that it is neither suitable nor conceivable that the body should be present; the second, which doubts the necessity of this presence. Luther replies that if one has to say of the real presence, *"es reimet sich nicht"* (it makes no sense), what is one to say then of the incarnation? "Is it conceivable that God be incarnate by the virgin, that Christ, the King of glory, before whom angels and creatures prostrate themselves, be crucified by sinful human beings on the cross? Then why not conclude that God did not become human or that Christ crucified was not God?" (*WA* 19, 486, 21)

Christ is at the same time seated at the right hand of the Father and present in the heart of human beings. In order to come down, he does not have to descend the stairs! The preaching which proclaims him as Lord over all creatures, sin, life, and death, makes him present to faith. Announcing certain views of Calvin, Luther can say, "Thus your heart is in heaven, not in some appearance or dream. For there where he is, you are also" (*WA* 19, 489, 30). If then he is present in the heart, which is "finer than bread" (*WA* 19, 490, 13—493, 24), why should he not also be in the bread?

But is Luther's argument very convincing or his thought very clear here? It seems that Christ comes into the heart with his glorified body (*WA* 489, 19, 6; 499, 24ff.), but it is possible also to get the impression that the believer is united with Christ both in faith and in heaven, by the very action of Christ—a concept defended by Calvin, except that for him the author of the action is the Holy Spirit. In any case, the difficulty for us consists of passing from the presence of Christ in the hearts of human beings to his presence in the bread and the wine. This is the point at which Zwingli opposes Luther. If it is not possible to deduce from Luther's reasoning any proof for this presence, it is at least possible to conclude that the presence of Christ in the bread and the wine is of the same kind as his presence in the heart of the believer.

In the second place, Luther recalls the incarnation of Christ, born of the Virgin Mary, a miracle even greater than his coming into the bread and the wine. He comes in the very body of Mary, not only in her heart. And it is by the Word that he comes there. It is just the same with the Eucharist. "As soon as Christ says, 'This is my body,' his body is there, by the Word and by the power of the Holy Spirit" (WA 19, 491, 13).

Finally, Luther appeals to the affirmations of Eph. 1:20ff. and Ephesians 4, according to which Christ "in his humanity is established above all creatures and fills all things" (WA 19, 491, 18). By the ascension, he has not gone upstairs; "The fact of a bodily ascension is only a sign (wahrzeichen)" (WA 19, 491, 29). The ascension has "placed him above all creatures and in all creatures" (WA 19, 491, 28). "But although he is everywhere in all creatures . . . yet he does not wish that I should seek him except in the Word. . . . He is everywhere,[14] but he does not want you to grope after him everywhere, only there where the Word is, there should you grope (tappen) . . . . Otherwise you tempt God and you practice idolatry" (WA 19, 492, 19-25). It is thus by the Word that Christ is bound to the bread and wine. It is there that we must receive him bodily (WA 19, 493, 7). Christ acts thus "because of faith" (WA 493, 27). In fact, for all his attempts to make intelligible the real presence of Christ on the basis of certain comparisons or from the glorified existence of the body of Christ present everywhere, Luther does not explain it. There is ultimately no other foundation than the Word of God. That is why he concludes in the following way: The Word of God is true; that is why your presumption (which makes you question the possibility of the real presence) must be false" (WA 19, 494, 12).

There is another objection concerning the necessity of the real presence. Why, ask his opponents, why not be content with belief in Jesus Christ who died for me, instead of believing further in a "baked God" (WA 19, 494, 17)? Here Luther invokes the impenetrable will of God. If the necessity for the real presence is put in doubt, then the necessity for the incarnation and redemption is put in doubt, since God would have been able to save us by his almighty power, by his Word and by faith without the suffering of the Son. But "God knows well how and why it was to be so. When he says it is necessary, then all creatures keep silence" (WA 19, 496, 14). It is necessary then to hold only to the Word of God, "to rest there like a child in its cradle" (WA 19, 498, 12), and not to do as the Enthusiasts do, destroying the words of institution.

If it is necessary to refer that which concerns the real presence to the impenetrable will of God, it is on the other hand, according to Luther, possible to ask about the usefulness of this presence and also about the use which must be made of the sacrament. Above all one must not make a work out of it (*WA* 19, 502, 24) by insisting as the Papists do on an adequate preparation for the sacrament. Using it in faith is necessary, that is to say, "You must believe not only that Christ is there with his body and his blood, but also that he is offered to you" (*WA* 19, 503, 11). Let those who receive the sacrament be sure that they are receiving the body and blood of Christ and that they receive it for the forgiveness of sins. "If then Christ is given to you, there is equally given to you forgiveness of sins and all that is acquired by this treasure" (*WA* 19, 507, 31).

Luther makes a distinction here between the public preaching which announces and commemorates the redemptive death of Christ and the sacrament. The first is addressed to the whole world; the second has a more personal character. "There it is given specially to you and to me" (*WA* 19, 505, 11).

The true purpose of the sacrament is to strengthen faith (*WA* 19, 508, 23). After having received the certainty, it is equally necessary to announce it to others (*WA* 19, 508, 24). But another product is love and brotherly communion. The sacrifice of Christ is an example for us. At the same time, the bread made from many grains and the wine produced by many grapes represent the desirable unity of Christianity (*WA* 19, 511, 20).

Dass diese Worte "Das ist mein Leib" noch fest stehen wider die Schwarmgeister [15] *(That these words "This is my body" hold fast against the Enthusiasts)*

The year 1527 saw the appearance of two writings of importance by Zwingli and Luther on the question which divided them. We shall deal here only with the christological arguments in Zwingli's work, *Amica exegesis*. According to Zwingli, Luther confused the two natures when he attributed ubiquity to the flesh of Christ (a property that belongs only to the divine nature), as if the body of Christ could be everywhere and fill the universe "as corn fills a sack" (*WA* 19, 493). In reality, the human nature is bound to a given place *(circumscriptio)*. If certain scriptural passages seem to attribute indistinctly to the two natures the functions and properties which belong by right to one of the two, this is only a manner of speaking designated in rhetoric as *alleosis*. This is when one speaks of one thing while thinking of another, or one speaks of two things at the same time, but thinks only of one of them. Thus there is *alleosis* when the Scripture says that the Word has become flesh (John 1:14). In reality, there is no beginning or becoming in God. This expression can only mean that the human has become God. *Alleosis* is applied equally to passages which deal with the death or suffering of Christ.

Zwingli emphasized that there is certainly one *hypostasis* or person, but that each nature retained its own character. And further, according to Zwingli, it is only to a hypostatic union that one could apply Luther's beloved simile of the iron and the fire. By the incarnation, God does not become human *(conversus)*, but he assumes a human nature. And Zwingli maintained that one must hold fast to the limited character of the body of Christ, or there is danger of falling into Sabellianism or Marcionism. If, further, the humanity of Christ is found everywhere, then it must follow that the elect, according to John 14:3, must be present in the Eucharist. This idea is still defended by Luther in his treatise on the Eucharist in 1519, but it now passes into the background because he insists far more on the uniqueness of Christ.

Zwingli also approaches the question of the ascension and of Christ "seated at the right hand of God." The ascension concerns only the human nature of Christ: in his divinity, he never departed, departing being a human function. What does it mean then to be "seated at the right hand of God"? Zwingli answers that question in words that can be translated from the Latin as, "It means to say, to be, to rejoice, to encourage the brethren, and, whether literally or figuratively, to be such as one who is situated in one place" (5, 696).

In an article which he appended to his *Amica exegesis* ("Friendly Criticisms of Luther's Preaching Against the Enthusiasts"),[16] it appears clear that, according to Zwingli, faith relates only to the divine nature, in the sense that it is trust in God alone. The humanity is only an earnest of grace. And especially, the role of the humanity is limited in time. It must satisfy *(vergnügt)* the divine righteousness and clear for us the path to God, but it is not offered to us in the Eucharist for the forgiveness of sins. For Luther, on the contrary, the humanity of Christ never ceases to have a fundamental significance for faith.

It can be asked whether Zwingli was at all happy about the way in which the debate switched to the christological plane.[17] It seems as though his fundamental preoccupation was rather with the nature of faith and the relation with God than with the way of understanding the mystery of Jesus Christ. But for Luther, who places Christ more and more in the center of the debate, it is precisely this mystery which is in question.

Luther's treatise, *Dass diese Worte* . . .[18] adds very little that is new for the interpretation of the words of institution. What is most original is Luther's exposition showing that the real presence was perfectly compatible with Christian faith in its totality and notably with the affirmation that Christ is seated at the right hand of the Father. On the other hand, there is found there also an interesting discussion of the usefulness of this presence.

It is necessary to agree, says Luther, on what is meant by "the right hand of God." The Enthusiasts, among whom he includes both Zwingli and Carlstadt, childishly imagine that Christ sits on a golden throne, beside his Father, wearing vestments and a golden crown! [19] But "Where is the passage of Scripture which requires the right hand of God to be in one place [only]?" (*WA* 23, 131, 28). On the basis of the scriptural witness it is necessary to oppose to the "localization" theory a quite different concept, according to which "the right hand of God is not a special place, where a body could or should be. But it is the almighty power of God which can be both nowhere and everywhere" (*WA* 23, 133, 19). "This divine power cannot and must not be enclosed and measured, for it is incomprehensible and immeasurable, beyond and above all that is and can be" (*WA* 23, 133, 26). At the same time, this power is present everywhere, to the extent that "God creates and activates and sustains all things by his almighty power and right hand, as our faith confesses" (*WA* 23, 133, 30). Such an activity presupposes the presence of God which Luther brilliantly ascribes (*WA* 23, 135). It is the presence of God himself—in his essence, for God's power cannot be separated from his right hand or his essence (*WA* 23, 139). For "beyond the creature, there is only divinity, itself one and indivisible" (*WA* 23, 139, 13). To support his thesis, according to which God is present both in heaven and in creation, Luther calls on the example of the incarnation, which he assumes all accept, and according to which God, while being in heaven, is present in his essence in the man Jesus (*WA* 23, 139, 24ff.). And Luther observes that in the incarnation, God did not descend into the womb of the

Virgin Mary, but that he was already to be found there as elsewhere (*WA* 23, 141, 11ff.).

But however interesting all these affirmations may be, Luther does not thereby shake Zwingli's position—except by his criticism of the concept of a localized heaven. In what concerns the omnipresence of God, the reformer of Zurich had no difficulty in following Luther, even if he had perhaps a slightly less dynamic idea of God. In fact, it was a question of knowing whether or not the body of Christ had any part in this ubiquity. Luther arrived at that position by noting the unique bond which binds the humanity of Christ to God. God is present in a special way in him. Only Christ can be called God himself, which distinguishes him from all other creatures. In him, God is present in a personal and unalterable way.[20]

Further, Luther argues in the following way: because the right hand of God is everywhere and the body of Christ is at the right hand of God, therefore the body and blood of Christ must also be everywhere.[21]

According to the witness of the gospel, Christ reigns also in his humanity, since he affirms that all had been given to him by the Father (*WA* 23, 145, 3ff.). Luther even goes so far as to affirm that, according to John 3:13, since the incarnation, the body of Christ "is both in heaven and on earth, already everywhere *(an allen en den)*. For he did not become another person by his glorification *(verklerung)*, he is omnipresent as he already was before" (*WA* 23, 147, 28).

The omnipresence of the body of Christ obviously explains his presence in the Eucharist. And Luther does not hesitate to say, "If Christ had not said at the Last Supper, 'This is my body,' the words, 'Christ seated at the right hand of God' would have required us no less to affirm that the body and blood could be there in the Eucharist as in all other places" (*WA* 23, 145, 13).

In passing, the reformer remarks that one must not think of the presence of Christ in the bread in a material sense, as the Enthusiasts do, comparing it to "wine in the barrel, bread in the oven, silver in the pocket" (*WA* 23, 145, 34). God has many possibilities to make two realities coexist in the same place. As examples, Luther takes the presence of children in the body of their father, the coexistence of color and light, the reflection in the mirror, the tree contained within the seed (*WA* 23, 147).

But, developing his idea of the ubiquity of the body of Christ, the reformer has to deal at the outset with an objection of some importance. Because of this ubiquity, could one not eat the body of Christ everywhere? [22] "There is a difference," Luther says, "between his presence *(gegenwärtigkeit)* and your action in taking him *(greifen)*" (*WA* 23, 151, 3). In fact, Christ is free as in the sunlight that passes through the windowpane. It is necessary to distinguish a general presence of God from his presence for human beings, for whom he binds himself by the Word to a particular place. That is what happened in the incarnation. "Just as the humanity of Christ seated at the right hand of God is now also in and above all things, according to the properties of being at the right hand of God," thus Christ has become "incomprehensible," "unless he binds himself for you, and invites you to a particular table by his Word, indicating to you himself the bread that you must eat" (*WA* 23, 151, 29).

Finally, Luther develops his conception of the glory of Christ. In the name of the glory of Christ, Oecolampadius had rejected the idea of Christ present in the Eucharist and maltreated by priestly hands. Ironically, Luther asks whether the glory of Christ consists of "being seated at the right hand of God on a velvet cushion *(sammet polster)* and listening to the songs of angels performing before him" (*WA* 23, 155, 16). No! the reformer forcefully replies.

The glory of Christ consists of his being present in the Eucharist. On the one hand, in order to confound the wisdom of the Enthusiasts, for according to the *theologia crucis*, the glory of God consists precisely in his self-manifestation in his weakness and the affirmation of his wisdom against all reason. On the other hand, his glory explodes in love by which he takes care of poor sinners, "to the point that, not only is he everywhere in and around us, over and beside us, but he also gives his own body for food, in order that he may so assure us with such a guarantee and console us, that our body too shall live eternally, because he has shared with us on the earth an eternal and living food" (*WA* 23, 155, 34ff.).

Hence the glory of Christ is revealed precisely in his weakness, by his incarnation and by his sacramental presence, thanks to which he saves human beings, body and soul.[23]

In the second part of the treatise, Luther refutes at length the objections of those adversaries who, making use of John 6:63, deny the usefulness of the flesh of Christ in the Eucharist. In reality Luther thinks, "the flesh" that "is of no avail" is not a thing, but the use that we make of things. "Flesh includes all that is in flesh, senses, reason, will, word, works. . . . All that is of no avail" (*WA* 23,

171, 18).[24] On the contrary, when Christ speaks of his body or his flesh, he always, according to Luther, adds the word "my." Further, to deny the usefulness of the body in the Eucharist would be to put the incarnation itself in question, for "flesh remains flesh, whether it be in the stomach, bread, the cross, heaven, spirit, or where you will" (WA 23, 175, 32). Why, in fact, should the flesh of Christ be useful only at the moment of his physical birth and not when it is received in the sacrament? [25]

Of course one must distinguish the spiritual eating from the physical eating. A purely physical eating would not only be useless, but harmful (WA 23, 179, 32). A spiritual eating, i.e., by faith, is in fact necessary.[26] But that does not do away with the physical eating. "Christ has brought both together, the Word and his body, to eat spiritually with the heart and physically with the mouth" (WA 23, 181, 36). The Enthusiasts, on the contrary, separated the Word from the body of Christ, the heart from the mouth and spiritual eating from the sacrament. Their error arises from their placing the spiritual in the object and not in the use one makes of that object. Now the flesh of Christ remains flesh, whether one grasps it by faith or by the mouth, being all the time still a spiritual flesh which, received in faith, is beneficial to human beings." [27]

The flesh remains flesh, and it is the same as that which Mary brought into the world and which we receive.[28] The adversaries retort that Mary saw the infant Jesus physically; the shepherds and Simeon equally saw him, while we see nothing in the Eucharist. "Would you teach your God how he should offer himself to you physically?" (WA 23, 191, 32), the reformer replies. "God has different ways of offering himself physically to human beings. He wishes to be born, physically and spiritually in Mary, but in our case, he offers himself in spiritual and bodily eating. He is thus as near to us physically as he was to them [Mary, Simeon, the shepherds]" (WA 23, 193, 10). Of course, we do not see him, but he has promised us that we shall see him at the end of time.

One may perhaps ask why God thus goes through the flesh in order to give us the Spirit and the new life. But that is a fundamental law of his activity. "The Spirit cannot be with us in any other way than by physical things, such as the Word, the water, the body of Christ, and his saints on earth" (WA 23, 193, 31). Thus Luther comments, "The body and flesh of Christ accord well with the Spirit, they even constitute the physical home of the Spirit, and by them the Spirit comes to others" (*WA* 23, 195, 3). "The flesh of Christ is special in that it is born not of flesh, but of the Holy Spirit. The Scriptures talk of no other human being like this" (*WA* 23, 201, 15).[29] "In this flesh is God: a God-flesh, a spirit-flesh. It is in God and God is in it, therefore it is living" (*WA* 23, 243, 31). It is because it thus contains God that this flesh was not able to be destroyed by death. Luther takes up again the patristic image of the humanity of Christ as the worm hiding the fishhook of the divinity. Thus the devil and death are caught.[30] But despite all this, the incarnation, now too the dwelling place of God, flesh-spirit, the flesh of Christ is not any less of the order of creation.[31]

It can never be stressed enough that Luther insisted not only on the flesh of Christ, but also on the bodily element in general. "Lutheran doctrine had never admitted the strict dualism that Western theology had affirmed ever since Saint Augustine.[32] In fact, the fundamental dualism is not that which opposes spirit to matter and to the body, but that which opposes faith to sin.[33] Where there is faith, all becomes "spirit." "All that goes to make up our body outwardly and physically, when God's Word comes and the act of faith is accomplished, is called to be spiritual. However bodily, carnal, or exterior a thing is, it becomes spiritual when the Word and faith come upon it . . . whether the thing we are using be physical or spiritual" (*WA* 23, 189, 8).[34]

At several points, the reformer develops the idea of the usefulness for our bodies of physically eating the bread. The heart (or the soul) and the mouth are nourished by the same flesh of Christ. "But the soul sees and understands well, that the body will live eternally, because it has partaken of an eternal food, which will not let it perish in the grave, nor crumble into dust (*WA* 23, 191, 25).[35] But Luther takes great care here to avoid a too materialistic conception and to insist on the uniqueness of this eating *(manducatio)*. Finally it is the question of the sovereignty of Christ that is at stake. The reformer thinks he can safeguard this in the following words: "Perishable food is changed into the body which eats it, whereas this spiritual food changes those who eat it into itself and makes them like itself, spiritual, living, and eternal" (*WA* 23, 203, 26).[36]

Hence we do not dispose of the flesh of Christ as we do of all other nourishment. Undoubtedly, he offers himself to us as food, but it is to transform us totally and graciously to his image. We are dealing here with a process that is eschatological in character, hidden still from the senses, but "We shall see him at the last day" (*WA* 23, 205, 24). Faith knows him already now.

On this subject, Luther links himself to certain Fathers of the church, notably Irenaeus and Hilary of Poitiers. He studied these authors, and Erasmus had just edited the writings of Irenaeus in 1526. At the same time, he had asked friends to collect for him those texts in which the Fathers expressed themselves on the subject of the Eucharist.[37] On the one hand, he repeats what they had said about the usefulness of the sacramental communion for the body (*WA* 23, 229, 27; 233, 1). On the other hand, he resisted the symbolic interpretation of the patristic texts which he found in Oecolampadius. He thus attempts to show, on the basis of a certain number of texts from Augustine, Tertullian, Hilary, and Cyprian, that all these authors intended to affirm the real presence of the body of Christ in the Eucharist.

One must note in the treatise the way in which Luther links the body of Christ to the Word of God. According to him, one could go so far as to envisage a work of this body without the Word, or a work which is bound only to an interior Word, like certain healings reported in the Gospels.[38] In fact, one cannot separate the body of Christ from the Word.[39] In the Eucharist, this body is not present without the Word. Therefore it is "useful because of the Word. Yes, even if the flesh of Christ were to be simply meat and God's Word called on us to eat it, it would still be useful because of the Word" (*WA* 23, 259, 14). But one might then ask whether the Word could work alone, without the flesh of Christ. The reformer says, No! "God gives us neither Word nor commandment which is not contained *(einfasse)* and presented to us in a thing which is outwardly corporeal. . . . In the same way, in the Eucharist there is given to us also the Word that the body of Christ is crucified for us and is contained in that bodily thing which is to be eaten. And this eating is useful for the forgiveness of sins" (*WA* 23, 261, 12-22).

But this forgiveness, this salvation, could it not be given to human beings without the sacrament? Luther concedes that it could be, if we consider it at the level of the freedom of God. But from this point of view, neither the presence of the body of Christ at the right hand of God, nor even the incarnation itself would be necessary. Who in fact would have been able to prevent God from setting us free by the act of his will, without preaching or the incarnation?

(*WA* 23, 267, 32). But as he has chosen the way of the incarnation, we must accept it.

The Treatise on the Lord's Supper (1528) [40]

In their reaction to the treatise that we have just analyzed, both Oecolampadius and Zwingli accuse Luther of falling into the errors of Marcion or the Docetic heresy, because, according to them, he attacks the reality of Christ's humanity, which is fulfilled and limited by the body of Christ. But both are embarrassed when required to say where the body of Christ is to be found. For they must clearly admit that "seated at the right hand of God" cannot be thought of in localized terms, with the body of Christ "imprisoned in a golden cage." In fact, one cannot know where the body of Christ is. That is Oecolampadius' last word.

According to him, the real presence does not serve the glory of Christ, quite the contrary. Certainly Christ is the bread of life for the believer, as the gospel of John says. But it is by the power given by the Word and by the inner light that he nourishes us, and not by his flesh. Zwingli also insists on the opposition between the flesh and the spirit of Christ. It is this spirit which prepares us for the resurrection, and not the bodily eating of his flesh.

Note that Zwingli introduces into the debate another rhetorical figure in order to interpret the texts which in the Scriptures apply to the whole person of Christ those properties which belong by right to only one of his natures. To the figure of *alleosis*, which has been used before, he now adds that of *ethopaeia*. This indicates the attribution to someone of a character which they do not have by nature. Thus there are in the Scriptures a certain number of anthropomorphisms by which one attributes, for example, suffering to God; or affirmations by which one seems to attribute to Christ's humanity conditions and acts, such as for example preexistence, which cannot belong to him except when preexistence is interpreted in the Platonic sense of an idea that is preexistent in God.

From the treatise of Luther *On the Lord's Supper*, by which he intends, once and for all, to express his thought on the subject of the Eucharist, we will identify the essential developments of his christology.

Zwingli had put forward the idea that one obtained forgiveness of sins only through the crucified Christ, and not by the bodily eating of his flesh as such. "That is what I hold also," replied Luther

(*WA* 26, 292, 34). To eat the body of Christ without faith is useless. But does the redemptive death of Christ on the cross exclude all other acts and ways by which Christ exists: the incarnation, the sitting at the right hand of God, the sacramental presence? "Hence we must never make anything of Christ, if we don't make of him someone who suffers eternally on the cross for our sin, so that we may not act against faith, believing according to other articles of faith that Christ is there, that he pardons sins. Now this spirit [Luther refers to Zwingli] wants to relate pardon only to the cross" (*WA* 26, 293, 32). Luther then takes up his distinction between *meritum* and *distributio meriti*, between the *factum* and the *usus facti*. This is to distinguish the realization of salvation on the cross from its announcement by the Word and sacrament.

Another argument of Zwingli is based on the words, "given for you." Christ has given himself in visible manner for us. He should then also be visible in the Eucharist if he were truly present. "We do not say," replied Luther, "that the body of Christ is in the Eucharist as or under the form in which he gave himself for us (for who would say that?), but that it is the same body which is given for us, not under the same form or in the same manner, but of the same essence and nature. For one and the same being can be here visible and there invisible" (*WA* 26, 298, 32ff.). That is one of the central points of the controversy. Zwingli strove to preserve the body with the properties which we know in it below—among others, its visible form. For Luther, everything depended on the identity between the dead Christ on the cross in his body and the present Christ in his body in the Eucharist.

It is necessary to stress with what violence Luther opposed the use of *alleosis* in christology.[41] In his criticism he did not at first proceed from the ubiquity itself, but he pointed to what according to him was an inescapable and fatal consequence of *alleosis:* attributing the suffering only to the human nature of Christ. When Zwingli did this, according to Luther, he denied the redemption. "The *alleosis* ultimately presents a Christ such as I should not want to be in conformity with him: i.e., a Christ who is no more in his life or his suffering than any other saint. For if I believe that only the human nature has suffered for me, Christ is for me a poor Savior; he has need himself of a savior" (*WA* 26, 319, 34ff.). Luther reasoned thus: redemption is accomplished by suffering on the cross. To exclude God from that suffering and to say that only humanity has suffered

is to make redemption rest only on humanity. "For he who is redeemed only by humanity is surely not redeemed, and will never
be redeemed" (*WA* 26, 342, 19). Of course, one may ask if divinity
is able to suffer and die. Reason is against it. And it is true that
considered by itself, divinity can neither suffer nor die. But one
must not consider it by itself, rather in its inseparable union with
humanity, "because divinity and humanity are one person in Christ.
Scripture, because of this personal unity, attributes also to the
divinity all that happens to the humanity and vice versa. And it is
truly so, they are equal in truth. For you must certainly say: this
person, i.e., Christ, suffers, dies. Now this person is truly God, that
is why one rightly says: the Son of God suffers. For although one
of the parties (if I may express it so) (the divinity) does not suffer,
the person who is God suffers nonetheless in the other party (the
humanity). Just as one says, 'The king's son is wounded,' even if only
his leg is wounded" (*WA* 26, 321, 21-29). It is only much later that
Luther will go deeper into these christological problems thus raised,
which had occupied the attention of the Scholastic theologians for
a long time. For the moment, it was a question of a cry from the
heart which repels the attack on the mystery of redemption which
he believed he could discern in the concept of *alleosis*.

Luther thus opposes to the Zwinglian christology a firm insistence
on the unity of the person of Christ. Redemption is at stake, as we
have seen, but so is the revelation of God. God has become one
person with humanity and can no longer be found outside this
humanity. That is one of Luther's dominant themes. "Where you
can say of a place, 'God is here,' you must also say, 'Christ the man
is equally there.' And if you would show me a place where God is
and not humanity, the person would already be divided, since I
would then be able to say, as if it were the truth: 'Here can be
found God who is not and never did become human.' But I don't
want to know anything about that God. For the consequences would
be that space and time would separate the two natures, one from
the other, and would divide the person. But neither death nor all
the devils have been able to separate them and tear them apart,
one from the other. And there would be for me a very poor Christ
if he were only in one place both a divine and human person,
whereas in all places he should be only a simple separated God and
a divine person without humanity. No, my friend, where you place
God, there you must place for me the humanity with him: you

cannot allow the one to be separated from the other. They have become one person and the humanity will not be separated off, like Master Hans taking off his clothes when he lies down to sleep" (*WA* 26, 332, 33-333, 10).

Following the discussion at another level, Luther remarks that there are different kinds of presence. He uses here a triple distinction introduced by the Scholastics and used especially by Occam. A thing can be present in a place *localiter* or *circumscriptive*, that is, "when the place and the body within it accord, join, and fit, just like the wine in the barrel" (*WA* 26, 327, 24). The second manner of presence is *diffinitive*, "incomprehensible, when the thing or the body cannot be comprehended in one place and cannot be measured by the space of that place where it is, but takes up more or less space" (*WA* 26, 327, 33). That is the case of angels or spirits or the resurrection appearances which are able to pass through closed doors. Finally there is the presence *repletive*, "supernatural, that is when a thing is at one and the same time absolutely in all places and fills all places, without however being measured or comprehended according to the space of any one place in which it is. This manner of presence is attributed to God only. . . . It is incomprehensible, beyond all measurement, beyond all reason, and can be maintained only by faith in the Word" (*WA* 26, 329, 27).

In order to participate in this omnipresence of God, humanity does not need to "extend itself and be stretched like a skin to cover all creatures" (*WA* 26, 333, 28), as Luther's adversaries were suggesting. That would be to misunderstand the nature of God. "God is not a bodily thing, but a Spirit above all things" (*WA* 26, 335, 1).[43] It is with him that Christ forms one unique person, not with a stone or a door! Christ participates then in the spiritual nature of ubiquity, "being more and deeper in the divinity than in the stone or the door" (*WA* 26, 335, 3). Given the spiritual and transcendent nature of God, the humanity does not have to "enclose the divinity or incorporate itself into it, as the carnal spirit dreams" (*WA* 26, 335, 8). In fact, the humanity never thus encloses the divinity so that it could be in one particular place or in all places. "But it is with God one unique person, in such a way that where God is, there also is the man. What God does, the man also is said to have done. What the man suffers is also called the suffering of God" (*WA* 26, 335, 26).

And Luther repeats: "Thus the body of Christ has three ways of being. First, the comprehensible, bodily way, so that he walked bodily on the earth. . . . In such a way he is not in God or with the Father in heaven, as the foolish spirit dreams. For God is not a physical space or state. It is about this way that the Bible speaks of Christ leaving the earth and going to the Father, etc. Second, the incomprehensible spiritual way, so that he takes up no space, nor gives any, but passes through all creatures as he wills. Third, the divine, heavenly way, so that he is a person with God. There all creatures are open and present to him, much more than they were in the second way" (*WA* 26, 335, 29–336, 10).[44]

Affirming the ubiquity on the basis of the personal union of the two natures, Luther writes: "We know well that he is in God and beyond all creatures and is uniquely one with God. But how that is so we know not. It is beyond nature and beyond reason, even beyond the angels in heaven. God alone knows and recognizes it" (*WA* 26, 336, 20). The secret can only be expressed with the use of certain images: the sparkle of the opal which appears to fill all of that precious stone, the one and only voice of the preacher which can reach different ears, the one image presented in the broken pieces of a mirror—there are images or analogies which can help us to approach the mystery of the ubiquity of Christ.

Finally Luther turns on his adversary and summons him to answer the following questions: "Where is the Scripture or the reason why the body of Christ should not have another way of being than the comprehensible, bodily way? . . . In the same way, where do we learn that the right hand is a particular place in heaven?" (*WA* 26, 340, 3ff.). The other question is as follows: "Christ is God and a human being; and his humanity, one person with God, has been totally assumed by God above all creatures, so that it cleaves to him. How is it then possible that God can be any place where he is not human? And how is it possible, without dividing the person, that it could be that here God is without humanity and there he is with humanity? For we do not have two Gods, but only one, and he is completely human according to one person, namely the Son" (*WA* 26, 340, 14ff.).

The conception of heaven is a precise point at which Luther differs from Zwingli as well as from Oecolampadius. According to John 3:13, Luther maintains, Christ was in heaven even during his earthly incarnation. But Zwingli protests: "Does one eat and drink in heaven? Does one die and suffer also in heaven? Does one sleep and take his rest also in heaven?" (*WA* 26, 344, 20). Luther replies, "The humanity of Christ from the body of his mother is higher and deeper in God and before God more than any angel. In this way it has been higher in heaven than any angel, because that which is in God and before God is in the heaven, exactly as the angels are, even while still on earth" (*WA* 26, 344, 26).[45]

Can one eat and drink, die and suffer, and yet be in the presence of God? And why not, Luther replies; otherwise it would be necessary to deny the union of the two natures.[46]

One must not think of heaven as a locality, but as existence in the presence of God and in God.[47] That is why not only Christ, but also "the Christians are at the same time in the kingdom of God and on earth" (*WA* 26, 422, 21), although they are not in the same way in God as Christ is, who is one with him in a unique way.[48]

An important question which is going to concern Luther later belongs in the realm of logic. Can one say that the bread is the body, while logically "two different natures *(Wesen)* can be only one nature, for what is an ass cannot be an ox" (*WA* 26, 439, 6). Would this not be contrary to what has been called the principle of identity? For the sake of logic, Luther observes, "The sophists have kept the body, but lost the bread" (*WA* 26, 439, 8), and taught the doctrine of transubstantiation. Wyclif, on the other hand, whose real thought Luther appears here to have misunderstood,[49] "keeps the bread, lets the body go, and says that the little word 'this' applies to the bread and not to the body" (*WA* 26, 439, 21).

For his part, Luther is at pains to show that "against all reason and fine logic" we must discern "that two distinct natures can be and must be called one nature" (*WA* 26, 439, 29). Logic must in effect submit to the Word of God and allow itself to be explained by it.

Luther then evokes several kinds of natures or unions, where there are sometimes coexisting two or several natures and one common nature. The strongest union is that which is designated "natural" unity by him, which is found only in the Trinity. In fact, "It is said of the unique Godhead that it is threefold, as three persons, which is far higher and harder against reason than to say that wood is stone" (*WA* 26, 440, 23).

Secondly, there is the union called "personal," which unites the humanity and the divinity of Jesus Christ. Union of a different kind from the first: "It is not the essential union of natures *(Naturen)*, for the two natures and the two essences *(Wesen)* are very different, but it is the personal union. For while there was not a single essence according to nature, there was nonetheless a single essence according to the person" (*WA* 26, 440, 41).

Luther talks of yet other forms of union such as the "unity of action" (*WA* 26, 441, 27), in which the wind and the flames of a fire are compared with the angels (Ps. 104:4). There is the "formal" union, in which the Holy Spirit is compared to a dove. Finally there is the "sacramental" union which unites the bread and the body of Christ. "It is not a natural or a personal union as in God or in Christ. Perhaps it is also a different union from that of the dove with the Holy Spirit or the flame with the angel. It is, however, also a union, a sacramental union" (*WA* 26, 442, 24). And a little later on, Luther brings this union much closer to the other two: "The bread is the body of Christ, just as the dove is the Holy Spirit and the flame is the angel" (*WA* 26, 443, 5).

Luther's conclusion is as follows: One must not follow only the logic which distinguishes the bread and the body, God and humanity, but also to follow the grammar, "which teaches in all languages that we speak thus: when two beings *(Wesen)* come into being, then language speaks of two beings in one single expression" (*WA* 26, 443, 14). This way of expression rests on a reality. "It is certainly true that the different natures that have been brought together into one truly receive by their conjunction a new and unique essence *(Wesen)*, according to which they are with reason called one essence or being, although each taken by itself has its unique particular essence" (*WA* 26, 443, 29). It is in this connection that Luther returns to the concept of *synecdoche,* to which we have already drawn attention.

The treatise ends with a confession of faith, very classical in style. We note the emphasis there placed on soteriology, the confession of trinitarian doctrine, the affirmation of the absolutely total humanity of Christ, "in everything and in every way a true human being as I am myself, like all others, save that he came without sin from the Virgin alone by the intermediary of the Holy Spirit" (*WA* 26, 501, 25-29).

Themes and Problems of Christology

The Real Presence, the Incarnation, and Salvation

On the basis of our analysis we can make a firm statement: the problem of the real presence is written into the continuous attention which Luther gives to the incarnation. The body and flesh of Christ, and not only his words or his spirit, have for him a fundamental importance. In a general way, he sees that the usefulness of the body is under attack in the criticism of his adversaries who impugn the real presence. By denying the necessity for the flesh of Christ in the Eucharist, one will deny it also to the incarnation of Christ himself. That is one argument which Luther does not cease to use.

His adversaries, on the other hand, rejected this conclusion. They obviously accepted the incarnation, but considered the flesh of Christ as belonging to the past. This flesh is limited by space and time and cannot be given to us as such today. One can say, as Luther does, that the incarnation continues in the sense that God continues to offer himself to us by the physical elements that are the bread and the wine of the Eucharist, i.e., the oral and physical character of the announcement of the gospel.[50] These physical elements have certainly not supplanted the humanity of Christ as such, but prolong it in some way, constituting his current way of being present.[51] The humanity cannot be present today as it was in the past in his incarnation, and Luther never stops saying that there exist different "modes of presence" for God and for human beings. It is present with physical elements in the sacramental union. The fact that in some way these elements prolong the incarnation is expressed by Luther in the parallelism which is established between the hypostatic union and the sacramental union. The former is of course much closer than the latter. But to put in question the latter is to put in question also the former. Luther also says that by the intermediary of these physical elements we are as close to Christ as were Mary and the disciples.

Why does Luther at this point insist on the body of Christ and on the real presence of this body? It is for him a fundamental concern which cannot be emphasized too much. We do not meet God outside of the man Jesus Christ, "in whom the whole fulness of God dwells bodily" (Col. 2:9). For that would be to move toward the naked God of speculation, while God wishes to come near to us for our salvation in the form of the flesh of the man Jesus, as he has appeared in history and as flesh present in the physical elements of the gospel, announced and in the sacraments. In Zwingli's admission that there is a presence of Christ in his divinity, but separated from his humanity, Luther discerns a grave danger to one of the fundamental principles of the faith, namely the revelation of God present in a hidden fashion in the flesh.

We have seen that Zwingli reacted quite differently. Of course, he was not in this matter a Deist, to the point of denying the revelation of God in Christ. But his faith did not demand to the same extent as Luther's did the presence of this humanity. He was content with the spirit of the historical revelation, the words of Christ and the meditation on the work of Christ accomplished in the past. More, it seemed to him that Luther's insistence on the presence of the body of Christ was highly suspect. According to him it threatened the spiritual nature of the object of faith. By definition, faith is concerned with an invisible reality; why then this strong insistence on the visible element? For Luther also, faith is concerned with invisible realities, but these are not outside the visible elements; they are hidden within them, while also attested by them. It seems to us quite wrong that Zwingli should reproach Luther for attaching faith to visible realities. In fact, it is not these realities themselves that interest Luther, i.e., the humanity of Christ and the sacraments, but what they carry hidden within them, namely, knowledge of God and salvation.

In this connection, Luther does not cease to insist on the necessity of faith and the Word which calls us to faith. God has not become visible in the humanity of Christ, neither have Christ and salvation become more so in the physical elements. Their presence is hidden, directed toward the last days when that presence will be visible.

Luther's conception becomes clearer when he shows how salvation is bound to the humanity, to the body, and to the flesh of Christ. As we have already seen many times, the role of Christ does not consist of him being in the first place, an example, a judge, or even a prophet bearing witness to God. His work is redemption, it is salvation. Now, that redemption is realized by him, by his suffering, by his real solidarity with sinful human beings, and by his active obedience to the Father. How would he have been able to realize all that without entering into our flesh, without partaking at all points of our human existence? Zwingli's attention was far less directed toward redemption itself. Of course, he believed it and

remained faithful to theological tradition. He speaks of the appeasement of God by the man Jesus and hence of "satisfaction." Nevertheless, at the heart of his thought there is a strong sense of the
"sovereign work of God," his *Alleinwirksamkeit,* which tends to
devalue the role of the human nature. All human certainty and trust
must rest on the divine nature as such. It alone saves us. What then
is the role of the human nature? "It is the guarantee of the divine
compassion," he writes in his *Amica exegesis.* It attests what is
realized only by the divine nature. It makes it known. From such a
point of view, it is evidently useless for the humanity of Christ to be
present for us today. What has been done can be attested by preaching. By meditation, we can go back to the Christ of history and to
the saving work that was then accomplished, while at the same time
receiving the effects of it by the present grace and power of God.

For Luther, the salvation of believers is and remains linked to the
flesh of Christ. It is necessary that this be given to them, because in
it alone they find their justification. It is not enough for us to see
that it is attested that God saves us, nor that we can be content to
receive only the benefits of the redemptive work of Christ accomplished in the past. We must receive Christ himself, Christ with his
flesh, because it was in his flesh that he accomplished redemption.
Everything depends then on the identity between the historic Christ
and Christ present, between Christ dead on the cross and Christ
who now constitutes my righteousness before God. The following
question can then be posed: If one so insists on forgiveness of sins
accorded by Christ present in the Eucharist, what becomes of the
work accomplished once for all on the cross? Has our redemption
not been realized by the historic Christ? Luther does not deny that,
but he maintains that Carlstadt with such arguments has turned
away from the real presence in order to meditate on the cross in the
past. That is precisely, according to Luther, what must not be done.
For his part, he distinguishes the realization of salvation which is
placed at a precise moment in time, from the attribution of this
salvation which can happen at any moment, when the present Christ
himself distributes the fruits of his work. But Luther places his
emphasis on the action of Christ, who on the one hand, offers himself for our justification by offering his present body, and on the
other hand, causes the birth of faith, by the Holy Spirit, faith which
unites human beings to Christ.

While recognizing for all the reasons given above the importance of the union of the believer with the body of Christ, one could ask whether it is necessary that the body and blood of Christ "descend" to human beings. Could it not be conceivable that the opposite direction be followed and God reunite persons to the body and blood of Christ, by the Holy Spirit, and give them the new life? Such will be the position of Calvin, who seems to us to be very much nearer to Luther on this point, because like Luther and unlike Zwingli, he has felt the soteriological importance of the union of the believer with Christ.

Luther cannot adopt this view because he fears a theology in which human beings are detached from the concrete realities in order to rise up to the naked God by their own efforts, thus falling again into the speculations of the Scholastics or into a theology of works in which human beings would rise up to God instead of believing in God coming down to them, in a hidden way. That does not necessarily put in question the view of Calvin. Whatever would have been the result of this confrontation between the two men, which regrettably never took place in history, it is necessary to underline the importance for Luther of this descent of God, this abasement by which God, who has realized salvation in Jesus Christ, comes today, offering this salvation by the intermediary of the person of Christ, present in these humble realities—the proclamation of the Word and the administration of the sacraments. We have seen that this abasement constitutes a major principle of the order of salvation developed by Luther in his controversy with Carlstadt. God first approached us by the humanity of Christ, by the water of Baptism, the bread and wine of the Eucharist, and by the proclamation of the gospel. And then he asks us to believe.

Since the 16th century it has often been asked if Luther had not overstated the role of the flesh of Christ and if he was not too dependent on certain conceptions of the early church. There are in fact striking analogies between certain statements of Luther and the thought of Athanasius or Irenaeus, for example. Luther himself notes them in his treatise, *Dass diese Worte*. . . . And it would be easy to find other parallels—with Saint Thomas, for example.[52]

At all times, these affirmations on the subject of the flesh of Christ have caused offense, particularly in the 19th century, when it was common to contrast the words and personality of Jesus, on the one hand, with his body, on the other. But this distinction is foreign to Luther. Salvation was realized by the whole person of Christ, and it is with the flesh in which he suffered for me that Christ is given to me in righteousness.

Another question is posed in connection with the flesh of Christ. Was not Luther led to value it in itself, quite apart from faith? Does he not speak of it as a flesh-spirit, full of life? Does he not go so far on one occasion as to say that in certain healings, such as that of the woman who touched the hem of his garment, the flesh of Christ acted by itself independent of faith or the Word? Luther appears there to have betrayed the fundamental principle of justification by faith. His adversaries reproached him with this after the publication of *Dass diese Worte. . . .* We do not think that this criticism is justified. Undoubtedly, the reformer, in opposing the spiritualism of his adversaries, gave great value to the flesh of Christ, a flesh of so great a value that in a limited number of cases it was able to bestow benefits, such as on the woman with an issue of blood. But in this case, was faith entirely absent? And Luther speaks also of an *interior* word in which she was able to trust. But repeatedly, he observes with vigor that the flesh of Christ by itself is useless if there is no human faith: worse, it is harmful, since if we really receive the body of Christ to eat it unworthily, that is to our judgment.

Our exposition so far would lead us to believe that the real presence of Christ was ultimately, for Luther, a postulate of faith before it was a reality attested by scriptural witness. In fact, this is not so. Luther directs our attention constantly to the "is" of the text of the words of institution. This text, according to him, is plain and simple, "in which we must dwell, like a child in a cradle." But this text and the affirmation of the real presence only corroborate what he knows from the witness of Scripture as a whole of the incarnation, of the justification by faith of the present Christ.

The real presence thus inserts itself into this general movement of the incarnation of God, which is not limited to the past incarnation of Christ. When it too is inserted into this movement, the real presence is equally the object of the same criteria as the past incarnation of Christ. Not more than it, can the real presence be proved as absolutely necessary. God is free; in order to save us he was not obliged to involve himself in the way of the incarnation and of the means of grace.[53] Redemption could have been effected in the same way as creation, that is to say, directly, without passing through the incarnation and without particular outward means. But that is not the way in which God involved himself. In his liberty he took another way. It is not our place to reproach him for it, as the Enthusiasts seem to want to do. "Now that your salvation comes through the humanity, through Word, through bread which is given in the Eucharist, who are you, thankless wretches, to ask why he did not do it some other way?" [54] What is at stake here is the concept of God himself. The adversaries seem to be concerned with the transcendence and the immutability of God, while the incarnation is secondary for them. For Luther, on the contrary, the image which he has of God is dictated by the incarnation. That lies at the basis of his knowledge of God.

On the other hand, like the incarnation itself, the real presence is seen from the perspective of the theology of the cross. We have drawn attention to this on several occasions. It is the nature of God to reveal himself by hiding himself, to choose, when he is saving humanity, the most humble means, such as the body of a man, the bread and wine. The all-powerful God works through weakness, shocking human reason and presumption. "God is a human being who wants to do that which is foolish and useless in the eyes of the world." [55] For Luther the opposition of his adversaries is part of the usual opposition of the wise according to the flesh against the action of God *sub contraria specie*. True faith, such as he envisages it, accepts the "unreasonable" ways of God, holds fast to the witness of the Word, and waits in expectation of the last day when faith will see what it has believed here below.

But one of the fundamental problems posed by Luther's conception of the real presence must be raised here, because this problem was at the center of the debate between Luther and his adversaries. It is that of the integrity of the body of Christ. We have shown, up to this point, the motives of faith which pushed Luther into an insistence, not only on the body of the earthly Christ, but on the presence of the body of Christ in the Eucharist. It is not a question of a new body, for it is the same body, in its different modes of presence, as that which was sacrificed for us on the cross. Now the whole problem lies there. On the basis of its union with the divine nature, this body, according to Luther, is present everywhere, and can therefore also be present in the Eucharist. But is such an omnipresent body still a human body, subject to the laws of space and time? Is this not to divinize the humanity of Christ in a way that is illegitimate and in fact to fall into the error of Docetism? That is the fundamental question which must be posed to Luther, and to

Lutheran theology in general, about the doctrine of the ubiquity of Christ. The reality of that question is keenly felt today by many Lutheran theologians.[56]

The Ubiquity of Christ and the Union Between the Two Natures

The real presence of the body of Christ is based on the "is" of the words of institution. It is the first and the last of Luther's arguments. At the same time, he attempts to show the possibility of this real presence by developing the doctrine of the ubiquity of Christ. In one passage, he even deduces the real presence directly from this ubiquity. This real presence, he remarks, would be imperative even if we did not have the words of institution.[57]

Thus we must ask how Luther explains this doctrine of ubiquity. Historically it seems that he owes it to his master, B. Arnoldi von Usingen. In fact, it goes back to Occam and to Gabriel Biel.[58] Whatever be the precise origin, one can detect here an Occamist theology, according to which God, *deus ex lex*, is not bound to his creation and is able to create a body which is limitless. In fact, Luther never stops arguing on the basis on the infinite possibilities of God. But another approach seems to us to be more important; it is christology properly so-called, more precisely, the union between the two natures. The reasoning we constantly find in Luther is the following: the divine nature is everywhere at work. The humanity must have its part in this omnipresence, for God can no longer be separated from the man Jesus, and that not only in redemption, but also in the general history of the world, in which he continues his work of creation. To admit that God can be in any place independent of the man Jesus would be, according to Luther, fundamentally to put in question the incarnation itself and the revelation of God hidden in the humanity. That would be to think that one can encounter God hidden in the humanity. That would be to think that one can encounter God beyond the humanity and to fall again into the speculation about the "naked God." It is important to note that God does not "dress himself" in order to meet us in the Word and in the sacraments, while he is "naked" in the creation and the law. Even when God is hidden, as he is in creation, he is united to the humanity of Christ. He does everything only through that humanity and as a function of it. Thus a doctrine of two realms which would place the humanity of Christ only in the realm of grace and not in that of the law does not seem to us to be in conformity with the ultimate intentions of Luther.

In any case, Luther puts all his emphasis on the inseparable unity between the divine nature and the human nature of Jesus Christ. We have shown the eagerness with which he is ready to combat Zwingli's *alleosis*, this rhetorical figure of speech which puts in question, according to Luther, the unity of the person of Christ.

Another aspect, fundamental for Luther, appeared in the course of the controversy. By separating the two natures, as Zwingli did, one could attack the reality of our redemption. By the *alleosis*, Zwingli had in fact been led to deny the suffering of God in the person of Christ. According to him, Luther had used an improper expression there—an anthropomorphism similar to what appeared in that other rhetorical figure of speech, *ethopaeia*. Now, Luther thinks that if God had not suffered, he would no longer have participated in the redemptive work, and then all certainty of salvation would collapse.[59] In fact, if it is not God himself who saves us in Jesus Christ, we are lost, then Christ is only one saint among others. Of course, there is no doubt that both reformers agreed that it was God who effected salvation. But according to Luther, God does this not by an exterior act of his almighty power, which the humanity has only to make known, but he does it in the weakness and suffering of the incarnation.

Luther makes it quite clear that the suffering of God must not be envisaged outside the concrete unity of God with human beings, realized in Jesus Christ. Taken by itself, metaphysically considered, God cannot suffer. From such a perspective, he is remote and immutable. But, for Luther, the God of whom faith speaks is the God present personally in Christ and participating in the suffering of the man.[60]

That is probably why Luther speaks of God in anthropomorphic terms. Zwingli for his part had drawn back from anthropomorphisms, while he introduced the term *ethopaeia* into the discussion. This figure is used when one attributes to someone a character which they do not have by nature. By this subterfuge Zwingli thought he could discard that which might be thought too concrete and anthropomorphic in the biblical affirmations about God. It was necessary then, according to him, to distinguish the being of God from the human way of expressing this being. But as A. Peters has remarked, "This distinction between our statements about God, bound to our humanity, and the being of God in himself always leads to a weakening of the concept of God existing as a person" ("Luthers Christuszeugnis," p. 76). It seems that a philosophical concept of God and his impassibility had here left its mark on Zwingli. Luther on the other hand has no fear of taking the biblical statements about God as they are without criticizing them. He rejects the concept of *ethopaeia* (WA 26, 342, 29). The humanity of Jesus Christ is not a curtain, behind which is hidden an impersonal and immutable God, but it expresses truly the heart, the very being of God.

One may well ask how we must conceive of the suffering of God in Jesus Christ. Does it not mean that God must have transformed himself into a human being? Luther says, no, the two natures are distinct. However, they are so united that the one participates in the properties and the actions of the other. And he tries to explain this with the help of images. Consider the human personality. There also, there are two distinct things which nonetheless are united: the soul and the body. Now what happens to the one concerns the other also. Suffering is never purely physical or purely moral. It is the same with Christ, God and a human being. Whatever happens to the Christ concerns the two natures.

On the other hand, the *alleosis* tears the Christ apart and makes of him two persons. "In our turn, we protest against those who divide Christ, as though he were two persons, a divine and a human" (WA 26, 324). Luther thus directs toward Zwingli the accusation which the Alexandrian theologians long ago directed toward their adversaries of Antioch. It is striking to see how, little by little, Luther comes to the point of putting Zwingli in the same boat with Nestorius.

In the treatises that we have just looked at, Luther does not enter too much into the mystery of the hypostatic union itself. At the most he brushes aside some ideas that he considers to be infantile. He declares himself basically in agreement with his adversaries in recognizing that the divinity does not "descend" concretely on the humanity in order to assume it. It was already present in the womb of Mary in the same way as it is always present everywhere. But it must be noted that the human nature does not circumscribe the divine nature. Yet, while his adversaries deduce from that a certain independence of the divine nature in relation to the human nature, Luther concentrates on the indissoluble union of the two natures by affirming that the humanity is, more than all other creatures, "in the divinity," participating in its ubiquity.[61] For the adversaries, to assume a human nature means that the divine nature keeps its distance from this human nature, since the humanity remains human, that is to say, limited by the laws of space and time. For Luther, on the contrary, the divine nature raises the human to itself and makes it participate in its activity.

It will be noted that the elaboration of the doctrine of ubiquity goes some way toward diminishing, for Luther, the place of the ascension. The glorification of the humanity is achieved already in the incarnation. In that the reformer is typically Johannine. In the foreground is Christ in glory, and he appears already in Christ in the flesh. Thus Luther will find already in the earthly Christ, ubiquity and other divine properties. Then the ascension merely attests a reality already existing since the incarnation.[62]

But one must, above all, ask about the conception of ubiquity which is elaborated by Luther. It seems to us that it is presented from two points of view. One could also say that it is necessary to distinguish the fundamental themes and the way in which they are conceived.

What are the themes in question? Since the incarnation, according to Luther, we do not meet God outside of Jesus Christ. In other words, the action of God is exercised in the world as a function of the man Jesus. He participates in the action of the Father and illuminates it. There where God is, there is found also the man Jesus. Ubiquity is at the very heart of a theology of revelation which considers the mystery of God revealed in Jesus Christ.

Ubiquity has also to be considered under the perspective of justification by faith. How are we justified by God? Not independently of the man Jesus, but by the offering of the sacrificial humanity of Jesus Christ, present through the Word and the sacraments. It is he who constitutes our righteousness before God. It is thus important that Christ be present as well in the Eucharist, in his humanity. That is inscribed in the very heart of Luther's theology. And this presence is possible if Christ participates in the ubiquity of God.

But difficulties arise because Luther considers this ubiquity, within the framework of the "communication of attributes," as a divine property communicated to the humanity. One might well ask how Docetism can be avoided. To communicate to the human nature a divine property, and that from the incarnation onward, renders it different from our humanity and appears to be in contradiction to that image of Jesus traced by the evangelists.

One will surely then have to ask whether Luther has not been led astray by a concept which is not adequate to express at one and the same time the true humanity of Jesus Christ and the almighty power of God which can by Word and sacramental sign render the man Jesus present wherever he will. God no longer wishes to be separated from the humanity of Jesus Christ.[63] The interpreter of Luther's thought must point out that a logical fallacy arises here. The theology of the cross, so important to Luther, underlines the true humanity of Jesus Christ. It is this which calls in question the concept of ubiquity, in the name of Luther's own views, to the extent that one makes of it a divine property which, communicated to humanity, threatens the integrity of the human nature.

This raises another question. Has the union of the two natures been so strongly stressed by Luther that there is a mixing or confusion? In other words, does Luther fall into Monophysitism? He had to defend himself against this accusation and never ceased to emphasize that he clearly distinguished the two natures as to their respective essences *(Wesen)*.

It must be acknowledged that he sometimes lacks precision in his vocabulary. He uses the term *Wesen* both for essence or nature and in the sense of being. "We do not mix the two natures in one being *(Wesen),*" he writes (WA 26, 324, 6). Each nature keeps its own essence *(Wesen).*[64] But a little later he writes, "Although there was not one being *(Wesen)* according to the nature, there is one being *(Wesen)* according to the person. And from that there comes two kinds of unity and two kinds of being *(Wesen)*" (WA 26, 340, 34). Luther makes clear the different uses of *Wesen,* but would it not have been better to avoid the possible ambiguities here?

The Concept of the Person in Luther's Christology

In the course of history, the term *person* has known different interpretations. In christology the controversies of the early church led to the Chalcedonian Definition, according to which the Son of God was the *hypostasis* which assumed human nature; in other words, only the *Logos* conferred personal existence on Jesus Christ. It is as united to the *hypostasis* of the Son of God that the man Jesus exists as person. The theologians have called this "assumption" of a human being into personal unity with the Son *hypostatic union.* Christ is thus the person of the Son existing in two natures, fully God and fully human.

Here we appear to have a fairly precise concept of the person, despite the inevitable theological divergence in detail. It is the *hypostasis* which is the person and enables the human nature to participate in the existence of the person by means of the incarnation. This concept of the person can be designated *ontological* or *metaphysical*.

But today when one speaks of person, generally it is no longer the divine *hypostasis* of the *Logos* which is envisaged, but the man as such in his relation to the world. Person, then, signifies conscious and free subject, moral personality. The concept of person has become psychological, moral, and phenomenological.

What is it with Luther? It is difficult to discern his thought, because he was not a man for definitions. He was capable of using the same term in different senses, as we have seen in connection with *Wesen*. An analysis of the texts on the Eucharist show that his attention was directed toward a "personal" union of the two natures. He was less concerned with the divine *hypostasis* than he was with the concrete totality which is the hypostatic union. "This man is true God, as an eternal, inseparable person come from God and humanity" (*WA* 26, 501, 11); "This has become one person, and the humanity is not separated from itself" (*WA* 26, 333, 8).

In such passages he underlines the unique "personal" bond which binds the human nature to God and no longer allows them to be separated.

It seems that the word *person* in Luther must indicate something concrete, the new being *(Wesen)* which accomplishes the work of salvation, and not the divine *hypostasis* itself. Does this alternative, in fact, effectively represent his thought? Is the personal union thus seen as conceivable without the doctrine of *enhypostasis* of the Logos in the human nature, that is to say, without the personifying element which is the divine *hypostasis?* The personal union does not result from the coordination of two metaphysical substances, a divine nature and a human nature, but from the movement of the Son, a free subject, who becomes incarnate in order to save human beings, determining by this design of love the personal existence of the man Jesus. Luther was powerfully attracted by the christology of the Alexandrians, a christology which concentrates, in Athanasius, on the *prolepsis*, that is to say, the "assumption" of the humanity by the Word.[65] The humanity is thus "surrounded" or "carried" by the divine person, whose instrument it becomes for the realization of salvation. Such a christology is found in Athanasius, as well as Saint Thomas [66] and in Article 3 of the Augsburg Confession.[67] We have already found this conception in Luther before the Eucharistic texts, e.g., in his commentary on Rom. 1:3-4, and we shall find it again when we come to analyze the *Disputationes*. Why should it be absent from the texts of the Eucharistic Controversy?

There is incontrovertably a new orientation. But before we come to examine that, it must be noted that the classic Alexandrian view concerning the assumption of humanity by the Word appears very neatly in the eucharistic texts. The principal writing, *On the Lord's Supper,* ends in fact with a classical confession of faith. We read there: "I believe and know that the Scripture teaches us that only the second person in God,[68] namely the Son, was made human, conceived without the cooperation of a man, by the Holy Spirit, and born of the pure and holy Virgin Mary, as of a true and natural mother. . . . Hence, neither the Father nor the Holy Spirit were made human, as certain heretics have taught. Also, God the Son has not only assumed *(angenommen)* the body without the soul (as certain heretics have taught), but equally the soul, that is to say, a completely perfect humanity. . . . This man is true God, as an eternal, inseparable person come from God and humanity." [69]

This text clearly shows that, for Luther, the incarnation means that the second person of the Trinity assumes the humanity. Other passages recall that the humanity of Christ rests in his divinity, is carried by the person of the Word and hence becomes a person: "Christ's body in the divinity is one person with God" (*WA* 26, 334, 19); "We have not two gods, but only one God and he is totally human according to the unique person, namely that of the Son" (*WA* 26, 340, 14ff.); "Now the humanity of Christ from the body of his mother was more highly and more profoundly in God and before God than any angel" (*WA* 26, 344, 9).

It will be noted also to what extent Luther takes certain images or expressions from a christology founded on the *enhypostasis.* Thus, for example, the image of iron heated by fire as expressing the humanity assumed by the divinity comes from John of Damascus, one of the principal post-Chalcedonian Alexandrians for whom the *enhypostasis* was the keystone of christology. Hence without Luther explaining at length, the classical idea, according to which the Word is the personal element in Jesus, is found in his writings.

This attitude, of which we have spoken, is shown in his insistence on the result of the *enhypostasis,* that is to say on the new and unique *Wesen* (being) which is Jesus Christ himself, a humanity united indissolubly to the divine *hypostasis.* His opposition to the views of Zwingli drove Luther to insist particularly on this aspect of his thought. In fact, Zwingli himself supported the affirmation of the early church: *"Unus autem, non conversione divinitatis in carne, sed assumptione humanitatis in Deum"* (Ath., 33), in order to highlight the freedom of the Word in relation to the humanity it assumed. He placed all his emphasis on the Word. The Word is the *persona* who realizes salvation, and can do this as well beyond the humanity of Jesus. Here Zwingli simply adopted a christological line which is found even among the Alexandrian theologians. In fact, although strongly uniting the divine nature to the human nature, Cyril and John of Damascus admitted no less than that, in his being and his action, the divine nature infinitely surpassed the human nature.

Luther on the other hand refused to consider the *logos asarkos,* i.e., the Word, apart from his incarnation. It is in personal union with the humanity that the Word saves us. It is this union itself, says Luther, which saves us because this is what accomplishes the work of salvation.

Luther's themes can be clearly recognized here. First, to refuse all reflection on the Word of God apart from his incarnation, for that would be speculation, that would be to speak of God outside his incarnation, detached from the place where God wishes to be found, the humanity of Jesus Christ. Further, the saving work is not realized by the Word alone—occasionally united to the humanity—but by the Word and the humanity intimately linked. Luther carries this to the point of saying that only the suffering of God thus united to humanity guarantees the reality of our redemption. This last point shows clearly in Luther's work it is not a question of a coexistence of two natures, but of an intimate union, which requires the possession in common of a certain number of properties. We touch here on the conception of communication of attributes. Certainly, and very curiously, this expression does not appear during the Eucharistic Controversy, but later, when Luther is paying greater attention to the history of the church, it will play a much more important role, after 1530. However, the characteristics of this conception do appear in the course of the Eucharistic Controversy. When Luther speaks of the suffering of God in Jesus Christ, he is concerned with the communication of a human property to the divinity, and when he speaks of the ubiquity of Christ it is the other way round, because he then makes the divinity communicate one of its properties to the human nature.

All these considerations now permit us to clarify what Luther meant by the *person*. His conception is without a doubt based on the traditional doctrine of *enhypostasis*. There would be no unity of the person if there were not the activity of the Word, assuming a human nature. But the attention of Luther is fixed even more on the result of this personifying activity, i.e., the communion between the two natures. Congar observes this when he writes: "In many places Luther is content to say that divinity and the humanity are one unique person in Christ. That is what is required by tradition." [70] It is in fact this personal communion, this one concrete whole, which realizes salvation, even though it is based on the eternal design of God, who was made manifest by the *enhypostasis* and whom I know only through this.

One may ask to what extent the concrete whole formed in Jesus Christ by the union of God and humanity is not a new reality, as if the person of Jesus Christ was a kind of third entity added to the two natures,[71] as if a new *Wesen* (being) resulted from this union.[72]

One must recognize that certain of Luther's expressions in these texts lack the accuracy that we find in his Latin writings, in which he uses traditional language. A detailed study of his Latin writings must be added to the consideration of these texts on the Eucharist in order to get to the heart of what Luther meant.

His ideas seem to us to be as follows: the person of the Son unites in itself the two natures, but in this hypostatic union a history begins, an intimate communion which Luther calls personal, in which the divine nature participates in the human suffering, and reciprocally the human nature participates in the divine ubiquity. The divine *hypostasis* thus truly descends into the history of human beings. It does not remain beyond them as an unchanging concept, but participates entirely in the history of Jesus of Nazareth. This is why Luther uses the term *person* in a double sense: on the one hand, to designate the eternal author of the act of redemption founded on the *enhypostasis*, namely the *Logos;* on the other hand, to designate the *concretum* in which, on the basis of the *enhyposta-sis*, the Logos and humanity are intimately united for our salvation.

The Lordship of Christ and the Real Presence

In the critical exposition of Luther's christological thought so far we have concentrated on the incarnation, the doctrine of the two natures, and the concept of the person. The lordship of Christ is another aspect of this controversy and must engage our attention, not only because it is an important christological theme in its own right, but also because the controversy about the real presence pushed Luther in a particular direction to develop, a bit more than in his earlier writings, his way of understanding the lordship of Christ.

One can show that this same theme, the lordship of Christ, according to Luther, leads necessarily to the real presence, while according to his adversaries, it excluded it. It is quite evident that what is at issue here is different conceptions of the rule of Christ. Two lines of thought are to be discerned in Luther. On the one hand, he shows that the rule of Christ, seated at the right hand of God, does not confine him to one place, but makes him present everywhere; as God himself is present, thus Christ is present in the Eucharist. On the other hand, he develops the idea that the real presence is not opposed to the lordship of Christ—his glory, Luther calls it—but translates precisely the very mystery of this lordship which is soteriological in form and is exercised for the benefit of human beings. The first line of thought led Luther to the certainty of the real presence on the basis of his interpretation of "'the right hand of God"; the second line led him there by consideration of the nature of the rule of Christ, which is based on love. Let us examine these two lines of thought in turn.

You will notice how much, in the course of the controversy, Luther insists on the lordship of Christ "over all things." It is a theme which, although it does appear in his earlier writings, here becomes one of primary importance. It is no longer only the lordship of Christ over the church by his Word or by his work of salvation, but also the cosmic dimension of the rule of Christ. He bases this affirmation of the active rule of Christ over the cosmos on the epistle to the Ephesians (particularly 1:20ff. and 4:10). But he is opposed to his adversaries in the way in which he conceives of this cosmic rule. In conformity with the doctrinal tradition of the church, both sides confessed that Christ rules because he is seated at the right hand of God. But what is the right hand of God? That is where the divergence appeared. To the "local" conception, which Luther detected in his adversaries, he opposed a conception in which the right hand of God appeared as the active presence of God in the midst of creation. That is how the rule of Christ is exercised. This rule is free, for Christ is not bound by a heaven conceived as a precise place, nor by an institution, nor by human beings. That is why his Word and sacraments can be active in all places, and not only in the bosom of the Roman institution. That is also why Christians are free, for their liberty rests on the limitless rule of Christ.[73]

Even while affirming that the rule of Christ is exercised by his intimate presence in the heart of the smallest as well as the largest of his creatures, Luther has taken care, as we have already noticed, to affirm the sovereignty of God and of Christ in relation to the creatures. In exercising his rule, Christ is "incomprehensible and immeasurable, beyond and above all that exists and can exist." [74] Christ is thus not localized concretely in the hearts of his creatures. He is present in them and above them in sovereign fashion. All our usual categories for expressing a presence prove to be inadequate.

Luther developed his conception of ubiquity in opposition to adversaries in whose work he thought he detected a localization of heaven where the body of Christ would be found to be enclosed. That was certainly a weak point in the system of Oecolampadius and of Zwingli, still paying respect perhaps to a pre-Copernican view of the cosmos. The embarrassment of these two men on this subject shows that they had recognized the difficulty.

But the fundamental motive which moved them seems to lie elsewhere. They were anxious to maintain the comparison of the glorified humanity of Christ with ours. How could we hope for the resurrection of our bodies, Oecolampadius asks, if the humanity of Christ were not a security for us? But how could it be if it were so different from other creatures that it participated in the ubiquity of God? Was this not to destroy the humanity of Christ and to accentuate unilaterally his divinity? It is necessary to do justice to this motive of faith which is expressed by the adversaries of Luther, even if their cosmology is debatable.

On the other hand, however, it is also necessary to emphasize that the ubiquity of Christ does not make him into a timeless reality, stretching him out in some way to encompass the entire universe. The ubiquity signifies that Christ is beyond the creatures and is present with them in what could be called a unique "eschatological" fashion.

However, it is legitimate to ask whether Luther succeeded in preserving the two biblical themes: first, according to which Christ is the new Adam, truly human although he is glorified, the place where the new creation begins; and second, the theme of the Lord participating in the action of the Father in the world and present in a particular fashion when the gospel is preached and the sacraments administered. Has this second theme not to some extent brushed aside the first?

It is legitimate also to ask whether the theme of the real presence of Christ in the Eucharist really required the elaboration of a doctrine of ubiquity, seen from the point of view of a property attributed to the human nature, and by which Christ participated dynamically in the action and in the presence of God in the world, always at the risk that the humanity thus present be dissipated into a spiritualism, ultimately contrary to Luther's own intentions.

Whatever one may think about these critical questions, the first problem that Luther had to face with his affirmation of the ubiquity of Christ was the following: how to pass from the ubiquity of Christ, reigning with the Father, to his personal presence in the Eucharist? Why search for Christ in the Eucharist if one could find him anywhere? Such was the objection which Luther met. In order to reply to it, he distinguished two kinds of presence of Christ: a presence in itself and a presence for us.[75] The presence of Christ in itself or his general presence in the heart of creation is a reality, but says Luther, it cannot be comprehended there, and he does not wish that human beings should seek it there. We find here the theme already raised by the liberty of Christ in relation to his creatures: he passes through them much as sunlight passes through the window, Luther says. And he draws attention to idolatry to which the search for Christ in creation or in a particular creature could lead. To this general presence is added the personal presence, by which Christ freely binds himself to a particular place by the Word. In the same way as the Son, in order to become incarnate, had bound himself to a particular humanity, Christ binds himself to a specific place, such as the bread and the wine on the altar, for our salvation. This bond is effected by the Word, which makes the elements the place where Christ wishes to give himself to us.[76]

It must be noted that the function of the Word is not to make Christ descend in some way from a given place into the sacrament, to lead him in some way into the elements. He is found there already because he is mysteriously present in the heart of creation with the Father, in order to reign over it. The role of the Word is twofold. On the one hand, it reveals Christ as being already present. On the other hand, it binds Christ, for our sakes, to the bread and the wine. He allows himself to be taken by us in the elements. We no longer have to grope about to find him. He has bound himself to the bread and the wine. Thus the Word has made the general presence of Christ into a saving presence, and it turns human beings away from all searching for Christ which would not be a personal encounter, realized by faith in this place and this time.

We have started first of all with the rule and general presence of Christ in the heart of creation in order to come to this particular presence realized by the Word. Along slightly different lines, Luther inquires, not about the cosmic rule of Christ and the ubiquity which allows this real presence, but about the sovereignty of Christ included in all concepts of lordship. Is there not an unbridgable opposition between the place of Christ after the ascension—his glory—and his real presence in the Eucharist? *"Es reymet sich nicht"* (it doesn't fit), said his adversaries. In other words, even if the real presence was possible (and how could one deny God the possibility?), that was contrary to the glory which Christ knew after his passion and since his ascension. Here we touch again on one of the principal themes put forward indefatigably by Oecolampadius, Zwingli, and also Schwenckfeld. It would be too great a humiliation for the glorified Christ to be delivered up in this way to sinners in the bread and the wine of the Eucharist. The whole question lies there: What is the glory of Christ? Is it manifest by the distance from humanity, by the enjoyment of a well-deserved and peaceful rest or heavenly joy—a conception denounced by Luther with irony against his adversaries—or rather should we conceive of it as this inexhaustible love which drives Christ toward human beings? That is the opinion which Luther develops with ardor and profundity.[77] The glory of Christ—that which is the true mark of his lordship—is not to be throned above all creatures, to surpass them all in power and beatitude, but to love them with that love which drove the earthly Christ to the sacrifice of the cross and which drives him still, even now, toward human beings in order to be present with them and to save them. The lordship of Christ is thus directed toward salvation. It is without doubt one of Luther's most characteristic themes, to see the lordship of Christ essentially from the point of view of salvation. At the same time, this lordship understood in this way must be brought into relationship with the cross. For his adversaries, the rule of Christ comes after the passion; for Luther, the rule of Christ, as he understands it, continues to operate under the sign of the cross. Christ rules in such a way as to call forth the irony of the proud and the irritation of the wise. . . . He rules by offering himself to sinners in the bread and the wine of the Eucharist, just as once he ruled by the cross.

It is important to note here how often Luther has really linked the Christ with the elements. In the treatise on the Lord's Supper of 1528, we have brought out how he was concerned to show how much Christ was united with the bread and the wine, and to preserve this unity or identity against both the doctrine of transubstantiation and against the spiritualism of his protestant adversaries who separated the body and the blood of Christ from the elements.

The sacramental union binds Christ to the bread and wine, to the extent that even the unbeliever receives him. That is the famous and controversial *manducatio* of the unworthy, even of those who deny God, which roused the indignation of his adversaries. Luther repeatedly insists that there is an indissoluble union between the bread and wine on the one hand and the body and blood of Christ on the other. He goes so far as to say, "Whoever eats the bread, not only eats but even crushes with his teeth the body of Christ and chews it while chewing the bread." [78]

Although he affirms the identity between Christ and the elements, he strives no less to preserve the mystery of it. The essential affirmation is this: "How he is in the bread, we do not know and we do not have to know." [79] It is not necessary to think of this presence in a crude way, like wine in the barrel.[80] Contrary to what his adversaries thought they found in Luther, he does not teach a *localis inclusio*. As we have seen, he takes the Occamist conception of a *diffinitive* manner of presence; in fact it is for him only a way of showing that God knows many ways of letting a body coexist with another in one given place. According to Luther, the presence of Christ cannot be localized, even if, following the usual categories of thought, the prepositions *in* and *sub* employed by him seem as though they must refer to a localized presence. The principal difficulty with such a conception obviously resides in the fact of postulating a real human body being present in a way that is neither corporeal nor localized. We have already drawn attention to this point.

Hence we have described the two poles of the extraordinary tension which characterizes Luther's conception. On the one hand, the identification of Christ with the bread and wine is pressed as far as it will go: whoever eats the bread, eats the body. On the other hand, Luther affirms the sovereignty of Christ which is not "enclosed" within the elements.

It seems to us that this tension is constantly present. Hence, Luther speaks of the corporeal *manducatio* of the body and blood of Christ, and adds at once that this does not mean a particular kind of nourishment, because it is not we who assimilate him to our human reality, but it is the Christ who transforms us to his image.[81]

While Zwingli would make of the Eucharist a commemorative meal, by which Christians remember Christ, Luther sets forth Christ present as "cook, waiter, food, and drink," all together at the center of this supper.[82] While his Roman adversaries would dispose of the Christ in order to present him to God in a kind of repetition of the sacrifice of the cross, Luther recalls the sovereignty of Christ who has already accomplished everything himself and comes to distribute the benefits of his work, by offering his body and his blood as a sign of the forgiveness of sins.

It must be emphasized to what extent all the affirmations of Luther touching on the presence of Christ in the Eucharist are ultimately placed in an eschatological perspective. What happens now is a mystery, realized and attested by the Word. This Word is to be understood as a promise, which one should believe. This promise accords forgiveness of sins by the body and blood of Christ given with the elements. The mystery of this presence and the corporeal and spiritual gift which it offers to human beings are placed in the context of faith. These realities attested by the Word are not visible and tangible; they are contrary to reason and experience. But one day we shall see the Christ now hidden beneath the bread and the wine, as we shall see also the new being that he has prepared for our body and our soul.

Notes

1   The Eucharistic Controversy has occupied the attention of many scholars and resulted in a large literature. We note only the following: A. W. Dieckhoff, *Die evangelische Abendmahlslehre im Reformationszeitalter*, vol. 1 (Göttingen: 1854); K. Barth, "Ansatz und Absicht in Luthers Abendmahlslehre" (1923), in *Die Theologie und die Kirche*, vol. 2 (Zurich: 1968), pp. 26-75; W. Köhler, *Zwingli und Luther*, vol. 1 (Leipzig: 1924), vol. 2 (Leipzig: 1953); E. Sommerlath, "Luthers Lehre von der Realpräsenz im Abendmahl," in *Ihmelfestschrift* (Leipzig: 1928), pp. 320ff.; E. Sommerlath, "Das Abendmahl bei Luther," in *Vom Sakrament des Altars* (Leipzig: 1941), pp. 95-132; P. Althaus, "Luthers Abendmahlslehre," *Luther-Jahrbuch* (1929), pp. 2ff.; P. Gennrich, *Die Christologie Luthers im Abendmahlsstreit* (Königsberg: 1929); H. Gollwitzer, "Luthers Abendmahlslehre" in *Abendmahlsgemeinschaft?* (Munich: 1937), 2nd ed., pp. 94-121; E. Bizer, *Studien zur Geschichte des Abendmahlsstreites im 16. Jahrhundert* (Gütersloh: 1940); H. Grass, *Die Abendsmahlslehre bei Luther und Calvin: Eine kritische Untersuchung* (Gütersloh: 1940), 2nd ed. (1954); E. Roth, *Sakrament nach Luther* (Berlin: 1952); V. Vajta, *Die Theologie des Gottesdienstes bei Luther* (Göttingen: 1952); R. Prenter, *Spiritus Creator* (Munich: 1954); A. Peters, *Realpräsenz* (Berlin: 1960); Th. Süss, *La communion au corps du Christ* (Neuchatel: 1968); H. Hilgenfeld, *Mittelalterlichtraditionnelle Elemente in Luthers Abendmahlsschriften* (Zurich: 1971).

2   "La christologie de Luther," p. 476.

3   Gennrich, *Die Christologie Luthers in Abendmahlsstreit*, p. 3.

4   "It seems to me that God, the Holy Spirit, even, knows no more, nor wishes to know more, than Jesus" (WA 18, 529, 6).

5   WA 23, 71, 16; 23, 253, 12-35; 23, 283; 26, 261-262; 23, 249, 14: "They are the marks of the devil." Luther himself reports that his opponents have been able to find 77 places in *Dass diese Worte . . .* where he brackets them with the devil! (WA 26, 402, 18) "For it is not Doctor Carlstadt who is important to me. It is not him whom I regard, but that one who has taken possession of him and who speaks through his mouth" (WA 18, 139, 9). On this subject see W. Köhler, *Zwingli und Luther*, vol. 1, p. 495.

6   WA 19, 354; 375; 401; 503

7   *The Adoration of the Sacrament of the Holy Body of Christ* (WA 11, 431-456).

8   *Against the Heavenly Prophets of Images and Sacraments* (WA 18, 37-214).

9   WA 9, 200, 15: "For Christ has laid down his power and his might in the sacraments, that one may seek and find the same there, according to the word, 'This is my body, given for you, for the forgiveness of sins.'"

10   On this subject see Köhler, *Zwingli und Luther;* J.V. Pollet, "Zwing-
      lianisme," in *Dictionnaire de théologie catholique.*
11   This reference is to the edition of Zwingli's works edited by E. Egli,
      G. Finsler, and W. Köhler (Leipzig: 1905).
12   On the subject of Oecolampadius, see E. Staehlin, *Das theologische
      Lebenswerk Oekolampads* (Leipzig: 1939).
13   "Sermon on the sacrament of the body and blood of Christ, against
      the spirit of the Enthusiasts" (*WA* 19, 482-523).
14   "Heaven and earth is his sack; as the corn fills the sack, so he fills
      all things" (*WA* 19, 493, 9).
15   *WA* 23, 38-320. We will refer to this as *Dass diese Worte.* . . .
16   Zwingli, 5, 763-794.
17   Köhler, vol. 1, p. 479, n. 2: "The whole christological exposition is
      conditioned by Luther's christology and is fundamentally far re-
      moved from Zwingli."
18   *WA* 23, 38-320
19   *WA* 23, 11
20   "For in him, God is not only present in his essence *(wesenlich),* as
      in all other human beings, but he also dwells corporeally in him,
      so that there is one person, God and a human being. And although
      I can say of all creatures, 'God is there,' or 'God is in that one,' yet
      I cannot say of them, 'That is God himself.' But of Christ, faith not
      only affirms that God is in him, but also, 'Christ is God himself.'
      Who kills Christ has killed the Son of God, God and the Lord of
      glory himself" (*WA* 23, 141, 24). Again, Luther says, "The whole
      fulness of deity dwells bodily in him, as St. Paul says in Col. 2:9.
      Thus outside Christ, there is neither God nor deity" (*WA* 23, 139,
      27). Hence, to deny the presence of Christ in his humanity would
      be tantamount to denying the very presence of God."
21   "So that where the right hand of God is found, there necessarily, the
      body and blood of Christ are to be found" (*WA* 23, 143, 32).
22   "If the body of Christ is in all places, well then, I may devour it and
      drink it in all the inns and cafés, glasses and pots, and there is then
      no difference between my table and the table of the Lord" (*WA* 23,
      149, 16).
23   "But the glory of our God is that he humiliates himself for our sake,
      descending to the deepest depths, into the flesh, into the bread, into
      our mouth, heart, and belly. And also for our sake he suffers, so that
      he is handled without honor, both on the cross and on the altar"
      (*WA* 23, 157, 30).
24   "Where in the Scripture the words 'flesh' and 'spirit' are set in oppo-
      sition to each other, the word 'flesh' cannot refer to the flesh of
      Christ, but to the old flesh, which is born of flesh" (*WA* 23, 193,
      35).
25   "I would gladly hear why the flesh of Christ should be of no use
      when it is eaten in the sacrament bodily, but quite otherwise when
      it is conceived bodily and born, when it lies in the manger, or is
      taken in the arms, or when it sits at table at supper, when it hangs

on the cross, etc. All these are outward manifestations and uses of his flesh in the same way as when it was eaten. What is better, that it be in the body of the mother, or in the bread and the mouth? If the one is no use, then the other can be of no use either. If useful is the one, it must also be of value in the other" (*WA* 23, 177, 25).

26   As examples, Luther draws on the birth of the child by Mary or the showing of Christ to the shepherds: all that would have been useless, even impossible, without the Word and faith (*WA* 23, 185-187).

27   "Whether the flesh of Christ is eaten bodily or spiritually, it is the same body, the same spiritual flesh, the same imperishable food, which in the Eucharist is eaten bodily with the mouth and spiritually with the heart" (*WA* 23, 203, 31).

28   God's flesh cannot be "cut up, divided, torn apart. It must be conceived, born, carried, eaten, and believed in one totality" (*WA* 23, 251, 32).

29   See also *WA* 23, 203, 14; 251; 21: "The flesh of Christ, full of divinity, of goodness, of life, and of eternal happiness."

30   "Death certainly tasted him once and tried to tear him apart and devour him. It could not, but rather the flesh of Christ tore open the belly and the throat of death in more than a hundred thousand places, so that the teeth of death were scattered and flew every which way, while the flesh of Christ remained living" (*WA* 23, 243, 31).

31   We cannot follow Gennrich, *Die Christologie Luthers im Abendmahlsstreit,* that "By its union with the divinity in the resurrection, the body of Christ is elevated above all creatures, as the humanity of the victorious Savior over death and sin, and is raised to the right hand of God. So that the spiritual flesh of Christ, which belongs to this elevated humanity, cannot be a creature" (p. 77).

32   Wendel, *Calvin,* p. 265.

33   "Our Enthusiasts, giddy and fickle in spirit, think that nothing can be spiritual that has to do with the material, and they claim that the flesh is useless" (*WA* 23, 193, 29).

34   "For even the devil, death, sin, and all manner of maledictions are no more than useful aids, when they are presented to us and we believe them within the framework of God's Word. Now death can only be useful to me, in body and soul, if I have with it the Word of Christ. . . . Should not then the body of Christ, which in itself is full of life, happiness, and God, be useful to me through his Word, at least as useful as death, sin, and the devil?" (*WA* 23, 259, 24).

35   "Since this poor old rotting sack, our body, also has the hope of resurrection from the dead and eternal life, it too must become spiritual, and all that is carnal in it must be destroyed and swallowed up" (*WA* 23, 205, 11). See also *WA* 23, 229, 27; 243, 31; 255, 16; 259.

36   "For in this eating, let me take a crude example: It is as when a wolf devours a sheep, and the sheep was such a strong meat that it

turned the wolf into a sheep! So it is with us, when we eat the body of Christ, spiritually and physically, the food is so strong that it transforms us into him, and makes persons who are mortal, sinful, and carnal, into persons who are spiritual, holy, and living. That is what we are already, but it is all hidden under faith and hope, not yet visible. In the last day, we shall see it" (WA 23, 205, 17). But it still remains true that the physical effects of the Eucharist are effective only by faith" (WA 23, 251, 21).

37 WA 23, 131, 2, 621. Although Luther did not know directly the writings of Gregory of Nyssa, his thoughts on the Eucharist are very close to those of this Father.

38 A little farther on he writes, "And even if it happened without the Word, the Word would still be necessary because it contains life and happiness" (WA 23, 267, 26).

39 "I will not allow anyone to separate the body of Christ from the Word for me" (WA 23, 257, 15).

40 WA 26, 241-509. Translator's note: The author has used the French edition, *Oeuvres de Luther: Labor et Fides*, vol. 6 (Geneva: 1964), pp. 13-185. Although for this translation the original German has been consulted throughout, the quotations are usually translated directly from the French.

41 "Beware! Beware of *alleosis*, it is the mask of the devil!" (WA 26, 319, 33) "Dame reason, the grandmother of *alleosis*" (WA 26, 321, 19).

42 See also WA 26, 342.

43 "We say that God is not such a being so extended, long, broad, thick, high, deep, but a supernatural being who cannot be fully comprehended or measured, who is, at the same time, totally within every grain and also beyond and outside all creatures. That is why there is no question of comprehending him here, for a body is much too vast for the divinity and indeed thousands of divinities could be held in one body. But also, a body is much too small to be able to encompass and contain any divinity. Nothing so small, that God is not smaller; nothing so large, that God is not larger; nothing so short, that God is not shorter; nothing so long, that God is not longer; nothing so broad, that God is not broader; nothing so narrow, that God is not narrower, and so on. He is an ineffable being, beyond and greater than all that human beings can describe or think" (WA 26, 339, 33).

44 "There we are with the humanity in a land different than when it went upon the earth, namely beyond and above all creatures, only in the divinity. . . . However, essentially it [the humanity] cannot be God, but since it reaches the essential God and holds to it above all creatures, and since it is there that God is, it must at least be God according to the person and thus be in all places where God is" (WA 26, 341, 4).

45 See also WA 26, 421, 7.

46 WA 26, 345, 18ff.

47 *WA* 26, 346, 35.
48 "It is his humanity, it alone, unlike any other, which clings in this way to God" (*WA* 26, 340, 38). "We know that Scripture places this unique human being, and no other, at the right hand of God" (*WA* 26, 349, 19).
49 On this subject see *WA* 26, 439, n. 2.
50 In this connection, it must be noted that, according to Luther, the bread and the wine are not the only privileged places in that which concerns the body and blood of Christ, really present. In a treatise of 1526, which is a sermon on the sacrament of the body and blood of Christ in opposition to the Enthusiasts, he places the water of Baptism, the preaching of the gospel as a spoken word (i.e., a concrete element), and the heart of human beings on the same level as we have seen him place the bread and wine of the Eucharist. An examination of his other writings confirms that this is so, even if he is mostly concerned with the bread and wine of the Eucharist.
51 Prenter, *Spiritus Creator*, p. 269: "The concrete signs of revelation are for the time between the ascension and his second coming the earthly and bodily way of existence of the humanity of Christ" (p. 269).
   Gennrich, *Die Christologie Luthers*, p. 28: "The humanity of Christ is, for Luther, not only the man Jesus of Nazareth, but all that represents a concretization of the infinite in the finite and the bodily, such as the 'virgin's womb,' the 'manger,' the cross, over and above the Scripture and the Apostles. All these outward and material things are, like the man Jesus, bearers of the divine Word, in which the eternal *Logos* is hidden and through which it works." "Now we have seen how, for Luther, the humanity of Christ, as a concrete fact, expressed in bodily form, stands in direct line with those 'outward signs' by which God reveals himself to human beings" (p. 146).
   Nilsson, *Simul:* "On the one hand, the humanity *(Menschlichkeit)* of Christ appears to signify, not only the historical and biological being of the man Jesus, which took form in a human body, but all of what Luther calls *indumenta Dei*, the Word, Baptism, and the Eucharist, for it is in these human things that God shows himself and acts toward us. Wherever such *species Dei* appear, they rightly indicate the humanity of Christ. On the other hand, Luther is never in any doubt of what he means by the humanity of Christ, even though the concept has a many-sided content and can refer to a multitude of *externa res*. In fact, all these have in common that they are a means of expression for the incarnation of the Word. It is only in the Word and by the Word that things and human signs can be called divine. In this way, it is possible for Luther to see all *apparitiones*, all *species Dei*, included and summed up *in homine Christo*" (p. 155). "The term 'the humanity of Christ' is the representative term for all of this divine incarnation, this Word which ceaselessly becomes human" (p. 156). See also p. 157.

52   Peters, *Realpräsenz*, p. 72; "Luther's Christuszeugnis," p. 82.

53   *WA* 23, 267, 32

54   *WA* 23, 268, 3

55   *WA* 19, 484, 13. Cf. 19, 389, 33: "The ways that God takes are ways of pure folly and insanity" (*WA* 19, 389, 33).

56   See Prenter, *Schöpfung und Erlösung*, p. 328.

57   *WA* 23, 145, 13

58   See Seeberg, *Dogmengeschichte*, vol. 3, pp. 789-791; Weber, *Grundlagen der Dogmatik*, vol. 2, p. 151, n. 1.

59   Congar, "La christologie de Luther," p. 478: "This is precisely the point which holds the passionate attention of Luther, and, one can say, his fervent religious intention. If he is eager to combat Zwingli and his *alleosis*, it is that in his eyes not only is the Chalcedonian Definition at stake—that discussion would not have moved him so much—but the reailty of our redemption is at stake. St. Athanasius argued against Arius in the following terms: if Christ is not truly God, he does not make us divine. St. Anselm added: the Christ can only satisfy if he is human, but he can only offer an adequate satisfaction if he is God. Luther never ceased to assert, if God did not die, we are not saved; it is not sufficient to say that the human nature suffered. That would make a paltry Savior! It is necessary to consider in Jesus the unique person of his divinity, both mortal and immortal. Not only is redemption negated if Christ is not truly God, as Arius imagined, but it is only effective if one can say, in all truth, that God suffered, that he was crucified."

60   "The divinity can neither suffer nor die. That is true. But, nonetheless, as in Christ the divinity and humanity are one person, Scripture attributes to the divinity all the characteristics of the humanity, because of this personal union" (*WA* 26, 320, 31).

61   *WA* 26, 344, 28ff.

62   Seeberg, *Luthers Theologie*, vol. 2, p. 332: "The bodily ascension here becomes a symbol *(Wahrzeichen)* of that omnipotence and omnipresence of the power of Christ."

63   Prenter, *Schöpfung und Erlösung*, p. 327: "Jesus Christ, in his true humanity, with all the limitations of a created being, is present in the Word of promise and the signs. The limits of his created being in space and time are not annulled, not replaced by an omnipresence (ubiquity) which belongs only to the creator. The union of the natures only indicates that the humanity of Jesus is bound up with the creating Word of God in an indissoluble union, so that this creating Word can make the humanity of Jesus present where and when he will. In reality, that also is what Luther teaches with his doctrine of ubiquity."

64   *WA* 26, 341, 9

65   Seeberg, *Luthers Theologie*, vol. 2, p. 359: "There is no doubt that Luther made every effort to render the correct catholic doctrine of the church, according to which the man Christ acquired his person-

ality from the person of the Son." P. 365: "The humanity acquires its person from the divinity."

F. Brunstaedt, *Theologie der lutherischen Bekenntnisschriften,* p. 41, characterizes Luther's christology in this way: "The basic idea of Luther was the unity of the person, which is the dominant note in *prolepsis* christology, or, if you wish to speak in terms of the history of dogma, Alexandrian doctrine."

66 Congar, *"La christologie de Luther,"* p. 473, 480.
67 Brunstaedt, *Theologie der lutherischen Bekenntnisschriften,* pp. 36ff.
68 See also WA 30, 3, 160.
69 WA 26, 500ff. In Luther's German, the last sentence reads, *"Und das solcher mensch sey wahrhafftig Gott als eine ewige unzurtrennliche person aus Gott und mensch worden."*
70 "La christologie de Luther," p. 477, n. 80.
71 Peters, "Luthers Christuszeugnis," p. 4: "According to Luther's controversial writings and confessions, written in the German language, it could appear that the 'I' of Christ was, as in Theodore of Mopsuestia, like a third entity, which was born of the coming together of the divine and human natures, as though Jesus Christ had become 'an eternal indivisible person, formed from God and humanity.'" See also WA 26, 501, 30.
72 "A new, united being" (WA 26, 443, 29).
73 WA 18, 211ff.
74 WA 23, 133, 26
75 WA 19, 492ff.; 23, 151ff.
76 "The power to consecrate comes not from our word as such nor from any kind of valid office, but from the Word of God who binds his Word to ours" (WA 26, 285). On this whole question, see Vajta, *Die Theologie des Gottesdienstes bei Luther,* pp. 182ff.
77 E.g., WA 23, 155; 26, 436.
78 WA 26, 442, 32: "Those who seize this bread, seize the body of Christ, and those who eat this bread eat the body of Christ; those who crush this bread with their teeth or with their tongue crush with their teeth and tongue the body of Christ."
79 WA 23, 87, 29
80 WA 23, 145, 34
81 WA 23, 203, 26. See also WA 26, 442, 35ff.: "But it remains always true that no one sees, touches, eats, or chews the body of Christ as one eats and tastes other, visible flesh."
82 WA 23, 271, 8

5

Change and Continuity
in Luther's Christology

The Impact of the Eucharistic Controversy
on Luther's Christology

At the beginning of the chapter devoted to the Eucharistic Controversy, we remarked that the controversy had only made clear the fundamental differences which already existed between the christology of Luther and that, for example, of Zwingli. That was to say that this christology had been already worked out, more or less clearly, when the controversy began. One must therefore be very careful in speaking of changes that took place in the course of the controversy. We are not dealing with fundamental modifications in the christological view of the reformer, but only changes of perspective, new themes appearing without upsetting the main line of his thought.

It is first of all noticeable that this controversy has pushed Luther to deal more specifically with christology as such, and particularly the person of Christ,[1] as well as to describe the union of the two natures from the point of view of the communication of attributes.

In the course of the controversy, Luther constantly returns to the theme of the *unio personalis* and of the one being which is Christ. From now on, he is no longer content simply to say that the humanity and divinity form one and the same person, but he will explain more precisely what that means for the humanity and the divinity thus united to each other. In this he links himself to traditional christology.

His christology not only becomes more technical, as we shall see in relation to the *Disputationes*, but all his attention is directed now toward the indivisible character of the two natures, the *indivisus* of the Chalcedonian Definition. Of course, he had emphasized this already in his earlier writings, such as the sermons on the church. Already in those sermons, we had seen the image of a man wounded in the leg, wherein suffering is attributed to the whole man. Luther uses this comparison again to defend the unity of the person of Jesus Christ against Zwingli's *alleosis*. In these sermons, Luther spoke more than once of the suffering of God in the concrete person of Jesus Christ. Nonetheless, he held more firmly to the separation of the two natures. He criticizes those who ascribe to the one nature that which belongs only to the other. But after the Eucharistic Controversy, Luther binds the human nature so tightly to the divine nature that it shares its ubiquity. Luther's enemies did not miss this development. In a letter of April 30, 1527, addressed to Zwingli, Bucer draws attention to Luther's sermon on Heb. 1:1-12, in which he asks that the two natures and their different properties be clearly distinguished.[2]

The change is shown again on another point. In his earlier works, Luther loves to say that it is necessary for us to rise from the humanity of Christ to his divinity. We have drawn attention to this point in relation to the sermons of 1519 and to the church postils of 1522. Luther is opposed both to that speculation which thought to reach God without passing through Christ, and to that spirituality of the imitation which places such emphasis on the humanity of Christ considered as an example that it succeeded in neglecting his divinity. Now, by insisting in this way on the necessity of rising from the humanity to the divinity, Luther himself, by separating the two natures, risked considering the incarnation a little after the manner of the Platonists, as the place where the idea is made known, but a place which it is necessary to leave behind in order to go on to the idea itself. In the course of the Eucharistic Controversy, Luther realized the danger that his earlier idea could present. Some years later, he therefore wrote, still under the shock of the dispute with Zwingli: "The Enthusiasts and Zwingli separate the divinity from the humanity of Christ. They teach a consideration only of the divinity and not of the humanity. But I believe in the Son of God in such a way that I do not tear him apart from the Son born of Mary. My faith is not only bound to the Son or God or to his divinity, but also to him of whom we say, he was born of Mary, who is the same as he who suffered for me. I do not want to know of any other Son of God than the one who was born from the Virgin Mary. I believe that the Son of God is wrapped up in the humanity and is one person, so that I must not separate the one from the other and say, that the humanity is of no value, only the divinity. . . . Many teachers have so taught, and I myself was such a teacher not long ago, excluding the humanity and thinking that I would do well to separate the divinity of Christ from his humanity. This is what once many great theologians did by flying from the humanity to the divinity of Christ, attaching themselves uniquely to this divinity with the idea that it was not necessary to know the humanity of Christ. But we must rise to the divinity of Christ and hold to it in such a manner as not to abandon the humanity of Christ, in order to arrive at the true divinity of Christ. Otherwise we fall from the ladder. Therefore you must know nothing of a God, nor of a Son of God, of whom it cannot be said, 'Born of the Virgin Mary,' and become human, as the Christian faith teaches. . . . And if someone wishes to separate him from the Son of God and make a wall between the Son of God and the Son born of the Virgin Mary, receive not that preaching and do not listen to it, but say: 'I know of no God or Son of God other than that of whom the Christian faith speaks when it says, "I believe in Jesus Christ" ' " (WA 33, 154-155).[3]

This text shows clearly the change of perspective. From the Eucharistic Controversy onward, Luther avoids saying that it is necessary to raise oneself from human nature to God. The only God that he wishes to know now is the one who is present in the flesh, that is, the concrete person of Jesus of Nazareth, in whom one can no longer dissociate the humanity from the divinity.

According to Luther, the ubiquity of Christ is based on the union of the two natures. The Son does not abandon the human nature, but makes it participate in his omnipresence. We have seen how much Luther develops this theme in the course of the Eucharistic Controversy. Now this is something new in comparison with the earlier writings. Of course, he emphasized, from his commentary of Rom. 1:3-4 onward, that the Son having assumed humanity meant that from his incarnation on, this humanity had acquired a true participation in the divine life and implicitly also in certain properties of God. Of course, one finds here and there, passages in which Luther underlines the participation of the humanity in the reign of

Christ.[4] But the explicit affirmation of ubiquity is absent from such passages, either because Luther had not yet elaborated this doctrine or because he had not felt the need to develop this theme until the Eucharistic Controversy. Even the earliest writings of the Controversy scarcely mention it. One of the first references appears in the treatise of 1523, *Vom Anbeten des Sakraments,* in which it is a question of the body which is found everywhere, *an allen Enden,* an idea which is going to be developed more and more in the course of the Controversy.

While the concept of ubiquity is developed more and more clearly, one can, it seems, discern a certain recoil on the part of the reformer from his insistence on the true humanity of Christ that one finds in the earlier writings of the Controversy. Not that he ever put in question the *vere homo* of the creed of Chalcedon. He links himself explicitly to that in the confession of faith with which the treatise on the Eucharist of 1528 ends, and he will defend it to the end against the Marcionites and other heretics who question the real humanity of Christ. We shall draw attention again later to this. In his commentaries and in his sermons, he will speak not only of the truly human body of Christ,[5] but also of his emotions and of his sufferings,[6] of his fear in the face of death.[7] In his 1544 commentary on Isaiah 53, which we shall be looking at again shortly, he also describes the Christ abandoned. He is both the king of glory and the one who submits to death and hell, confronted by the wrath and even the hatred of God.[8] One cannot maintain that the emphasis which is so poignant in the commentary on Psalm 22 in the *Operationes* will not be found again after the Eucharistic Controversy. In fact, the theology of the cross is a theme which dominated Luther all his life.

However, a certain development takes form in the sermons on the church in relation to Luther's affirmations on the human limitations of Christ. In these sermons, Luther thinks that Christ could be ignorant of certain things. In relation to Matt. 20:23, he points out that this passage concerns the "pure" humanity. The word "pure" has disappeared by the edition of 1528. In that of 1540, John 14:28 is no longer cited in order to characterize the humanity of Christ. We have seen how in the church postils Luther had striven to conceive of a certain evolution in the level of the humanity of Christ, basing this on Luke 2:40-52. This interpretation by Luther continues into the 1540 edition. But as J. Köstlin has noted, the affirmations in the home postils which refer to the infant Jesus take another direction.[9] There it is a question of Jesus, our good God, submitting to his mother, not because he must, but because he really wished to submit. In the conversations in the Temple with the scribes and Pharisees, the child Jesus "pretended that he had learned from his mother what he said [to the Pharisees]." [10] But in fact it was a pretense, because he knew everything since his birth.

We have already observed that another change had taken place in the course of the controversy: it concerned the attention given to the cosmic lordship of Christ. The earlier writings presented Christ from the point of view of soteriology proper, recalling the way in which he had saved human beings, his link with justification by faith, his lordship over the church by the Word and sacraments. It is a point of view which of course continues until the very end in the work of Luther. But the lordship of Christ now takes on a cosmic dimension. Christ is associated with the creative work of the Father, not only as the second person of the Trinity, but as a human being seated at the right hand of God. The Eucharistic Controversy drove Luther to broaden this perspective. For the believer, Christ is not only the lord of the church and the Savior of each individual believer, but, thanks to this activity of Christ in the church and in faith, the history of the world unfolds with the hidden participation of Christ and can be understood as the result of this participation.

In general, one can say that after the controversy the lordship of Christ is emphasized more and more, to the detriment, it would seem, of his role as *exemplar* or the new Adam. We have pointed out that in the writings before the controversy, Christ was both, on the one hand, the Lord, the Son made flesh, who saved human beings by the Word and sacraments, and on the other hand, the new human being in whom appeared, through the cross and resurrection, the image of a new reality, to which we must be conformed. Equally, one will have noted the comparison of Christ and the saints in the sermon on the Eucharist of 1519. In contrast to this, in the controversy with Oecolampadius on the Eucharist, Luther insists on the difference between the glorified Christ and the saints.[11] We shall never be one person with God. Christ is present in the Eucharist, but the elect are not (Oecolampadius had suggested they were) in order to show the weakness of Luther's position. From now on, the saints are separated from him. Their souls remain, waiting for the last day.[12]

The humanity of Christ is now seen more and more from the point of view of the sacrament, as bearer of grace, rather than as *exemplar* to which we must be conformed. Of course it would be wrong to think that the perspective of Christ as *exemplar* disappeared from this point on. In the sermon of 1527 on Gen. 1:24ff., for example, Luther designates Christ as "the heavenly Adam, to whom we must be conformed." [13] But one will note that, in contrast to the earlier writings, the accent is placed more on the glorified aspect of this humanity than on the way from the cross leading up to the resurrection. Christ is the first heavenly human being, in whom everything that he says, does, and suffers becomes heavenly, and he also makes us, who are "incorporated" in him by faith, into heavenly persons.[14] More than in the past, the humanity of Christ is now described from the point of view of his eschatological accomplishment. As for the theme of the conformity of Christians to Christ, that passes into the background, without quite disappearing. Considerations of the redemptive work of Christ and of the flesh of Christ take on much greater importance and, without denying the *vere homo*, the uniqueness of Christ begins to appear much more strongly.

Despite the changes that we have indicated, the fundamental themes of the christology remain. We shall mention three briefly, because we shall have occasion to return to them.

What remains above all is the bond between Christ and justification by faith. Christ is our righteousness, the gift of God for our salvation and not the example of the judge. This theme dominated Luther's thought already when he combatted the spirituality of the imitation of Christ. It is on this point that he opposed Carlstadt. In the next chapter we shall see with what vigor he continues thus to associate Christ with justification by faith, placing him under the gospel and not under the law. Here we are dealing with a truly permanent aspect of his thought.

In the second place, the theme of the revelation of God in Christ continues to dominate Luther's thought. One can even say that this theme is more strongly emphasized as a result of the Eucharistic Controversy, and in this sense, that Luther now refuses to "rise up" from the humanity to the divinity, and holds only on to God who is become flesh and who remains bound to this flesh for all eternity.

Finally, we think that the theme of the theology of the cross continues. Admittedly, it is only a kind of corollary to the theme of the revelation of God in Jesus Christ, because it underlines the tension between the majesty of God and the weakness of the place where he wishes to meet with us. But it is certainly this theme which leads Luther to reject a concept of the lordship of Christ in which this lordship is situated in his glory, far from the weakness of the flesh and from human sorrow. Of course one can get the impression that a certain deification of human nature tends to threaten the basic principle of the theology of the cross, which affirms the revelation of God hidden in the weakness of the humanity, but not transforming this human weakness into the divine glory. Nonetheless, in the course of the Eucharistic Controversy itself, the dominant role of faith and the Word and hence the hidden presence of God in Christ and in the Eucharist is emphasized. What is meant here is less the historic incarnation of Christ itself, in relation to which a dangerous evolution seems to be effectively outlined in the sense of the communication of attributes, than the presence and work of Christ in the Eucharist. They are placed under the cross and not in glory, they must be attested by the Word, until that day when we see Christ face to face.

The Revelation of God in Jesus Christ and the Mystery of the Hidden God: The Treatise *De servo arbitrio* and Its Place in Luther's Theology

All along our analyses of the different writings of Luther have underlined the importance for him of the centrality of the fact for him that in Jesus Christ it is God himself who offers himself to human beings, revealing the saving plan he has for us. We have noted the constant exhortation of Luther to hold to God present and revealed in Jesus Christ and to turn away from all speculations about God comprehended apart from Christ. But we must also, with Luther, emphasize that the presence of God in the humanity of Christ is a hidden presence, accessible only to faith.

At the same period when Luther was so strongly opposed to Zwingli and all those who, according to him, separated the divinity of Christ from his humanity, he wrote, in 1525, one of his most important writings, the treatise, *De servo arbitrio*.[15] It is written in opposition to Erasmus and his answer to the question of free will. In the course of the discussion, Luther makes a number of statements about the hidden God, whom he distinguishes radically from the revealed God. It is scarcely possible to pass over in silence the difficult problems posed by this text, and we cannot deal with them without giving here an exhaustive treatment of this question which has so often been worked at by Luther scholars.

Let us recall first of all the principal statements made by the young Luther on the subject of the revelation of God in Jesus Christ. We have seen that he never ceases to oppose certain mystics and speculative theologians on this point. He reproaches the mystics for wanting to approach the *Verbum increatum,* that is, God separated from the incarnation. As for the theologians whom he designates "speculative," they reason about God and his properties, elaborating their ideas of God, sometimes on the basis of his works in creation, sometimes from reason itself which postulates a supreme being and thereby attributes a certain number of properties to him.

Of course, Luther did not deny that natural human beings have some knowledge of God based on the works and the law of God— we shall return to that. In fact, this knowledge, as the apostle Paul shows, has not led to the adoration of God, but to idolatry. That is why God chose another way to reveal himself to human beings in order to save them. He presents himself to them, hiding his glory under the weakness of the cross. Basing himself on Exod. 33:18-23, Luther says that it is necessary for us to see the *back* of God, that is to say, in his weakness, and not to see his *face* directly, that is to say his glory.[16]

Instead then of recognizing God on the basis of his works, a possibility which has not led human beings to true worship and which is now in fact lost to us, and instead of serving him by works, it is necessary hereforth to find him in the sufferings of Christ and to serve him by accepting the sufferings of the Christian life itself. Thus the theology of the cross is found to be opposed to the theology of glory.

It is characteristic of God to act *sub contraria specie,* that is to say, to be powerful in weakness, to rise in humiliation, reveal himself by hiding himself. We have constantly emphasized this in relation to the humiliated Christ who is at the same time the lord of glory, as for example in connection with Luther's defense of the real presence in the Eucharist, where the lordship of Christ is affirmed precisely when he allows himself to be present in the humble realities of the bread and the wine.

It must be shown that the principle of the theology of the cross not only dominates the works of the young Luther, but that it is found to the end in his works. We shall return to this in analyzing his commentary on Isaiah 53, which is dated 1544.

It is not difficult to find support for Luther's affirmations on the subject of the hiddenness of God. "Truly thou art a God who hidest thyself" (Isa. 45:15) was clear enough to Luther. The Nominalist tradition had particularly insisted on the "hiddenness" *(abscondite)* [17] when it emphasized his freedom in relation to his creatures, in connection with the reason and the laws which human beings wished to impose on him. One often finds Luther in agreement with such a concept of God. In fact, he also emphasizes, as we have seen, the freedom of God, who freely chose the incarnation as a way of salvation. But with Luther, the essential emphasis is not on God apart from his revelation, but on his hiddenness within the framework of this revelation. That appears to come clearly from his working out of the theology of the cross. God is hidden there *sub contraria specie,* because he neither wishes nor can be known here below directly, face to face, but only indirectly by the faith which clings to the Word announcing to human beings the hidden presence of God in the weakness of the humanity of Christ. From such a perspective, it is evident that the God who hides himself is the same as the one who reveals himself. He hides himself precisely in order to be accessible to human beings in a way that will lead to their salvation, so as not to crush them by his majesty seen directly, and yet be present in his majesty in a way that is close to humanity. Thus Luther will speak of God's "alien" work *(opus alienum),* by which he hides himself, but which he effects by virtue of his proper work *(opus proprium),* which is truly revelation. [18]

In the name of such a conception and because he has himself experienced the terrifying approach to God by a person without Christ, Luther never ceases to warn against speculation. In connection with this there appears more and more the strong feeling of apprehension about what he calls the "naked God." [19]

It is God, not clothed in flesh, not incarnate, presenting himself in the nakedness of his majesty, in this light, which crushes human beings. Now this light will only be accessible to us in eternity. We have noted in the church postils that it is the same light as that hidden in the humanity of Christ. Now God makes himself actual and hides himself in the humanity of Christ, then in the outward signs of the bread and the wine, of the water and the Word, as we have just seen in connection with the Eucharistic Controversy.

It is then necessary to turn us from the naked God, says Luther, from this God who is also *Deus vagus,* that is to say, omnipresent and incomprehensible, in order to bring us near to God where he becomes actual for us, in the humanity of Christ and in the outward signs.

But the passage in the treatise *De servo arbitrio* which deals with *Deus absconditus* (the hidden God) indisputably goes in a quite different direction. And it is to this passage that we must now turn.[20]

Luther's thoughts on *Deus absconditus* take as their starting point the exegesis of Ezek. 33:11: "As I live, says the Lord God, I have no pleasure in the death of the wicked, but that the wicked turn from his way and live." Erasmus used this passage to support his view of the free will of human beings, who are called to turn toward life. But according to Luther, he transformed the text into an exhortation and confused the gospel with the law.[21] According to Luther's interpretation, it is rather a word of the gospel, i.e., a promise of grace addressed to sinful human beings, conscious of their sin and fearful of the judgment. Luther points out that Ezekiel does not say, "God has no pleasure in the sin of man," but "I have no pleasure in the death of the wicked [the sinner]" (*WA* 18, 683, 35). It is in this way that human beings afflicted with sin are consoled.

But it is here that the fundamental problem arises: How can one reconcile the saving intention of God thus affirmed with the fact that human beings are damned? Erasmus attributed it to the free will and thus resolved the problem. Since Luther denies the free will, the question posed concerns the unity of God. Erasmus asks whether this means that God is divided within himself. Is it the same God who deplores the death of his people who also determines this death? It is this question which leads Luther to introduce the concept of *Deus absconditus,* an expression which he will use in two ways, and to distinguish a double will of God. "It is necessary to discuss God or the will of God which is preached, revealed, offered, adored in a different way *(aliter)* from the way in which one discusses God who is not preached, not revealed, not offered, not adored. To the extent that God hides himself and does not wish to be known by us, he does not concern us. For it is truly said: *Quae supra nos, nihil ad nos* (What is beyond us is nothing to us) (*WA* 18,

685, 3ff.). The God who is neither preached nor revealed is the *Deus absconditus in majestate* (God hidden in majesty) (*WA* 685, 21).

One is struck by the force with which Luther distinguishes the two wills of God, even puts them in opposition to each other, and to a certain extent introduces a double reality in God. There is on the one hand, the God of the gospel, the God of revelation, of preaching, over whose weakness the Antichrist can vaunt himself (*WA* 18, 685, 8). It is this God who is known and who enters into relation with us *(commercium, oblatus)*. It is the God who is clothed with flesh, as with a garment, in order not to crush us and who enters into the situation of the death of sinners in order to set them free.

But on the other hand, there is God himself *(Deus ipse)* who must be distinguished from his Word. It is the God above whom none can rise, for "All things are in subjection to his powerful hand" (*WA* 18, 685, 13). "God does many things which he does not reveal to us by his Word. He desires many things also which the Word does not reveal to us that he wishes them. It is thus that he wishes not the death of a sinner, according to his Word; but he wishes it according to his inscrutable will" (*WA* 18, 685, 27). This is the God whose will is "inscrutable and incomprehensible" (*WA* 18, 685, 32), who does not wish to relate to us and does not wish that we should seek any such relation with him, because it is necessary "to leave him in his majesty and in his essence" (*WA* 18, 685, 15).

The ideas that we have just presented have always embarrassed Luther scholars. One cannot in effect deny that the concept of *Deus absconditus* bears a different significance here from that in the theology of the cross. It is not a question of the hiddenness of God in his revelation, that is to say the dialectic so characteristic of the theology of the cross, where God hides himself in order to reveal himself, just as he dies in order to give life. In the passage we have just examined, the *Deus absconditus* is opposed to the *Deus revelatus*. He is not in the Word, he is beyond it. Are we dealing here, as for example Ritschl maintains, with Luther's "falling back" into Nominalism, returning to the *Deus exlex* of Occam, placing oneself above all law and all knowledge? That is not a very satisfying explanation. The will of God which is subject to no explanation and no reason is not therefore arbitrary as such. Luther emphasizes the liberty, not the arbitrariness of God. One can only speak adequately of the "*Deus absconditus*" of the *De servo arbitrio* by placing it within the structure of Luther's overall thought, of his affirmations on the subject of God and the nature of faith.

But before attempting to give an explanation, one must not only underline the change of his concept of *Deus absconditus* in relation to the theology of the cross, but also the difficulty which here arises for his thought in general.

One can ask oneself, as Althaus does, whether a shift of emphasis has occurred in relation to the scriptural witness.[22] In effect, this describes as a mystery the fact that God hardens hearts. But Luther goes further when he affirms a will of God which expresses itself in contrary effects. Paul speaks of a hardening which is not necessarily a definite rejection (Romans 11). Luther, on the other hand, speaks of an eternal damnation, of a predestination to salvation and another to perdition. But is this double predestination, thus systematized, really scriptural?

And further, does not the distinction made between God incarnate and *Deus ipse* put in question the foundation of faith itself, which finds its assurance precisely in the encounter with God himself present in the humanity of Christ and there offering the salvation which corresponds to the true nature of his heart? In the passage in question in *De servo arbitrio*, there appears the idea of a will of God which is hidden and not directed toward salvation. Are we concerned again with making possible a faith confronted with the dialectic of God who reveals himself in hiding himself, or rather with a dualism which is really a contradiction in God himself and can only destroy faith?

It must be recognized that the passage in question leads to misunderstanding and seems to fit into the general pattern of Luther's thought with difficulty. However, it is necessary to separate out the motives which prompt him when he presents the concept of *Deus absconditus* in the way that we have seen here.

First of all one can observe that Luther seems to go along with Erasmus when he says that we must not concern ourselves with the mysteries that are in God. "Whatever be the design, the why and the wherefore of the inscrutable will of God, it is not for us to research them, to choose them ourselves, to concern ourselves with them or to touch them, but only to fear and to adore" (WA 18, 686, 2).

Is this not a reserve equally appropriate toward all thought which would systematize the hidden purpose of God, as for example the

double predestination, where Luther himself seems to venture too
far? But is this to affirm that the *Deus absconditus* is "God in himself," who is excluded from entering into relation with human beings? It does not seem so. One can rather establish that with Luther
the *Deus absconditus* belongs necessarily to the revelation of God
and conditions the nature of faith. In fact, if the *Deus absconditus*
does not wish to be and cannot be the object of speculation, he can
at the very most be the object of adoration and prayer on the part
of the believer. He is thus in some way a particular aspect of the
object of faith, at the same time as he determines faith in its character as faith.

The hiddenness of God in the sense of the treatise *De servo arbitrio* underlines the liberty of God in his revelation and his act of
salvation. God is not obliged to become incarnate or to save human
beings as *Deus praedicatus*. It is against the background of the *Deus
absconditus* that these acts of God acquire their full dimension, i.e.,
they are affirmed not only as saving realities which in some way
exhaust the being of God, but as acts of his mysterious love, absolutely free and miraculous.

The grace of God, his revelation and his saving acts cannot be
deduced from the nature of God himself. One can also say that the
reality of God is greater than the action by which he gives himself
to human beings. Thus grace cannot become a self-evident reality,
a general idea by which faith reaches the point of a knowledge
devoid of fear and anxiety, because it can only be that existential
movement by which human beings flee from the hidden God to the
revealed God, from fear to assurance.

Hence the majesty of the *Deus ipse* repeatedly forces us to the
Deus praedicatus. Certainly God is bound to his Word for our salvation, but without renouncing his deity, i.e., his majesty and his
freedom. In this majesty, he does not wish to be recognized by us.
He is inaccessible to us, because he wishes to be. He wants to be
reached only in his Word. Faith is precisely this attitude which
respects the freedom of God and does not cross the limits fixed by
God. It holds itself to the place to which God binds himself in order
to encounter human beings.

Thus interpreted, the concept of *Deus absconditus* is integrated
into the overall pattern of Luther's thought. He emphasizes the
freedom of God that we have constantly highlighted when speaking
of the incarnation. He determines faith by placing it in tension be-

tween love and fear. It thus appears that, from Luther's point of
view, it is necessary to speak of a double hiddenness of God. There
is that of the theology of the cross, i.e., of the revelation of God in
which God hides himself in order to reveal himself, because here
below we are not able to see him directly and because by definition,
faith is in hidden realities. But there is also the hiddenness which is
part of the being of God, such that he is distinguished from human
beings. It is this hiddenness which attracts the speculation of unbe-
lief, it is the consuming fire which burns the curious spirits who try
to penetrate it. Faith, on the contrary, by which human beings recognize and adore the deity of God, bows in adoration before this hiddenness and holds to revelation.

We have tried to place the concept of *Deus absconditus* such as it
appears in the heart of the theology of the cross and such as one finds
it in the passage we considered in the treatise *De servo arbitrio*. But
what of Luther's later development of thought? The theology of the
cross has too often been limited to Luther's earlier works. On the
other hand, the later Luther strongly criticized the concept of *Deus
absconditus*. From this point of view it is possible to discern an evolution which is said to be characteristic of him.[23] But this requires
a much closer examination, meanwhile being satisfied with showing
the direction which, in our opnion, a more detailed study should
take.

In his commentaries on the epistle to the Galatians of 1531 and
on Genesis, for example, we find a whole range of fairly powerful
warnings against the concept of *Deus absconditus*.[24] In the middle of
his Latin commentary on Genesis, Luther quotes the line of his
famous hymn, "A Mighty Fortress"; "Ask who this may be: Lord of
hosts is he! Jesus Christ, our Lord, God's only Son, adored" (*LBW*
228 [© 1978 *Lutheran Book of Worship*]) (*WA* 43, 463, 7). But
what do these warnings mean? Do they not simply repeat what
Luther has insisted on from the beginning, namely that one must
not speculate about God, to rise to the naked God, but only to hold
to the God revealed in Jesus Christ? It is not the concept of *Deus
absconditus* which is rejected, but every approach to God which
would search for God beyond or apart from Jesus Christ. Such
searching is in fact diabolic and will lead human beings to destruction (*WA* 43, 458, 36ff.).

But what does Luther mean when he strongly insists that there
is no other God than the God revealed in Jesus Christ? It seems to

us that he does not there deny the hiddenness of God as such, in the sense that we have seen it in the treatise *De servo arbitrio*. But he does reject the dualism which would oppose an incomprehensible and perhaps hostile God to a Savior God. Such a dualism would undermine all assurance. For Luther it is essential that it is the real God himself whom we meet in Christ. "God for us" is not opposed to "God in himself"—or again the saving act of God reflects the very being of God in himself, even though this being in its mystery is not exhausted by the saving act, so far as we are capable of understanding it. There is certainly—and it must be underlined—a reaction in Luther against all attempts to penetrate to the *Deus absconditus* apart from revelation, but the reality of the *Deus absconditus* is never thereby denied.

To what extent can one affirm that the theology of the cross, with its insistence on the *Deus absconditus,* passes to the background in the later Luther? Without wishing to deny that the insistence on this theme is weaker in the period of the Heidelberg Disputation or again in the *Operationes,* we do not however think that this is a fundamental reorientation of Luther's thought, in all his works. We have emphasized it again in relation to the Eucharistic Controversy, we shall find the question coming up again when we examine his commentary on Isaiah 53. It would be possible to cite other texts.[25] It remains understood that, for Luther, God, Jesus Christ, and the realities which they determine, such as the church, salvation, the Christian life, are placed under the cross, offered to us *sub contraria specie*. They are hidden, and they require faith. At the same time that this orientation remains, there seems to appear a new emphasis which insists on the reality of the revelation in Jesus Christ as revelation. The early Luther insisted above all on the hiddenness as such, at the same time as he insisted on the judgment directed to natural human beings, a judgment under which was hidden grace. Now, it seems it is affirmed more clearly that we know God and his saving intentions truly in Jesus Christ, that the announcement of the gospel is forgiveness, not judgment hiding forgiveness.

Walther von Loewenich observed that the simultaneity disappeared behind a temporal succession. What does that mean? The theology of the cross of the early Luther highlighted the simultaneous presence of judgment and grace, God hidden and God revealed. In the later writings, Luther is more concerned with a temporal succession.

264   Change and Continuity in Luther's Christology

As an example, von Loewenich takes the different ways in which Luther uses the term *posteriora*.[26] We have seen that in the Heidelberg Disputation, thesis 20, Luther used this term, which he had taken from Exod. 33:18ff., to designate the hidden aspect of God. But it is very clear that the *posteriora Dei* and the face of God are not two different realities. When we encounter God "from behind," it is still him whom we encounter. We are before his face, which is only hidden until the last day. Later, according to von Loewenich, a shift has occurred in the thought of Luther. Examining the *Commentary on Genesis,* one would discover the following idea: it is necessary first of all to see God "from behind," i.e., to meet him in his sufferings, in order to be able to go later, much further, and to discover his face.[27] Without questioning such a change of perspective, it should be possible to ask however if there is not also the perspective of succession in the early Luther, when he affirms, for example, that it is necessary first of all to go to the humanity of Christ and then to rise to the divinity. On the other hand, von Loewenich himself indicates that the perspective of simultaneity has not entirely disappeared in the later works of Luther. We are undoubtedly here in the presence of a necessary dialectic. On the one hand, it must be emphasized that the *posteriora Dei* does not present us with another God, but that there we encounter God himself who is hidden in order to be revealed. On the other hand, revelation implies a certain change on the side of human beings, by which they go from the hidden aspect of God toward the light, when God will present his face directly.

However that may be, it seems to us that the essential modification is to be found elsewhere. A certain shift occurs in the sense that Luther fixes his attention no longer only on the dialectic *sub contraria specie* of the revelation of Jesus Christ, but that the later Luther insists more on the law as an instrument by which God brings death and hides himself, while in Jesus Christ he brings life and reveals himself fully. The *posteriora Dei* are now the law and creation.[28]

The revelation of Christ is now found to be emphasized more as revelation. In fact the negative pole of judgment or the hiddenness of God is put essentially outside Christ, in the law, while in Christ God reveals himself and saves human beings. Of course, Christ also is an instrument of God to judge human beings, he accuses them because he has accomplished the law perfectly. But the principal accent is now placed on the revelation by Christ of the saving intentions of God.

It would be wrong, however, to affirm an absolute change or to try to locate it. We have already discerned the distinction between law and gospel in the *Commentary on the Epistle to the Hebrews,* which belongs to the same period as that in which Luther most strongly affirmed his theology of the cross. We found this again in his later writings when the dialectic between the hidden God in creation and the law, and the revealed God in Jesus Christ, is dominant. What we are really talking about is rather a change of emphasis.

Concerning the relationships between creation and the law on the one hand and the gospel, properly so-called, on the other, one can make the following remarks: Luther is able to affirm, on the basis of works of creation and those of the law, that reason has a certain knowledge of God.[29] It is a knowledge which Luther qualifies as *legalis,*[30] or again as *generalis,*[31] because reason does not know the particular action of God in Jesus Christ. Through true knowledge of God, one knows him in his love, made manifest in Jesus Christ. It is only in Jesus Christ, and from this point of view, that Luther is able to say that we see the heart or the fact of God or that we can respond to the question: In what way has God taken pity on us? It is only in Jesus Christ that one discovers the cause of the creation or its meaning. It is as though one knew the power and the ability of a prince without knowing his intentions or his feelings.[32]

Commenting on Rom. 1:23ff., Luther admitted a certain knowledge of God among the pagans.[33] But he had equally shown that the natural knowledge of God had turned to perversion, in the sense that human beings had not been content to adore the mysterious God, certain of whose properties appeared to them through the works of creation. Following the apostle, Luther called that idolatry into which the pagans fell. One of the particular forms of idolatry stressed by the reformer is justification by works. Therefore, the true revelation of God in Jesus Christ is not only a revelation which complements that which people know already from nature on the subject of God, but it is opposed to this knowledge. In fact, in Jesus Christ God must first of all destroy a certain number of false ideas about God and salvation that human beings had formed. That is where the theology of the cross is rooted.

Sometimes Luther insists on the perversion of relationships between God and human beings which are based on reason and the works of creation. Sometimes he shows that by knowledge of God apart from Jesus Christ one does not truly know him, because such knowledge ignored his intentions. From this point of view, one could talk of the hiddenness of God in the heart of creation.

Finally, it must be noted that God can use the creation and the law in the movement by which he stirs up faith and determines it as faith. Several times we have already shown that faith is situated in the dialectic between the hidden and the revealed God, between judgment and grace. In the theology of the cross, we saw that this dialectic was situated in Christ himself. It can also include the law and the hidden God of creation. Then human beings, disquieted by the law of conscience and confronted by the wrath of God who accuses them, flee to Jesus Christ, where God reveals himself to be love. In the next chapter, we shall examine more closely this dialectic between law and gospel.

Notes

1   Harnack, *Luthers Theologie,* p. 103: "The basic ideas of his chris-
    tology, like those of his doctrine of the Eucharist, are clear for him
    since the early years of his Reformation works, but it is only in the
    struggle against the Enthusiasts (i.e., since 1525), and in the Eu-
    charistic Controversy (since 1527) that his doctrine of the person
    of Christ developed."
2   Köhler, *Luther und Zwingli,* vol. 1, p. 545.
3   See also WA 30, 3, 23ff.
4   E.g. the 1518 commentary on Psalm 110 (WA 1, 693, 1ff). See also
    WA 10, 1, 1, 150, 12.
5   WA 46, 634; 631ff.
6   E.g. 43, 131, 1; 47, 212, 18; 46, 633ff.
7   WA 41, 573, 17; 46, 102, 35; 52, 735, 23. See also the following
    chapter, section 3, "The Saving Work of Jesus Christ."
8   WA 40, 3, 7111ff.
9   *Luthers Theologie,* p. 147.
10 WA 52, 107, 39-108, 1
11 A. Peters, *Realpräsenz,* p. 85: "Christ the high priest stands unique-
    ly isolated in the heavenly sanctuary."
12 WA 43, 359; 21, 31; 360, 34
13 WA 24, 50
14 WA 47, 172ff.
15 *The Bondage of the Will,* WA 18, 551-787.
16 On this subject see the *Heidelberg Disputation* (WA 1, 361ff.),
    particularly theses 19 and 20.
17 Translator's note: The author coins the word *l'abscondité,* from the

Latin *abscondite,* to express the fact that God is hidden. We shall use the term "hiddenness."

18   *WA* 1, 112, 10ff.; 138, 13ff.

19   On this subject see Althaus, *Die Theologie Martin Luthers,* pp. 31-34.

20   Among those studies which have approached the question, see especially: Von Loewenich, *Luther's Theology of the Cross;* M. Doerne, "Gottes Ehre am gebundenen Willen: Evangelische Grundlagen und theologische Spitzensätze in *De servo arbitrio,*" *Luther-Jahrbuch* 20 (1938):45-92; H. Bandt, *Luthers Lehre vom verborgenen Gott* (Berlin: 1957); Althaus, *Die Theologie Martin Luthers,* pp. 238-248; K. Schwarzwäller, *Theologia crucis: Luthers Lehre von Prädestination nach De servo arbitrio* (Munich: 1970).

21   *WA* 18, 683, 24ff.

22   Althaus, *Die Theologie Martin Luthers,* p. 241.

23   Thus, for example: Siggins, *Martin Luther's Doctrine of Christ,* pp. 80-81.

24   Von Loewenich, *Luther's Theology of the Cross,* pp. 39-43.

25   E.g. *WA* 18, 633, 14; 31, 1, 51, 21; 249, 15; 43, 140, 28ff.; 392, 16ff.

26   Von Loewenich, *Luther's Theology of the Cross,* pp. 40-42.

27   E.g. 43, 460, 26ff.; *WA* 44, 601, 18ff.

28   *WA* 46, 672, 24ff.: "This is a knowledge of God from the left side *(auff der lincken seiten),* for from the law one knows that a God exists, but he is a God who turns his back on us; therefore turn yourself round and see what is the true face of God, or what is his will. For it is only in Christ that he is truly seen, namely that all who wish to acquire eternal happiness must confess that they are sinners and damned, and they must hold firmly him who is full of grace and truth, in order that we through him may obtain grace and truth."

29   *WA* 8, 629, 23ff.; 19, 205-207; 40, 1, 607-608

30   *WA* 19, 206, 7ff.; 466, 68, 11

31   *WA* 40, 1, 607, 28

32   *WA* 40, 2, 458, 30. The passage continues: "The creation of the world and the power of God is openly presented to our eyes. But the heart of the matter is to know to what end and for what purpose God has created the world."

33   *WA* 56, 176ff.

6

The Victory of Christ
and Justification by Faith
According to the Commentary on
the Epistle to the Galatians of 1531[1]

The Climate of the Commentary

In his introduction to the modern French edition of Luther's commentary, R. Esnault rightly remarks that "the reason for this new commentary has nothing to do with the regular progress of a pre-established academic program" nor is it motivated by a "difficulty inherent in the text." [2] Luther is anxious to arm the tender conscience against the heresies which pervert the gospel. To Rome, the original adversary, has now been added the Enthusiasts. Luther never ceased to maintain that Rome and the Enthusiasts. found themselves in accord in their attack on the gospel, which he himself characterized as having justification by faith as its essential doctrine. "These foxes are joined by their tails, but their heads are different. Outwardly, they pretend to be great enemies, but inwardly they conceive, they teach, and they defend the same opinions against Christ, the only Savior, who alone is our righteousness." [3]

It was the struggle against the Enthusiasts, then against Zwingli, which above all had held Luther's attention in the period 1524 to 1530. The hope of a reconciliation with Rome had not been entirely abandoned, and that is shown most clearly by the rather conciliatory character of the Augsburg Confession of 1530. But this was rejected by the Catholic theologians and the emperor. Luther was deeply affected.[4] From this moment on, his attacks on Rome became particularly sharp. That is seen already in this Commentary of 1531 and even more clearly in the Smalcald Articles of 1537.

But behind Rome, the emperor, and the Enthusiasts—and Luther speaks often also of the Anabaptists—there rises for Luther another adversary, far more dangerous than human beings, Satan himself. It is he who "rangeth about seeking to devour us." [5] It is he who seeks by all means to deface the gospel,[6] to seduce, that is to say, "to introduce into the heart a false opinion of Christ." [7] One may be astonished at Luther's naive "mythology" or minimize the place that the reality of Satan held in his life and thought. But it is a fact which the historian must take account of: Luther saw the history of the world as an incessant combat in which Satan sought to attack the good creation of God. This combat finds a particular expression in the struggle which Satan conducts against the Christ who came to save God's creatures and restore a fallen order.[8] It is in this dramatic ambiance that Luther elaborates his thought.

It is the gospel itself, we would say, that Satan attacks in order to destroy the church. Now, the gospel is no other than the announcement of justification by faith: "I mean the doctrine that we are redeemed from sin, death and devil, and made partakers of eternal life, not by ourselves (and certainly not by our works which are less than ourselves), but by the help of another, the only-begotten Son of God, Jesus Christ." [9]

Luther never stops proclaiming that it is this article of justification which constitutes the foundation of the church. He speaks of "this one solid rock which we call the doctrine of justification." [10] It is the only point which he thinks cannot be conceded in his quarrel with the pope. "Wherefore if the Pope will grant us, that God alone by his mere grace through Christ doth justify sinners, we will not only carry him in our hands, we will also kiss his feet. But since we cannot obtain this, we again in God are proud against him above measure, and will give no place, no, not one hair's breadth, to all the angels in heaven, not to Peter, not to Paul, not to a hundred emperors, nor to a thousand popes, nor to the whole world." [11] There is no other weapon "against sects, or power to resist them, but only this one article of Christian righteousness. If we lose this article, it is impossible for us to withstand any errors or sects." [12]

Now this fundamental article of the faith is once again under attack from Satan through Rome and the Anabaptists, according to Luther, for he envisages history in its totality as an incessant struggle against the truth of the faith expressed by the article of justification by faith.[13] "Therefore most necessary it is, chiefly and above all things, that we teach and repeat this article continually. For it cannot be beaten into our ears enough or too much.[14] Without ever tiring of it, Luther on the slightest provocation which the text gives, proceeds to develop the article of justification by faith, which according to him "is properly the dominant theme of the entire Commentary." [15]

We would say that the theme of justification by faith occupies a central place in the commentary. But it must also be emphasized that Luther characterizes in yet another way that which is central to his thought. He writes, "For the one doctrine which I have supremely at heart, is that of faith in Christ, from whom, through whom and unto whom all my theological thinking flows back and forth, day and night. Not that I find I have grasped anything of a wisdom so high, so broad and so profound, beyond a few meagre rudiments and fragments." [16] It is really Christ who is the subject of this epistle.[17]

The fact that Luther speaks sometimes of justification by faith, sometimes of Christ himself *(fides Christi)* as the center of faith, reveals that basically these are only two faces of the same reality. Justification by faith is only a way of expressing the reality of Christ, and conversely, one cannot speak truly of the reality of Christ without relating it to justification by faith. In fact, it is precisely as Savior, that is to say, as the one who alone accomplishes my salvation and calls for faith, that Christ is the center of the Scripture, which leads us to the very heart of justification by faith. On the other hand, to separate this theme from Christ would be to disregard it, to forget that the faith which justifies is that which apprehends Christ present and makes of him and of the Christian "one and the same person," as we shall see again.

We must finally make some remarks on the framework within which the thought of Luther is elaborated, the "abundant riches" of the exposition in that particular kind of literature which is the biblical commentary.[18] It is a form based on a course of lectures, which permits theological discussion at some depth. Luther does not spare the students. He discusses at length and repeatedly the Scholastic doctrine of *fides caritate formata* [19] and other theological opinions current at the time.

In addition, it appears that the "doctrinal element," properly so-called, gained a special importance in the thought of Luther. In this connection M. Greschat compares Luther with Melanchthon. Instead of envisaging the action of Christ only from the point of view of his Word, which makes him present to believers, Greschat maintains that, starting with the commentary which we are here studying, Luther would have accorded a much more important place to the words concerning Christ. Faith would then be the acceptance of a truth about faith, and justification would be not only an act or the object of a confession of faith, but also the subject of a doctrine.[20] Moreover, Greschat thinks that at this period and in connection with the article of justification, Luther was much under the influence of Melanchthon.

This thesis is interesting, but has not entirely convinced us. On the basic content, one can certainly detect the care with which Luther taught a doctrine of justification by faith, but does one really find many texts where "faith consists partly of an intellectual appropriation of an *objectivum* and at the same time as an attitude in which human beings are moved and seized by the content of this Word?" [21] In spite of all, the foremost of these two tenses seems to be used very little. The opposition which Luther establishes again and again between a historical faith and a saving faith reinforces us in our reservations.[22] The historical faith is precisely a faith which apprehends Christ as an *objectivum*, while saving faith is that by which human beings become one with Christ and truly recognize in him the Savior because of what he has done for the believer.[23]

Of course, we must take into account the academic framework within which Luther's thought moves in this commentary and a possible comparison with Melanchthon (a comparison whose scope must still be precisely defined). It is also necessary to emphasize all that is "non-academic" in this commentary. We think as much about the importance of the "mythological" element as about the existential dimension which constantly comes through in this commentary (as it does in that on the epistle to the Romans!).

One is struck by the way in which Luther personifies faith, the devil, sin, death, and by the images or *quasi* mythological turns that he employs on these subjects. Death, this tyrant, engages in combat with Christ, but encounters in him an immortal life.[24] Satan wishes to devour Christ, but it is Christ who on the contrary devours him.[25] Satan, sin, death, and even the law and wrath of God are designated as "monsters" *(monstra)*. Christ struggles against them,[26] bearing "the extreme cruelty and tyranny of the law." [27] Christ is the new law which devours the other law that held us captive; [28] or again, "It is as if Paul said: O law, if thou canst accuse me, terrify me, and bind me, I will set above and against thee another law, that is to say, another tyrant and tormentor, which shall accuse thee, bind thee and oppress thee. Indeed thou art my tormentor, but I have another tormentor, even Christ, which shall torment thee to death; and if you are ripped apart, then I am free through Christ. In the same way, if the devil thrashes me, I have a stronger devil who will thrash him in turn. When the strongest devil fights his competitor and triumphs over him, then am I at liberty." [29] In another place, Luther speaks of the astonishing combat *(mirabile duellum)* "when the law, a creature, struggles against the creator." [30]

The interpreters of Luther's thought are at one in their comments on the abundance of mythological images and figures in the *Commentary on the Epistle to the Galatians*.[31] How is that to be explained? Is it enough to compare Luther with the early church and to speak of reading he could have done at that time on the subject? Are there not more profound reasons why Luther to such a point personified sin, the law, and death? Karin Bornkamm seems to us to have explained this in the most convincing manner. According to her, the personification of the powers, particularly striking in this commentary, would be due to the fact that in this commentary Luther inserts the believer directly into the history of Christ. Justification, according to her, would consist of participating in this history, which "understood as a struggle and a victory, ends up, of itself, at the personification of the powers, i.e., the law, sin, death, which attack and are vanquished. In Christ, believers have another law, which silences and imprisons the law that accuses them; they have a death which kills its death; they have the one who in his own body disarms its death; etc." [32]

The mythological figures and the personification of sin, the law, and death seem not to have caused Luther to fall back into a naive and uncritical world of magic. There is a direct correlation between the struggle of Christ against the powers and the struggle against sin and the hostile powers. With Luther, mythology does not exclude the existential, it expresses it and inserts it into history, the fabric of a combat which opposes God to Satan.

Another point characteristic of this commentary must also be stressed. It is striking to ascertain how much the teaching presented is bound up with the religious experience of the reformer himself. That is, of course, nothing new. Luther has always and consistently been a theologian gripped to the greatest degree by the truth which he communicates. But that needs underlining when it happens also in an academic work. He appeals to his own spiritual experiences.[33] His exposition gives an important place to the temptations.[34] One also feels how often Luther is conscious of finding himself in an eschatological situation and having soon to appear before the throne of God.[35] He lives and thinks in the perspective of the judgment to come. It is from this point of view that he would preserve the article of justification by faith alone.

When Luther describes the tension (that we shall look at more closely in the next chapter) between judgment and grace, between law and gospel, he does not do so as an observer at some distance, nor as a theologian operating coldly with the help of more or less adequate formulae. He lives this tension in his own consciousness.[36] Personal experience enters here to an astonishing degree into the theological exposition, without thereby reducing it to the level of mere autobiography.

Law and Gospel

Among the powers which oppress sinful human beings in their consciences, the law occupies a particular place.[37] When one thinks of the importance given to the law in the epistle to the Galatians, it is not surprising that this commentary takes up the theme at many points. But the law, particularly in opposition to the gospel, generally plays a preeminent role in the thought of Luther.[38] Our exposition of Luther's christology would be incomplete if it did not show that Christ saves us by liberating us from the law. But we must first of all make clear what Luther understands by the law and where he places its activity.

Generally, by the term law one designates an imperative force or rule imposed on living beings or matter. Laws thus regulate the relationships between human beings. At that level, Luther affirms that the law is absolutely necessary, "in order to punish transgressions." This is what he calls the first use of the law.[39] But what about the law at the level of relationships between God and human beings?

In many places, Luther is content to envisage the law as the quintessence of the will of God. As such it can be said to be inherent in conscience, and its content is identified with the Mosaic law. From this perspective, the law is good and is not opposed to the gospel.

But another perspective opens up because of sin, and it is this which dominates Luther's thought. For sinful humanity, the question which is posed concerns salvation and the way that leads to it. Can the law fulfill this function, that is to say, help human beings to overcome the separation from God, by the observation of rules and the accomplishment of the works which it prescribes? No! says Luther with energy. For human beings in their sinful reality, the law is *lex non impleta,* and because of that a *lex accusans.* The law which we encounter in the concrete reality of our situation as sinners is characterized by its accusing function. In speaking thus of the law, Luther is less concerned with its contents than with the function of this law by which human beings are accused—even destroyed—by the law which makes them aware of their sin.

This function—Luther calls it "office" *(Amt)*—is desired by God. And Luther says: The proper use *(Amt)* and end therefore of the law is, to accuse and condemn as guilty such as live in security, that they may see themselves to be in danger of sin, wrath and death eternal, that so they may be terrified and brought even to the brink of desperation, trembling and quaking at the falling of a leaf; and in that they are such, they are under his law." [40] "The law is the hammer of death, the thundering of hell and the lightning of God's wrath." [41] "It increaseth sin, it worketh wrath, it accuseth, it terrifieth and condemneth." [42]

How is this function of the law accomplished? "For the law requireth perfect obedience unto God, and condemneth all those who do not accomplish the same. Now, it is certain that there is no man living which is able to perform this obedience; which notwithstanding God straitly requireth of us: the law therefore justifieth not, but condemneth." [43]

The law then becomes the revelation of sin; it unveils it. "It shows sin (which without the law is dead)." And Luther stresses that, "I speak not here of that speculative knowledge of hypocrites, but of a true knowledge, by which we see the wrath of God against sin, and feel a true taste of death."

Besides, even if—an impossible hypothesis—a human being managed to fulfill all the commandments, the accusation would not disappear. In fact, what remains is the manner in which the law was observed. It is not accomplished if it is observed in a spirit of slavery. God wants his will to be accomplished with a joyous and spontaneous liberty, which is precisely what is not possible for a sinful person who is seeking to observe the law. The person "cannot enjoy the freedom of the Spirit, or grace, except he first put upon him the new man by faith in Christ." [44] There are persons who even in accomplishing the law, deny it because they are destitute of faith and the fear of God, which are the conditions of this liberty of which we have just spoken.[45] "That is to say, that hypocrites do the law, and yet in doing it they do it not; for they understand this word 'doing' according to the moral grammar, which in divinity availeth not. Indeed they work many things, but of their own presumption and without the knowledge of God and faith." [46]

Thus human beings encounter the law as a law which has not been accomplished and which in consequence accuses them. But it not only unveils the sin, it even provokes it—in the sense that human beings accused by the law of God begin to hate this God. Hence, the law leads to death and not to life. For the purpose of justifying human beings before God, it is not only useless, but positively harmful. Of itself, it opens up no possibility of new life for human beings.

It must be noted that this destructive office of the law is not the result of the human misunderstanding of it in its essence according to the will of God. It is the will of God himself that this accusing law work in this way, unveiling and even provoking sin. But in the light of the gospel, we shall see that this function of the law is only the alien or unusual work of God, who in some way is only preparing for his proper work, which he will realize through Christ and by the proclamation of the gospel.

Such is then the distress of human beings; to be cornered by the law and the wrath of God, to be without excuse before God, to be condemned to sin and despair. But it is in this distress that the Word of the gospel resounds. Liberation is offered to human beings thus accused. When the law accuses and exacts an impossible obedience, the gospel, God's verdict with regard to human beings, says to them: Your sins are forgiven you. Why are they? Why this liberating Word from God? Because Jesus Christ has assumed the existence of human beings before God. Because he is this life of obedience, of which human beings were not capable. At the same time, he is the one against whom the assaults of the law were shattered. He has "dashed out the teeth of the law." [47]

The gospel sets a limit to the law,[48] in the sense that the accusing function of the law is annihilated. By the gospel, God acts in some sense against the law. In fact, the law was accomplished and its accusing power was vanquished by Jesus Christ. The gospel is then the incessant proclamation of Jesus Christ and his work of salvation.

The gospel does not exact works on the part of human beings, but refers him to what Christ has done for them. "This gospel teacheth me, not what I ought to do (for that is the proper office of the Law), but what Jesus Christ, the Son of God has done for me: to wit, that he suffered and died to deliver me from sin and death." [49]

It is, moreover, the gospel alone which allows us to place the law within the plan of God. The destruction which it works appears to be good sense when one considers it as a preparation for the reception of the gospel. Luther then takes up again the statements made by Paul on the subject of the pedagogic role of the law. It is as we have already indicated above, the "alien" work of God, in the service of his "proper" work, which is to save human beings by the work of Jesus Christ and by the proclamation of the gospel. "That is why," Luther writes, "when the law terrifies the conscience and sin accuses it and strikes it; then it is time to say: There is a time to die and a time to live; there is a time to listen to the Law and a time to despise the Law; there is a time to hear the Gospel and a time to be ignorant of the Gospel. Let the Law now depart and let the Gospel come; for there is now no time to hear the Law, but the Gospel." [50]

Again the thought of Luther can be explained by presenting it from the perspective of justification by faith. By wishing to be justified by his works, human beings remain shut up within themselves, in what they do or wish to do. The law which accused them confronts them both with the wrath of God and their own sin; it shows them their works which can only accuse them, because they remain always insufficient in the eyes of God.

The new life, offered by the gospel, is realized in faith, that is to say, precisely through this attitude of human beings who no longer regard themselves, but who find their real life in another who is Jesus Christ. That is why, commenting on Gal. 2:20, Luther says, "Wherefore we must learn in such conflicts and terrors of conscience (forgetting ourselves and setting the law, our life past and all our works apart, which drive us to the consideration of ourselves only to turn our eyes wholly to the brazen serpent Jesus Christ crucified, and assuredly believe that he is our righteousness and life." [51]

Faith can thus be described as that movement by which human beings flee from sin and to law, in order to go to Christ. Commenting on Gal. 2:16, Luther writes, "Therefore when the law accuseth and sin terrifieth him, he looketh upon Christ, and when he hath apprehended him by faith, he hath present with him the conqueror of the law, sin, death and the devil: who reigneth and ruleth over them, so that they cannot hurt him." [52]

The way which leads from the perdition of human beings accused by the law to salvation passes through faith, which is attached to the work of Christ. This way must be taken again and again, with the sure and certain knowledge that if the law was indeed overcome in Christ, human beings are forever detaching themselves from Christ, or rather the devil is trying to obscure the gospel, to worry human beings by temptation, to sow doubt in their spirit.

Luther sets himself strongly against the way described by the Scholastics, who subtly distinguish between the work of human beings and that of God, the human merits and the help of grace: "With all his religious rabble of sophists and schoolmen, the Pope sees and teaches that by the merit of congruence we must come to grace, and that afterward by the merit of worthiness we are received into heaven. Here saith the Christian: this is not the right way to justify us, neither doth this way lead to heaven. For I cannot, saith he, by my works going before grace, deserve grace of congruence, nor by my works following grace, obtain eternal life of worthiness: but to him that believeth in Christ, sin is pardoned and righteousness is imputed. This trust and this confidence maketh him a child of God and heir of his kingdom; for in hope he possesseth already everlasting life, assured unto him by promise." [53]

The law accuses and the gospel liberates, the law demands works, the gospel offers as a gift Jesus Christ and forgiveness. Oppositions of this kind could be multiplied. Under these circumstances one is hardly astonished to find that Luther insists on emphasizing the distinction between law and gospel. Many interpreters of Luther think that these two terms and the dialectic they imply express the basic structure of his theology and that in certain respects, this is another presentation of the theme of justification by faith.[54]

We frequently find this distinction between law and gospel in the commentary we are studying in this chapter. It would be impossible to understand Luther's christology fully without reference to it. It appears particularly clearly, for example, in his comment on Gal. 2:14, where he writes: "This place touching the difference between the law and the Gospel, is very necessary to be known, for it containeth the sum of all Christian doctrine." [55] To distinguish the law from the gospel is to distinguish two kinds of righteousness: the active righteousness and the passive righteousness, the first being that of works exacted by the law and valid here below in human relations; the second, resting on faith in Christ and concerning our relationship to God." [56] The two levels must be distinguished with the same care as heaven and earth: [57] "If we mark well this distinction, neither the one nor the other shall pass his bounds, but the law shall abide outside heaven; that is outside the heart and conscience: and contrariwise, the liberty of the Gospel shall abide outside the earth; that is to say, outside the body and its members." [58] The preaching of faith is opposed to that of the law.[59] "The Law never bringeth the Holy Ghost, but only teacheth what we ought to do; therefore it justifieth not. But the Gospel bringeth the Holy Ghost, because it teacheth what we ought to receive." [60] "The Law is good and profitable, but in his own proper use: which is first to bridle civil transgressions, and then to reveal and to increase spiritual transgressions. Wherefore the law is also a light, which sheweth and revealeth, not the grace of God, not righteousness and life; but sin, death, the wrath and judgment of God. . . . Contrariwise, the Gospel is a light which lighteneth, quickeneth, comforteth and raiseth up fearful minds. For it sheweth that God for Christ's sake is merciful and gracious." [61]

We find this distinction between law and gospel again in the care with which Luther preserves the image of Christ the Savior in contrast to Moses the lawgiver and distinguishing it from that of the judge and from the example to be followed. Luther never tires of saying that Jesus Christ is not Moses or another lawgiver, but a Savior.[62] Pesch has rightly observed that this opposition is yet more radical in the later works of Luther, among which must be included the commentary which we are here studying.[63] Luther often reproaches the papists for having made Jesus Christ into a tyrant more severe than Moses himself.

To make of Jesus Christ an example to follow would be to fall into the same error. It is necessary to distinguish the Christ as an example from the Christ as a gift, a distinction which we have already often met. Luther again recalls how necessary this is.[64] It is vital, particularly in times of tribulation and temptation, as when he writes, "I wish not to hear of nor receive any other gift than that of Jesus Christ who died for my sins and has given me his righteousness." [65] Or again, he opposes the Christ, made sin for us, to the Christ of the Sophists who make of him an example to be followed.[66] Tirelessly, Luther opposes the *propria definitio Christi* to the false images of Christ which have this in common, that they have joined Christ and the law. Now, in the life of human beings before God, only Christ can dwell in the conscience, while "the ancient dweller, Moses, must be evicted." [67]

The Saving Work of Jesus Christ

Salvation Accomplished in the Life, Death, and Resurrection of Christ

Luther describes the saving work of Jesus Christ in very different ways. First we shall give a general view of this diversity and then look more closely at the most important passage related to the work of Christ, namely the commentary on Gal. 3:13. Luther presents Christ as the mediator who "loves to the point of giving himself for us: who is also our High Priest, that is to say, a mediator between God and us miserable and wretched sinners." [68] The priesthood and offices of Christ consists of "pacifying God, to make intercession for sinners, to offer himself a sacrifice for their sins, to redeem them." [69] Christ is not "a new lawgiver . . . but the Son of God, who not for our desert or any righteousness of ours, but of his own free mercy and love, offered up himself a sacrifice for us sinners, that he might sanctify us for ever." [70] It will be noted that the office of mediation is not limited to the incarnation, properly so-called, but continues in the present intercession of Christ who is "our everlasting High Priest, sitting at the right hand of God and making intercession for us." [71]

The mediation of Christ is necessary because an immense gulf separates the holy God from sinful human beings: "And the offence is such, that God cannot pardon it, neither can we satisfy for the same. Therefore between God (who of himself is but one) and us there is wonderful discord. Moreover, God cannot revoke his Law, but he will have it observed and kept. And we, which have transgressed the Law, cannot fly from the presence of God. Christ therefore hath set himself a mediator between two which are quite contrary and separate asunder with an infinite and eternal separation, and hath reconciled them together. And how hath he done this? He hath effaced the handwriting which condemned us by ordinances, that is by the Law, and he hath fastened it to the cross." [72]

How has Jesus Christ disarmed the accusation which the law, the instrument of God, levels against us? Both by accomplishing it perfectly and by submitting to the oppression of the law by his passion, in our flesh. "He was made under the Law, that he might redeem us who were under the Law." [73] "He changeth not the voice of the Law, nor hideth the same with a veil as Moses did, nor leadeth me out of the sight of the Law; but he setteth himself against the wrath of the Law, and taketh it away, and satisfieth the Law in his own body, by himself." [74]

The continuation of this passage which we have quoted above shows that the law cannot be overcome unless it is first fulfilled, but just like the wrath of God, it must also be undergone as a punishment. This punishment Jesus Christ has suffered for us, in our place. Yet being innocent, he has disarmed both the law and the wrath of God. "Jesus Christ is God and man, who fighting against the Law, suffered the utmost cruelty and tyranny thereof. And in that he endured the burden of the Law, he vanquished it in himself." [75]

The saving work of Christ is also described as a combat. "The true and proper office of Christ is to wrestle with the Law, with the sin and death of the whole world." [76] The salvation of human beings depends on the victory of Christ who is "victor over Law, sin, our flesh, the world, the devil, death, hell and all evils." This victory which is his, he has given to us. "That is why these tyrannies and our enemies which accuse us and terrify us, cannot however reduce us to despair, nor condemn us; for Christ whom God the Father raised up from the dead, is our righteousness." [77]

The work of Christ is thus described in different ways, both from the point of view of mediation, Christ suffering under the wrath of God and accomplishing the Law, and from the point of view of combat, led against the powers which oppress human beings.

The expression *meritum Christi* appears in a number of passages.[78] Luther can say that "Jesus Christ by his death and his resurrection . . . has merited for us the forgiveness of sins, righteousness, liberty and life." [79] But in speaking thus he intends only to contrast Christ, the source of salvation, "who has satisfied abundantly," [80] with those who thought they could be saved by their works.

"Now the Law with all the works and righteousness thereof, is but as a farthing if compared unto Christ; who by his death and resurrection hath vanquished my death and hath purchased unto me righteousness and everlasting life." [81]

The most characteristic passage and the most significant in the commentary we are studying is certainly that in which Luther comments on Gal. 3:13: "Christ redeemed us from the Law, having become a curse for us." [82] We shall find there all the issues that we have so far raised and dealt with, in addition to a particular insistence on the real solidarity of Christ with sinners, his struggle against the law,[83] and his victory.

Luther emphasizes that "the unspeakable and inestimable mercy of God" is the origin of the work of Christ among "us unworthy and lost men." [84] It is this mercy which sets in motion the history of salvation. And Luther places this initiative of God, by which he sends Christ to save human beings, in time. Therefore he writes: "Our merciful Father, seeing us to be oppressed and overwhelmed by the curse of the law, and so to be holden by the same that we could never be delivered from it by our own power, sent his only Son into the world and laid on him all the sins of all men, saying: Be thou Peter that denier; Paul that persecutor, blasphemer and cruel oppressor; David that adulterer; that sinner which did eat the apple in Paradise; that thief which hanged upon the cross; and briefly, be thou the person which hath committed the sins of all men; see therefore that thou pay and satisfy for them." [85] In our last chapter, we shall return to this when we consider the drama that unfolds in this way between the Father and the Son, their "cooperation" in the work of salvation. Let us once more, from this new perspective, repeat that the Son who is made flesh does not assume only the general conditions of a human existence, but clothes himself as with a garment, as Luther says, "wrapped in my sins, yours and those of the whole world." [86] And, in fact, Luther can say: "for thou hast not yet Christ, although thou know him to be God and man; but then thou hast him indeed when thou believest that this most pure and innocent person . . . hath taken my sinful person upon him, borne thy sin, thy death, thy curse." [87]

In his body he carries the sins of all. Hence, "He is not now an innocent person and without sin, is not now the Son of God born of the Virgin; but a sinner, which hath and carrieth the sin of Paul, who was a blasphemer, an oppressor and a persecutor; of Peter, who denied Christ; of David, who was an adulterer, a murderer and caused the Gentiles to blaspheme the name of the Lord." [88] Thus Christ is no longer to be considered as an individual and private person,[89] but as "the person for all men," [90] where all sins are gathered together and judged. It is not only when all has been accomplished on the cross and by the resurrection that human beings appear as the beneficiaries of the work of Christ in order to receive the fruits of this work. The benefit is present in the person of Christ from the moment of the incarnation. In fact, at no point has Jesus Christ lived and worked for himself. Every action and every moment of his existence is determined for our salvation. We and our sin are present in his life. Basically, Christ must therefore be considered from the point of view of his work. Any reflection on the person of Christ which would omit this work is false from the start. Christ is entirely with us and for us. From his birth, we are in him with all our sin.

On what biblical basis does Luther rely to affirm such things? He appeals to Isaiah 53, according to which, all our iniquities are laid on the servant of God. Luther also refers to certain Psalms where the psalmist confesses sins (40:13; 41:5; 69:6). And we have seen already that he does not hesitate to put these passages into the mouth of Christ. And finally, among the New Testament passages there is above all 2 Cor. 5:21, which speaks of Christ as being made sin for us.

Luther evidently feels himself obliged to refute traditional interpretations which try to water down the sense of such passages as Gal. 3:13. Beginning with his commentary on Gal. 3:13, Luther attacks the interpretations of Jerome and the "popish sophists," who "seeking, as they would seem, with a Godly zeal to turn away this reproach from Christ, that he should be called a curse or execration" [91] and using all kinds of exegetical means, try to make Paul or Deut. 21:23 say things other than what they want to say.

According to Luther, everything is perfectly clear if you distinguish Christ as an isolated person from Christ "for us." By the first meaning, Christ was in fact innocent, but having carried the person of the sinner, he is that no longer, and is rightly condemned to hang on the cross. The sophists who wished to separate Christ from sins and sinners reduced him in reality to the level of an example and deprived the believers "of this saving knowledge of Christ and most heavenly comfort, namely that Christ was made a curse for us, that he might deliver us from the curse of the law." [92]

For his part, Luther makes much of the consolation resulting from the fact that the sins are no longer in us, but on him.[93] Because they have been removed by this one man, Jesus Christ, God sees them no more in the world.[94] "If the sins of the whole world be in that one man Jesus Christ, then they are not in the world." [95]

Since, then, Christ is truly charged with sins and is a sinner in the sense that we have just seen, then the punishment which he will bear is something other than a legal fiction; his death is not only the last stage of an obedience which will have been perfect up to the very end. There has been a real judgment of sin present in him. "Here now cometh the law and saith: I find him a sinner, and that such a one as hath taken upon him the sins of all men, and I see no sins else but in him; therefore let him die upon the cross. And so he setteth upon him and killeth him." [96] And a little further on, "For unless he had taken upon himself my sins and thine, and the sins of the whole world, the law had no right over him, which condemneth none but sinners only, and holdeth them under the curse. Wherefore he could neither have been made a curse nor die, since the only cause of the curse and of death is sin, from which he was free. But because he had taken upon him our sins, not by constraint, but of his own good will *(non coacte, sed sua sponte),* it behooved him to bear the punishment and wrath of God." [97]

It must also be noted that the fact of assuming the sins of the whole world is reflected in the consciousness of Christ. By binding the reality of things to the consciousness that human beings have of that reality, Luther takes the side of Nominalism, while at the same time he anticipates modern thought. It is not sufficient to consider things in themselves, but to distinguish the consciousness that human beings have of them. More and more, this appears as the central location of reality itself.

When speaking of the wrath of God or of sin carried by Christ, Luther is not content to describe these in an objective way, nor to describe the consequences at the level of the physical sufferings endured by Christ. Above all, he describes their eruption into the consciousness of Christ. He does not only suffer in his flesh the punishment which is attached to sin. He lives in himself the separation from God. We have already pointed out this perspective in relation to the community that Luther made on Psalm 22 in his *Operationes*.

This idea reappears here when Luther writes: "For it is a terrible thing to bear sin, the wrath of God, malediction and death. Wherefore that man who hath a true feeling of these things, as Christ did truly and effectually feel them for all mankind, is made even sin, death, malediction etc." [98]

And it is typical that Luther should cite the Psalm to show how Christ has borne the evil in our place: "Embracing us miserable and lost sinners, he took upon him and bore all our evils, which should have oppressed and tormented us for ever; and these cast him down for a little while, and rose over his head like water, as the prophet in the person of Christ complaineth when he saith: 'Thy wrath lies heavy upon me, and thou dost overwhelm me with all thy waves' (Ps. 88:7). Again: 'Thy wrath has swept over me; thy dread assaults destroy me' (Ps. 88:16)." [99] Apart from those passages, Luther did not further develop his thought on the consciousness of Christ.

Sin, wrath, and death rest on Christ. But they do not remain in him. In his very person a struggle unfolds whose issue is nothing less than the salvation of humanity. In a great panorama, where the mythological motifs of the early church reappear, Luther describes the battle which opposes "the highest, the greatest and the only sin" to the eternal righteousness; [100] "death the omnipotent Empress of the whole world" to life; [101] "the eternal grace and mercy of God in Christ to the curse, which is the wrath of God upon the whole world." [102] In many other passages, he adds to these hostile powers the law, which is the instrument of the wrath of God.[103] And he speaks of a battle which Christ wages against the law.

The issue of such a combat cannot remain undecided. "Here one of them must needs be overcome and give place to the other, seeing they fight together with so great force and power." [104] Luther seems to have taken up again the theme of the devil being deceived when he writes a little later: "This tyrant, sin, flieth upon Christ and will needs swallow him up, as he doth all other. But he seeth not that he is a person of invincible and everlasting righteousness. Therefore in this combat *(duello)* sin must needs be vanquished and killed, and righteousness must overcome, live and reign." [105]

The same of course can be said of the opposite of life to death, of blessing to curse. "Christ the power of God, righteousness, blessing, grace and life, overcometh and destroyeth these monsters, sin, death and the curse, without war or weapons, in his own body and in himself." [106]

The drama of salvation thus leads to the resurrection. God not only makes known there that he has accepted the sacrifice of Christ, but there the Son truly lifts up his head again, life triumphs over death. "Because he was a person, divine and everlasting, it was impossible that death should hold him. Wherefore he rose again the third day from the dead, and now liveth for ever; and there is neither sin or death in him any more, but pure righteousness, life and everlasting blessedness." [107] Once more we can discern the importance which the resurrection assumed for Luther, as for the early church.

Therefore when faith considers Christ, his righteousness and the way by which he has accomplished salvation, it must consider the incarnation, as well as the passion and resurrection. In the thought of Luther, one does not appear without the other; they support each other and elucidate each other. The incarnation is already the passion, in this sense that Christ became human in order to assume our sinful condition, and the passion supports the resurrection, for it deals with a combat led by the Son of God from a freely accepted distress to a promised victory.

One understands also why the priestly theme and the theme of combat fit so closely into one another in the very image of this profound unity that there is in Luther's work between incarnation, passion, and resurrection. From the beginning to the end, the work of Christ is the struggle of the love of God against his wrath and against the forces which have power over human beings because of the wrath of God. This struggle is not conducted from outside, but within our flesh. It is led by Christ who makes a gift of his life. From the incarnation, Jesus Christ despoils himself and offers himself to God for human beings, by carrying their sins. But this sacrifice is the extreme means to which the struggle of love has recourse.

The Actualization of Salvation by Christ Present: The Unity with Christ in Faith

As we have already noted in connection with the priestly office of Christ, Luther speaks of the work of Christ in the past and in the present. This office is not limited to the suffering on the cross, but it continues in the present intercession of Christ.

On the other hand, Luther never tires of saying that Christ comes with his incarnation, his passion, and his resurrection, and then salvation. He comes by the Word, i.e., by the announcement of the redemptive events. Commenting on Gal. 3:7, he writes: "And today also Christ is present for some and for others he is yet to come. To all believers, he is present; to the unbelievers, he is yet to come, neither doth he profit them anything at all: but if they hear his word and believe, then he is present unto them, he justifies and saveth them." [108] "He setteth him forth by the word; for he cannot be apprehended in any other way than by faith." [109]

It will be noted to what degree these texts—and others could be cited [110]—bind salvation to the actual coming of Christ by the Word and to his presence in faith.[111] Christ comes himself by the Word. It is his personal presence which is important. It is not enough to benefit from the effects of his work, but rather from his presence. He has realized this presence himself. The church with its preaching is only the instrument which he uses in his sovereign way.

The presence of Christ is not thought of as static. In fact, Christ is present because he is always the one who comes. It must be said that he comes. Thus Luther speaks of the daily advent of Christ: "Just as Christ came once into the world in the time before appointed, to redeem us from the hard and sharp rule of our schoolmaster; even so he cometh daily unto us spiritually, to the end that we may increase in faith and in the knowledge of him, that the conscience may apprehend him more fully and perfectly from day to day." [112]

It is by faith that human beings have part in this saving reality which is Christ present in his Word. This faith is a union with Christ. Luther emphasizes this particularly in the *Commentary on the Epistle to the Galatians.*[113]

The most significant passages on this subject are found in the commentary on Gal. 2:16-21. In different and repeated ways, Luther there underlines the close bond between Christ and the believer. The expressions and images which he uses are borrowed from contemporary language used to describe marital union. Christ and the believer are united intimately *(conjunctissimmi)*, they adhere *(conglutinatio)* to one another, they cleave *(inhaesio)* to one another, they "become one body and one spirit." [114] By thus describing the union between Christ and the believer with the help of these categories of marriage, Luther obviously joins himself to a long Christian tradition which appears, for example, in Ephesians 5, as well as in the spirituality of the medieval mystics. But it will be important to establish the reason why Luther is thus led to emphasize the union between Christ and the believer, and that lies in his conception of justification by faith.

Let us look again at some passages in which Luther insists on the reality of this union. "Faith therefore must be purely taught: namely, that by faith thou art so entirely and nearly joined into Christ, that he and thou art made as it were one person; so that thou mayest boldly say: I am now one with Christ, that is to say, Christ's righteousness, victory and death are mine. And again, Christ may say: I am that sinner, that is, his sins, death etc. are mine, because he is united and joined unto me, and I unto him." [115]

The care he takes to emphasize the union, even the quasi-identification of Christ with the believer, brings Luther to the point where he hesitates. When defining faith as "a sure trust and confidence of the heart, and a firm consent whereby Christ is apprehended; *so that Christ is the object of faith*," he adds the comment, "or rather he is not the object, but as it were, in the faith itself Christ is present." [116] In fact, to speak of Christ as the "object of faith" puts in question that intimate presence of Christ which Luther does not cease to preach.

It may well be asked why Luther expresses himself in this way. Does he not thus abolish the distinction between Christ and the believer, confusing that which must not be confused? Before seeing how Luther discards a mystical interpretation of his thought, it is necessary to note that he intends it to explain his conception of justification. According to him, justification cannot rest on a quality inborn in human beings. That was the concept which he thought he found among the Scholastic theologians. Nor can it be reduced to the mere nonimputation of sin to persons by God, who in his goodness does not take human sin into consideration. Justification cannot be put into action by an absent Christ who is situated in the heavens or exists only in the imagination. [117] Preeminently, according to Luther, justification is bound up with the personal presence of Jesus Christ. As Pesch wrote in relation to Luther's thought: "It is 'with' Christ that human beings possess righteousness, salvation, and communion with God." [118] If then there is justification by faith, it is not because faith as a human attitude is the new quality meriting the divine favor, but "faith is justified, because it apprehendeth and possesseth this treasure, even Christ present." [119] Again, Luther can say that it is Christ "which furnisheth and adorneth faith, or which is the form and perfection of faith." [120]

He goes so far as to say, "If therefore in the matter of justification thou separate the person of Christ from thy person, then art thou in the Law, thou abidest in it and livest in thyself and not in Christ, and so thou art condemned of the Law, and dead before God." [121]

What can be said except that we cannot present ourselves before God outside the person of Jesus Christ? Our new life consists of living with Christ, resting our sins on him, and receiving his righteousness, of presenting Christ to God as our righteousness. Thus Christ does not justify us by acting on us in some way from outside, but by being present in faith. In faith, I must say that he is my Savior and my righteousness. It is this way of considering Christ which makes the difference between a historical faith and a saving faith. The historical faith in fact reduces Jesus Christ to the status of an object detached from the observer, because he is placed in the past and because he is considered as a reality in general. On the other hand, a saving faith takes hold of Christ" [122] as a reality which is addressed personally to me [123] and as a reality which is present in a sphere which I can and must penetrate and within which I can and must exist. Opposed to this is the historical faith which separates Jesus Christ from human beings. That is why this faith, characteristic of the relationship which the devil and impious human beings have with Jesus Christ, is dead. [124]

Although we have insisted very strongly on the true union between Christ and the Christian faith, it would be wrong to think of an absorption of Christ by the Christian. In Luther's perspective Jesus Christ remains distinct from me. Certainly he is present in faith, he is my righteousness before God, the new human being to whom I am called to conform more and more. However, the Christian does not progressively absorb Christ, but is transformed into Christ's image.

It must be noted that the union between the Christian and Christ is realized by the Word, not by a "Christianization" of a mystical or sacramental order, but by the creation in the course of the Christian life of a new person on the basis of what Jesus Christ is and has done and according to his likeness.

It must also be noted that Luther clarifies his conception of the union between Christ and the Christian in the following terms: "But here must Christ and my conscience become one body, so that nothing remain in my sight but Christ crucified and raised from the dead. But if I behold myself only and set Christ aside, I am gone." [125]

This text permits us to define Luther's thought in the following way: Jesus Christ is the person in whom I exist before God. He is the content of my conscience. I exist as a new person, not by confusing myself with him, but by considering him in faith, by turning me away from myself in order to carry me toward him, who is simultaneously the basis and likeness of the new life to which I am called.

God and Humanity in Jesus Christ or the Author of Salvation

According to a very common interpretation of Luther's christology, especially among Catholic authors, it would be necessary to emphasize the unique and sovereign action of God in the work of salvation wrought by Jesus Christ. Basing himself on "Swedish protestant theologians," Congar thus defines "the Lutheran conception of redemption as that of a drama which is played within Christ, within the reality of his death and resurrection, but whose only actor is basically God. The humanity of Christ is the theater of this drama; the cross and the resurrection are the acts or the scenario; the devil is caught and conquered in his own trap. But the dramatic conflict is played out in God himself as a conflict between righteousness and grace, wrath and love. Thus all is of God in the redemption. The sacrifice and the satisfaction are not offered to God by Christ in his human nature. It is God himself who, in Christ, satisfied and triumphed over the devil.[126]

If such an interpretation were right, it would in effect reduce the humanity of Christ to the place where the all-powerful action of God was accomplished. It would not be possible to say with truth that God operates *through* Christ, but only *in* him.[127] In this understanding of the thought of Luther by Congar it is difficult to see how modalism can be avoided. It is always *God,* in effect, who is active in the creation as in the redemption, without any apparent differentiation of persons, without any direct relationship, face to face, between the Father and the Son, without all this drama in which the Father, the Son, and the Holy Spirit act for the salvation of human beings. But is this really the thought of Luther?

Without stopping to examine the fact that Congar is far too dependent on the interpretation given by Aulén, who has been and will be criticized for emphasizing the role of the divine nature at the expense of the human nature, let us look at Luther's thought itself.

Luther does emphasize that God *is* in the humanity of Jesus. He contended as much against the Arians who devalued the divinity of Jesus Christ [128] as he did against those who reduced Jesus Christ to the level of an example to be followed. If God had not been present in Jesus Christ, then his passion would have had no salutary effect for us. There is nothing in this affirmation which does not conform to the tradition, and it would be false to deduce from it that Luther was a modalist or that he left no place for the free activity of the man Jesus.

In fact, it is still necessary to examine the texts again and to ask how the work of salvation is realized. It is accomplished within the framework of a drama which takes place between the Father and the Son, but it is a drama passing through this earth, through the incarnation of the Son, through his free obedience as a human being, through his sacrifice freely accepted, and through his act of suffering.

The initiative is taken by the Father. "He has sent his Son," [129] "He has not spared him, but given him freely for us," [130] "this most pure and innocent person is freely given unto thee of the Father to be thy High Priest and Savior." [131] Luther even imagines a kind of declaration by the Father to the Son: "be thou the person which hath committed the sins of all men; see therefore that thou pay and satisfy for them." [132]

But Christ is not only a passive object thrown in some way by God into the world and punished by the Father, and neither is he simply the place where "God" is present. He goes to sinners in free obedience to the Father. Thus Luther emphasizes both the love of the Father who is the author of our salvation and the love which moved the Son, who wished to be the companion of sinners,[133] who takes on himself all our sins.[134]

An action is thus set in motion. God sends the Son, who freely obeys out of love for the Father and for human beings. God places our sins on him; [135] the Son receives them of his own free will. "He has taken our sins upon himself without being constrained, but of his own free will." [136]

First, an important point should be accepted: it is not "God," thought of in the modalist sense, who is the author of the work of salvation, but the Father acting through the Son and the Son acting in the incarnation, obeying the Father and in solidarity with human beings. Looking at things in this way does not put in question the principle according to which all three persons of the Trinity always act together *(opera divina ad extra sunt indivisa)*. Hence we do not forget that we encounter the trinitarian God in Jesus Christ, but it does become evident that salvation is a drama which unfolds between the Father and the Son. Thus the incarnation is seen in a perspective both personalist and historical.

But there is a second point which must also be made clear. It is the free and spontaneous action, the active role, of the humanity of Jesus Christ. Certainly, Luther strongly emphasizes the action of God in Jesus Christ. Nevertheless, he does not thereby wish to exclude the human activity of Jesus, but rather to oppose the work of Jesus Christ, raised up and given by God, to our works and our righteousness. "For God hath laid our sins, not on us, but on his Son, Christ; therefore they cannot be taken away by us." [137]

By this affirmation, Luther does not wish to deny the human activity and liberty of the man Jesus.

The victory is won, not only by the presence of God in the man Jesus, although that is an indispensable condition, but also by the fact that Jesus Christ has freely obeyed. But there is not only this free human obedience; it is also, although Luther does not expressly say this, the translation onto the plane of human history of the eternal love of the Son for the Father. There is also the activity of the man which is itself revealed in the sacrifice. Jesus Christ not only bears the sin and the punishment which God imposes on him, but "he freely offers himself to God." [138] "He gives himself up for us." [139] He presents the sins in his body.[140]

To reduce Jesus Christ to the level of a passive victim on whom the punishment falls would be a travesty of Luther's thought. On the contrary, the activity side of Christ's suffering must be emphasized. He wishes it, he chooses it, he offers himself to God and to his plan. In Jesus Christ the eternal love of the Father acting through the Son in favor of human beings, and the love of the innocent man offering himself to the Father, meet and are united.

In Luther we do not find reflections on the relations between God and humanity in Jesus Christ, that is, reflections about the way in which relations must be envisaged between divine activity and human activity. But what does reappear here is one of his fundamental preoccupations: not to separate them! While, as we have seen, he constantly insists in his Eucharistic writings on the unity of the person, he insists equally also on the inseparable unity between the action of the man and the action of God in the work of salvation.

It is sufficient for us to state that the saving work of Jesus Christ is realized through a drama in which the creative love of God is at work, but also through the human obedience and human activity of Jesus Christ. In addition, just as Luther's theology always stands under the sign of the cross, so his christology is always eschatologically oriented, i.e., it refuses speculation about the relations between God and humanity in Jesus Christ, in order to wait for the full revelation when we shall no longer live by faith but by sight.

We have attempted to show that the saving work is accomplished by Jesus Christ, God and a human being, and that the human activity and freedom of Jesus Christ is far from being devalued, as has so often been said of Luther. But our exposition would not be complete if we passed over in silence some texts where the role of the divine nature is found accentuated to the point where the role of the human nature appears to be minimal.

In the course of a long exposition of Gal. 3:10, Luther is led to write about those who wish to be justified by works: "Therefore while they go about to do the law, they not only do it not, but also deny (as I have said) the first commandment, the promises of God, the promised blessing of Abraham; they renounce faith and they go about to make themselves blessed by their own works: that is to say, to justify themselves, to deliver themselves from sin and death, to overcome the devil, and violently to lay hold on the kingdom of heaven. And this is plainly to renounce God, and to set themselves in the place of God. For all these are the works of the Divine Majesty alone, and not any creature either in heaven or on earth." [141]

What is the meaning of this text? In fact, Luther is contending against the persons who exalt human activity while reducing the grace of God to the level of an aid, and who try to "make themselves blessed by their own works," that is to say, to constitute for themselves a merit which they could present before God. It is to this attitude that he opposes the initiative and activity of God. He it is who is the author of salvation.

To affirm that is not to oppose God to the man Jesus, but to oppose grace to wrath, salvation to sin. The human activity of Jesus Christ is found included within the saving activity of God. In effect, to affirm that God is the author of salvation is not, for Luther, to exclude the activity of the man Jesus, but it is to combat the idea of merit. As D. Löfgren rightly notes, "Luther has no quarrel with the activity of the human in the reconciliation accomplished by Christ, but only with the activity of the man conceived as *meritum,* i.e., against the purely sentimental view of Christ which was common in the current medieval spirituality directed toward the passion of Christ, which put a false accent on his humanity." [142]

We find an analogous point of view in Luther when he writes a little further on in this commentary, "For to overcome the sin of the world, death, the curse, and the wrath of God in himself, is not the work of any creature, but the divine power. Therefore he which in himself should overcome these, must needs be truly and naturally God." [143]

Luther, in opposition to the Arians, only affirms here the *vere deus.* The victory realized in Jesus Christ was only possible because he is fully God. One must not mutilate the divinity as the Arians did, nor make it pass into the background as the spirituality based on the imitation of Christ tended to do.

But to affirm that Jesus Christ is truly God is entirely in conformity with tradition. And, let us repeat, such an affirmation does not in Luther's thought automatically exclude human activity. To accentuate the activity of God unilaterally in the work of salvation "is to risk making Luther's conception of the sovereignty and love of God into a purely abstract idea." [144]

We must examine one final passage, without doubt the most difficult to interpret. It concerns the commentary on Gal. 3:10.

Luther there criticizes justification by works. The full weight of the text bears on the doctrine of justification by faith and not on christology as such. That must be noted at the beginning. In order to make quite clear what he means by justification by faith, Luther comments that "the Holy Ghost speaketh diversely of faith in the Scripture: sometimes (as a man would say) of an abstract or absolute faith, *fides abstracta vel absoluta,* sometimes of a concrete, compound or incarnate faith, *composita vel incarnata.*" [145] It is the abstract faith, i.e., considered independently of works, that justifies, although it would never do so without works. In order to clarify this distinction between abstract faith and compound *(composita)* faith, Luther appeals to the christological dogma. According to him, there are two ways of considering Christ, "Sometimes, the Scripture speaks of Christ as God and sometimes as a Christ, compound and incarnate." [146] It is to the divinity alone that is attributed the creation,[147] and abstract faith corresponds to the divinity thus considered in itself. Just as the divinity alone acts in creation, so also abstract faith alone justifies.

But one does not speak only of Christ according to his divine nature, any more than one confines oneself to abstract faith. In the Scripture, it is a question of the compound person of Christ, i.e., composed of "divinity joined to humanity." [148] In the same way it is a question of compound faith, i.e., faith acting in the works.

On the christological level the question is at once posed as to whether a particular role is recognized for the humanity of Christ. Luther points out that one says that the man Jesus created the heaven and the earth, for example. But can one really say that? In fact, Luther observes that "man in this proposition is a new word and (as the schoolmen themselves do grant) hath relation to the divinity: that is to say, this God that was made man, hath created all things. Creation is attributed only to the divinity (of Christ), for the humanity doth not create; and yet notwithstanding it is truly said that the man created, because the divinity which alone createth is incarnate with the humanity, and therefore the humanity together with the divinity is partaker of the same properties. Therefore it is well and godly said: this man Jesus Christ brought Israel out of Egypt, stroke Pharaoh, and wrought all the wonders from the beginning of the world etc." [149] All is thus attributed to the man because of the divinity.

The concern of Luther is to show that, in fact, the divinity alone creates. Speaking of the man Jesus in the context of the creation is only a way of speaking. It is a way of expressing the identity of this God who acts with the God who will become incarnate. Only God creates all things.

Of course, "eternal and infinite power *(regnum divinitatis)* is given unto the man, Christ," [150] but "it is not because of his humanity, but because of his divinity. For the divinity alone created all things, without any help of the humanity *(humanitate nihil cooperante)*.[151]

The process of justification must be understood in analogy with christology, as we have just expounded it. Faith is, of course, concrete, i.e., accompanied by works, in the same way as the divinity is bound to the humanity. And yet it is faith, considered in an abstract manner which justifies. "Faith is . . . the divinity in work, person and members, as the one and only cause of justification, which afterward is attributed to the matter because of the form, that is to the work because of faith." [152]

In his exposition of the christology of Luther, Congar dwelt particularly on the passage that we have just briefly analyzed. "What interests us at once in this text," he writes, "is the affirmation that the only effective reality in the salvation accomplished in Jesus Christ is the divinity, while the humanity is assigned no part in the order of efficiency. Even in Christ, the human is in no way a cooperator with God and author with him of the work of salvation, although it is effected through him, through a communication or participation with him." [153] Hence, according to Congar, it is at the level of christology that the fault is located which separates Luther from Catholicism. For Catholicism cannot follow the reformer when he speaks of the *Alleinwirksamkeit* of God. The doctrine of justification by faith is only an application on the level of soteriology of a fundamental choice already made at the level of christology.

The importance of the problem requires that we give careful attention to the passage to which Congar refers.

It will be asked first of all whether the doctrine of justification by faith alone is derived, as Congar maintains, from christology. One has always had the impression that Luther appeals to christology, looked at from a certain angle, in order to explain his doctrine of justification by faith. This is equally the view of Manns in the penetrating analysis which he has given to our passage.[154] He speaks of an *ad hoc* christological construction which appears to him to be "too forced" *(zu gewaltsam)* and "too much in contradiction to other christological affirmations, to consider it as an expression which is theologically valid for an understanding of Luther's thought." [155]

For our part, we have noted above a collection of passages where Luther clarified the human activity of Jesus Christ, the role played by his free obedience and by his sacrifice in the realization of salvation. Under these conditions it is permissible to emphasize the commentary on Gal. 3:10, where the accent is placed above all on the doctrine of justification, in order to minimize the role of the human nature in Christ?

It will be noticed, on the other hand, that in our passage Luther's interest is concentrated almost entirely on those acts which are accomplished by the divinity alone, i.e., the creation or the liberation of Israel. It is thus in effect that the analogy between the *solus deus* of the christology and the principle of *sola fide* of the doctrine of justification by faith is convincing. As has been clearly established by Manns, the facts of the suffering, death, and resurrection are passed over or take second place. They appear only under the mythological form of the hook (the divinity) and the worm (the humanity) on which the devil throws himself, only to be vanquished. Now when it is a question of the human activity of Jesus, the humanity of Christ appears again from a quite different angle in the commentary.[156] This is the case, as a general rule, when Luther is not called on to defend the *fides nuda.*[157] But preoccupied as he is in the commentary on Gal. 3:10 with the doctrine of justification by faith, he gives there only an incomplete exposition, even crude and warped, of his christology, since he presents the humanity of Christ only with the image of the bait. Hence, the human activity of Christ, his obedience, his suffering, the sacrifice that he made to the Father of his person, his solidarity with sinners, all the constitutive elements of his christology as we have already seen many times scarcely appear. In the same way there is a danger that there will appear an abstract idea of the *Alleinwirksamkeit* of God in which one no longer sees the activity of God exercised through the human activity of the Son become human, by which the human is enclosed rather than excluded.

Finally, it is important to examine the affirmations in our passage about the victory of Christ over sin and death. In fact, as we have already noted, Luther hardly deals with this subject and confines himself to using the old image of the hook and the bait, which allows him to put all the emphasis on the divinity, letting the humanity be merely the bait which deceives the devil by hiding on the hook, which is the divinity. After having affirmed the *solus deus* and the *nihil humanitate cooperante* in relation to the creation, Luther continues: "nor did the humanity conquer sin and death, but the hook hidden under the worm, whereon the devil did fasten, conquered and devoured the devil, which sought to devour the worm. Therefore the humanity alone could have effected nothing, but the divinity, joined with the humanity *(divinitatis humanitati conjuncta sola)* alone did all these things, and the humanity because of the divinity *(propter divinitatem)."* [158]

Here, Luther's thought does not seem to be very clear. Certainly, one cannot say in the perspective of redemption, *sola humanitatis.* "It was not the humanity which conquered sin and death." As we have already stressed, this passage is concerned with a christological affirmation of the most traditional kind, adopted by Luther from the early church. If Jesus Christ had not been God he would not have been able to save us. But does that mean that the humanity is basically useless? Does it participate in redemption only as an inanimate instrument, whose only role is in some way to hide the all-powerful activity of God? Is it necessary to interpret the *sola divinitatis* of Luther in such an exclusive way? The thought of Luther is hardly explicit on this subject. He uses the expression, *divinitas humanitati conjuncta sola*. The divinity which saves me in Jesus Christ works only when united to the human nature. In other passages, Luther shows more clearly the importance of this human nature for our redemption, although that does not in any way minimize the primordial role of the divinity. But here he is preoccupied with the concern to preserve the doctrine of justification by faith alone and by analogy to insist on the *solus Deus* of redemption. Hence, he scarcely asks the question about the real humanity of Christ, nor about the way in which this humanity is included in the work of redemption.

Notes

1   Luther's first series of lectures commenting on the epistle to the Galatians was published in 1519. This commentary depended largely on St. Jerome and Erasmus. (*WA* 2, 436-618.) Luther dealt with the epistle a second time in 1523, when he departed from them both. The present commentary was published in 1535 from lecture notes taken by one of the students during the series of lectures in 1531 (*WA* 40, 1, 33-688; 40, 2, 1-184). The English text used in this chapter is the revised Middleton text published in 1575. It is contained in an edition prepared by Philip S. Watson (London: James Clarke and Co., 1953). Page references throughout are to *WA* and to this English version (noted as *MT*).

Among the works that have dealt particularly with this commentary, we would mention the following: Althaus, *Die Theologie Martin Luthers*, pp. 183-203; Karin Bornkamm, *Luthers Auslegungen des Galaterbriefes von 1519 und 1531: Ein Vergleich* (Berlin: 1963); P. Manns, "Fides absoluta—Fides incarnata: Zur Rechtfertigungslehre Luthers im Grossen Galaterkommentar," in *Reformata Reformanda*, Festchrift für Hubert Jedin, vol. 1 (Münster: 1965), pp. 265-312; M. Greschat, *Melanchthon neben Luther*, Studien zur Gestalt der Rechtfertigungslehre zwischen 1528 und 1537 (Witten: 1965), pp. 80-109; O.H. Pesch, *Die Theologie der Rechtfertigung bei Martin Luther und Thomas von Aquin* (Mainz: 1967).

2 Martin Luther, *Oeuvres,* vol. 15, Labor et Fides (Geneva: 1969), p. 7. Cf. *MT* 1-15.
3 *WA* 40, 1, 36
4 Greschat, *Melanchthon neben Luther,* p. 80: "From the point of view of the theology of history, Luther interpreted the rejection of the Augsburg Confession by the emperor and the empire as the last stand of Satan in his resistance to the lordship of Christ."
5 *WA* 40, 1, 39
6 *WA* 40, 1, 53-54; 40, 1, 113-114; *MT* 30, 67.
7 *WA* 40, 1, 322, 1; *MT* 194-195; see also *WA* 40, 1, 580ff., *MT* 366.
8 On this whole question see A.E. Buchrucker, "Nullus Diabolus—Nullus Redemptor: Die Bedeutung des Teufels für die Theologie Martin Luthers," *Lutherischer Rundblick* 16 (1968):150-160; H. Obendieck, *Der Teufel bei Martin Luther* (Berlin: 1931); H.M. Barth, *Der Teufel und Jesus Christus in der Theologie Martin Luthers* (Göttingen: 1967).
9 *WA* 40, 1, 33; *MT* 16.
10 *WA* 40, 1, 33, 16; *MT* 16.
11 *WA* 40, 1, 181; *MT* 107-108.
12 *WA* 40, 1, 296; *MT* 177.
13 *WA* 40, 1, 34; *MT* 17.
14 *WA* 40, 1, 72; *MT* 40.
15 Esnault, *Oeuvres* 15, p. 8. A similar point is made by Philip Watson, editor of the *MT:* "In 1531 Luther seems to have decided to lecture again on the epistle because he felt that the centrality of the doctrine of justification by faith had been somewhat obscured during the controversies of the preceding years" (p. 5).
16 *WA* 40, 1, 33; *MT* 16.
17 *WA* 40, 1, 82; *MT* 46.
18 *WA* 40, 1, 33, 1; *MT* 16-17.
19 "Faith formed and furnished with charity." See *WA* 40, 1, 239ff.; *MT* 141ff.; *WA* 40, 1, 286; *MT* 17; *WA* 40, 1, 421, 29ff.; *MT* 262.
20 Greschat, *Melanchthon neben Luther,* pp. 95-99.
21 Greschat, *Melanchthon neben Luther,* p. 97.
22 E.g., *WA* 40, 1, 285; *MT* 170. Greschat is of a different opinion and he writes: "Luther, like Melanchthon, understands faith as a combination of *fides historica* (historical faith) and *fiducia* (trusting faith)" (p. 98).
23 On this question see K. Bornkamm, *Luthers Auslegungen,* pp. 176-223.
24 *WA* 40, 1, 439, 28; *MT* 273.
25 *WA* 40, 1, 440, 2, 15; *MT* 273-274.
26 *WA* 40, 1, 400, 2; *MT* 273-274.
27 *WA* 40, 1, 469; *MT* 291.
28 *WA* 40, 1, 270; *MT* 160.
29 *WA* 40, 1, 279; *MT* 165-166.
30 *WA* 40, 1, 565, 18; *MT* 356.
31 G. Jacob, *Der Gewissensbegriff in der Theologie Luthers* (Tübing-

en: 1929), p. 39, where he speaks of the impenetrability and great
abundance of mythological images by which the powers of darkness are characterized; Althaus, *Die Theologie Martin Luthers*, pp.
183ff., where the author speaks of the work of Christ as a combat
against the powers and finds his principal source for this in the
Commentary on the Epistle to the Galatians; K. Bornkamm, *Luthers
Auslegungen:* "There is no doubt that, in the course of the *Commentary on Galatians*, one can observe how the argument takes a
deliberate turn toward the use of mythological images."

32   K. Bornkamm, *Luthers Auslegungen*, pp. 166-167.

33   E.g., the way in which he refers to the experience of his youth,
when he approached Christ as a judge (*WA* 40, 1, 265; *MT* 157).

34   *WA* 40, 1, 271; *MT* 160-161; K. Bornkamm, *Luthers Auslegungen*,
pp. 157-234.

35   *WA* 40, 1, 35; *MT* 17: "Hence, I am willing to do my duty and
let this extremely verbose Commentary be published in order to stir
up my brethren in Christ against the wiles and malice of Satan, who
in these last days has become so infuriated at the recovery of the
sound knowledge of Christ."

36   Peters, *Glaube und Werk*, p. 38: "Luther does not describe the tension between law and gospel, between judgment and grace, merely
as an interested observer, nor does he seek as a systematic theologian to press them into manageable formulae, but he suffers through
them to the point of breaking, to the edge of self-annihilation, and
in this way he transports them by prayer into the *eschaton*.

37   It can be questioned whether it is right to translate the terms
conscientia or *Gewissen*, which are used by Luther, as *conscience*.
It must be made clear that by *conscientia* Luther does not mean
only the faculty to discern good from evil in an accomplished act
or one yet to be done, but the very life of human beings before God,
their most intimate beings, their hearts. When Luther uses the word
conscientia, he means it to include both the moral or psychological
conscience *and* the extent to which all the faculties of a person are
present in an encounter with God. It is in this *conscientia*, conscience understood in this way, that the experience of faith lives.
On this subject see G. Jacob, *Der Gewissensbegriff bei Luther*
(Tübingen: 1929); K.J.E. Alanen, *Das Gewissen bei Luther* (Hel-
sinki:1934); E. Hirsch, "Drei Kapitel zu Luthers Lehre vom Gewissen," *Lutherstudien* 1:9-220; E. Wolf, "Vom Problem des Gewissens
bei Luther," *Peregrinatio* 1:81-112; Peters, *Glaube und Werk*.

38   For the place and meaning of the law in Luther's thought, see espe-
cially W. Joest, *Gesetz und Freiheit* (Göttingen: 1951); P. Watson,
Um Gottes Gottheit (Berlin: 1952), pp. 125-129; G. Heintze, *Lu-
thers Predigt von Gesetz und Evangelium* (Munich: 1958); L.
Haikola, *Usus legis* (Uppsala—Wiesbaden: 1958); M. Schloemann,
Natürliches und gepredigtes Gesetz bei Luther (Berlin: 1961);
Pesch, *Die Theologie der Rechtfertigung bei Martin Luther und
Thomas von Aquin*, pp. 31-76.

39   See his commentary on Gal. 3:19 (*WA* 40, 1, 487ff.; *MT* 302ff.).
40   *WA* 40, 1, 257, 19; *MT* 151. And a little later, "So the law can do nothing else than strip us bare and make us culpable" (*WA* 40, 1, 258, 31; *MT* 152). See also *WA* 40, 1, 403; *MT* 249; *WA* 506, 24; *MT* 316; *WA* 513ff.; *MT* 320ff.
41   *WA* 40, 1, 482, 24; *MT* 299-300.
42   *WA* 40, 1, 400, 17; *MT* 246.
43   *WA* 40, 1, 257; *MT* 152. See also *WA* 40, 1, 428ff.; *MT* 266-267.
44   *WA* 40, 1, 45, 29; *MT* 24.
45   *WA* 40, 1, 399, 18; *MT* 245-246.
46   *WA* 40, 1, 419, 17; *MT* 259.
47   *WA* 40, 1, 276, 13; *MT* 163.
48   When, following the apostle, Luther puts this idea forward, it is quite clear that it concerns not only the ceremonial law, but "the whole law, whether it be ceremonial or moral, to a Christian is abrogated utterly, for he is dead unto it" (*WA* 40, 1, 268, 24; *MT* 159).
49   *WA* 40, 1, 168, 20; *MT* 101.
50   *WA* 40, 1, 209, 24; *MT* 124.
51   *WA* 40, 1, 282, 33; *MT* 168.
52   *WA* 40, 1, 235, 23; *MT* 138.
53   *WA* 40, 1, 236, 23ff.; *MT* 139.
54   G. Ebeling, "Die Grundformel theologischen Verstehens," *Die Religion in Geschichte und Gegenwart,* vol. 4, p. 507; Peters, *Glaube und Werk,* pp. 77ff.: "The conscience must be set free from confidence in its own work, and also from despair of itself. It must also be liberated from the slavery of the 'Thou shalt not,' which is why Luther is careful to distinguish between the law and the gospel"; Pesch, *Die Theologie der Rechtfertigung,* pp. 31-35, 66-76.
55   *WA* 40, 1, 209, 16; *MT* 123. See also *WA* 40, 1, 207, 17; *MT* 122.
56   *WA* 40, 1, 45ff.; *MT* 24.
57   *WA* 40, 1, 207ff.; *MT* 122ff.; see also *WA* 40, 1, 393ff.; *MT* 242.
58   *WA* 40, 1, 208, 16; *MT* 123.
59   *WA* 40, 1, 329; *MT* 200.
60   *WA* 40, 1, 336, 33; *MT* 205.
61   *WA* 40, 1, 485, 26ff.; *MT* 302.
62   *WA* 40, 1, 232; *MT* 137; *WA* 248ff.; *MT* 146-147; *WA* 260-261; *MT* 154-156; *WA* 298-299; *MT* 179-180; *WA* 503; *MT* 313-314.
63   Pesch, *Die Theologie der Rechtfertigung,* p. 54.
64   *WA* 40, 1, 389-390; *MT* 239-241.
65   *WA* 40, 2, 42, 29; *MT* 470.
66   *WA* 40, 1, 434; *MT* 270.
67   *WA* 40, 1, 262, 9; *MT* 155.
68   *WA* 40, 1, 299; 24; *MT* 179.
69   *WA* 40, 1, 297, 34; *MT* 178.
70   *WA* 40, 1, 298, 14; *MT* 178.
71   *WA* 40, 2, 6, 19; *MT* 444.
72   *WA* 40, 1, 503, 34ff.; *MT* 314.

73   *WA* 40, 1, 428, 27; *MT* 266.
74   *WA* 40, 1, 503, 19; *MT* 313.
75   *WA* 40, 1, 569, 14; *MT* 358.
76   *WA* 40, 1, 569, 18; *MT* 358.
77   *WA* 40, 1, 65, 12; *MT* 36.
78   *WA* 40, 1, 264, 21; *MT* 156; *WA* 265, 13; *MT* 157; *WA* 571, 19; *MT* 360.
79   *WA* 40, 2, 22, 24; *MT* 456.
80   *WA* 40, 1, 232, 32; *MT* 137.
81   *WA* 40, 1, 305, 17; *MT* 183.
82   *WA* 40, 1, 432-453; *MT* 268-282.
83   This is hardly surprising when one thinks of the place that the law occupies in the epistle to the Galatians.
84   *WA* 40, 437, 19; *MT* 272.
85   *WA* 40, 1, 437, 25; *MT* 272.
86   *WA* 40, 1, 436, 24; *MT* 271.
87   *WA* 40, 1, 448, 20; *MT* 279.
88   *WA* 40, 1, 433, 28; *MT* 269; *WA* 40, 442, 33; *MT* 275.
89   *WA* 40, 1, 448, 17; *MT* 279.
90   *WA* 40, 1, 437, 25; *MT* 272. "The man for others."
91   *WA* 40, 1, 432, 20; *MT* 268.
92   *WA* 40, 1, 434, 21; *MT* 270.
93   *WA* 40, 1, 437, 18; *MT* 272.
94   *WA* 40, 1, 438, 12; *MT* 272.
95   *WA* 40, 1, 438, 24; *MT* 272. See also *WA* 40, 1, 445; *MT* 277.
96   *WA* 40, 1, 443, 1; *MT* 272.
97   *WA* 40, 1, 443, 16; *MT* 275.
98   *WA* 40, 1, 449, 17; *MT* 279.
99   *WA* 40, 1, 452, 16; *MT* 281. "For the law being in his principal use and full of power, set upon Christ, and so horribly assailed him, that he felt such anguish and terror, as no man upon the earth had ever felt the like" (*WA* 40, 1, 567, 26; *MT* 357).
100   *WA* 40, 1, 439; *MT* 272-273.
101   *WA* 40, 1, 439; *MT* 273.
102   *WA* 40, 1, 440; *MT* 273.
103   *WA* 40, 1, 73, 12; *MT* 40; *WA* 40, 1, 273-274; *MT* 161-162; *WA* 40, 1, 503ff.; *MT* 313-314; *WA* 40, 1, 564ff.; *MT* 355ff.
104   *WA* 40, 1, 439, 15; *MT* 273.
105   *WA* 40, 1, 439, 23; *MT* 273.
106   *WA* 40, 1, 440, 21; *MT* 273-274.
107   *WA* 40, 1, 443, 31; *MT* 276.
108   *WA* 40, 1, 379, 14; *MT* 233.
109   *WA* 40, 1, 545, 34; *MT* 344.
110   *WA* 40, 1, 545, 24; *MT* 344; *WA* 40, 1, 130, 18; *MT* 77; *WA* 40, 1, 332, 33; *MT* 202; *WA* 40, 1, 401, 2; *MT* 247.
111   W. Joest, *Ontologie bei Luther*, p. 389: "The *Christus praesens* is the reality of our salvation *by* the Word (not *as* Word). . . . Christ

reveals *(eröffnet)* his presence to us by the Word. Just because it is his own presence, it is only by the Word and faith."

112   *WA* 40, 1, 536, 8; *MT* 337; *WA* 40, 1, 10ff.; *MT* 338.

113   K. Bornkamm, *Luthers Auslegungen,* p. 98: "The idea of the close bond of the believer with Christ is more strongly emphasized (from 1519 onwards) as the principal basis of his affirmations"; Pesch, *Die Theologie der Rechtfertigung,* pp. 234-248; Joest, *Ontologie bei Luther,* pp.. 370-382; Althaus, *Die Theologie Martin Luthers,* pp. 186-190; 200-203. But in opposition to this, E. Seeberg, *Grundzüge,* p. 118: "It is only in his early period that Luther insisted on justifying faith as effective union *(Einigung)* with Christ." M. Greschat also notes the importance for him of union with Christ, but he thinks that the expression of Luther's thought became more doctrinal than mystical: "In contrast with his earlier statements, the description of the union of the believer with Christ has now to a considerable extent exchanged its mystical attire for a rational mode" (p. 101). Both Seeberg's and Greschat's theses prompt certain reservations, but they are both right in noting that the concept of Christ as the "alien" righteousness of the believer gained in significance and that the idea of conforming to Christ has less emphasis in the later writings of Luther.

114   *WA* 40 1, 284, 20ff.; *MT* 170.

115   *WA* 40, 1, 285, 24; *MT* 170.

116   *WA* 40, 1, 228, 33; *MT* 134.

117   "Vain therefore is the speculation of the sectarians, concerning faith, which dream that Christ is spiritually, that is speculatively in us, but really in heaven. Christ and faith must thoroughly be joined together. We must be in heaven and Christ must live and work in us. Now he liveth and worketh in us, not by speculation and naked knowledge, but indeed and by a true and substantial presence *(non speculative, sed realiter, praesentissime et efficacissime)*" (*WA* 40, 1, 546, 23; *MT* 344).

118   Pesch, *Die Theologie der Rechtfertigung,* p. 244.

119   *WA* 40, 1, 229, 22; *MT* 135. See also *WA* 40, 1, 165, 3-19; *MT* 99; *WA* 233, 3-17; *MT* 137.

120   *WA* 40, 1, 229, 28; *MT* 135; *WA* 283, 26; *MT* 168.

121   *WA* 40, 1, 285, 15; *MT* 169-170.

122   Pesch, *Die Theologie der Rechtfertigung,* p. 235, rightly points out that this formula occurs more frequently in the later works of Luther. In the commentary we are here studying, *apprehendere Christum* occurs frequently: *WA* 40, 1, 228, 10-15; *MT* 134; *WA* 40, 1, 229, 1-10, 22, 29; *MT* 134-135; *WA* 40, 1, 233, 21; *MT* 138.

123   For the importance of *pro me,* see: *WA* 40, 1, 299, 9; *MT* 179-180: "Let us say only this word 'me,' 'for me,' in order to comprehend with a sure faith and not to doubt: 'for me.' " *WA* 40, 1, 448, 2; *MT* 279: "Therefore all the weight and force hereof consisteth in this word, 'for us.' We must not then imagine Christ to be innocent, and as a private person (as the schoolmen and almost all the Fathers

have done) who is holy and righteous for himself alone. True it is indeed that Christ is a person, pure and unspotted: but thou know him to be God and man: but then thou hast him indeed when thou believest that this most pure and innocent person is freely given unto thee of the Father to be thy High Priest and Savior . . . that he might bear thy sin, thy death, thy curse, and might be made a sacrifice and a curse for thee, that by this means he might deliver thee." See also WA 40, 1, 85, 26ff.; MT 48; WA 40, 1, 91, 16ff.; MT 52; WA 40, 1, 299, 29ff.; MT 180.

124   WA 40, 1, 285, 20; MT 170.

125   WA 40, 1, 282, 21; MT 167.

126   Congar, *La christologie de Luther*, pp. 466-467.

127   It is one of the weaknesses of many Catholic theologians that they address themselves not only to Luther, but to protestant christology in general; e.g., Wilhelm Averbeck, *Der Opfercharakter des Abendmahls in der neuen evangelischen Theologie* (Paderborn: 1967), pp. 787ff.

128   WA 40, 1, 441; MT 274-275.

129   WA 40, 1, 437, 21; MT 272.

130   WA 40, 1, 303, 31; MT 182.

131   WA 40, 1, 448, 22; MT 279.

132   WA 40, 1, 437, 21; MT 272.

133   WA 40, 1, 434, 17; MT 269.

134   WA 40, 1, 433, 23; MT 269.

135   WA 40, 1, 337, 13; MT 206.

136   WA 40, 1, 443, 19; MT 275. See also WA 40, 1, 434, 17; MT 269: "of his own accord *(sponte)* and by the will of the Father."

137   WA 40, 1, 437, 13; MT 271.

138   WA 40, 1, 298, 17; MT 178.

139   WA 40, 1, 299, 24; MT 179; WA 40, 1, 303, 21; MT 182.

140   WA 40, 1, 297, 22; MT 178.

141   WA 40, 1, 404, 29; MT 249.

142   Löfgren, *Die Theologie der Schöpfung bei Luther*, p. 261.

143   WA 40, 1, 441, 16; MT 274. See also WA 40, 1, 569, 25ff.; MT 359.

144   Löfgren, *Die Theologie der Schöpfung*, p. 251, and a little later he writes: "The wrath is not directed against the humanity as humanity, but against the contempt and abuse of the love and the grace of God. Luther never needs to emphasize the sovereignty of God to make clear the littleness of humanity, but only to underline the fact that human beings are called to receive the salvation of the grace of God. And, alternatively, he never needs to emphasize the littleness of humanity to highlight the transcendent sovereignty of God, but only to show the love which is God's total gift to the sinner" (p. 252). And similarly, earlier, he writes, "God and the creature are not absolute opposites, even if they are not identical, the distance between God and the creature lies not so much in their ontological structure as in the opposition of creatures to their subordination to the Creator, a subordination willed by God" (p. 49).

145 *WA* 40, 1, 414, 27; *MT* 256.
146 *WA* 40, 1, 415, 11ff.; *MT* 256.
147 *WA* 40, 1, 416, 12; *MT* 257.
148 *WA* 40, 1, 417, 34; *MT* 258.
149 *WA* 40, 1, 416, 10ff.; *MT* 257.
150 *WA* 40, 1, 417, 29; *MT* 258.
151 *WA* 40, 1, 417, 30; *MT* 258.
152 *WA* 40, 1, 417, 27; *MT* 258.
153 "La christologie de Luther," pp. 465-466.
154 Manns, "Fides absoluta–fides incarnata," pp. 265-312.
155 Manns, "Fides absoluta," p. 274.
156 Manns, "Fides absoluta," p. 275: "The neutralizing of the human participation of Christ such as we find it in our comparison, cannot therefore be taken without further examination, as typical of Luther's christology."
157 Manns, "Fides absoluta," p. 274.
158 *WA* 40, 1, 417, 31; *MT* 258.

7

Luther and the Christological Tradition of the Church[1]

The Texts: Content and Editing

The studies devoted to the thought of Luther after 1530-1535 are far less numerous than those dealing with the preceding period. Is this partly due to prejudice against writings like the *Disputations,* which are considered to be more academic or even Scholastic? Or perhaps there is the general feeling that everything is already found in the young Luther and that the "old" only repeats less well the affirmations of youth. Or perhaps there is a lack of sympathy with the conservative tendency in the later Luther, particularly after the Eucharistic Controversy. For our part, we are convinced that the christology of the old Luther cannot be passed over in silence.

The period that we are studying here seems to us interesting from several points of view. First, Luther shows more and more interest in the study of church history. At the christological level, it is of the greatest importance to see the result of the confrontation between his own thought and tradition. Certainly, Luther always appealed to tradition. We have already emphasized that. But so far, he had written no history of dogma, such as the *Treatise on the Councils and the Churches* of 1539.

The *Disputations* belong to the same period. There we see Luther in his role as teacher, and his christology appears within the framework of an academic tradition. The *Disputations* are in the form of

typical academic exercises in which one attacks and defends theses
on a given theological subject. These exercises were introduced
into the university during the Middle Ages and had fallen into dis-
use in Wittenberg by the year 1520. They were reintroduced in 1533
and practiced with more or less success by Luther himself.[2]

He gives a great importance to the *Disputations*. They must establish the proof that the Reformation lies within the classical tradition
of the *fides catholica* (*WA* 39, 2, 93, 1); they must defend faith
menaced by the devil (*WA* 29, 10; 97, 5; 266, 21),[3] struggle against
heresies present and future (*WA* 7, 7), and make Lutheran Christians, particularly the theologians, capable of responding to attacks
(*WA* 6, 17). The work then is both an exercise in rhetoric or discussion and an occasion to expound the doctrine clearly in view of
misrepresentations of which it had become the object.

What are these misinterpretations? They are certainly those of
Rome. We noted in the preceding chapter that the rejection of the
Augsburg Confession by the established church had greatly affected Luther. Therefore the opposition to Rome became more and
more virulent with him, as witness, for example, the Smalcald
Articles of 1537. It can also be detected in the *Treatise on the
Councils*, in which Luther emphasizes that the popes took little
part in them—they were called by the emperors—and that they had
only a small part in elaborating the doctrines that resulted from
them, which proves the necessity of cutting the papacy down to
size! But while squaring off against the church of Rome, Luther
never ceases to declare his attachment to the early church and to
insist on what is common to the churches of the Reformation and
the church of tradition. He continues to think that there is no discord on the subject of the Trinity, nor of the incarnation.[4] The
Augsburg Confession was content to use the creeds of the early
church on this subject, and the Smalcald Articles did the same. The
later Luther does not only study the history of the councils, in the
course of which these creeds were elaborated; he also comments on
them [5] and often appeals to them in the *Disputations*, which are
always centered on the classical christological confession. Luther
thinks that if there is discord with Rome on the subject of christology, then it is more in relation to the work of Christ. In fact, because
it denies justification by faith, the Roman doctrine did not, according to him, place sufficient emphasis on the unique character of
this work.

The fact that Luther remains linked to the early church in his christology and trinitarian doctrines does not prevent him, as we shall see, from serious reservations about the terminology nor from thorough discussion of the way in which the christological doctrine was developed in the Middle Ages, particularly with Occam.[6]

This attachment to the early church, which stems from a deep conviction and not only tactical considerations, enables Luther to defend himself against the charges of having introduced new doctrines. It also enables him to struggle against new adversaries, in the heart of Protestantism, who minimized the doctrinal tradition of the church and put in question certain accepted dogmas by introducing doctrines that Luther judged to be new and heretical.

So he continues to attack Zwingli. The Zurich reformer was, of course, dead by 1531, and the Concord of Wittenberg in 1536 had established an agreement with Bucer and others favorable to Zwingli's views. But the opposition to Zwingli's ideas remained strong with Luther until his death. In the *Treatise on the Councils and the Churches,* for example, he identifies Zwingli with Nestorius,[7] and a little before his death he reaffirmed once more his implacable opposition to Zwingli.[8]

But new Protestant adversaries, who pushed certain positions of Luther to an extreme, arose after Zwingli's death. Thus the Antinomians affirmed that Christians can dispense entirely with the law, especially in its use as a moral guide.[9] There are several disputations directed against them.[10] It is also at this period that the debate with Osiander takes place. It is known that Osiander, a convinced follower of Luther, thought of justification as real communication (and not only forensic) of the righteousness of Christ to the faithful in whom he dwells. From this point of view, all the emphasis was placed on the divinity of Christ at the expense of his humanity. These views of Osiander were made the subject of the disputation on justification in 1536.[11]

On his side, Schwenckfeld ever since 1538 had circulated the idea that the glorified humanity of Christ was not a *creatura,* thinking that thereby he would take up again certain affirmations made by Luther in his debate with Zwingli. In the disputation of 1540 (*WA* 39, 2, 93-121), Luther saw himself obliged to parry this attack, not in order to convince the ignorant heretic (which he took Schwenckfeld to be), but in order to dissipate the misunderstanding which Schwenckfeld's teaching had caused.

From 1543, Luther's attention is fixed more particularly on trinitarian questions. Servetus and Campanus were certainly far away from Wittenberg, but their ideas spread and confused the people.[12]

Apart from the disputations in which he took up this question, Luther also wrote a kind of commentary on the last words of David, *Von den letzten Worten Davids*. It is more a treatise essentially devoted to trinitarian questions than a commentary. We also find there traces of anti-Semitism, often violent. In effect, what Luther reproaches the Jews with is, among other things, the denial of the divinity of Jesus Christ and therefore of the Trinity. He reckons them among the adversaries which the theologians faithful to the Holy Scriptures must combat. We shall also consider this writing, which clarifies the way in which Luther approached trinitarian problems.

Luther and the Early Church: Some Notes on the *Treatise on the Councils and the Church* [13]

The matter of a council had found much interest in the Protestant camp. It seemed to offer a means of overcoming the schism that was developing in the church, as a consequence of the Reformation and to avoid having the pope, from the side of the Roman Church, acting as sole judge in the affair. But could one accept an invitation to a council sent out in 1536, when one knew that the pope had made quite clear that he reserved the right to have the last word? The question of the authority of the council was thus clearly posed. From the beginning, Luther was far more skeptical of the possibility of a council than were his friends. But it was only in 1539 that he expressed in a more detailed way his views on the question, after the research he had undertaken on the subject of the councils of the early church.

In his treatise, Luther prepared himself by a detailed study of the Fathers.[14] He applied himself to the councils by studying the *Ecclesiastical History* of Eusebius of Caesarea, circulated in the West in the Latin translation of Rufinus. But this history does not go beyond the beginning of the fourth century. He also used the *Tripartita* of Cassiadorus, a kind of synopsis of the works of three Greek historians of the church, but that did not go as far as the Council of Chalcedon. In addition, Luther made use of the *History of the Popes* by Platinus (which he observed to be too favorable to the popes), as well as the *Canones,* the decisions of the councils, as they were incorporated into the collection of ecclesiastical law by Gratian. But his most recent source, and the one which he considered the most satisfactory, was the work of a Franciscan monk, Pieter Crabbe, which appeared in 1538 under the title *Concilia omnia tam generalia quam particularia.*[15]

More than once, however, Luther complains about gaps in his sources or about their bias. He was in fact confronted with the major problem of understanding those whom the church had condemned as heretics and whose ideas were often known only through quotations selected by their "orthodox" adversaries.

What is Luther's verdict on the Fathers and the councils in general? He points out inequalities and contradictions between councils and Fathers.[16] And above all he observes that in no council and in no Father is the Christian doctrine present in its entirety.[17] The Council of Nicaea dealt only with the divinity of Christ. That of Constantinople proclaimed the divinity of the Holy Spirit. That of Ephesus established that Christ was not two persons, but only one. The Council of Chalcedon, for its part, set forth the two natures of Christ.[18] Only one source contains the totality of Christian doctrine: that is the Scriptures. It is therefore always necessary to turn to them.[19]

After this general judgment, we must ask ourselves what authority Luther ascribes to the councils. For him it is clear that the fundamental authority rests in the Holy Scriptures.[20]

They are the norm and the source. "It is better to drink directly from the source than to drink from the stream that comes from it" (*WA* 520, 3), he writes, following St. Bernard of Clairvaux. The councils must work on the basis of Holy Scripture. Without the Scripture they are the councils of Caiaphas, of Pilate, and of Herod (*WA* 606, 21). All that the councils affirm is already there in the Scriptures—for example, the divinity of Christ (*WA* 552, 6ff.). If it were not the case, the affirmations of the councils would have had little effect (*WA* 552, 16). The four articles defended by the council are already proclaimed, abundantly and powerfully, in the one gospel of John (*WA* 605, 21).

What then can be the meaning or purpose of a council? Luther's conception of it is quite simple.[21] A council assembles, not to create new articles of faith, but to conserve the old and condemn the new.

All else that the councils have done at the level of the organization of the church and the episcopacy, fixing the date of Easter, etc., concerns only a particular period of time. Moreover, measures taken by a council in addition to this can be harmful if they institute laws, i.e., new works to accomplish which threaten the doctrine of justification by faith. The proper role of a council then is to defend, on the basis of Scripture, one of the truths of the Christian faith, a truth which has been menaced by heresy.

What we have just seen of the general attitude of Luther to the early church can appear to be somewhat negative. But it must not be forgotten that by the *Treatise of the Councils,* Luther wished to make his coreligionists more realistic. The hope, often deceptive, in a council which would make possible the union of the divided church, was still very much alive among Christians, both Protestants and Catholics. Luther, for his part, appeared skeptical. This is what explains the general tone of the *Treatise on the Councils.* But that does not mean that Luther was not consciously bound to the early church. We shall see this better as we now come to study his way of interpreting the christological subjects of what he called the four great councils.[22]

We shall not be able to show in detail Luther's lively and critical way of attempting to reconstruct the history of the councils, the part played by the emperor, the characteristics of the heretics who were condemned, the different episodes. We shall not be able to go very deeply into the question to what degree Luther seemed to understand what was at stake, nor examine his method of interpreting different heresies. These are hermeneutical problems which are only beginning to be studied.[23] We shall then study the four councils at the level of christology.

The Council of Nicaea [24]

It had for its principal purpose, to preserve the ancient doctrine of the divinity of Christ.[25] Luther's passionate interest in this article is well-known. If Christ were not God, he would not be able to save us.[26] On this subject, the Council of Nicaea only repeated, as is proper in matters of faith, the biblical affirmations.

But what did the Arian heresy mean to Luther? It taught that Christ was a creature.[27] And Luther showed that such a teaching was incompatible with acknowledging the divinity of Christ and his preexistence before all creatures. For Arius, Christ was God in the same way as Moses and the saints were. And he was before all creatures, that is to say that, for Arius, he was created and made before them. And where the Nicene Creed speaks of Christ "begotten, not made," Arius could subscribe to this in the measure that he established a parallel with Christians who are also born of God. For Luther, the example of Arius shows clearly that it is not enough to confess the divinity of Christ, but that it is even more necessary to be precise about what one means by it. It is in this perspective that Luther selects the *homoousios* as the central point of the Nicene Creed.[28] He uses this term in the traditional sense, that is, that it expresses for him also the unity of essence between Father and Son.

Luther lingers over this question when he refers to a dispute between Arius and Athanasius. When Arius wished to remove this word *(homoousios)* because it is not found in the Scripture, Athanasius replied that one does not find his terms there either, i.e., *innascibilis, ingenitus deus,* by which Arius sought to distinguish between the Father and Christ.

In this connection, Luther remarks that in divine things, one must teach nothing that is not found in the Scripture. But that does not exclude the use of nonscriptural terms,[29] particularly when arguing with heretics.[29] "Then it is necessary to summarize the meaning of Scripture in a few brief words, where several verses have been used, and to ask whether they hold Christ to be *homoousios*, which in many words is the clear meaning of Scripture, words which they pervert among their friends with many erroneous glosses, while confessing them freely before the emperor and in the midst of the council" (*WA* 572, 26). Note in this remark of Luther the decisive manner in which he defends the term *homoousios*. There is only one single passage in which he seems to show some reserve about this term, and even then only conditionally: *Quod si odit anima mea vocem homoousios nolim ea uti, non ero haereticus.*[30]

We do not think that this conditional remark expresses the basic thought of Luther. He certainly shows himself critical of the terminology, but then so does Athanasius at the beginning of the controversy with Arius, when he excuses himself for using a nonscriptural term.[31]

But as we have just seen, Luther recognized that it was necessary to use this term to drive Arius into a corner. It was both necessary and legitimate. In fact, the scriptural principle does not forbid the expression of evident truths by means of nonbiblical terms.

The Council of Constantinople

This council proclaimed the divinity of the Holy Spirit in opposition to the Macedonians. According to these heretics, "the Holy Spirit would not have been truly God, but a creature of God, by whom God set in motion, illuminated, consoled the hearts of human beings and did all those things which Scripture says of the Holy Spirit" (WA 575, 17).

Luther does not go very deeply here into the doctrinal questions. He deals mainly with other aspects of the council, emphasizing particularly its independence from Rome.

The Council of Ephesus

This is the council which most held the attention of Luther, since according to him, it went to the very heart of the christological question.

Can one call Mary *theotokos,* mother of God? That was the starting point of the conflict. By replying negatively to this question, Nestorius and his friends had stunned the general assembly of Christians. They concluded that he did not regard Christ, born of Mary, as truly God, but simply a man (WA 582). Thus he was condemned, and according to Luther, rightly, because with this view he had taken over the heresy of Arius and sharpened it. According to Luther, that would be the usual way of presenting Nestorius.[32]

Luther attempted to correct this false picture of Nestorius and to deal with the question more profoundly by seeking to go beyond the positions defended in this way by his sources. First, he established from his sources that Nestorius had in fact professed the divinity of Christ, because those who condemned him accused him of dividing Christ into two persons, God and a human being (WA 584, 8). But according to Luther, this reproach also is unjust. In fact, Nestorius did not teach two Christs, but only one, as the writings devoted to the question affirm with equal clarity (WA 584, 19-34).

It was necessary then to take up the question again and to see why Nestorius had been condemned. Luther did this in two steps. He first examined *theotokos* as such and broadened the perspective by general considerations of the communication of attributes.

It is the *theotokos* that led to the condemnation of Nestorius. He did not wish to call Mary God's mother, because Christ did not derive his divinity from her . . . or Christ did not have his divinity from her as he had the humanity from her" (*WA* 585, 32).

Of course, Luther agreed, Christ had not derived his divinity from Mary, and yet one can say that God is born of Mary, as a child is the child of a woman in body and soul, even though the soul itself is not derived from the mother. On the basis of the personal union between God and human beings in Jesus Christ, one must say that she has brought him into the world, "Mary has nursed and cradled God, and she has prepared bread and soup for him" (*WA* 587, 14).

The error of Nestorius was thus fundamentally this: he has denied the communication of attributes. Thus Luther broadens the discussion and leads it to this point which he regards as of central significance. Because God and human beings are united in Jesus Christ, the one participates in the properties of the other. When the man Jesus dies, it is God who dies. We shall come back to this question of the communication of attributes later. Let us note here that Luther accuses Nestorius at this point of lacking in logic. In fact, he would have admitted the *antecedents*,[33] that is, Christ as a single person, but refused the *consequences*, that is, the communication of attributes. "It seemed too terrible a thing for him to hear that God should die" (*WA* 589, 7).

That is why, in the eyes of Luther, the council did not condemn the heresy in its full extent. In fact it had seen only a single "attribute," i.e., the *theotokos*. But Nestorius had denied others to which Luther in the Eucharistic Controversy had given great attention already, i.e., "death, the cross, suffering, and all that does not accord with divinity" (*WA* 590, 28). Luther is thus led to put Zwingli and Nestorius in the same bag.

This is not the occasion for us to evaluate at length the judgment of Luther on Nestorius. He did not place the patriarch of Constantinople in the general context of the struggle of the School of Antioch, particularly with Apollinarius, who did call into question the full humanity of Christ. But note the care with which Luther does justice to Nestorius, applying to him criteria of judgment which prefigure the methods of a modern history of dogma.[34] It is known that at this period a certain rehabilitation of Nestorius was in progress.[35] It is recognized today that his adversaries wronged him in reproaching him for speaking of Christ as two Sons. "Like Theodorus, Nestorius refused to speak of 'two sons,' just as he refused to see in

Christ a *purus homo,* adopted by God, or elevated by his merits to the dignity of Son of God." [36] But he is so attached to the distinction of the natures that one often has the feeling that he sees in Christ only two natures simply juxtaposed, united by a conjunction which is purely external.

This is the point that Luther emphasized with vigor for reasons generally known. By introducing into his criticism of Nestorius the conception of the communication of attributes, Luther made a historical error. Although it was lurking among the Alexandrian theologians, this concept was not fully elaborated until later. But for Luther the fact is significant. All the evolution of the christology of the early church tends, according to him, toward this concept. To the extent that one does not affirm it, one remains a Nestorian. By not accepting it, one calls in question the incarnation itself, that is to say, the union between God and humanity.

The Council of Chalcedon

Luther complains particularly about the lack of information on the subjects dealt with at this council. He claims that his sources leave him lacking.[37] He is obliged to make use of the *History of the Popes* by Platinus, which he judges to be too favorable to the popes.

According to this source and the letters of Pope Leo I, it would seem, Luther says, that the calling of the council was provoked by the teaching of Eutyches that Christ was only one person, according to the divine nature *(allein in göttlicher natur)* (WA 593, 17). The council corrected this and taught that Christ is one person in two natures, which corresponds in the eyes of Luther to good doctrine (WA 593, 19). If we are to believe the sources, Eutyches admitted that the divinity, after having taken the humanity upon itself and after having become the Christ in one person only, absorbed the humanity. Christ would thus be only God and not a man. Luther admits that he cannot clearly understand this. Eutyches certainly taught the doctrine of two natures since he affirmed that the divinity took the humanity upon itself. But what did he mean when he taught that afterward a single divine nature remains in the incarnation? Luther does not find clear information about this in the documents that he was able to study.

That is why he tried himself to reconstruct the heresy of Eutyches.

According to a letter of Pope Leo, Eutyches taught a heresy exactly opposite to that of Nestorius.[38] Very curiously, Luther concludes that Eutyches must have refused to attribute the attributes of the divinity to the humanity, that is to say that he must not have admitted that, for example, Christ is also creator of the world according to his humanity. Whereas Nestorius refused to attribute the attributes of the humanity to the divinity, Eutyches did the opposite.

Even taking account of the fact that it is rather difficult to discern, still today, the exact thought of Eutyches [39] (if he had a thought?), it must be recognized that Luther has not grasped the error of the Archimandrite condemned at Chalcedon. He is, in effect, opposed to Nestorius by his emphasis on the unity of Christ to such a point that his divinity absorbed his humanity. The flesh of Christ is not, according to him, consubstantial with ours. Certainly he did not intend, as Apollinarius did, to remove from Christ the rational soul, but by professing "one nature only" in the incarnate Christ, he was already crossing over Monophysitism. On this point, Eutyches could appeal to Cyril of Alexandria, but the latter's formulae were better balanced and more able to preserve the humanity of Christ.[40] On the other hand, Eutyches seemed to have fallen back into the errors of Apollinarius and to have misunderstood the persistence of the human nature of Christ.

It is striking to see that Luther failed to detect this tendency in the thought of Eutyches. Was it because he himself tended in certain respects toward Monophysitism? Or because in his eyes, ever since the confrontation with Zwingli, the essential danger was too great a separation between the two natures? That is why he reproaches Eutyches for something for which he could only with difficulty be blamed. He reproaches him for failing to bind sufficiently strongly the humanity and the divinity, since, according to Luther, he refused to apply the attributes of the divinity to the humanity. In reality, Eutyches had so strongly bound them together that humanity disappeared! This is a point that Luther did not see. We might add that he could not see it, because he was above all attached to the idea of the unity of Christ. Moreover, Luther feels himself ill at ease with Eutyches. He has the feeling that he has not completely understood him. And he does not have much respect, it seems to us, for the Council of Chalcedon.[41] That of Ephesus was enough for him!

The Doctrine of the Trinity

Taken as a whole, the ideas of the reformer on the Trinity have been little and inadequately studied. Congar can justly observe that "the works devoted to a study of his doctrine of God do not present us with a comprehensive or thought-out theology of the Trinity." [42] There is a tendency to pass rapidly over Luther's attitude to the doctrine of the Trinity, either to emphasize his soteriology or to underline the dialectic between the hidden and the revealed God (e.g., Th. Harnack). [43] Or again, one expects to find a deformation of the doctrine of the Trinity in Luther. Thus K. Holl has accused him both of modalism and of subordinationism. [44] Others, while they find the classical doctrine of the Trinity in Luther, generally think that it is to be found there as a "foreign body." [45] Even a historian as conscientious as Köstlin, who offers one of the best expositions of Luther's doctrine of the Trinity, [46] reproaches him ultimately for depending more on the doctrinal tradition than on the Holy Scripture. [47] This judgment should be revised—at least in the sense that for Luther there is in this matter no contradiction between the two sources. Luther would not have adopted the classical doctrine of the Trinity if he had not found it firmly based in the Scriptures, and notably in the Old Testament. [48]

Given the slight attention devoted by the scholars to the doctrine of the Trinity in Luther or the often dubious conclusions at which they arrive, it is not difficult to understand the questions and doubts of Congar: "Has Luther a correct trinitarian theology? Has he a precise doctrine of the Trinity?" [49] Basing himself on a certain number of Protestant works and on his own research, he is able to write a little further on: "Luther is not a man for the mystery of the Trinity, he is for 'God' and that suffices for him. . . . He refused to occupy himself with speculations about God; he wishes to understand God only in Jesus Christ, that is to say, in the victorious act of love and the gift whereby he became my righteousness and my salvation." [50] And he thinks he can make use of a certain number of formulae which deviate dangerously from traditional trinitarian formulae.

The opinion thus advanced is fair insofar as it emphasizes the attention given by Luther to the revelation and saving activity of God. But it is false insofar as it fails to see to what extent this saving activity of God not only presupposes, in Luther, the classical trinitarian and christological doctrines, but is exercised precisely within the framework of an action between the Father, Son, and Holy Spirit. Of course, Luther affirms, with the tradition: *Opera ad extra sunt indivisa.* At the same time, however, the Father sends the Son who obeys the Father and whose work is made effective, in the present, as salvation by the Holy Spirit. It is not simply "God" who acts, but it is God—Father, Son, and Holy Spirit—in the framework of a drama within God himself, with which human beings find themselves associated.[51]

It can be asked to what extent it is legitimate or necessary to speak, as tradition does, of the immanent Trinity, i.e., of God in himself. Would it not be sufficient to speak of the revelation of the trinitarian God in history? Is that not primarily what Luther did? There can be no doubt that Luther started there. If he speaks of the Trinity, it is on the basis of revelation and scriptural witness, but it must also be said that he does not content himself with speaking of the economy of the Trinity, as Melanchthon does, but that he speaks also of the immanent Trinity, or of the eternal relationships between the Father, the Son, and the Holy Spirit. Is there then a reason other than Luther's inborn traditionalism? It seems to us that this characteristic has its origin in the logic of his thought about revelation. Everything depends on the fact that the accomplishment of salvation, realized by the Father, the Son, and the Holy Spirit is determined in the very eternity of God. If there are two "Gods"—the God who saves and God in himself—the assurance of salvation would be put in question. And that is where modalism ultimately leads, wherein the Father, the Son, and the Holy Spirit are reduced to different modes by which the divinity is manifest in history. But in its essence it remains beyond revelation. A division arises between God as he is and God as he acts. That is why it is also necessary to speak of the "immanent" Trinity, even if, faced with the mystery it is only possible to speak with hesitation and inadequately. But it appears that the saving act of God in history only translates what God is from all eternity, that is to say action between the Father, the Son, and the Holy Spirit.[52] Considering things in this way, Luther could not avoid speaking of the immanent Trinity. We must now see how he speaks, and where he places himself in relation to tradition.

In the period which interests us here, Luther approached the trinitarian problem quite often—particularly after 1543. It was not

the conflict with the traditional church that provided the occasion—
on this point he considered himself at one with the Roman Church—
but it was rather that the doctrine of the Trinity was called into
question as much by the Jews and Turks [53] as by such adversaries
as Servetus. Because of these attacks it is necessary to defend the
faith, Luther said to those who thought it was a sin to discuss the
Trinity.[54] The question is dealt with in several of the *Disputations,*
and also in the writing devoted to the last words of David, which it
is interesting to compare with the *Disputations.*

It will be noted that the *Disputations* give a large place to questions of terminology. We have already shown that, according to Luther, the first task of theology is to express as adequately as possible,
the mysteries of the faith, taking careful account of the changes in
meaning which words applied to God require. On the other hand,
Luther concerns himself with the questions disputed by the theological schools of the Middle Ages, which gave him the opportunity
to clarify his own interpretation of the traditional doctrines of the
church. In the writing devoted to the last words of David, Luther
strives, above all, to illuminate the scriptural witness to the Trinity. That is where we shall begin our interpretation.

"I would believe neither the writings of Augustine nor those of
the Master of the Sentences," Luther declared, "if the Old and New
Testament did not clearly bear witness to this article of the Trinity." [55] But how do they bear witness? Luther observed that the
world was created by the Word, as testified by Genesis 1 and
John 1.[56] This Word, existing before the creation, was not created,
but was with God; it was itself God, while it was throughout a different person from the Father (*WA* 54, 57, 3ff.). In another passage,
commenting on 2 Sam. 23:2-3, he states that the Trinity appears in
that passage too. There the Spirit of the Lord speaks through David
about the God of Israel (the Father) and the Rock of Israel (the
Son) (*WA* 54, 35; 31ff.). Very often Luther also reasons in the following manner: a supreme and eternal rule is promised to the Messiah; now such an honor belongs to God alone; the Messiah must
then be God, even though he is a different person from the Father
(*WA* 54, 35; 44, 15). The same reasoning is found in connection
with the invitation addressed by God to the man Jesus to sit at his
right hand (*WA* 54, 51), or when Luther refers to the vision of
Daniel, seeing on the clouds a man to whom is accorded an eternal
and heavenly rule (*WA* 54, 47, 38ff.), or again when it is a question

of the house of God which the Messiah will construct. This will be more beautiful than the heavens and the earth, which is why its constructor, the Son of David, must also be God, although a person other than the Father (*WA* 54, 40, 26ff.).

Here we leave to one side the way in which he proves the divinity of the Holy Spirit.[57] It is also important to note that beside the scriptural witness are placed the signs and works destined to make known the Trinity to the eyes of faith.[58] In fact, God uses creatures in order to reveal himself as the trinitarian God. These must be considered from two points of view: "absolute" (as creatures of God, a work of the three persons met in the Trinity); or "relative." Under this last aspect, God uses them as images or revelations of the three persons considered separately.[59] In this way, the dove is an image of the Holy Spirit only,[60] and the man Jesus is specifically, since the hypostatic union will never cease, the sign of the Son only.[61]

Here Luther no longer follows Augustine, as he still did in a sermon of 1514 (*WA* 1, 20, 1ff.) in order to discern vestiges of the Trinity, either in human beings or in nature.

The signs of which we have just spoken have meaning only because they accompany and confirm the Word. Like the Word, they address themselves to faith.[62] It is faith that allows us to know, here below, the mystery of the trinitarian God, who one day will be accessible to our sight.[63]

We must now look more closely at the way in which Luther expounds the doctrine of the Trinity. "But the basis *(Grund)* of faith is that you believe there are three persons in the one sole God, and each person is similarly fully and solely God, in such a way that the persons are not confused and the nature *(Wesen)* not divided, but there remains distinction of the person and unity of the nature" (*WA* 54, 64, 27). Here he agrees completely with Athanasius, whose creed he had recalled a few pages earlier (*WA* 54, 57, 26ff.). One finds again with Luther a then current Scholastic distinction when he places the following words in the mouth of Christ: "*Ego et Pater unum sumus, sed non unus; unum id est una essentia, unus hoc est una persona*" (*WA* 39, 2, 314, 17).[64]

Luther observes that the unity of the Trinity goes beyond the unity we meet at the level of the creatures or that of mathematics (*WA* 39, 2, 287, 17).[65] And yet it does concern three persons. In order to express this paradox, Luther insists that there must be a new grammar and a new vocabulary. "*Cessat etiam numeri ordo:*

unus, duo, tres" (The order of the numbers cease to be 1, 2, and then 3) (*WA* 39, 2, 303, 24).

It must be affirmed that, on the one hand, all the divinity *(tota divinitas)* is present in one person taken in isolation, and on the other hand, no person is the whole of divinity (nulla persona esse sola divinitas) (*WA* 39, 2, 287, 21). In the first case, one refers to the divine nature, which is the very being of God; in the second case, one envisages one of the persons. On the basis of the unity of the divine nature, each person is in himself truly God. But one cannot isolate one person in relation to the other. "Even if sometimes it is the person of the Father which is revealed, sometimes that of the Son, sometimes that of the Holy Spirit, it is still the one, sole God revealed in three persons" (*WA* 54, 88, 3).[66]

In other words, there where one of the persons is found, the others are also present. "Whichever person you name, you have named the one sole God in three persons" (*WA* 54, 65, 6).

These considerations take on a particular importance when seen from the point of view of the incarnation. The humanity of Jesus is the work of the three persons of the Trinity.[67] Luther has taken over the traditional formula: *opera ad extra sunt indivisa*.[68] But it is the Son only who assumes the humanity, as Luther frequently stresses.[69] And he takes over an image from Bonaventura, who speaks of three girls of whom only one put on a dress, with the help of the other two.[70] According to Col. 2:9, in the man Jesus "the whole fulness of deity dwells," "and yet thereby the Father and the Holy Spirit are not robbed of this same divinity, but they are with the Son and the man Christ, one sole God" (*WA* 54, 60, 21).

Luther remains faithful to the tradition when he speaks of intertrinitarian relationships. It is within the framework of these relationships that the Father, the Son, and the Holy Spirit must be distinguished, and not in their action with regard to the creature. He is faithful to the thought of St. Augustine when he writes: "What distinguishes the Father is that he is the Father and does not derive his divinity from the Son or from any other source. . . . What distinguishes the Son is that he is Son and does not derive his divinity from himself, nor from any other source than from the Father only, since he is born from the Father eternally. . . . What distinguishes the Holy Spirit from the Father and the Son is that he is the Holy Spirit who proceeds *(ausgehet)* eternally from the Father and the Son" (*WA* 54, 58, 15ff.).[71] It is thus their reciprocal relationships that distinguish one from the other of the three persons of the Father, Son, and Holy Spirit. That is the Augustinian doctrine, taken over by Peter Lombard and by Saint Thomas. Can one say that Luther has gone farther? Does one find again with him the tendency of the Eastern Church, in which the *per se* of each person is more strongly marked? We had already posed this question. It seems to come up again here when he declares that the Father is "the origin *(Ursprung)* or the source *(Quelle)* of the divinity" (WA 54, 64, 3).[72] The expressions *Ursprung* and *Quelle* recall certain Greek theologians, such as Basil or Origen. It would also be possible to make a comparison with the terminology of Dionysius the Areopagite, who speaks of the Father as the source of the divinity, and calls him the fount of light, from which the Son and the Holy Spirit come out like flowers.[73] It is known that in the 12th century, Richard of St. Victor took over certain of these ideas when he founded a movement that had some influence in the 13th century and which sought to establish the necessity of the three persons on the basis of the divine nature.[74]

In fact, it seems to us very difficult to assign a place of importance to this term *Quelle*. It is only an image used to express the fact that the Father is Father, because he derives his divinity from no one, but he gives it to the Son. All the speculations that can be found in Eastern theology with regard to the divinity as source of life and light are absent from Luther's thought. In general, as we have emphasized above, he holds to the Augustinian doctrine of relationships. In the same way, he refuses, as we have already seen, to make the three persons of the Trinity derive from the nature of God.

One of the trinitarian questions most hotly debated in the Middle Ages was that posed by Peter Lombard in Book I, Distinctio 5: Did the Father engender the divine nature, or did it engender the Son, or did it engender itself? The response of Peter Lombard, contested on this point by Joachim di Fiore, was as follows: *essentiam divinam nec generare nec generari* (the divine nature is neither engendered nor engenders). That really means that only the Father can engender, not the divine nature. The Fourth Lateran Council had adopted the position of Peter Lombard. Twice Luther makes this sentence by Peter Lombard the center of his *Disputations*.

In the disputation devoted to John 1:14 in 1539, Luther declares his agreement with Peter Lombard.[75] According to human logic, it should in fact be necessary to conclude from the two statements *pater in divinis generat* and *pater est essentia divina* that the divine nature engenders. But the majesty of God is placed beyond such a syllogism. By divine nature what must be understood here is *tota trinitatis et majestas Dei*.[76] Now, it is the Father alone and not the entire Trinity which engenders.[77]

But a few years later, Luther appears to have changed his mind. In the disputation of Georg Major and Johannes Faber in 1544, he takes the side of Joachim di Fiore, pointing out that Peter Lombard should not have introduced a new idea. It would have been enough to understand the phrase *essentia generat* as "relative," as applying to the Father, and not as "absolute." Augustine and Hilary had both taught that clearly enough with the phrase *essentiam de essentia, lumen de lumine relative intelligi, non absolute* (understanding the nature of nature, the light of light, not absolutely, but relatively).[78] Koopmans tried to compare Luther with the Cappadocians, for whom the nature is what the three persons have in common, while these three persons are described as individuals.[79] Joachim di Fiore, whom Luther here defends, had in fact followed the Cappadocians, and this would explain his nearness to them. Luther's Augustinianism would then be less evident here.[80] In any case, it does not seem to us that there is a necessary contradiction here between the positions taken by Luther in 1539 and in 1544. In both cases, in fact, he affirms that it is not the divine nature (whether it designates the intertrinitarian life or the nature taken *absolute*) that engenders. This would in effect have been absurd, since the engendering takes place at the level of intertrinitarian relationships, and not that of the Trinity turned *ad extra*. But if one envisages the nature *relative* —that is, in relation to the Father in his existence as Father—one can affirm that the nature engenders. Such an affirmation is not excluded in the disputation of 1539, but it is only affirmed as such in that of 1544.

We shall end our exposition by showing that, at several points, Luther insisted that our reasoning and our current vocabulary were inadequate to express the mystery of the Trinity.

In the Disputation of 1539 he had to face the argument: *"In Deo nihil est caducum neque accidens. Qui dicunt Deum esse patrem et filium tribuunt Deo accidens. Ergo vos ponitis accidentia in Deo"* (In God nothing is void or caused. Whoever says that God is Father and Son ascribes change to God. Therefore you attribute causal happening in God) (*WA* 39, 2, 20, 1). That is human reasoning that one cannot apply to God. To be Father and Son belongs to his eternal being; to his "substance" as Augustine said. The same argument appears under another form in the disputation of 1544: "*Quicquid generatur, est subjectum passioni. Deus autem non patitur. Ergo non est generatio in divinis*" (Whoever is engendered is subject to suffering. But God does not suffer. Therefore there can be no engendering of the divine) (*WA* 39, 2, 307, 25). There again, Luther remarks, a new vocabulary is imposed. If one wishes to speak of suffering and action, it is necessary to do so in a language appropriate to the intertrinitarian life and not following our normal categories. One finds the same kind of argument when he rejects the idea that the birth of Christ makes of him a creature (*WA* 39, 2, 104), or that birth places him in time (*WA* 39, 2, 293, 3ff.).

Examining the terminology used by Luther to describe the mystery of the Trinity, one is struck both by his traditionalism and by his profound dissatisfaction with the way in which the doctrine is expressed.

The traditionalism appears particularly in the *Disputations,* since they are in Latin. If the German texts seem at times to leave room for equivocation on Luther's traditionalism because he is there obliged to use new words, such as *Wesen,*[81] this equivocation is soon removed when one returns to his Latin texts. We find there terms inherited from tradition and notably by the medieval schools. He speaks of the Trinity, of person, of essence, of consubstantiality, setting himself in the Latin tradition.[82] The term *person* corresponds to what the Greeks call *hypostasis.*[83] There are *tres subsistentes personae, una autem divinitas* (three subsisting persons, but only one divine being).[84]

At the same time, however, Luther suffers from the inadequacy of these terms to translate the reality which he is aiming at; often he has to deal with terms which are not scriptural, such as Trinity. But nonetheless, it is necessary to use *pro captu infirmorum* these inadequate terms.[85] "*Trinitas macht ein seltsam cogitation, man muss aber propter infirmos et docenti cause also reden*" (The word *trinitas* seldom helps in thinking, but it must be used for want of a better and for the sake of the teaching).[86] If anyone does not want to use the term *person* or *hypostasis,* let them do as they please, so long as they express the matter clearly.[87] "*Rem mussen wir behalten, wir redens mit Vocabeln, wie wir wollen*" (We must keep true to the matter, but we use what vocabulary we wish).[88] Recall the insistence of Luther that terms take on a new meaning when one speaks of God. "Let the order of the numbers cease to be one, two, three. What is valid in creation respecting the numerical order, place, or time has no validity here. Therefore one must deal quite differently here and constitute other forms of speaking than is natural. Here, not only order, but coeternity, coequality, image, nature must be quite new." [89]

The Incarnation

Luther holds expressly to the tradition of the church in order to confess Jesus Christ to be true God and true human being.[90] The care with which he studies the councils of the early church shows the extent to which he takes this doctrinal tradition seriously, although he suffers from the inadequacy of the terminology and from the way in which the "moderns," the Scholastic theologians and particularly the Occamists, interpreted and refined the christological doctrines of the early church.[91]

It is necessary to emphasize again the incessant effort of Luther in the *Disputations* to make clear the miraculous reality of the incarnation. Philosophy can neither justify the incarnation nor put it in doubt. To the argument that philosophy should be able to attribute to God the possibility of incarnation, because it had already attributed all power to him (WA 39, 2, 8, 10, 24, 29), Luther replies in the following manner: "Even when it ascribes almighty power to God, philosophy cannot say, the same person is creator and creature, God and a human being" (WA 39, 2, 8, 20–9, 19). But since philosophy ascribes incomprehensible attributes to God, could it not concede to him the possibility of incarnation? (WA 39, 2, 14, 15). Luther replies, basing his answer on the fact that no philosophy has so far conceded incarnation to God (WA 39, 2, 14, 20). Certainly the human intelligence and imagination could have conceived an idea of the articles of faith, but not affirmed them with confidence in their reality (WA 39, 2, 15, 4). The incarnation is a fact, not because it has been thought by human beings, but because God has realized it.

The fact precedes the thought. Such thought has to let itself be corrected, transformed, and reoriented by this unique and new reality, which shocks our usual way of thinking. *Nulla est proportio finiti et infiniti* (nothing has the dimensions both to finitude and infinity) is a current philosophical axiom. But Luther does not discuss it. For him, the reality itself of the incarnation renders such a discussion superfluous, so that he simply refers to the argument and never returns to it again (*WA* 39, 2, 35ff.; 9, 2ff.; 9, 20; 112, 15ff.; 14, 34ff.).

Of course, an infinite distance separates God from human beings. Far more than the philosopher, the theologian must increase this distance. But, as R. Schwarz remarks, "The abyss between God and human beings is far deeper for Luther, when he speaks of Christ, than it is for the philosophers. In his eyes, the statement *Deus est homo* is to a much higher degree a *praedicatio disparata* (absurdity) than the statement *Homo est asinus* (humanity is an ass), while the philosophers [Occamists] treat the two statements on the same level." [92]

Yet, one must say *Deus est homo*, precisely because the miraculous reality of the incarnation imposes itself. As we have seen, it is the Scripture which bears witness to the incarnation. Faith is content with this witness.

We must now examine how Luther thinks of the incarnation.

And first of all, who is incarnate? That is the first question to ask. In the disputation of 1540, one of his opponents reasoned thus, "*Natura divina est factus homo. Divina natura est trinitatas. Ergo ...*" (The divine nature has become human. The divine nature is trinitarian. Therefore . . .) (*WA* 109, 23). Is it then the whole Trinity which becomes incarnate? To this Luther replied no. It is the divine nature which becomes incarnate in the person of the Son. And a little further on, he observes that the divine nature can designate either one person of the Trinity or the whole Trinity, the *tota divinitas*. When dealing with the Trinity, we cannot say that the divine nature is dead. But we can say that of the divine nature in reference to one person of the Trinity, *quando capitur pro persona* (*WA* 39, 2, 110, 10). Luther returns to the question in a disputation of 1544: "Not the Father, nor the Holy Spirit, but the Son become human") (*WA* 39, 2, 279, 30). And in this context, he insists on the incomprehensible character of this affirmation. The same idea recurs in one of the theses of another disputation of the same year: "*Sola filii persona assumpserit hominem*" (Only the person of the Son has assumed humanity) (*WA* 39, 2, 287, 24).

But can one really confess the divinity of Jesus Christ? Can one say that in this respect he is placed on the same level as the Father? Do not the descriptions of the incarnation and the relationships between the Father and the Son in the Holy Scripture tend in the other direction? Here Luther has to reply to a number of classical arguments used in the course of theological debates. There is no variation in God, according to the epistle of James (1:17); but there is change in the Son, since he became human. How could he then be God, for in God there are no *accidentia*? (*WA* 39, 2, 22, 12; 111, 3). Luther responds by saying that for God, the incarnation is not necessarily to be located at the level of *accidentia*. In the unity with humanity in Jesus Christ, the divinity is like the *substantia* (*WA* 39, 2, 111, 8). It does not change its nature. That is what determines the person of Jesus Christ in his own being. The incarnation does not introduce a change in God. The Son can thus be incarnate while still remaining God.

But yet another argument is held against him: "If the Son was of the same substance as the Father and had the same power as he had, then the Scripture would not say that all things would be summed up in him" (*WA* 39, 2, 20, 15; 104, 4). To that Luther replies: "Although he is one *(idem)* with his Father, all things are subject to him by the Father, because he was made flesh, suffered, and was crucified for us" (*WA* 39, 2, 20, 21), or again, "Whatever relates to his ministry and humanity, in his divinity he is, in fact, equal in power with the Father" (*WA* 39, 2, 104, 6). That is the answer he always gives when his opponents make much of the limitations of Christ attested by Scripture (*WA* 39, 2, 102, 10ff.; 111, etc.).

The most delicate questions arise when it is a question of being more precise about the manner of the incarnation, that is to say, the respective place of the Word and the humanity, the nature of this humanity, and that of the unity realized in Christ. The Occamist theologians were very attached to the study of these questions. The christology of Luther is clarified when it is compared to certain Occamist developments on the same subject. We shall refer here to the detailed study of R. Schwarz to which we have already directed attention.

At the basis of Occamist christology, as of that developed by Luther, lies the traditional concept that in the hypostatic union, the person of the Son does not assume a human *person* at the incarnation, but a human *nature*. The problem is to know how the human nature is united to the divine person.[93] Occam rejected the idea that the human nature is in some way melted with the Christ into one

sole person, so that the human nature also becomes *persona Christi.*
Rather than admit such an idea, Occam thought that one could as
readily conceive of the human nature becoming an ass! Occam and
his disciples Pierre d'Ailly and Gabriel Biel, for their part, understood the hypostatic union quite differently. The human nature does
not become, according to them, *persona Christi,* but is carried and
elevated *(sustentificatur)* by the *persona divina.*

According to Gabriel Biel, as earlier for Bonaventura, the *persona
divina* constitutes for the human nature what he calls a *suppositum,*
that means it allows it to live as an individual existence. It is in that
that the human nature is carried and elevated *(sustentificatur)* by
the *persona divina.*

The hypostatic union thus conceived as *suppositale* union is distinguished from personal union in that the human nature does not
become a person. That is excluded because according to the Occamists one cannot attribute the existence of a divine person, who is not
created, to human nature which is created. But the human nature
brings something to the *persona divina* which carries it. It confers
on it a concrete appellation *(denominatio concretiva).*

Whereas in 1509 Luther, commenting on the *Sentences* of Peter
Lombard, showed himself in agreement with the Occamists' christology, he began to oppose it in the course of these *Disputations*
that we are now studying.

For example, he opposed the moderns in the theses of the disputation of 1540, when he accused them of *insulsius* (tasteless) discourse (*WA* 39, 2, 95, 32) by saying "*humanum naturam sustentari
seu suppositari a divina natura, seu supposito divino*" (human nature is sustained either by support from the divine nature or support
from the divine) (*WA* 39, 2, 95, 34). According to Luther that does
not adequately translate the mystery of the hypostatic union. He
thinks that by assuming human nature the Word makes the human
nature participate in his personal being.

Luther accentuates the unity of the two natures in the unique
person of Jesus Christ. Even though they are distinct, yet they are
united in one and the same person. Luther also uses the terms *con-
jungi* and *conjunctio* in order to designate the unity (*WA* 39, 2, 98,
6ff.; 101, 8; 101, 19; 102, 3; 106, 26ff.; 114, 15ff.). The two natures
constitute one and the same person and the person of Christ is composed *(constat)* of the divinity and the humanity (*WA* 39, 2, 100,
18; 110, 22). For Luther the hypostatic union is not reduced to the

suppositale union, for the two natures are united *"personalitur"* in the unity of the person (*WA* 39, 2, 98, 6ff.). We shall have occasion to see that, in the eyes of the reformer, it is the communication of attributes which constitutes the only adequate and legitimate expression of this unity. Whereas in philosophy, God and humanity are two persons, in Christ the humanity and the divinity constitute only one and the same person. Philosophical logic is not therefore suitable in theology (*WA* 39, 2, 100, 13).

But what does Luther mean exactly by the word *persona?* It is difficult to find any detailed explanation in his writings. In the same disputation as that from which we have just quoted is found the following sentence, *persona est res per sese existens* (person is something existing in itself) (*WA* 39, 2, 117, 23), a definition which one can compare, as R. Schwarz does, with that of Richard of Saint Victor [94] and Duns Scotus. In its union with the Son of God who has assumed it, the humanity takes part in the existence as *persona*.

A question arises here in connection with the word *homo* as applied to Christ. What does one mean by that? Luther thinks that this term takes on a new meaning here, because it signifies *personam divinam sustentantem nostram humanam, ut albus significat homunem sustentantem albedinem* (a human person sustaining our humanity, as a white person signifies humanity sustaining whiteness) (*WA* 39, 2, 10, 30), or again *Christus homo significat personam divinam incarnatam* (the man Christ signifies a divine person made flesh) (*WA* 39, 2, 10, 35). On this subject, one can make the following remarks: First of all, it will be noted that Luther distinguishes a philosophical and a theological sense of the term *homo*. In philosophy, it indicates the *persona per se subsistentem* (person existing in himself) (*WA* 39, 2, 10, 28). In theology, on the contrary, attention is directed, not precisely toward the entity *humanity*, considered in itself, but toward the concrete whole where the human nature has been assumed by the divinity. Hence, *Christus homo, id est, persona divina, quae suscepit humanam naturam* (The man Christ is a divine person who assumed human nature) (*WA* 39, 2, 117, 35).

The difference in meaning of the term *homo* in theology and philosophy also becomes apparent when the two terms *homo* and *humanitas* are set over against each other. According to Luther, the two are identical in philosophy (*WA* 39, 2, 116ff.). Not in theology. *"Homo hic in concretis significat humanam naturam, quia est*

persona, sed humanitas non significat personam" (humanity signifies human nature in the concrete, because humanity is a person,
but humanity does not signify a person) (*WA* 39, 2, 116, 3). In
other words the term *homo* implies that of humanity, because the
Son who becomes incarnate and whom one may designate by the
term humanity, assumes a human nature. But this human nature is
not *homo,* for *homo* signifies a person. But *humanitas* does not, although it may assume such a form (*WA* 39, 2, 115, 1). Thus, in
common with the general theological tradition, Luther stresses that
one cannot say that the Son of God has assumed a *homo,* otherwise
there would have been two persons (*WA* 39, 2, 116, 7). It is a
natura humana that he has assumed. Equally, according to Luther,
that verse of the "Te Deum" must be understood in this way, where
it reads, "When you took upon yourself to deliver humanity" (*WA*
39, 2, 116, 26ff.). *Humanity* is here taken in the sense of *humanitas,
quae non est subsistens, sed assumpta* (humanity, which is not supported, but assumed) (*WA* 39, 2, 117, 33).[95]

It can also be pointed out how Luther criticized the Scholastic
theologians for the way in which they used the term *homo.* According to him, they used it sometimes to designate "the created human
race," and sometimes God *sustentantem humanam creaturam* (*WA*
39, 2, 10, 9).[96] This is the *aequivocatio* which he was still practicing
himself in his commentary on the *Sentences* of Peter Lombard and
which he criticizes in the *Disputations.* But Luther does not think
that the term *aequivocatio* applies in this case. In theology, the term
homo has a precise and unequivocal sense, because it designates the
divine person who assumes our human nature (*WA* 39, 2, 10, 29ff.).
The *aequivocatio* must be avoided, for it is the mother of errors
(*WA* 39, 2, 28, 10).

The elaboration of a christology has at all periods posed the problem of the humanity of Christ. Does it concern a humanity consubstantial with our own? Does the doctrine of the *anhypostasie,* which
affirms that Christ finds a personal existence only because the human nature subsists in the unique *hypostasis* which is the Word,
not mutilate this humanity? That question must be posed to all who
hold the doctrine of *anhypostasie* [97] and therefore to Luther.[98] The
question of the integrity of the human nature must also be raised
when one thinks of the close unity which is found binding the two
natures. Is there not a risk of divinizing the human nature? Luther
denies this. When his adversary claims that the humanity of Jesus

Christ is only an accident, because Paul says that Christ came "in the likeness of men" (Phil. 2:7), Luther replies that, on the contrary, Paul wished to prove by that that Christ was *verus homo qui patiebatur, loquebatur sicut homo* (true human being who suffered and spoke even as human beings do) (*WA* 39, 2, 114, 12). Of course, Christ was not subject to original sin and concupiscence. But this does not call in question the reality of his humanity (*WA* 39, 2, 107, 4ff.; 118, 26). He is born of *(ex ea)* the Virgin Mary and not by her *(per eam)* (*WA* 39, 2, 31, 29-35).

It is above all in his discussion of the term "creature" that Luther develops his thought on the subject of the true humanity of Christ. Can one speak of Christ as a creature?

It is worth comparing Luther's thought with other theological views on Christ as creature. It is known that the Arians had envisaged a certain subordination of the Logos to God, in the sense that he was conceived as a creature of God *('ktisma)*, even though the first creature, supreme and created *ex nihilo*. It goes without saying that Luther will seek to separate himself from such a view (*WA* 39, 2, 21, 21; 29, 17; 94, 28; 127, 21).

But the affirmation, *Christus est creatura* was a matter of discussion even among the most orthodox theologians. It was in fact a kind of case study on which the analytical spirit and logic of the Occamists could be exercised. That is why Gabriel Biel treats this subject at such length. According to him, *creari* must be understood here, not in the sense of *creatio ex nihilo,* which is to be reserved for the unique creation of the world, but in a larger sense concerning the way in which God has opened up from *non esse* to *esse*. In philosophy and in theology, a distinction is made between *creator* and *creatura*. As R. Schwarz shows, Biel can with difficulty admit that *Christus est creatura,* since *Christus,* the subject of the affirmation, is a person having two different natures, while according to Biel the human nature, created and assumed, must be distinguished *realiter* (in a real sense) from the divine person who assumes it. Can one say both that *Christus est creator* and *Christus est creatura?* Would it not be necessary to refine this last statement by saying that according to his humanity, *Christus est creatura?* But to satisfy Biel, it has to be admitted that the designation *creatura* can be applied to the subject directly or only indirectly. When one says that Christ is *creator,* then that refers to the divine person. One cannot then go on to say that he is *creatura,* without further qualifying that by saying, "according to his humanity." But if the designation refers mediately or indirectly to the subject, it is then possible to affirm *Christus est creatura,* for that implies that it is only in respect of the human nature that has been assumed that the divine person can be qualified as a *creatura.* Thus only the statement, *Christus est creator* can be made without qualification. As for the statement *Christus est creatura,* it must be handled with all the care that we have indicated. There again, Luther goes beyond the Occamist position, because for him the hypostatic union is not reduced to the *suppositale* union, but it is truly a union within the person and it finds adequate expression in the communication of attributes, conceived *realiter.*

But we must present also another view, antagonistic to Luther, that of Schwenckfeld. He thought that, in his glorified human nature, Christ was no longer a creature, the unity between the divinity and the humanity being such that the former had in some way absorbed or radically transformed the latter. But if one affirmed that the humanity was a creature, then Christ was no more than *homo* and could not therefore be *redemptor generis humani* (redeemer of the human race). This argument can be found presented in the disputation of 1540, provoked by the ideas of Schwenckfeld (see especially *WA* 39, 2, 100, 1ff.). Moreover, Schwenckfeld remarked that since Christ can be adored, that proves that he is not a creature (*WA* 39, 2, 105, 25ff.).

Schwenckfeld thought that he was being faithful to the ideas Luther himself had put forward concerning the ubiquity of Christ. In fact, he possibly intended only to carry Luther's reasoning to its logical conclusion, by divinizing the humanity of Christ. But Luther did not recognize himself in this view and vigorously attacked Schwenckfeld's position. There can be no question for him of mixing the two natures, falling thereby into what one must call the Monophysite heresy.

Let us now examine the thought of Luther on the subject of the statement, *Christus est creatura.* Luther does not place himself with the Occamists. For them it is primarily a question of logic. The traditional words and the usual distinctions must keep their meaning in theology, which means a clear distinction must be made between creator and creature. Luther places himself with respect to the unique gift which is the mysterious unity of the creator and the creature in Jesus Christ. In order to express this mystery he rejects the "ancient language" *(lingua vetus),* that is to say, the language of philosophy in which "creature" represents that which "the creator has created and from which he is separated" (*WA* 39, 2, 105, 4ff.; 94, 19ff.; 118, 14ff.). In this sense one cannot speak of Christ as a creature without falling into the Arian heresy (*WA* 39, 2, 94, 31ff.). And Luther cannot adopt the current definition of the word "creature" (*WA* 39, 2, 118, 14ff.; 105, 5ff.), precisely because in Christ the creature is not separated from the creator (*WA* 39, 2, 118, 21ff.). When speaking of Christ, it is necessary to give to the term "creature" a new sense which would not consider the creature as an entity taken in itself, but as the unique unity by which it is bound to the creator: *Nos conjungimus creatorem et creatoram in unitate personae* (We join creator and creature in the unity of the person) (*WA* 39, 2, 120, 14). According to Luther, it is all there: one must consider this mysterious unity in which the creator and creature are *unus et idem* (one and the same) (*WA* 39, 2, 105, 7ff.). The divinity has truly caused the creature to enter into its own existence as *persona.* The Christ is then both creator and creature in the indissoluble unity of personal existence.

Luther dissociates himself from Occamist distinctions. R. Schwarz notes that unlike Biel, it is of little importance to Luther whether one says, *Christus secundum quod home est creatura* (Christ to the extent that he is human/ is a creature) or *per humanitatem* (by his humanity), or *in humanitate* (in his humanity): one can just as well say, *Christus habet creaturam* (Christ inhabits a creature) or *assumpsit creaturam* or quite simply, *humanitas Christi est creatura.* Here all the logical and terminological distinctions break down.

For Luther, this does not mean the mixing of the two natures, as ultimately Schwenckfeld did. Luther continues to teach that it is the divinity which creates and that it is the humanity which is created, but one cannot isolate the divinity from the humanity. They are united in one and the same person. That is why Luther can say of this one and the same person both that he is creator and that he is creature.

According to Luther, the unity of God and humanity in Jesus Christ finds its most adequate expression in the doctrine of the communication of attributes. It is this doctrine and the way in which Luther interpreted it that we must now examine.

The Communication of Attributes

This theory seems to have had a great importance for Luther. We have already shown this in relation to his *Treatise on the Councils*. The communication of attributes appears there as the decisive point of the controversies and development of christology in the early church. In the sense that Luther intends it, it becomes a kind of touchstone of true theology.[99] It was K. O. Nilsson above all who in recent times insisted on the importance of the communication of attributes in Luther's thought. It is at the center of his exposition of Luther's christology.[100]

Luther did not, of course, invent this theory, which was current in the theological tradition of his day. Before seeing what Luther made of it, it is useful to look briefly at what it meant before his time.[101]

It was a hermeneutical problem which led to the use of the concept in the early church. From a christological point of view, it was necessary to explain the fact that the biblical texts attributed, on the one hand, properties rightly reserved for God to the man Jesus, and on the other hand, human imperfections to the Son of God. This problem became more acute because one carefully distinguished the two natures in other respects. The idea of a closer communion between the two natures, inhabiting one another and communicating their properties reciprocally, seemed to offer a solution to the hermeneutical problem with which we are dealing. Is it necessary, however, as Regin Prenter does, to attribute the origin of the theory of the communication of attributes to the latent Docetism of the early church?[102] This explanation can hold in certain cases, e.g., Cyril of Alexandria, but is it really the origin of this concept (Prenter calls it *der Grund*)? We doubt it, although it cannot be denied that the communication of attributes has tended to favor Docetism. But the motives on which it is founded seem to us to be legitimate, such as we shall show again in relation to Luther. It is not possible to deny that there are hermeneutical problems such as we have raised above.

The idea of an interpretation of the divine and human properties seemed necessary, if one did not want to sacrifice the real union of divinity and humanity in Christ, as it is testified in Scripture. It is known that the Cappadocians, in this regard, had forged a number of images (iron/fire, for example) which Luther picked up together with the whole of the tradition. Gregory of Nazianzus spoke of an interpenetration, of a circular movement *(perichorèsis),* but it is above all John of Damascus who developed this concept. The division between the Alexandrians (Cyril, John of Damascus) and the Antiocheans is most clearly shown in the different ways in which they conceive of the communication of attributes. Thus the Alexandrians thought principally of the action of the divine nature with respect to the human nature: the penetration takes place only in one direction and there is the risk of a certain Docetism, as Prenter has already noted in connection with Cyril of Alexandria. On the other hand, the theologians of Antioch envisaged the *perichorèsis* as the communication of the properties of each of the two natures to the person who is common to them both. They did not envisage an exchange between them. The whole christological dilemma breaks out in connection with this exchange. To deny it is to put in question the real unity of the God-man, but how can we avoid Monophysitism if the exchange is affirmed? This question was to hold the attention of medieval theologians. In general they admit a form of exchange, but they do their utmost to explain exactly what they mean. The West is more reserved than the East in this regard, less reticent with regard to Monophysitism. As Otto Weber shows, the communication of attributes is very often considered as a particular form of expression *(eine bestimmte Weise der Aussage)* (p. 146). Such is notably the case with Saint Thomas, followed on this point by Calvin and also to a certain extent by Zwingli, who emphasizes the *alleosis.* Thus one weakens the sense of the reality of the exchange and directs attention toward the way in which it is expressed, the language. In effect, this expresses the reality only imperfectly, as Calvin was able to say of this concept that it was *impropris, licet non sine ratione* (improper, even without reason).[103] The identity of view between Calvin and Saint Thomas is well illustrated by an image devised by the latter; to say that an Ethiopian is white makes nonsense as a general proposition, but makes sense when what is meant is *albus secundum dentem* (white so far as his teeth are concerned).[104]

It is not always easy to follow the way in which the idea of the communication of attributes developed after Saint Thomas.[105] Was there even a development? According to H. A. Oberman, "Nothing essential was added after Saint Thomas Aquinas, who presented and studied this problem so clearly; neither Oresme nor Biel con-

stitute an exception in this regard." [106] Of course, theologians such
as Occam, Nicholas d'Oresme, d'Ailly, and Biel took a great interest
in this question, but it would appear that they did so without adding
anything new.[107]

An important point must be mentioned here because we shall
come to it again with Luther. It is to know whether the communication of attributes concerns the two natures or the unique person of
Jesus Christ. Saint Thomas concluded that it was in the latter sense.
The uncreated cannot be encompassed or comprehended by the
created *(finitum non capax infiniti)*, that is why one cannot conceive
of a communication of attributes by considering the two natures.
One cannot say, for example, of the human nature as nature that it
is "creator," because it is a creature; nor that it has not been conceived. One can say that only of the person of the Son. Later, it will
be said that one can only conceive of the communication of attributes *in concreto*, that is to say, in the person of the God-man and
not *in abstracto*, in relation to the two natures which are presented
to us in this person. In Luther, we have already met the problem
of Christ *creatura* and seen the reply he gave to it. It will be necessary to take up this problem again in the perspective of the communication of attributes.

How does Luther understand this? He explains himself rather
often after 1530. Apart from the *Disputations* and the *Treatise on
the Councils*, we must take into consideration, as Nilsson has, such
texts as the sermons, particularly a sermon on Col. 1:18-20 in 1537
(*WA* 45, 297ff.), the commentaries on John 1–2, John 3–4, John 14–
15, as well as the commentary on Genesis. One can say without
exaggeration that the communication of attributes is one of the
key concepts of Luther's christology after 1530, although it was
basically present in his thoughts already before that date.

It will be noted that Luther is opposed to any conception of the
communication as purely nominal. For Zwingli, it was possible to
attribute to the person that which belonged by right to only one
of the two natures. But there it is only a question of a rhetorical
figure, a *praedicatio verbalis*. We have already drawn attention to
the opposition between Zwingli and Luther. For Zwingli, who insisted on the distinction and separation of the two natures above all,
it was impossible to envisage *realiter* that God had been able to
suffer or that the man Jesus had been able to create the world. He
could only envisage a *communicatio nominalis* and make use of the

alleosis to explain the attribution to the two natures of that which belongs only to one.

In relation to tradition, Zwingli seems to have given a more rational turn to the communication of attributes, by reducing it to a figure of rhetoric. Saint Thomas had gone further, and it seems that his position can be found again with Calvin. According to these two, the communication of attributes is not simply a figure of rhetoric. It is founded on a real communication of the properties of the two natures to the one person of Christ and to his work. But, as we have already seen, there is no communication between the natures themselves. It seems to us that Nilsson is wrong to neglect the differences between Calvin and Zwingli.

If one now examines Luther's position, it is necessary to emphasize not only the opposition to Zwingli, but also the fact that he seems first of all to follow the Thomist tradition, by saying that what is attributed to one of the two natures is found in the whole person of Christ. "Because God and humanity are one sole person," he says in the 1537 sermon on Col. 1:18-20, "it must be said that the person of Christ carries *(führe)* the properties of the two natures. . . . Hence, that which appertains individually to one of the two natures must be attributed to the whole person" (*WA* 45, 300, 37ff.). It is in this sense that we must understand Luther's parable: when a dog bites a child in the leg, one says quite rightly that it is the child who has been bitten, even though the bite was only on the leg. "Because God and a man are one person, one Christ, one Jesus, one Son of God and Mary, and not two persons, not two Christs, not two Jesuses, not two Sons, the result is that the properties of the two natures in Christ must all be, and in the same manner, attributed to the person" (*WA* 45, 301, 21-25).

It seems to us that in what concerns their understanding of the communication of attributes, Luther and Calvin find themselves at one on another point: their insistence on soteriology. Nilsson has shown quite clearly that when Luther defines or clarifies the properties of the two natures, he never envisages them only as metaphysical properties, like immutability to define God as distinct from human beings (i.e., the traditional properties), but that he prefers to consider those properties which play a role in the work of Christ.[108] "He cites biblical passages which tell of human properties concerned with birth, crucifixion, death for human redemption, but each time he emphasizes those divine attributes which concern reconciliation and forgiveness of sins." [109]

In the language of Lutheran orthodoxy, one would say that what is meant by that is the *genus apotelesmaticum,* that is the kind of communication of attributes which attributes all the activities of Christ not to only one of the two natures, but to the unique person of the Savior. Now this *genus apotelesmaticum* is found equally clearly at the center of Calvin's thought, while Zwingli refused it for the sake of preserving the *Alleinwirksamkeit* of God. From Zwingli's point of view, humanity could only bear witness or make known what the divinity alone realized.

But Luther goes further than the communication of attributes from nature to person. There is for him the idea of a real communication of attributes between the two natures themselves. Of course, it is necessary to note the distinction made by Luther himself between a communication *in abstracto* and a communication *in concreto.* Envisaging the divinity in an abstract fashion, i.e., as not bound to the humanity in Jesus Christ, it is necessary to say that God does not suffer. In this same way, this humanity, considered *in abstracto,* i.e., in itself, cannot create. [110]

We have already pointed out above the care with which Luther distinguishes, on the one hand, the natures taken in themselves, and, on the other hand, the natures united in the person of Christ. But as Nilsson has rightly noted, this distinction between the *abstractum* and the *concretum* brings Luther no nearer to the thought of Zwingli. Luther is not content to proclaim a *communicatio nominalis,* nor to attribute to the person what rightly belongs only to one of the natures. [111]

He goes further by conceiving in the person of Christ the communication of attributes as a real communication of the properties of one nature to the other nature considered in itself. [112] Of course, he does not always express himself with great clarity. Studying in depth a number of texts, one concludes that only the communication of attributes from the nature to the person is meant, and that is accepted, traditional, and orthodox Lutheran teaching, called *genus idiomaticum.* But it is necessary to recognize that he has gone further than the first two genera recognized by orthodoxy, by Calvin and Melanchthon, and that he envisages also a *genus majestaticum,* [113] as also a *genus tapeinoticon.* These expressions are not found in Luther and they must be used with care, but they can help to express his thought. The *genus majestaticum* is the communication of the properties of the divine nature to the human nature. One of the most striking texts in this respect is found in the *Table Talk*. Of course, it is necessary to show reserve concerning the authenticity and fidelity of this source, but corroborated by other sources, better attested, the *Table Talk* can in certain respects be very revealing. "As for what happens to and befalls this person Christ," the reformer writes, "it happens to and befalls both to this God and to this man. From whence it comes that these two natures in Christ communicate their attributes and their properties the one to the other; that is to say, that which is the peculiar property of one nature is communicated also to the other. That is why one says justly of the natures that they are attached to one another, intertwined and united." [114]

The communication of the concrete properties of the divine nature to the human nature permits the human nature to receive ubiquity, that is to say that like the divinity it can be present everywhere. It is "beyond the creatures," Luther said in the Eucharistic Controversy; it no longer submits to the laws of space and time. We have already studied this conception closely when analyzing the Eucharistic texts. In the communication of attributes, as Luther understands it, there is a theological foundation, although it can be presented without this foundation, as was the case with Gabriel Biel, to whom it appears to go back.[115]

Following Luther, Lutheran orthodoxy will insist on the *genus majestaticum,* by which those divine properties which can be are attributed to the human nature. In effect, it is not possible in every case; for example, the immortality and the power to create are excluded (Formula of Concord, VIII).

On the contrary, it will not follow Luther in attributing the properties of the human nature to the divine nature. That can be called the *genus tapeinoticon.* Orthodoxy will refuse this concept because in its eyes it would constitute a limitation of the divine nature. But one of the characteristic traits of Luther's christology is to envisage a kind of participation in Jesus Christ of the divine nature in human weakness. In that passage from the *Table Talk,* from which we have already quoted, we read again that the sufferings of our human nature "are communicated, attributed, and given to the divine nature," [116] and farther on, "that it is true and right to say that God is born, suckled and bred, sleeps in the cradle, is cold, walks, falls, wanders, wakes up, eats, drinks, suffers, dies, etc." We have already drawn attention to similar passages which speak of the suffering of God.

The originality of Luther must be recognized on this point. Of course, by affirming, as he did, a communication of attributes, he took over the Eastern tradition, the concept of the *perichorèsis,* by which the natures are united as fire and iron. He thus joins with the current flowing from the Cappadocians to John of Damascus, by way of Cyril of Alexandria. But from the perspective of the Greek theologians, the movement went only one way, from the divine nature to the human nature, carrying with it a certain Docetism. Under the influence, to a certain extent, of Platonism, these theologians insisted on the immutability and impassibility of God. It is only in the course of the theological struggle over Patripassianism that one will envisage the movement going also in the other direction, so that the suffering of humanity is *communicated* to the divine nature.[117] As we have already seen, Luther turns himself resolutely away from the Platonic image of a God who is immutable and impassible. In this regard there are very deep passages in his writings where he marvels at this mystery, incomprehensible even to the angels, that God has truly suffered in Jesus Christ (*WA* 39, 2, 279, 26; 340, 16; 43, 579ff., etc.).

Such affirmations continue to attract the attention of modern theologians, even those of the so-called "death of God" school. A theologian like Paul Althaus rejects the communication of attributes, but he is sensitive to the *genus tapeinoticon.* He reckons, however, that by affirming the humiliation of God in Jesus in this way, the communication of attributes "is itself destroyed as a metaphysical theory and tends to become a christology of paradox." [118]

One may ask why Luther accorded so great an importance to the theory in question.

He has made use of this traditional concept (even modifying it as we have seen) in order to set in relief a certain number of themes fundamental to his thought. For him, there is first of all, the revelation of God in Jesus Christ. The unity of God and humanity in Christ must be so strongly emphasized because from now on God wishes to be found no longer apart from the man Jesus. In opposition to the Enthusiasts, Luther can say, *"Deus sine carne nihil prodest"* (God without flesh avails nothing).[119] He goes so far as to criticize an earlier stage of his own thought, when he so often sought

for the way to rise from the human toward God. Of course, then he
already had the same idea on the revelation of God in Jesus Christ,
but after the Eucharistic Controversy, this expression seems to him
to be in danger of separating God from humanity! Thus he writes,
"We cannot touch or grasp the divine majesty, any more than we
would wish to touch or grasp a devouring fire. . . . That is why he
has presented his flesh to us, in order that we may attach ourselves
to it and to a certain extent be able to touch and comprehend it.
. . . Therefore do not listen to those who say that the flesh avails
nothing. Reverse this word and say that God without the flesh avails
nothing. For it is on the flesh of Christ from the Virgin's womb that
your eyes must be fixed, so that you may take courage and say:
'I have known nothing of God, neither in heaven nor on earth, apart
from the flesh, sleeping in the Virgin's womb'. . . . For otherwise
God is in all ways incomprehensible, it is only in the flesh of Christ
that he can be grasped." [120]

The theory of the communication of attributes is intended to emphasize the fundamental theme that since the incarnation, there is
no longer any valid relationship with God which is not also a relationship with the man Jesus. There where God reveals himself, the
man must be present also. Because Zwingli had here introduced
separation, Luther had put the communication of attributes at the
center of his christology.

This theory expresses another fundamental theme of Luther's
theology. It allows him to emphasize the fundamental unity between
creation and redemption. The man Jesus created the world; [121] in
Christ, God died on the cross. Such paradoxical statements can be
made within the framework of the communication of attributes.

That is to say no less than that from the beginning the creative
activity of God, in the person of the Logos, did not occur independently of the man Jesus, but in union with him. Here we touch
on the very difficult question of the preexistence of Christ. It is certain that Luther shows great reserve with regard to the idea of a
separation between the eternal Word of God and the humanity, as
it appears when one speaks of the *logos asarkos* (word without
flesh) or of the *extra-calvinisticum*. It can be said that from all time
when one speaks of the relationship between the Father and the Son,
one thinks of the Son as human. The hypostatic union was certainly
an event in history, but from all eternity the Son is defined in relation to the incarnation. He acts always as he acted through the man

Jesus. That is what he means by the concept of preexistence, and it is that which Luther wants to emphasize.

Thus the unity is realized between the God who creates by his Word and the Word made flesh. The creation as well as the redemption are accomplished in union with the man Jesus. He not only appears in order to follow God to accomplish his work of redemption in the person of the Son, he is already the one by whom the world was created. Thus the incarnation leads not only to the cross and to the work of redemption, but it must also reveal the meaning of creation.

And on the other hand, in Jesus Christ, it is God who suffers and dies. In this way the union between creation and redemption is again emphasized. It is the creative Word who is crucified and who suffers in union with the man Jesus. There is thus no rift between the creative work and the work of redemption; he who suffers on the cross is the creative Word. From this point of view it is not wrong to give to a study of the conception of "God" in Luther's thought such a title as "The Crucified Creator." [122]

The communication of attributes can also, in Luther, be considered from a third point of view which might be called the soteriological perspective. The work of redemption is accomplished by God and by the man within the indissoluble union of the two.[123] For the believer, it is essential to know that the acts and exploits of the man Jesus are not those of some saint or superman, but that they are the acts and exploits of God. And on the other hand, the God who saves me must not be sought anywhere except in the form of the man Jesus. On this point, Luther opposes both the Enthusiasts and Zwingli. We have already seen that Zwingli had a conception of the *Alleinwirksamkeit* of God, in which the man Jesus in fact participates only as an accessory in the work of redemption. In some way, he makes it known, but for Zwingli he is not himself the God who saves human beings.

Fourth, we should like to show that according to Luther, the communication of attributes destroys the traditional metaphysical conception that human beings make about God and makes room for the living God proclaimed by the Holy Scripture. It is within the framework of this theory, as we have seen, that Luther speaks of the suffering of God. Thus with him there appears the image of a God who struggles and who truly participates in creation. This image replaces that of the impassible God of the Platonic tradition or of the God *ens summum* (highest being) or *causa prima* (first cause). The theory of the communication of attributes allowed Luther to give a kind of theological foundation to these ideas, which however he also expressed independently of this conception.

Finally, the theory of the communication of attributes tries to express in its way the uniqueness and the particularity of the humanity of Jesus. Of course, his humanity is part of history; his humanity is of the same nature as ours. But as we have already indicated above in connection with the preexistence of Christ, this humanity is unique in that it was elected by God. It finds itself in the same way placed in some sense above time. It has a priority in relation to all other creatures.

All these reasons can explain why Luther took over the idea of the communication of attributes. But has this theory obscured or even distorted his thought?

From a traditional point of view, it must be admitted first of all that it is not always easy to understand in what sense Luther uses this theory.[124] For, most of the time, he uses it in a very traditional way, attributing to the person in his concrete existence that which properly belongs only to one nature. We have already noted that. In other passages, however, he goes much further and admits a reciprocal communication of the properties between the two natures themselves. But it is well to note that Luther knows nothing yet of the differences between the three *genera* and also that one cannot always tie Luther down rigorously to specific categories of his thought. But it must be recognized that he does not draw back from what later will be called the *genus majestaticum* and the *genus tapeinoticon.*

Now, one might well ask whether he does not tend toward a certain Monophysitism, that is toward a certain confusion of the natures. The communication is so emphasized that certain expressions lead us to believe that his thought is tending in this direction. In the sermon already cited on Col. 1:18-20 of 1537, Luther says: "One speaks of the communication of attributes when one unites and mixes *(vermischt)* the properties of the two natures in Christ, in the same way that one unites and mixes the natures, God and the man, in one person" (WA 45, 297). Often he replaces the term *communicatio* by such expressions as "communion," "mixing," "confounding," "exchanging," etc. Without doubt, Luther will continue to protest against the accusation of Monophysitism. He will not cease to

emphasize that he knows well the distinction between the two natures and that he intends to preserve it. But it must be recognized
that his expressions often lack clear definition and that his manner
of using the theory of the communication of attributes brings him
dangerously near to Monophysitism.

Equally it must be asked to what extent he can avoid the charge
of Docetism, if a divine property such as ubiquity can be attributed
to the human nature.[125] Althaus is perfectly right to pose the question: "How can the properties of one nature be attributed to the
other without changing it, so that it ceases to be a human nature?
The *genus majestaticum* divinizes the real humanity of Jesus. A man
with the divine properties of omnipotence and omniscience is no
longer a man. The mystery of the person of Jesus finds itself ration-
alized by a metaphysical construction which destroys the real
humanity. It is in total contradiction to the picture of Jesus in the
Gospels." [126] What concerns the participation of God in the "properties" of the human nature, such as suffering, as we have already
emphasized, can undoubtedly be better expressed otherwise than
by the theory of the communication of attributes. In fact, this theory
risks leading thought in a direction which is subject to criticism.
Thus in the 19th century, certain "kenotic" theologians appealed to
the *genus tapeinoticon* of Luther's christology in order to go still
further and defend the idea, according to which the Word, by being
incarnate, lost some of its divine properties. Surely there is an im-
passe there which is due not to the theme of the suffering of God,
but to a way of thinking which envisages the union of God and this
man in terms of communication of properties. When we come to the
root of this theory, it is necessary to be precise about what we mean
by the death or suffering of God. Or again, to be clear how to express both the historicity of God (his becoming and his death in the
union with the creature) and also his eternity. This question separated Calvin from Luther, the supporters of *extra-calvinisticum*
from those who held the *genus tapeinoticon*.

All things considered, it is the conception of the communication
of attributes itself which calls for certain reservations. It must be
asked whether the biblical image of an active God who suffers,
who forgives sins, and who is human, is best rendered by such a
speculative theory of properties attributed to the two natures and
often determined outside the biblical revelation. Luther did not
escape the difficulties inherent in this theory. To attribute, as he

does, ubiquity to human nature is an abstract view, hardly faithful to the biblical perspective which describes the history of God and his people, a history which culminates in the man Jesus in whom God offers himself to the world and destroys the powers which enslave it.

Luther himself warned against those who wished to enclose the mystery of the hypostatic union within a metaphysical construction. As he says, that mystery is a *res ineffabilis*.[127] Even the angels cannot comprehend it.[128] According to him, a new theological language is required to attempt to express the mystery. It might be asked whether the language of Luther himself answers this demand.

Excursus: The Logic of Theology

Theology has for its object the study of God revealed in Jesus Christ for faith. There is no other God. Theology must observe the rule: *bene notandum est et maxime observandum quod extra Christum non est Deus alius* (emphasizing and observing that outside Christ there is no other God) (WA 39, 2, 25, 17). Theology is not to speculate on the idea of God, but on the God who, in all his majesty, is really present in the humanity of Jesus Christ (WA 39, 2, 106).

It can be said that theology is based on a fact. That fact is the God given in Jesus Christ. Philosophy, on the other hand, cannot accept the incarnation because there is no common ground between the finite and the infinite (WA 39, 2, 14, 34; 112, 19, etc.). As Luther says, making his own a thought from Occam: the idea of God becoming human is as contrary to the spirit of philosophy as that of God becoming an ass (WA 39, 2, 3, 5).

On the contrary, theology starts from this mysterious given that in Jesus Christ the creator and the creature are effectively and really one. The philosophic axiom, *nulla propertio finiti et infinititi* (no property can be both finite and infinite), must give place to the reality which goes far beyond the common ground of the finite and the infinite, because it consists of the unity between the two.[129] This unity is thus the given foundation, and for Luther the christological problem consists above all in expressing this in the most adequate fashion.[130] But before looking at this aspect of the question, another point must be given due attention.

It goes without saying that the given, on which theology rests, is accessible only to faith. The articles of faith are based on the Word of God and call for faith (*WA* 39, 2, 5, 9; 269). They are opposed to reason (*WA* 39, 2, 4, 2). It is precisely there that theology is distinguished from philosophy. Philosophy is surrounded by reason, while theology occupies itself with *credibilia, id est quae fide apprehenduntur* (things to be believed, i.e., that which is apprehended by faith) (*WA* 39, 2, 6, 26). Luther can say, "We walk in the clouds of the Holy Spirit" (*WA* 39, 2, 104, 17), or again he can describe the difference between theology and philosophy in the following manner; the one concerns things visible, the other things invisible (*WA* 39, 2, 15, 8). Again, he affirms that it is as necessary to distinguish philosophy from theology as it is to distinguish the law from the gospel. Philosophy has its validity in the realm of laws, but from the point of view of salvation it leads to legalism (*WA* 39, 2, 13, 12, etc.). It is not qualified to express the gospel, i.e., the incarnation, eternal life, justification, etc. (*WA* 39, 2, 14). The law is thus the domain of philosophy; the gospel (the promises), on the other hand, is the domain of theology (*WA* 39, 2, 26, 4, 35).

But there is a dialectical relationship between the law and the gospel. The former must not only be distinguished from the latter, it also plays a positive role in relation to it. Thus Luther can qualify the idea of the law as identified with philosophy with the description *paedagogum ad Christum* (Gal. 3:24) (*WA* 39, 2, 27, 17; 34).

Again, Luther can emphasize that philosophy and theology deal with different subjects: they are different but not contradictory. They do not militate against each other (*WA* 39, 2, 26, 29).

The distinction between philosophy and theology crystallizes especially around the problem of the double truth which had so agitated thinkers in the Middle Ages and particularly the Occamist theologians.[131]

We do not find a great development in Luther on this subject.[132] But in the disputation of 1539 he opposes the Sorbonne several times, a place which he calls the *mater errorum* (*WA* 39, 2, 3, 7), but which considered itself *idem esse verum in philosophia et theologia* (to be the very truth in philosophy and theology) (*WA* 39, 2, 3, 7). He observes that if in the domain of mathematics or philosophy (*WA* 39, 2, 5, 13ff.) the truth is not always the same, how much more will this be the case in the relationship between philosophy and theology (*WA* 39, 2, 5, 33ff.).

Since the object of philosophy is not the same as that of theology, the methods of approach will therefore be different also. Philosophy studies its object, that is to say the idea of God, the laws, etc., with the aid of reason. And the typical development of its thought is in the form of syllogisms. Luther here shows himself very familiar with these traditional theological exercises where the syllogism had an important place, particularly in the Occamist school. In the course of the *Disputations* he does not cease to repeat that the syllogism is not suitable in the field of theology (*WA* 39, 2, 4, 19; 5, 8, 12, 29; 30, 15ff.).[133] In fact, the syllogism allows one to establish the necessity of the incarnation (which according to Luther would put the liberty of God in question) and to question its possibility. This is simply a verbal game in which the thinker does not start from the facts offered to faith, but which moves within certain rules of logic. Now these things correspond to human reason, but not to the reality of God made human in Jesus Christ. In this matter it must be said that *Deus non sit subjectus rationi et syllogismis, sed verbo Dei et fidei* (God is not the subject of reason and syllogisms, but of the Word of God and faith) (*WA* 39, 2, 8, 5; 30, 15, etc.). The syllogistic argument is not false in itself, but we are concerned here with a matter far too mysterious and specific for it to be encompassed by a syllogism.[134] That is why Luther demands that the form of the syllogism or philosophical reason should be treated as Saint Paul said women should be in church—that is, they should be quiet (*WA* 39, 2, 4, 19)! In the articles of faith it is the *affectus fidei* and not the *intellectus philosophiae* which must be exercised (*WA* 39, 2, 5, 39). And again Luther can say that we must follow "the grammar of the Holy Spirit" (*WA* 39, 2, 104, 24ff.).

All that does not mean denying the possibility of theology making use of a rational language, so long as it espouses the reality which is the object of faith, that is to say, so long as it imprisons the intelligence in obedience to Christ [135] and that it allows the Holy Spirit to dictate the rules of grammar. Luther does not wish to eliminate dialectic from theology, otherwise he would not have reintroduced the practice of disputations. But he insists that the dialectic must be the servant of theology (*WA* 39, 2, 24, 24; 36). In other words, theological exposition must express the logic proper to its subject matter, namely to God made one with the man Christ Jesus.

But it is evident that theology represents a particular language. Its task is to examine this unique and specific reality which is God united to humanity in Jesus Christ. Luther is very conscious of the difficulty of this task. In fact what is envisaged is ineffable and incomprehensible (*WA* 39, 2, 105, 4), incomprehensible even to the angels (*WA* 39, 2, 98, 13ff.). Even to express this reality in analogies is improper (*WA* 39, 2, 96, 3). In truth, one must not rely on analogies any more than on etymology, but simply let oneself be led by the Holy Spirit (*WA* 39, 2, 109, 6; 112, 31). It is the Spirit who prescribes the manner by which to speak.

Is that to say that theology must be an endless creation of new words, different from those used in philosophy? Luther does not exclude the possibility of creating new words, better suited to the intended reality than certain old words. However, most of the time he is content to make use of traditional terms such as *creatura, homo, humanitas, imago,* etc., but insisting on the following fundamental rule: *Omnia vocabula in Christo novam significationem accipere in eadem re significata* (Every word in Christ takes on a new meaning in the thing which it describes) (*WA* 39, 2, 94, 16ff.).[136] What does that mean if it is not that the given reality, Christ, the God-man, gives a new and specific meaning to the terms employed? That is, for example, the case with the term *creatura.* Current usage understands by that a distinct being separate from the creator, namely God. In Jesus Christ, on the contrary, the term takes on a new meaning, because there the creature is united with the creator in a way that is inseparable (*WA* 39, 2, 105, 5ff.; 118, 11ff.).

Similar observations could be made about other traditional terms. In every case, the rule applies that the expressions referring to the creature (and *mutatis mutandis,* the creator) take on a new meaning when applied to Christ, in whom the creature and the creator are one.[137]

Thus the purpose of the *Disputations* appears clearly to be: to formulate the truth of the faith, taking into account the specificity of this unique theme, which is the unity of God and humanity in Jesus Christ, revealed to faith.

Notes

1 Apart from the *Treatise on the Councils* (*WA* 50, 488-653), we shall study especially the following *Disputations:* that on the *Sentences* of Peter Lombard, *Verbum caro factum est,* 1539 (*WA* 39, 2, 1-33); the *Disputatio divinitate et humanitate Christi,* 1540 (*WA* 39, 2, 92-121); the graduation disputation of Georg Major

and John Faber, 1544 (*WA* 39, 2, 284-336). We shall occasionally quote from certain passages taken from the sermons Luther devoted to John 1-2 (*WA* 46, 538-789), John 3-4 (*WA* 47, 1-231), and John 14-15 (*WA* 45, 465-733). The *Commentary on the Last Words of David* will be used to clarify the trinitarian doctrine of Luther (*WA* 54, 16-100). The other texts from the same period that we use in the course of this chapter will be referred to in passing.

The following works have been of special value to us in our research: J. Koopmans, *Das Altkirchliche Dogma in der Reformation* (Munich: 1955); K. O. Nilsson, *Simul: Das Miteinander von Göttlichem und Menschlichem, in Luthers Theologie* (Göttingen: 1966). R. Schwarz, "Gott ist Mensch," Zur Lehre von der Person Christi bei den Ockhamisten und bei Luther," *Zeitschrift für Theologie und Kirche* (1966):289-351. See also U. Gerber, *Disputatio als Sprache des Glaubens* (Zurich: 1970), pp. 197-296.

2   See the introductions to *WA* 39, 1 (x-xi) and 39, 2 (ix-xxvii).

3   Unless otherwise noted, all references are from *WA* 39, 2.

4   In 1543 he wrote concerning the Trinity and the incarnation: "This article has remained pure in papism and with the Scholastic theologians in a way that we have no quarrel with them on this account" (*WA* 54, 64, 19).

5   *WA* 50, 255-283

6   It must be noted on this point that Luther also comments that the Fathers have here and there spoken unwisely (*incommode*) about the mysteries of the faith (*WA* 98, 22ff.), but they must be interpreted correctly and their thought must not be perverted as it is, according to Luther, by the papists and by Schwenckfeld (*WA* 112, 5). But nonetheless he concedes a greater liberty to the Fathers of the church than he does to the Scholastics (*WA* 99, 1-5; 105, 9-11; 112, 4-6), because the theologians should be more careful in their terminology than the Fathers. Cf. Schwarz, "Gott ist Mensch," pp. 290-291.

7   *WA* 50, 591, 9ff.

8   *WA* 54, 142, 17: "As for me, as I go to my grave, this is my witness before all which I wish to carry before the throne of my dear Lord and Savior, Jesus Christ: that I have condemned and driven from my mind, those Enthusiasts and enemies of the sacrament: Carlstadt, Zwingli, Oecolampadius, Schwenckfeld, and their adherents, wheresoever they be, as it is ordered in Titus 3:10: "As for a man who is factious, after admonishing him once or twice, have nothing more to do with him."

9   *WA* 50, 599, 5ff.

10   *WA* 39, 1, 334ff. (1537-1540)

11   *WA* 1, 78ff.

12   *WA* 39, 2, 285ff.; 290, 15

13   For an introduction to this treatise, see the selected works of Martin

Luther, edited by H. H. Borcherdt and G. Merz, 3rd ed., vol. 7 (Munich: 1963), pp. 139-146.

14   *WA* 50, 519, 18ff.
15   "All the councils, taken as a whole as well as individually" (*WA* 50, 501-505; 592-593).
16   *WA* 50, 520, 12; 542, 19
17   *WA* 50, 546, 14
18   *WA* 50, 546, 15ff.
19   "If you have all the councils, then you are nonetheless not thereby a Christian, because they give you too little. If you have all the Fathers, then they too do not give you enough. You must look into the Holy Scripture, in which everything is given to you richly, or in the catechism, in which these things are given in an abbreviated form, but one finds there more than is given in all the councils and all the Fathers" (*WA* 39, 2, 618, 30).
20   "It [the Holy Scripture] must remain master and judge" (*WA* 520, 7; 525, 23); "If the Holy Scripture had not been written and preserved, the church would not have survived for long with only the councils and the Fathers. And as proof of that: From where did the Fathers and the councils learn what they taught? Do you think that they invented it in their time or that the Holy Spirit gave to each one of them anew each time? On what did the church stand before the Fathers and the councils?" (*WA* 547, 2)
21   See *WA* 39, 2, 606ff.
22   *WA* 522, 18ff.; 543, 6ff.; 606,1
23   F. W. Kantzenbach, "Kontroverstheologische Methode und Denkform bei Luther (nach der Konzilschrift von 1539)," in *Festschrift für Franz Lau* (Göttingen: 1967), pp. 154-171.
24   *WA* 39, 2, 548-575
25   *WA* 551, 13; 552, 17; 559, 32
26   *WA* 562, 12
27   *WA* 550, 26; 570, 15
28   "When they went to the heart of the matter, that Christ was *homoousios* with the Father, equal and identical power, then there was no more loophole, crack, or subterfuge that they could find. *Homoousios* means the same essence or nature, a single essence and not double. That is how the Fathers in the council defined it. In Latin it is sung as *consubstantialis*, others speak of it as *coexistentialis* or *coessentialis*" (*WA* 50, 571, 23).
29   The same observation is found in the *Disputations*, e.g., *WA* 39, 2, 109, 20.
30   "If I do not like the sound of the word *homoousios*, I am not thereby a heretic," written against Latomus (*WA* 8, 117, 20ff.). For this whole question, see Congar, "La christologie de Luther," p. 481, n. 97. Also, Harnack, *Luthers Theologie*, vol. 2, p. 147, n.a; Watson, *Um Gottes Gottheit*, p. 226, n. 1; Koopmans, *Das altkirchliche Dogma*, pp. 52-53; Prenter, *Spiritus Creator*, pp. 181ff. Among recent Catholic studies devoted to the doctrine of the Trinity and

the attitude of the reformers to it, we point out the exposition presented in *Mysterium Salutis*, vol. 2. L. Scheffzyk there recognizes the fidelity of Luther to tradition and calls his exposition of the doctrine of the reformers, "The defense of the doctrine against modern rationalism" (p. 195). It can however be asked whether he is right in affirming, "This desire to give a more living presentation of the mystery within the framework of the history of salvation has as little success with Luther as with the other reformers" (p. 195).

31   The Migne Edition of patrology, *series Graeca*, 25, 454.

32   "Like everybody else, I had come to think that Nestorius had denied the divinity of Christ and had considered him to be only a man, as the decrees of the council and all the papist writers had said" (*WA* 583, 28).

33   *WA* 588; 590; 597

34   Kantzenbach, p. 156.

35   A. Grillmeier, "Das Scandalum oecumenicum des Nestorius in kirchlichdogmatischer und theologiegeschichtlicher Sicht," *Scholastik* 36 (1961): 321-356.

36   Thomas Camelot, "De Nestorius à Eutychès," in *Das Konzil von Chalkedon* (Würzburg: 1951), p. 221.

37   "No trustworthy historical writing takes us as far as this. The *Ecclesiastica* stops at the First Council of Nicea; the *Tripartita* and Theodoretus takes us only as far as the Third Council of Ephesus, and from there on we are entirely dependent on what the popes say and their historians, who are very difficult to believe for striking and evident reasons" (*WA* 592, 30).

38   *WA* 594, 7; 602, 12

39   On this subject see Camelot, "De Nestorius à Eutychès," pp. 234-250.

40   Cyril spoke of the nature as one from the God-Word become human, but his precise formula is, *ek duo physeôn eis* (from two natures one).

41   "What must one do, when even this council was lost? The Christian faith must not sink because of it. For that would be to lose more and something much more useful than this council" (*WA* 602, 7).

42   "La christologie de Luther," p. 476.

43   Cf. Löfgren, *Die Theologie der Schöpfung*, p. 35: "Too little attention is paid to Luther's doctrine of the Trinity in Luther research, because the dominant tendency is to make all the affirmations of Luther either 'christological' or 'existential.'" See also Nilsson, *Simul*, p. 310.

44   Karl Holl, *Gesammelte Aufsätze*, vol. 1, 6th ed. (1932), p. 72, note. Neither of the two accusations seem to us to be well-founded. How can Luther be modalist when he so often criticizes Sabellianism? Moreover, all his expositions devoted to the question of the Trinity distinguish in a most orthodox manner between the three persons. In answer to Holl, see Prenter, *Spiritus Creator*, pp. 183-187, n. 25; p. 356; Nilsson, *Simul*, p. 177, n. 29.

45   Elert, *Morphologie des Luthertums*, vol. 1 (Munich: 1931), p. 191.
46   Köstlin, *Luthers Theologie*, vol. 1, pp. 68-76; vol. 2, pp. 92-95.
47   Köstlin, *Luthers Theologie*, vol. 2, p. 84.
48   Althaus, *Die Theologie Martin Luthers*, p. 175.
49   "La christologie de Luther," p. 480.
50   "La christologie de Luther," p. 480.
51   This is the point of view that appears in the most recent research, which rightly emphasizes that Luther moves from the economic Trinity to the immanent Trinity, that is to say that he speaks of God in himself only from the basis of the history of revelation. But what is important to note, and this is being increasingly recognized today, is that Luther teaches that God reveals himself as a trinitarian God. Thus Peters writes: "It is not an academic christology, but the self-revelation of the triune God which forms the beginning, the middle, and the end of all Luther's considerations" (*Luthers Christuszeugnis*, p. 97). Löfgren, *Die Theologie der Schöpfung*, p. 214: "Luther's adherence to the traditional doctrine of the Trinity is firmly anchored in his concept of revelation as act and not simply an adjunct to it; the idea that God only makes use of the creation in order to bring to a favorable outcome his action with human beings is placed systematically within the framework of the trinitarian doctrine." See also A. Peters, "Die Trinitätslehre in der reformatorischen Christenheit," *Theologische Literaturzeitung* 94 (1969):561-570.
52   Prenter, *Schöpfung und Erlösung*, p. 42: "If one speaks only of the economic Trinity and thereby passes over in silence the immanent Trinity, then God in his eternal being has no part in the language of worship. Such a conclusion would open up all kinds of speculation about the "hidden" God, who in that case would not be identified with God, the Father, Son, and Holy Spirit, who is revealed in history. But if the ancient trinitarian theology, despite the strangeness and inadequacy of its expressions, dared to make affirmations concerning the eternal being of God, it is saying that the God revealed in history, the economic Trinity, is the one who is from everlasting to everlasting."
53   WA 54, 68
54   WA 39, 2, 29, 10; 97, 5
55   WA 39, 2, 305, 9
56   These two passages attest the Trinity in a particularly clear way, according to Luther (cf. WA 54, 65ff.).
57   See Prenter, *Spiritus Creator*, pp. 177-187; 238-245; Marc Lienhard, "La doctrine du Saint-Esprit chez Luther," *Verbum Caro* 76 (1965):11-38.
58   WA 54, 61, 19: "He has given us his Word and Holy Scripture, confirmed by great miracles and signs and acts, in order that we may learn from them." Prenter rightly underlines the fact that Luther's incessant effort to establish the scriptural foundation of the doctrine of the Trinity shows how concerned he is, not with dead

formulae, but with that which is alive and given, inseparably bound up with the revelation of God in history (*Spiritus Creator*, pp. 180-181).

59   WA 61, 27ff.
60   WA 61, 38ff.
61   WA 63, 3ff.
62   WA 54, 64, 37: "In this, faith must hold to the Word. Reason can do nothing here, except to say that what is impossible and contradictory, that three persons can each be fully God, and yet there be no more than one God, and only the Son is human."
63   WA 54, 61, 17
64   WA 39, 2, 110, 5: "I and the Father are *unum*, but not *unus* [one nature, but not one person].
65   WA 39, 1, 22, 1ff.: "Mathematics is the most inimical of all to theology." See also WA 22, 21-29.
66   WA 54, 88, 36: "The person of the Son has been revealed and has become human in a specific *(unterscheidlich)* way."
67   WA 54, 60ff.; 37, 26
68   "The works of the triune God are indivisible" (WA 54, 59, 17; 60, 5; 63, 27; 65, 23; 88, 17).
69   WA 54, 41, 7; 64, 39; 88, 17; WA 39, 2; 279, 26ff.: "Christ alone is not the whole *(tota)* Trinity"; 39, 2, 110, 9; 288, 24; 287, 24ff.; 304, 4.
70   WA 54, 60, 31ff.
71   See also WA 54, 63, 30ff. and note his acceptance of the Western *filioque* clause.
72   See also WA 54, 69, 20.
73   Cf. Seeberg, *Dogmengeschichte*, vol. 2, 317ff.
74   Seeberg, *Dogmengeschichte*, vol. 2, pp. 408ff.
75   WA 39, 2, 28ff.; 17, 17ff.
76   "The whole Trinity and the majesty of God" (WA 39, 2, 17, 26; 18, 4).
77   WA 18, 8
78   WA 287, 29ff.; 288, 1ff.; 295, 13ff.; 316-317
79   Koopmans, *Das altkirchliche Dogma*, p. 63.
80   But Koopmans himself is very reserved on this point in his final conclusion: "But it is not necessary to conclude from these two examples [he had quoted another text where Luther speaks of *relationes* as *res*, i.e., things], that Luther had adopted the Greek trinitarian doctrine rather than the Latin. One can only affirm a tendency in this direction. And there are many affirmations, which the Cappadocians, for example, would not have been able to agree with, that stand in opposition to this tendency. But the tendency is there, in spite of all, an inheritance, no doubt, from the Scholastics."
81   On this subject see Congar, "La christologie de Luther," p. 481.
82   WA 39, 2, 30, 1-14
83   WA 30, 10, 305, 17

84 *WA* 30, 11
85 *WA* 305, 16
86 *WA* 305, 19
87 *WA* 305, 17
88 *WA* 305, 22
89 *WA* 303, 24ff.
90 *Disputatio de divinitate et humanitate,* 1540, thesis 1 (*WA* 39, 2, 93, 2): "The Catholic faith is this, that we confess one unique Lord Christ, who is true God and truly human."
91 *WA* 39, 2, 95, 32ff.
92 Schwarz, *Gott ist Mensch,* p. 343. Disputation on John 1:14, thesis 3 (*WA* 39, 2, 3, 5).
93 Schwarz, *Gott ist Mensch,* pp. 293ff.
94 "We say that the person exists in its own right alone, according to a particular manner of rational existence" (Migne, Latin, 196, 946, from Richard Vict., *de trinitate,* 4, c. 24). Schwarz, "Gott ist Mensch," p. 306: "By *'existere'* of the person in the texts of Luther, one will first understand, while waiting until all the elements of the concept of 'person' in Luther are clarified, simply the concretization which the nature undergoes in the existence *(Dasein)* of the person."
95 On this subject see Koopmans, *Das altkirchliche Dogma,* pp. 84-85.
96 For the discussion concerning the *aequivocatio,* see also *WA* 11, 16, 24ff.
97 On this discussion see D. M. Baille, *God Was in Christ* (London: Faber, 1961), pp. 85-93. See also Emil Brunner, *The Mediator* (London), pp. 265ff.; 318ff.; 345-354. Also, Althaus, *Die christliche Wahrheit,* vol. 2, pp. 225-226; Prenter, *Schöpfung und Erlösung,* pp. 384-385.
98 Koopmans thinks that Luther is close to Cyril of Alexandria and highlights the anti-Humanist character of the doctrine of Anhypostasis (p. 86).
99 *WA* 39, 2, 13-21; 20, 19ff.; 11, 21-26; 12, 4-8, 27-30
100 Nilsson, *Simul,* "The heart of Luther's theology is the communication of attributes. For it expresses the relation between the human and the divine, and Luther reckons it to be inevitable, unless we wish to make of Christ, either a perfect super-man or a terrifying God-judge" (p. 228). "It is the *communicatio idiomatum* by which Luther's whole system of theological thought stands or falls. The *communicatio* must not be understood as an accessory, more or less important, to the main theological structure. This is a matter of the utmost importance in understanding Luther. The *communicatio* is not a doctrine in itself which one might derive by careful and diligent study from the thought of Luther about the unity of Christ's person and work. The doctrine of the *communicatio idiomatum* is not merely a consequence of the unity in Christ, but an expression of this unity itself and the whole basis on which, according to Luther, life and happiness rests."

101 On this subject see F. Franck, "Communicatio idiomatum," *Real-Enzyklopädie für protestantische Theologie und Kirche* (1878), vol. 3, pp. 326-334; A. Michel, "Communication des idiomes," in the *Dictionnaire de théologie catholique*, vol. 7, col. 595-602; O. Weber, *Grundlagen der Dogmatik*, part 2, pp. 145-148.

102 *Schöpfung und Erlösung*, p. 186.

103 Calvin, *Institutes 2, 14, 2, quoted by Weber, Grundlagen der Dogmatik*, vol. 2, p. 146.

104 *Summa Theologiae 3, 16, 8*

105 On this subject see Schwarz, *Gott ist Mensch*, pp. 313-334.

106 Oberman, *Spätscholastik und Reformation*, vol. 1, p. 245.

107 Schwarz, *Gott ist Mensch*, pp. 348-349.

108 Nilsson, *Simul*, pp. 231-233; 243-245.

109 Nilsson, *Simul*, p. 243. The two natures are united in one person "for the salvation and redemption from eternal death" (WA 47, 76, 27).

110 WA 40, 3, 707, 22-27: "If I speak rightly saying that the divinity does not suffer, the humanity does not create, then I speak of something in the abstract and of a divinity which is separated. But one must not do that. Abstract concepts should not be cut loose, or our faith will become false. But one should believe in a concrete sense *(in concreto)*, saying this man is God, etc. Then the properties are rightly attributed." WA 40, 3, 709, 24-26: "Then it is rightly said: the human nature is adored, not in the abstract but in the concrete sense, for it is one person with the divine nature, and one cannot adore God without adoring the man [Jesus]." Nilsson, *Simul*, p. 257: "It is only the indissoluble unity of the person which makes possible the communication between the natures."

111 Nilsson, *Simul*, p. 256.

112 Nilsson, pp. 237, 241, 249, 256.

113 Lutheran orthodoxy follows him on this point. It distinguishes three *genera* in the *communicatio idiomatum*: genus *idiomaticum*, *apotelesmaticum*, and *majestaticum*.

114 *Tischreden* 4, 67ff. (Aurifaber 1541.) Or in WA 47, 199, 19-28: "We have often said that we should learn to contend against the Enthusiasts. You know that there is the *communicatio idiomatum*, that in the Lord Christ there are two natures, and yet only one person, and that these two natures have and hold each other's properties and even share them with each other." Thomasius, *Dogmatik* 2, p. 219: "For the idioms of the divine and the human natures appear to be impossible to unite, but it is not as if the person of Christ was only the place where they were together; on the contrary, the natures, united personally in that person, commune the one with the other, and thereby share their properties (which are inherent in them) one with the other; now this communication is real and reciprocal" (vol. 2, p. 219).

115 Weber, *Grundlagen der Dogmatik*, p. 151: "Luther probably has to thank his teacher Bartholomeo Arnoldi von Usingen for the doc-

trine of ubiquity; it goes back to Gabriel Biel. In the background is to be found the notion of *Deux exlex,* who is not even bound to his own proper work and therefore, contrary to what the Thomists think, can very well create a body which is unlimited."

116   *Tischreden* 4, 68, 18ff.

117   On this question see W. Elert, *Der Ausgang der altkirchlichen Christologie,* pp. 71-132.

118   Paul Althaus, *Die Christliche Wahrheit,* vol. 2, p. 238.

119   *WA* 25, 107, 4-19; 1532-34, in the disputation of 1540, *The Word Is Made Flesh,* he enunciates the following rule: "It must be remarked and observed with the greatest seriousness that, outside Christ, there is no other God" (*WA* 39, 2, 25, 17).

120   *WA* 25, 106, 33-107, 11

121   *WA* 39, 2, 93, 2-9; 101; 280, 16

122   Torgny Bohlin, *Den korfästa Skaparan* (Stockholm: 1952).

123   Nilsson, *Simul,* p. 228: "Because for Luther all depends on the fact that Christ, who is truly the united, divinely human redeemer, has accomplished the work of salvation *pro nobis,* and because the unity of this action *(Einlichkeit)* is itself closely bound up with the unity of the person, to which the *communicatio* teaching is central, therefore the *communicatio idiomatum* is the heart of Luther's theology."

124   Congar rightly brings this out in his "La christologie de Luther": "It is not always easy for a Catholic theologian to appreciate the accuracy or inaccuracy of these Lutheran formulae on this matter of the communication of attributes. On the other hand, he finds there statements that he can make his own with a good conscience; on the other hand, he detects a certain unease and a feeling that things are being said that he cannot accept" (pp. 479-480).

125   Prenter, *Schöpfung und Erlösung,* p. 326: "This leads inevitably to Docetism, to the idea that in spite of all, his humanity is of a different kind from ours." We have presented a similar criticism of the christology of orthodox Lutheranism as it is expressed in the Formula of Concord (Article 8) in "Die Verwerfung der Irrlehre und das Verhältnis zwischen lutherischen und reformierten Kirchen" in *Gemeinschaft der reformatorischer Kirchen: Auf dem Weg,* vol. 2 (Zurich: 1971). See particularly pp. 116-129.

126   Althaus, *Die christliche Wahrheit,* vol. 2, p. 227; in the 5th ed. (1959), 223; *Die Theologie Martin Luthers,* pp. 173-174.

127   *WA* 39, 2, 297, 26ff.

128   *WA* 98, 7ff.

129   *WA* 112, 15: "However, we do not make so much of the relation *(proportionem)* between the finite and the infinite, but rather we establish the unity."

130   Schwarz, p. 309: "Theology must not treat the personal union as a speculative problem, but as a linguistic task *(Sprachaufgabe).* Therefore Luther can consider the development of the doctrine in the early church simply from the point of view of whether, con-

sidered from all sides, the interpretation was consistent with the *communicatio idiomatum.*"

131   *WA* 39, 1, p. 229 (note by editor Hermelink): "The assertion that something can be theologically false and philosophically true, and *vice versa,* is attributed by the later Scholastics to a pupil of Occam named Robert Holcot. The Thomist school in its entirety rejected this because it is a contradiction in terms." See also Bengt Hägglund, *Theologie und Philosophie bei Luther und in der oecumenistischen Tradition: Luthers Stellung zur Theorie von der doppelten Wahrheit* (Lund: 1955).

132   He has already taken up his position in the course of the disputation in 1537 (*WA* 39, 1, 229, 27ff.).

133   Th. Süss, *Luther,* pp. 48-49.

134   *WA* 39, 2, 4, 31: "Not because of some failure in the syllogistic form, but because of the quality and the magnitude of the material, which cannot be enclosed within the narrowness of reason or syllogisms."

135   *WA* 39, 2, 4, 6: "The entire intellect (and without doubt also philosophy) must be imprisoned within obedience to Christ."

136   See also *WA* 39, 2, 5, 35; 19, 34; 29, 32; 105, 9ff.; 303, 23–304, 9. We find an equally revealing passage in a disputation of 1537, where Luther comments on the use of physical terms *(causa, forma,* etc.), in theology: "If you wish to use these words, clean them well first, if you like, take them to the bath! And even then, you could never use them without danger and great harm, because they are dangerous and remain so. When the words of physics are introduced into theology, they lead ultimately to Scholastic theology" (*WA* 39, 1, 229, 16ff.).

137   Schwarz, "Gott ist Mensch," p. 334: "All the attributes of created being obtain a new meaning in Christ, although the thing designated, i.e., the created being, retains its identity in Christ. . . . Words like *homo, humanitas, passus,* etc., become new words when they are said of Christ. They describe the same things as in nonchristological talk, but in a new and different way."

8

Jesus Christ, Crucified and Risen, Our Lord and Savior

Luther did not spend his last years only in ceaseless conflict with the Occamists and other traditional theologians, forging his philosophical and theological weapons in the arsenals of combat. He continued to preach, to write treatises, and to comment on the Holy Scripture. We shall study one of the most beautiful of these commentaries and show that, compared with the years of his youth, the great reformer's religious inspiration had not abated. The fundamental themes of his thought, which the *Disputations* had only brought out in a more technical way, appear very clearly in this commentary.

It is the *Commentary on Isaiah* 53 of 1544.[1] In spite of lengthy and somewhat repetitive treatment of philosophical problems, partly due to the text on which he is commenting, this commentary sums up rather well the major themes of Luther's christology. The text is certainly not Luther's, but comes from Rörer, whose faithfulness is not always above suspicion. But the themes which are dealt with are so characteristic of Luther and are corroborated by so many other texts that one can without hesitation consider these pages as authentic expressions of his thought.

According to Luther, Isaiah 53 refers to Christ himself, that is to an individual person. He criticizes the interpretation of Nicholas of Lyre, and of Thomas Aquinas, who like the Jews, relate this passage to the Jewish people. According to Luther, it does not relate to Christ in his body, that is to say to Christians either, even though he is clear that Christians must be conformed to Christ.

Christ and the Word: The Theology of the Cross

The first theme that Luther deals with is the prophetic and teaching office of Christ. *Ecce servus meus intelliget* (Behold, my servant perceives) is how the Vulgate renders Isa. 52:13a. Of what does the activity of Christ consist? First of all, to be for the Jewish people a preacher and a doctor of the law,[2] to teach the way in which eternal life may be received, to forgive sins, and to set free from death and the devil.[3]

But, for the moment, what Luther wants to emphasize by this is less the content of Christ's preaching than the fact of the preaching. The only weapon by which this Messiah reigns is precisely the Word, to the great indignation of the Jews, who expect a quite different kind of Messiah.[4] Now since the incarnation it is quite clear (as Luther notes) that the lordship of Christ is exercised only by the Word and by faith. "That is why it is vain for you to expect another rule, which would be without the Word and beyond the Word and which would consist of a wisdom conforming to this world and which would be exercised by a power and by arms of flesh" (WA 40, 3, 689, 3).

Again we find the fundamental importance of the Word in connection with the glorification of Christ. One could think that this glorification would have disengaged the rule of Christ from the dimension of the Word and make the Messianic glory which the Jews awaited so long follow the humiliation and the weakness of the incarnation. But Luther remarks that the ascension of Christ is equally accomplished by the Word and by faith. Undoubtedly there is a personal glorification of Christ, a change in his circumstances, because he no longer submits to humiliation and the cross, and because he rules at the right hand of the Father. In fact, this glorification of the person of Christ himself (to which Luther will return later) is of less importance than that other glorification which is effected by the proclamation of the gospel to the whole world and by the faith and the praise of the believers who contribute to glorifying Christ.[5] Luther can speak of the parallelism between two kinds of glorification and also emphasize in another connection that the glorification of Christ according to his person had as its purpose the glorification by faith.[6]

Hence the resurrection and the ascension, of course, make Christ enter in a very real way into his effective rule over all things. But this rule remains hidden. It must be announced by the Word and believed by faith. It is only when Christ thus encounters the faith of human beings that he will have truly attained the goal which he has fixed for himself, a glory proclaimed and acknowledged, and which by this fact itself transforms the believers according to his image.

The King as Servant: The Servant as King

The identity of the king with the servant is an intolerable paradox for reason, which "cannot comprehend how he who appears as the most poor and most miserable servant is also the king" (*WA* 40, 3, 695, 19). Only those who believe in the witness of the Word can grasp this mystery.[7]

It is in his commentary on Isaiah 53 that Luther dwells explicitly on this paradox, or, as Luther says it, "this scandal for reason"—that the king should be identified with the servant. Who in fact is "the arm of the Lord," who according to this verse, must be revealed? No other person than the suffering servant! That is the affirmation which made the Jews stumble. "What kind of a Messiah is this? they ask the Christians. You affirm that the true God, the Creator of heaven and earth is a servant of God, 'cursed' by God, wounded, struck by him, crucified. If he is God, he cannot be the servant; if he is the servant, he cannot be God, particularly such a servant, vile and despised to the very depths of hell. He who has created the angels and 'all things,' can he die and descend into hell, as you teach and believe?" (*WA* 40, 3, 701, 27)

There we stand at the center of the debate, at the very heart of the theology of the cross, that fundamental principle of Luther's theology which, from the beginning to the end, determined his thought: God revealing his glory in the suffering humanity of Jesus Christ, in the humiliation of the flesh, in the bread and the wine of the Eucharist. The principle is always the same.

"The one and the other is true: true God, arm of the eternal, and yet the most miserable of servants" (*WA* 40, 3, 701, 37). But who is this who authorizes Christians to affirm such things, so contrary to reason and to the ideas which reason forms about God and his glory? It is the Holy Spirit, who after the resurrection revealed that we were truly dealing with God.[8] The conviction of Christians, thus founded on the action of the Holy Spirit and on faith, affirms "this incredible thing, namely that the most miserable son of David is also the son of the king of glory, of God in the highest heaven, that he is the Messiah nailed to the cross and dying there, that he is subject to all the demons, and that he suffers even the most extreme humiliation, that among all the sins of the world there is not one that was not made his, that he did not impute to himself, that he did not assume and carry, but also that he who carried all these sins was the true 'arm of the Lord' and the God glorified and blessed for ever and ever" (WA 40, 3, 702, 20-26).

It is in order to express this central idea of the theology of the cross and of his entire concept of salvation that Luther recalls the union of the natures and the communication of attributes, protesting against all those who, from Nestorius to Schwenckfeld, according to him, impugned the unity of the person of Jesus Christ. *Non enim dividenda et distrahenda est persona filii Dei et Davidis. Sed debemus credere et confiteri, quod illae duae naturae sunt unus filius, quia sunt jam unitae unione hypostatica* (For the person of the Son of God and David cannot be divided or rent asunder. But we must believe and confess that the two natures are one Son, because they are already united in the hypostatic union) (WA 40, 3, 703, 3ff.).

Given the union of the natures in one single person, it is possible to say that God was born of Mary and that he was crucified. The theory of the communication of attributes only underlines this union of the two natures in one and the same person, so much so that one can say that "this man created the stars; that God cried in the manger; that this man is creator and governor of the angels; that he who created all things sucked at the breast of his mother, and that he slept in the manger" (WA 40, 3, 704, 5). "That is the principal article of our religion" (WA 704, 8).

Luther does not go any further with the question of the communication of attributes, but the fundamental idea which appears once again can be grasped through this passage. It consists of safeguarding, at all costs, the identity of the Lord with the servant and not separating God from the suffering man, but encountering him in the one who is the most miserable of all persons.

Passion, Glorification, and Rule of Jesus Christ

Jesus Christ not only suffered at the time of his passion, but his entire life was a suffering. Very often, he wept with pity and was moved with compassion.[9] He assumed the suffering caused by our sins, and not only the sins of tax collectors and prostitutes, but, as Luther makes quite clear, the sins of the saints. And Luther praises Isaiah because, better than the three evangelists and scarcely less well than John, he described not only the suffering of Christ, but also its causes and its effects.[10]

One finds again in this commentary ideas which the reformer has many times affirmed on the subject of the wrath of God which Jesus bore, the pains of hell that he felt, and the assaults of Satan which he underwent.[11] Because the innocent Son of God has thus suffered, he acquires for us, peace, and salvation.[12] Only he could do that, as the "person, eternal and infinite, one drop of whose blood would have been sufficient to save the entire earth . . . that is the Son of God . . . the chastisement of the Son of God, and not that of a prophet, of a patriarch or of an angel. The price *(pretium)* paid is too high. Christ is a very rich redeemer" (WA 40, 3, 717, 27ff.).

Commenting a little further on, on v. 10 ("It pleased the Lord to bruise him"), Luther insists that the suffering of Christ corresponds to the will of God. "God has willed to 'crush the serpent's head,' that is, to destroy the rule of the devil, of sin, of death, in order to build the rule of righteousness, of salvation, of eternal life" (WA 40, 3, 732, 1). The drama of Christ crucified is not then an accident, nor even one human tragedy among others, nor the fruits of the wickedness of the Jews; it corresponds to the saving will of God. The *causa finalis* is our salvation (WA 40, 3, 732, 8). "Christ does not die in order to be reduced to ashes, but to fill the whole earth with righteousness, salvation, and life, and to reestablish the kingdom of heaven. He did not die in order to perish, but to give his life for our sins, to be, as Paul says, an expiation *(hostia)* for our sins. The will of God was that he be victim, reconciliation *(placatio)*, ransom, redemption, price of our sins. For the wrath of God could not be appeased or put off except by so great a victim, namely the Son of God who could not sin. There was no other sacrifice by which God could be appeased, other than this victim who gave his life" (WA 40, 3, 732, 17-25).

But Christ was not a passive victim, an object tossed about by the

Jesus Christ, Crucified and Risen, Our Lord and Savior

wrath of God. He not only offered himself in sacrifice, but "he made himself sin, our victim" (*WA* 40, 3, 733, 1). Without insisting too much on it, Luther says that Christ gave proof of an active human obedience. He offers himself in sacrifice by an effort of his will and by a love which freely goes out to meet suffering because he seeks solidarity with sinful human beings. "Because he has become our victim and, for our great good and greatest happiness, sweats blood" (*WA* 40, 3, 737, 22), he is glorified and can rejoice in his victory over the powers. "Christ will see the fruit of his passion and of the resurrection, namely the church, victorious over death, sin, and the devil" (*WA* 737, 1).

It is because of the propitiatory suffering of Christ and of his intercession on our behalf that the Father forgives us and is found to be reconciled to us.

Moreover, Luther takes over in an original way, a traditional idea, found already in Gregory of Nazianzus, who said: that which is not assumed is not healed.[13] For the church Father, that refers above all to the body itself; for Luther, it refers to the life and death as such and of submission to the law. "The cross and suffering have been sanctified by his innocence" (*WA* 40, 3, 713, 33). From now on, there is no longer anything in life or death which has not been sanctified by Christ.[14]

But what of the death of Christ? Can one say that the Son of God has really died? In the proper sense of the word it is only the human nature that has died a real death. "And yet, it is right to say that the Son of God has been put to death" (*WA* 40, 3, 721, 27). Taking account of the unity of the person, it is even possible to speak of the death of God.

But at the same time, it must be affirmed that Christ could not be killed "because he was himself the living God" (*WA* 721, 28). "I die indeed for you, and in dying I live, because I am God and a human being. Death can bite and kill me, but it will not be able to hold me" (*WA* 721, 29-31).

The glorification of Christ is his resurrection and his entry into another life, in which he is no longer in submission to the chains of hell, sin, and death and where the law is abrogated.

But Luther's interest is primarily in the lure that Christ exercises in our favor. "That is why he is seated at the right hand of God the eternal Father, not only so that by sending the Holy Spirit he may heal us by the imputation which accords us forgiveness of our sins because of his death; but also in order that he may be efficacious in us and make us pass from sin to righteousness, healing both soul and body . . . that we may serve God with ardor in all piety and holiness of life" (*WA* 726, 24-30).

Christ and the Law

Once again, Luther stresses the accusing role of the law: "It does not testify to us that we are on the good way, but that we are under the wrath of God and involved in the struggle with sin" (*WA* 40, 3, 720, 7). God has charged the law to drive us toward the Son of God, not to give us grace, but to make us long for that forgiveness which is accorded only in Jesus Christ.[15]

The victory of Christ brings the accusations of the law to an end. Under the effect of the wrath of God, the law had its place among those powers which oppress human beings. By this victory, Christ liberates us from the *lex damnatrix et accusatrix* (*WA* 40, 3, 742, 18), so that believers no more fear this tyrant, but live in the peace of a good conscience and in the joyous assurance that nothing can oppress them anymore nor separate them from God.

And once more, Luther makes clear how Christ has won the victory over the law "not only by the merits of his own power which renders him righteous, but also by conforming with the letter of the law *(jure)*, because the law which has assailed him and accused him of being a sinner has been condemned. Thus Christ has delivered us, yes us too, from the curse of the law, because he joined himself to us and espoused *(copulatur)* us. And before God he has taken on himself all our sins. Hence, the law accuses him and condemns him as a sinner . . . the law takes him prisoner and shuts him up: thus death, sin, the devil, hell consider him as a sacrilegious being and condemn him. But what happens? He rises from the dead and his adversaries hear him say [to the devil]: 'I am the Son of God; I am innocent and righteous. You seduced Adam in paradise; I have taken on myself the sins of the whole world, and I have offered myself as a victim because of these sins. What rights have you over me?' Then Satan and death are obliged to say: 'We have sinned, we have accused an innocent person, killed someone who had done no wrong. . . . Hence death itself is killed, the devil himself is strangled, hell has despoiled itself' " (*WA* 40, 3, 744, 2-28).

Luther now takes care to eliminate a misunderstanding about his teaching on the law to which some of his early affirmations about the law had given rise among certain of his followers. In fact, some of his followers had understood his opposing of the law to the gospel as meaning that, according to the reformer, all laws are abolished for the Christian. This would place the Christian above the civil laws and the rules governing the coexistence of people in the city and in the family. That is why Luther says quite clearly that, "Christ does not suppress the ordinances of the family, economic life, and civil institutions" (*WA* 40, 3, 740, 12). It is not these laws which he wishes to destroy, but the works of Satan.[16] When the law, sin, and death are vanquished, the civil order and the family remain.[17] And Luther recalls that Christ confirmed this order by the intermediary of his apostles.[18]

Justification by Faith

In this commentary, Luther is not content simply to describe the redeeming sufferings of Christ and his work. He shows also how human beings participate in them, that is to say, "how, by what means, we attain the fruit and purpose of this work" (*WA* 40, 3, 738, 1). There is no other way than the knowledge *(notitia)* of Christ. It is by "faith alone, and not only the historic faith, which can equally be that of the devil, who also believes in God, after the manner of the heretics. But it is a knowledge *(cognitio)* of the order of experience *(experimentalis)*" (*WA* 40, 3, 738, 4). This faith is of the same order as that "knowledge" Adam had of his wife, *non speculative aut historice, sed experimentaliter* (neither speculative nor historical, but experimental) (*WA* 738, 8).

Luther remarked in this connection that the Hebrew verb *jada* is often translated into Latin as *doctrina* and one sees in that a "knowledge which is true and living, which I cannot limit to what is heard or explained" (*WA* 738, 10). The knowledge in question is a personal experience, an assurance. "It enters into my heart, that I may hope and not doubt, be quiet and know that Christ has died for me. This is not the traditional faith *(historica fides)*, which is not accompanied by this experience, nor this kind of feeling. The true faith affirms: 'My beloved is mine and I seize him with joy' . . . This is a vision, not only speculative, but based on experience and by which the soul and the body are set in motion, feeling a renewal and movement of life" (*WA* 738, 12-20).

It is by attaching themselves in this way to Jesus Christ that human beings are saved. Outside this faith, they are those lost sheep that v. 6 speaks of. Before his discovery of the gospel, Luther formed part of this flock of lost sheep, among whom are also, according to him, the Jews and the pope. "Of faith in Christ, of the power and the fruit of the passion, of the Eucharist of the Lord, of Baptism, nothing was rightly taught. Therefore, I was forced to justify myself by ever greater zeal, by means of my own works; I did not eat, nor drink, nor sleep; others did not have this bad conscience, were not exercised with such terrors; but I feared the last day and the wrath of God and hell. . . . The more I labored, the more I accumulated idolatries. I was not able to see Christ because the Scholastics had taught me that there was no hope for forgiveness of sins and salvation except in our works. So I lost the crucified and was seized with horror at seeing his face" (*WA* 40, 3, 719, 30ff.).

Now Luther proclaims that the only justification of human beings resides in the person and work of the man who was crucified and risen for them. That is why, when Christ comes, "the heart finds rest and peace and says: it was for my sake that Christ was punished and smitten, in order that I might be holy and at peace" (*WA* 40, 3, 720, 20).

With this central idea in Luther's thought, the *Commentary on Isaiah 53* closes. Luther urges his readers one last time to direct their attention to Christ alone. "Therefore, we must no longer regard ourselves, nor consider our sins, but act as though we knew nothing of them and turn ourselves toward this special 'Michael' (the archangel), that is to say, someone who is as God and who has borne our sins and, yet more, has risen from the dead, seated at the right hand of God, he sends to us the Holy Spirit and renders us all holy and righteous and gives us life and righteousness. . . . Therefore, there is no more sin in Christ and in those who believe in him.[19] Of course it is not entirely rooted out of the flesh, but it will no more be imputed to it. . . . The chief and essential part of our existence is Christ himself in whom our body will be entirely liberated from sin and from death, when the worms consume the death, and sin, and the misery of this body" (*WA* 40, 3, 745, 1-14).

It seems to us that this commentary we have just analyzed contains the principal themes of Luther's christology and soteriology. There again is stressed the importance of the Word and of the faith for every true approach to the reality of Jesus Christ: the theology of the cross, which presents to us God the Savior in the image of a suffering human being, while at the same time, it proclaims the glorification of Christ by the resurrection; the proclamation of the gospel; and the gift of the Holy Spirit.

Luther shows us the work of Jesus Christ, who, by his suffering and his resurrection, reconciles us with God and triumphs over the law, over death, the devil, and sin. Reflections on the person of Christ, with the help of the communication of attributes, insert themselves into the fundamental orientation of the theology of the cross and Luther's soteriology. It deals in fact with assuring thereby the reality of our salvation, because God himself in the person of the Son has known the infirmity of the human condition in the suffering of the Messiah who identifies with sinners. God has entered into this suffering, in order to save us, by enabling us to benefit from his victory.

Faced with the law and the other powers which try to enslave them and separate them from God, Christians grasp Christ who is the only righteousness that they can present before God. Thus they live a new existence and wait for the day when they will be entirely free from sin.

It will be noted that the subjects we have just recapitulated are found already in the young Luther. We have given evidence, from the earliest writings, of the theology of the cross; the role of the Word; the unity of incarnation, cross, and resurrection; the importance of justification by faith; the bond between the work and person of Christ; the way in which Luther envisages the work of Christ. Despite the variations which here and there, on individual points, can be found and of which we wrote in Chapter 5, the essential elements remain. Luther remained a kerygmatic theologian to the end, concentrating above all on the work accomplished by Christ on our behalf and emphasizing the necessity of a faith, striving to make known this work by the proclamation of the gospel and thus making persons enter into a new existence before God and human beings.

Notes

1   *WA* 40, 3, 685-746 *(Enerratio* on Isaiah 53 [1544], published in 1550).
2   *WA* 40, 3, 688, 6
3   *WA* 40, 3, 689, 8ff.

4   *WA* 40, 3, 688, 5ff.; 693, 3: "The prophet thus says that the Messiah, the arm of the Lord, will be a very poor, a very humble servant, who has nothing but the Word and who reigns only by means of the office of the Word." *WA* 40, 3, 699, 1ff.: "What has the king done to you? With what weapons has he supported you? Where is his armament, his army, his power? It is his Word, which is spread by the mouths of children, so that they freely submit to him."
5   *WA* 40, 3, 690ff.
6   *WA* 40, 3, 691, 35ff.
7   *WA* 40, 3, 697, 13ff.
8   *WA* 40, 3, 702, 2-6; 705, 19
9   *WA* 40, 3, 712-714
10 *WA* 40, 3, 715
11 *WA* 40, 3, 715, 14ff.
12 *WA* 40, 3, 717, 20ff.
13 Ep. 101, 7 (Migne Greek Patrology, 37, 182)
14 See also *WA* 37, 59, 1
15 *WA* 40, 3, 718, 28ff.
16 *WA* 40, 3, 741, 4
17 *WA* 40, 3, 740, 12
18 *WA* 40, 3, 740, 13
19 This affirmation seems to put in question the principle of *simul justus, simul peccator* (justified and yet a sinner), which is inherent in the doctrine of justification by faith, which Luther taught. In fact, the subsequent text shows that this is not the case. Of course, Christ takes away all sins, by forgiveness, but these sins have not yet entirely left human beings.

9

Conclusions and Perspective

Christology and Soteriology

We have seen how greatly Luther placed the accent on the saving work accomplished by Christ. Lost human beings, separated from God by the abyss of sin, subject to the divine wrath, enslaved to sin, the law, and death, are faced by the love of God, who has sent the Son. He came to share our conditions of existence; the innocent became one with sinners; he offered himself to the wrath of the Father and bore our punishment for sin; he triumphed over the law, the devil, and death. Coming to us when the gospel is proclaimed, he offers himself to faith as the righteousness we present before God, he triumphs over the powers who enslave us and he renders us in conformity with his death and with his resurrection.

Such, described in summary fashion, is the soteriological perspective of the reformer. Within the framework of this perspective, he explores a number of questions about the person of Christ and relates himself to the christological tradition of the church. It is important from the beginning to stress the intimate link between christology, reflection about the person of Christ, and soteriology, teaching about the work of Christ. These two aspects of the mystery of Christ are really inseparable: one might even say, in certain respects, that they are identical.

In fact, we have seen that, according to Luther, the incarnation did not mean only that Christ had taken a human body, but that

371

from the beginning he had been subject to the law and had assumed the sin of human beings. Thus the incarnation coincides with the redemption. In this connection it is still necessary to recall the many passages in which Luther affirms that we really know Christ only in that moment where we acknowledge what he has done for us. Thus the work of Christ is the key which opens the door to the mystery of his person. That is why Luther is so concerned that Christ be recognized as gift, as savior—and not as judge—before he is followed as example.

To underline in this way the fact that Luther's christology is above all soteriology, that it is determined by the saving work accomplished by Jesus Christ, is not to deny that Luther had reflected a great deal on questions concerned with christology as such, i.e., on the divinity and humanity of Christ, as well as their union in the person of Jesus Christ.

Nothing in our study allows us to confirm the widely propounded thesis, according to which, there is a contradiction in Luther between a soteriological christology and a "technical" (i.e., ontological) christology, such as St. Thomas taught. In this matter of the natures, their properties, and their union, certain Protestant theologians of the last century tried to oppose the soteriological and biblical christology of Luther to that of the early church, with its metaphysical language. In order to explain this opposition they called on the famous words of Melanchthon: *Hoc est Christum cognoscere, beneficia ejus cognoscere* (to know Christ is to know his benefits).

Some Catholic theologians, like Congar, have taken account of this opposition between the two types of christology, not of course to rejoice at it, but to deplore the absence of a fully elaborated christology in Luther, i.e., the absence of a study of the mystery as such and of an ontological or terminological reflection on the concepts of *natura,* of *persona,* and even of the concept of *God.*

We think we must object to this opposition which has been established between the two types of christology by theologians so diverse. Because he insists so much on the work of Christ, Luther has been led to refine his way of understanding the person of Christ, and on the basis of this work he has rediscovered the profound meaning of traditional christology. Admittedly, he did not start out from a well-constructed christology, from a carefully elaborated doctrine of the person of Christ, to go on to work out in detail the way in which he understands the work of Christ. From the beginning, and in conformity with the biblical testimony, he fixes his attention on the saving acts of God, among which the incarnation has a central place. But we believe that we have shown that Luther did not stop at a christological "agnosticism." He tried to be precise about the mystery of Christ. Unlike Melanchthon, he did not stop at the threshold of the mystery. He spoke of the immanent Trinity and not only of the "economic" Trinity. He raised questions about what were the divinity and the humanity of Christ, about the union between the two natures. Of course, he was pushed into certain developments, for example in the communication of attributes, by polemics in which his opponents had ensnared him. But Luther was well aware that it was not enough to describe the work of Christ without saying something about the one who accomplished this work. It is soteriology itself which demands a christology in the technical sense of the word. It is precisely in order to preserve the reality of our salvation that Luther considers it necessary to affirm clearly that Christ was God and a human being and to be clear about what is meant by that.

We have, of course, seen that for the most part, Luther's thoughts on christology were not really technical or speculative. His thought is rather "kerygmatic," i.e., it affirms a certain number of things, on the basis of the biblical witness, without always tending toward a very elaborate system, nor toward terminological precision which might well have been desirable because of the transition from Latin into German. All the same, the Eucharistic Controversy and the *Disputations* do reveal a "technical" christology. What emerges from these texts is that Luther never felt he was innovating anything in christology. If he spent years clarifying his thought on this point, it was not because he saw it as a matter for discussion, for he shared with Rome the current christological tradition. It was the Eucharistic Controversy which obliged him to express himself on the union between the two natures and to emphasize this union which was a fundamental reality of his faith, because for him it was above all important to join the savior God to the man Jesus. It was then that he sought concepts that would allow him to emphasize this. Quite naturally, he seized on the communication of attributes, which was available to him; also quite naturally, he thought it appropriate to study the christological tradition of the church and to clarify, particularly in the *Disputations,* his own agreement with it. This shows that he scarcely innovated—apart from allowing a direct communication between the two natures in the unique person of Christ.

One can nevertheless wonder whether the christological concepts used by Luther—for example the communication of attributes—were a service or a disservice to his thought, as it appears in his earlier writings, or again whether these concepts did not make him evolve his thinking toward a much stronger emphasis on the divine nature, to the detriment of the human nature. It seems to us that the modifications pointed out in Chapter 5 cannot be denied.

The Divinity of Christ

In conformity with the christological tradition of the church, Luther begins by confessing the divinity of Jesus Christ. This, according to him, is attested by the scriptural witness and confessed by the creeds of the early church. It could never be placed in doubt. We have often pointed out how insistently Luther emphasized the divine character. It is at the very center of his faith. If Christ was only human, he could not save us; he would be only one saint among others. God alone, in fact, can accomplish the work of redemption. Such is the reasoning which Luther shares with theologians as diverse as Athanasius and Anselm. Luther thought that he could discern in those who, at that period, emphasized the human side of Christ, considered as an example to be imitated, an attack on the fundamental principle that we have just enunciated. That is why he vigorously opposed all the spirituality of imitation and with force insisted on the divinity of Christ. In the face of a christology which favored the humanity of Christ, as a model to imitate or an image to inspire, Luther linked himself to the dogmatic christology of the early church.

The insistence on the divinity of Christ is also explained by the attention given existentially to the revelation of God. Luther is the man who experienced the wrath of God, who wrestled with the mystery of predestination, who sought the Father. He is not only seeking a piety, a kind of bond with Christ. He is seeking out God himself. But where could one find God more clearly revealed, and especially revealed in his love, than in the man Jesus? We have emphasized many times how Luther opposed those who thought they could go to God apart from the man Jesus. Whether they be mystics or speculative theologians, they contravene the express will of God.

And instead of encountering the God of love, they founder when they come near to the "naked" God. For his part, Luther intimately linked the divinity to the humanity of Christ. He did so to a greater extent than the theological tradition. One does not find in Luther the emphasis called, since Calvin (although known long before him), *extra-calvinisticum,* the conception according to which the Word was both present in the humanity of Jesus and apart from him. In Luther, the divine *hypostasis* is radically linked with the humanity of Christ, allowing it to participate in his activity, but no longer acting outside that activity.

Luther was not content, in conformity with the theological tradition, simply to confess the *vere deus* of Christ. Occasionally, a certain number of reflections are found in his writings on what must be understood as the "being of God." It is, above all, from the point of view taken from Genesis, the being of the creator. That is what distinguishes God from human beings. God is creator of life and of salvation. That is, one could say, his very nature. Luther has not hesitated to speak, again in conformity with tradition, about the two natures of Christ and their respective properties. Thus he has spoken of the omnipresence and the omnipotence of God. But, in fact, he expresses himself most often, like Hebraic thought, in active terms. God is everywhere, God suffers, God saves. These are the properties of God! The biblical language has thus renewed the traditional categories from within, without making them obsolete. But Luther does not ask only in some neutral way about the nature of God. His fundamental problem is, as we have shown, to know the intentions of God toward him: in other words, he poses the question of the wrath of God and the love of God. The real meaning of the "divine nature" of Christ consists for human beings in its revelation of the love of God beyond his wrath. In Christ I encounter the love of God himself, but this love is revealed through the suffering assumed by Christ, through which he reveals the wrath of God, which he bears and takes away.

Certain theologians, like Congar, have criticized what they call the lack of precision in Luther with regard to the Trinity. They mean that he only speaks of God in Jesus Christ, without making precise that it is only a question of the *hypostasis* of the Son, who is incarnate. Is this criticism justified? We think not. There is no doubt that Luther insisted above all on the divinity of Christ in order to emphasize that it is God who saves us, and not Christ as a human example. He also wishes to emphasize that we really encounter God and his loving intentions in the humanity of Christ. But such affirmations, which may appear to be "modalistic" are not, in fact, made at the expense of the traditional trinitarian dogma. We have pointed out how often Luther emphasized that only the Son had become human. We have also shown the importance in Luther's soteriology of the drama in which the Father and the Son confront each other. Salvation is accomplished within a personal and historical framework, where the Son seems to separate himself from the Father in order to be in solidarity with sinful human beings, for whom he is both victim of the wrath of God and sign of his love. This is an aspect of Luther's thought which is too little studied and to which we have drawn attention constantly.

The Humanity of Christ

While he affirms the true divinity of Christ, Luther never ceases to insist on the reality of his humanity. Sensitive to the concrete, he constantly drew attention, especially in his preaching, to the ordinary human daily life of Christ, in his preaching, referring to his physical limitations, his work, his family life, his condition as a Jew, and all the other traits of the life of Jesus as reported in the Gospels. In contrast to modern christologies, he had no doubts caused by historical and textual criticism and was in no way hindered from producing a picture of the humanity of Christ which is often very much alive. He used the occasion to oppose those who made of Jesus a superman and minimized the reality of his humanity. It is however true that the Eucharistic Controversy led him to neglect somewhat the humanity of Christ. We have detected a certain shift of thought at this point.

We have pointed out that in contrast to the majority of traditional christologies and thanks to the discovery of subjectivity, also under the influence of Nominalism, Luther paid rather great attention to the psychological consciousness of Christ. The suffering which he endured on the cross is expressed in his consciousness and Luther points out there the feeling of abandonment which invaded Christ, subject to the wrath of God. One knows how much the consciousness of Christ held the attention of the theologians of the 19th century. Schleiermacher and others built their christological systems on the consciousness that Christ had of his divine sonship; that leads, in the 19th century, to what has been called the "personality" of Jesus, characterized essentially by his consciousness of himself. The personality, thus defined, is often opposed to the body or to the flesh of Christ.

It is striking to see that Luther is unaware of such an opposition. The humanity of Christ is both his consciousness and his body. When, in the course of the Eucharistic Controversy, his adversaries minimized the flesh of Christ in favor of his words or his spirit, Luther reacted violently. There is no longer an incarnation if the flesh is devalued. There is no longer true humanity if the body of Christ is discounted. It is in fact in his consciousness and in his body that he suffered and that the redemption was accomplished. And the body is the means, the sign, by which the reality of salvation accomplished on the cross is most clearly attested and communicated to us to this day.

We have frequently indicated, in the course of our study, that in order to characterize Christ's humanity. Luther was not content to speak of his body or soul, i.e., of general, but static, anthropological conditions. For Christ to be human means equally to enter into our human condition, to be subject to the law, and to take the consequences of sin, which are the wrath of God, the assaults of Satan and death. Of course, Luther is perfectly clear in saying that Christ did not himself sin. At the same time, however, he emphasizes his solidarity with sinful human beings. From the beginning the humanity of Christ is thus described with the aid of active, even moral categories. This humanity, which is voluntary submission to the law, is suffering and solidarity with other human beings.

The Union Between the Two Natures

Luther insists on the real humanity of Christ, but of course his interest is not in the humanity alone. The role of the man Jesus is important because by his mediation, God approaches human beings and acts on their behalf. In other words, Luther's prime interest is in the union between the two natures of Christ. He stresses this union constantly. In Christ, God and human beings have become one single person, a new being. A new concept of the "person" seems thus to emerge, in which the person appears as the concrete whole, formed by the two natures and acting for the salvation of human beings. In fact, Luther has not renounced the classic conception of *enhypostasis,* according to which the *hypostasis* of the Word, the second person of the Trinity, subsists in a divine nature and a human nature, assuring the union between them and constituting the personifying subject of the entity Jesus Christ. A certain number of passages show that this classic conception remained present in Luther's christology. At the same time, however, his attention bears less on the eternal Word and the action of *enhypostasis,* than on its results, namely the concrete person of Jesus Christ who saves me, whom I encounter in faith and in whom I find God.

We have pointed out in the course of our study that from the Eucharistic Controversy on, Luther emphasized more strongly the union between the two natures. According to him, his adversaries divided the person of Christ, by thinking that they were able to encounter God apart from the man Jesus Christ, because they affirmed that, in the Eucharist, Christ was present only in his divine nature. Luther was thus pressed to emphasize yet more strongly than before the union between the two natures, while a little earlier, in the year 1522, he had still insisted on the need to distinguish them carefully. It is no longer necessary to dwell at length here on the reasons of faith which pressed Luther to maintain so strongly the unity of the two natures. It concerns both the full revelation of God, truly present in Jesus Christ, and the reality of our salvation which is sure only if God himself acts for us. This action is really attested only if one can say, on the basis of the unity of the person, that it is not only the man Jesus, but God himself who suffered for us.

When Luther tried to express the mystery of this union, he hesitated, it seems to us, between two divergent tendencies. On the one hand, he considered, particularly in his early works, the presence of the divinity in the humanity, from the point of view which one could call eschatological. He described it as a hidden presence, as a mystery, which needs to be revealed by the Word and which we shall only grasp in its modalities in the last day, when we shall see the divinity which is now hidden in the humanity. The conception of the communication of attributes can itself be described from an eschatological perspective, in which the natures are distinct and yet united, as we have shown in our consideration of the *Commentary on the Epistle to the Romans.* In this way, Monophysitism and Docetism are discarded, while at the same time an unprecedented tension is set up in the doctrine of the two natures in which the divine power and human weakness coexist, a tension which is certainly resolved at Easter and when the mystery is unveiled by the proclamation of the gospel, but which is not entirely revealed until the end of time. This perspective, which characterizes what we have called Luther's theology of the cross, permits us to maintain the necessary distinction between the two natures, which must not be confused, although they are closely united.

But in order to describe the bond between the two natures, traditional theology offered Luther the concept of communication of attributes. He used this concept, even in his earliest works, without thereby calling into question the eschatological perspective which we have just outlined. It was the Eucharistic Controversy which introduced a certain change on this point. The communication of attributes came to assume a greater importance, because it was a question of expressing the real presence of Christ, God and a human being, with the aid of a category which bound the humanity and the divinity together indissolubly. This concept provided that a certain number of properties, both human and divine, can be attributed either to the totally concrete person, or to the other nature. This seemed to offer a way out. In fact, by interpreting it in this latter sense, one could envisage the communication to the human nature of that property of ubiquity which is characteristic of the divine nature. One could also, at the same time, make the divinity participate in the sufferings of the humanity, more perhaps than in the perspective outlined above, in which there appeared the tension between the divine majesty and the human weakness.

We have indicated the difficulties which accompany the theory of the communication of attributes. The principal one is undoubtedly that of an illegitimate divinization of the man Jesus, to whom is attributed the divine property of ubiquity. Because he wants to be precise about the indissoluble union of the two natures, with the aid of the categories of the communication of attributes, Luther, it seems to us, contradicted the eschatological perspective which in other respects so largely dominates his thought, right up to his latest writings. There, at the very heart of his thought, we find a fracture which must be noted.

The Humanity of Christ and Salvation

The role of the human nature in the accomplishment of salvation has until now been left too much in suspense. The important part played by this nature in such a system as that of St. Anselm as well-known, and also the way in which St. Thomas and the Scholastic theologians tried to integrate it into the work of salvation by speaking of a cooperation of the human nature with the divine nature and as a "second cause." So the question of the meaning of the incarnation itself is posed.

It will first be noted that for Luther, the incarnation belongs to the so-called "historicity" (*Geschichtlichkeit*) of God. There is no doubt that Luther did not cease to emphasize the liberty of God, who, according to him, could have saved human beings other than by the incarnation and the cross. At the same time, however, he emphasizes the extent to which the incarnation allowed God to participate fully in human history and thus to show that he is a reality other than the impassible, transcendent being imagined by the Greeks. To some extent, then, the incarnation corresponds to the very being of God, who from all eternity is action between the Father, the Son, and the Holy Spirit. The incarnation of the Son manifests this confrontation of the Trinity at the level of human history and allows God to be discovered precisely through the history of Jesus, confronted with the wrath of God and subject to human condition. What must be emphasized with Luther, more than we have done so far, is the trinitarian dimension of the incarnation and of the revelation of God.

Because God, in the person of the Son, and by those relations which bind the Father to the Son, thus comes near to human beings in human terms, relations of faith between God and persons are possible. In effect, God "puts on" humanity, enters into our history by the incarnation and by the cross. This is not the "naked" God who has to be discovered by speculation or by the mystics, but God made flesh, who reveals himself here below only by the Word and only to faith. Thus the humanity of Christ makes possible relations of faith between God and human beings, as we have frequently emphasized in the course of this study.

But is this all that one can say about the meaning of the incarnation? Has the humanity no other role than that of hiding the "naked" God and allowing God to realize his eternal being in time? What precisely is the role of the humanity in the realization of salvation?

The Son becomes incarnate in order to reveal the love of God to human beings who are subject to his wrath. That is Luther's first perspective, which could be called the Johannine: "He who has seen me has seen the Father" (John 14:9). The man Jesus, who is also the eternal Son become flesh, thus reveals in a human language, by human gestures and acts, the eternal love of the Father, which remains even when the wrath of God submerges the Son. The humanity is thus the instrument of the divinity, used to reveal, within the conditions of historicity which we have indicated above, the profound being of God.

But from another perspective, the drama itself of the accomplishing of salvation is envisaged. There, Luther describes Christ, who is delivered up to the wrath of the Father, bearing the punishment deserved by sinful humanity and reconciling God and humankind. He speaks also, from another point of view, of the victorious combat, led by Christ against the law, sin, the devil, and death—those powers which enslave human beings because of the wrath of God. Now how could the Son truly take our sins upon him and bear the wrath of God, how could he triumph over the law and death, if he had not become human? Of course, he could have saved human beings as he created them, that is, without participating in their human condition. But that is not the way that God wished to follow, because he wished to appeal to faith. Hence, to become human means for Christ to clear the way for the love of God, bearing his wrath and his punishment, in the place of all human beings and as one of them, paying the price of grace and vanquishing the law, sin, the devil, and death, from within, deceiving them, as Luther says, following the early church.

We return now to our initial question. In the work of salvation, thus envisaged, in which the humanity holds an essential place in order to allow the Son to overcome the wrath of God by submitting to it and also to the assault of the powers, how must one think of the "cooperation" of the humanity? Is it simply the place where the drama of salvation unfolds, the revealer of the victorious combat led by the Son, or did Luther have in mind a cooperation between the two natures, as St. Thomas envisaged? We do not think that it is possible to limit Luther to this alternative.

He hardly ever speaks of a "cooperation" between the two natures. This way of thinking is foreign to his thought. But he has greatly stressed the human activity of Jesus Christ, who at the same time expresses the attitude of the eternal Son. He described the active sacrifice of the Son in becoming human, who delivered himself to the Father, who submitted himself freely to the human condition, and who bore the wrath of God. How could an action, which had a personal and historical (in the sense of *geschichtlich*) character, take place unless it were within the relations composed of liberty, faith, and hope between the Father and the Son, himself become human? Luther does not seem to have considered the two natures of Christ as two entities, which had in some way to be harmonized. If our interpretation is correct, it seems that he admitted a purely human will in Christ, which expressed in history and in the conditions of a human existence the eternal will of the Son.

Christ and the Church

We must again examine an important christological question, that of the relation between Christ and the church, between Christ and Christians. This question we are now going to look at is at the heart of differences between Catholics and Protestants. We have pointed out in the course of this study the extent to which Luther emphasizes the lordship of Christ over the church, a lordship which is expressed preeminently by the Word, thanks to which Christ manifests his presence. But we have equally shown that it is not only necessary to emphasize the liberty of Christ or his transcendence in relation to the church, but also his humiliation. In effect, he binds himself to these earthly realities, which are the voice of a human being, the bread and the wine of the Eucharist, the water of Baptism. These realities, in a way, constitute the continuance of his earthly incarnation. It is not, then, the institution, the ministry, or the teaching office which directly continue the incarnation of Christ, but what Article 5 of the Augsburg Confession calls the "means," by which the Holy Spirit is given. The teaching office and the institution are situated with respect to these means.

But what of the relations between Christ and the Christian, between him and what is traditionally called the mystical body? The direct link between Christ acting by the Word, the individual Christian, and the importance of faith, must be emphasized. By the Word, Christ offers himself to human beings as their righteousness before God. He lives in people and preserves them from the wrath of God. At the same time, he draws them, in faith, in death and life, conforming them to his cross and his resurrection. He presents them to God in the prayer by which he stands as Son eternally before God the Father, and, in the liberty which he confers on human beings, he moves them to service and humiliation. He is thus, for them, both sacrament (because he is their righteousness before God and liberates them from the hostile powers) and example (in the sense that he leads them to follow on the path of service). It is thus that, by the Word and by faith, the body of Christ is constituted, i.e., the assembly of believers.

The Christology of Luther and the Biblical Witness

Finally, we would like to situate Luther, on the basis of our study, with respect to the general christological tradition of the church.

First, it must be emphasized to what degree Luther's christology is rooted in the biblical witness. Most of his works are biblical commentaries and sermons. He never ceased to interpret the Holy Scripture and always in reference to Christ himself. To a biblicism which places all the biblical passages on the same level, he opposes, not modern historical criticism which recognizes different sources and distinguishes authentic passages from others considered to be inauthentic, but a *Christo-centrism*. This Christo-centrism, which is very marked, places and judges different texts according to whether they bear witness directly or indirectly to Christ.

The major biblical accents are found again in Luther's christology. We must content ourselves here with a few brief remarks. When he defines the divine nature on the basis of its creative action and describes its omnipresence in such a lively way, it is the Old Testament which inspires him, and particularly Genesis and the Psalms. In his sense of the concrete and in his sense of action, the spirit of Luther is very close to that of the Hebrew mentality. It was in Genesis also that he thought he found the passages on which he based his doctrine of the Trinity. Finally, the Psalms and Isaiah 53 have contributed preeminently to Luther's very human portrayal of Jesus Christ. By placing the penitential psalms in the mouth of Christ himself, he was able to describe, much more radically than the theological tradition, Christ's submission to the wrath of God and his real solidarity with sinners.

When examining the relationship between Luther and the New Testament, it seems to us that one must avoid favoring one or the other part as the source of his inspiration. Certainly, in his concept of justification, one cannot deny his dependence on Paul. But this must not be taken as the primary source of his inspiration in matters of christology. From this standpoint, we believe that we have been able to show that all the main New Testament emphases are to be found in Luther's christology. It is true that the role of the Synoptics seems to have been much less important from the Eucharistic Controversy onward.

At first, it seems that Luther's thought draws predominantly on the witness of John's gospel. The insistence on the incarnation (the Word made flesh), on the revelation of the Father by the Son, on the divinity present in the humanity in hidden fashion, on the importance of faith and the Word—these are themes common to Luther and John. Particularly in the context of the Eucharistic Controversy, there must be added the care that Luther takes to emphasize the glory of the earthly Christ, somewhat at the expense of his glorification by the resurrection and the ascension. There again is an orientation which is fairly typical of John's gospel.

And yet, Luther gave careful consideration also to the Synoptics. From where else could he have drawn the realistic descriptions of the human life of Jesus which we found in his sermons, if not the Synoptic Gospels? He also found there, more than in John, that "subordination" of the Son, become human, to the Father, his temptations, and above all the account of his passion which, with the christological interpretation of the Psalms, holds so great a place in Luther's christology, particularly in the first period of his activity.

Besides Isaiah 53, it is in Paul that he found the theological explanation of the sorrows of Christ: he was made sin for us. Luther sometimes understood this text literally, by showing in his commentaries on the Psalms, where the existential aspect of Christ confronted by the wrath of God dominates, and also in his Pauline commentaries, that Christ literally assumed the sin of human beings and bore the sufferings which were the consequences of that sin.

Luther thought that he found the idea of preexistence in Paul and in John. It is also Paul, particularly in Rom. 1:3-4 and Phil. 2:5-11, who contributed to his doctrine of the different states of Christ.

One can wonder to what extent Luther has made use of the Pauline statements about Christ: the new human being, firstborn of all creatures, etc. The theme of Christ as *exemplar,* to which we must be conformed, often held his attention, particularly in his earlier works. Later, the lordship of Christ and the insistence on the uniqueness of Christ caused this essential theme to pass somewhat into the background.

It can be said that in a very large measure, Pauline thought deter-mined Luther's soteriology. Both men saw the work of Christ as reconciliation between God and human beings, as a victory over sin, death, and the devil. Luther recovered from the epistle to the Gala-tians an idea which had been rather neglected by tradition, namely the opposition between law and gospel, and the victory of Christ which disarmed the law of its function as accusor.

Finally, it will also be noted that Luther is very close to "Pauline mysticism" when he stresses, with the apostle, that the new life is given to us by union, in faith, with Christ. But for both men, this is not mysticism, properly speaking, but a union realized by the Word and in faith. As regards justification by faith, it is hardly necessary to stress here the spiritual kinship which binds Luther spiritually to Paul. There is, of course, still the question of whether the perspec-tives are not a little different. Paul insisted more on the presence of the new reality, while Luther remained at the *simul justus, simul peccator* by stressing the eschatological perspective of a new life, which certainly has already begun, but which will only know its completion at the end of time.

Again, one can point out the importance of the priestly theme in Luther, which brings him close to the orientation of the epistle to the Hebrews, particularly in its rootedness in the Old Testament and its insistence on the temptations of Christ. As for the theme of the lordship of Christ over the church and the world, a theme so typical of the epistle to the Ephesians, this appears several times in Luther's writings, as we have already shown. Luther, of course, emphasizes particularly lordship over the church and the Christian life in general. He does this by insisting on the role of the Word, the liberty of Christ in relation to the institutional church, as well as on the priestly and sacrificial office of Christ, the Lord of the Chris-tian life. Luther's affirmations concerning the cosmic lordship of Christ are more scattered. We pointed them out in the course of the Eucharistic Controversy, in which Eph. 1:19ff. and 4:10 were used to explain the ubiquity of Christ, which in a certain way made it possible to describe the cosmic lordship of Christ.

Luther and the Early Church

The fact that Luther's christology is clearly rooted in the Bible does not mean that in any way he scorns the theological tradition which, with the aid of new categories, attempted at different periods to clarify and "translate" the biblical witness relative to Christ. On this subject, we have analyzed the different conceptions, defended by Luther, in his *Treatise on the Councils and the Churches*.

We find that he again uses the christological vocabulary of the early church. He speaks of *homoousios*, of *hypostasis*, of natures and persons, of Trinity, and of the communication of attributes, while at the same time retaining the right, on occasion, to criticize the terms on the basis of the biblical witness. Evidently, with him, one is in the presence of an important phenomenon: all these terms, in a sense, lose their original meaning, because an important cultural change is in the process of taking place. Luther himself makes the transition from Latin to German. The cultural unity of the world of the early church and of the Middle Ages is giving way to pluralism. In addition, the time of the great systems of thought is over. It is now the period of the Humanists, who pursue a new study of the texts, including the text of the Bible. The way is opening up for the discovery of history and the subjectivity of human beings. A number of these aspects are announced both by medieval piety and by Nominalism. They appear in Luther and oblige us to distinguish between his christological thought and that of the early church.

Yet it is not possible to designate Luther's taking over of the christological vocabulary of the early church as simply "formal." When he speaks of the two natures of Christ or the Trinity, it is, for him, a question of expressing, however imperfectly, yet legitimately, in conformity with the biblical intentions, the mystery of Christ. He never considered the creeds of the early church to be obsolete. At the most, he felt called to interpret them with the help of his doctrine of justification by faith.

In the course of this study, we noted how much Luther was permeated by the thought of the Fathers of the church. First of all, St. Augustine must be cited, but also Athanasius, Chrysostom, Irenaeus, Gregory of Nazianzus. A more thorough study would show in detail the significance of these influences. The stressing of the flesh of Christ, the resurrection, the victory over death, sin, and the devil, the theme of the *admirabile commercium*—even that of a certain "deification" of human beings—all these subjects show a definite kinship between the thought of Luther and that of the early church.

This may sometimes be indirect, through medieval authors such as Peter Lombard. Is it necessary to mention, finally, the affinities between the Monophysite tendency in Luther and certain aspects of post-Chalcedonian christology? Luther has gone beyond the Latin Middle Ages with its rather Nestorian tendency, back to an earlier Eastern christology, emphasizing the unity between the two natures and developing, in the course of the struggle over *Patripassianism*, the conception of the communication of attributes, even the theme of the suffering of God.

Luther and Medieval Christology

Several times, in the course of our study, we have tried to place the christology of Luther in relation to Anselm's, showing that Luther, like Anselm, had a more radical concept of sin than the early church, and that also like him, he conceived of the necessity for a reconciliation of God with human beings. But one does not find Anselm's well-constructed system entirely in Luther. In Anselm, God seems to a certain extent subject to the law. Rather than satisfying the law, we find in Luther the need to appease the wrath of God, a theme to which Luther attached far more importance than Anselm. This wrath is appeased by the action of the Son offering himself to the Father in order to bear the punishment instead of sinful human beings.

At the same time, there appears with Luther, as distinct from Anselm, a certain reserve in regard to the necessity and the logic of the incarnation and the work of Christ. There is there, if you like, a certain Nominalist heritage, in the sense that the liberty of God is more stressed. In fact, one must not exaggerate the influence of Nominalism in Luther. Very often, that which is attributed to Nominalism is in Luther only a return to the biblical image of God living free in his acts.

When one compares the thought of Luther with that of St. Thomas Aquinas, a comparison which has become more frequent in recent years, one comes across many similar statements. Between the master of high Scholasticism and the reformer, we find Nominalism, an accentuation of subjectivity, under the influence of a certain number of tendencies in medieval spirituality, as well as an undeniable biblical renewal, due largely to the efforts of the humanists. A weakening in the influence of the philosophy of Aristotle should also be noted.

The insertion of the *believer* into the theological horizon is far more important than in St. Thomas. The latter is to some extent more "objective," and he concentrated more on the mysteries of faith, on *fides quae creditur* (faith because it is believed), and not on *fides qua creditur* (faith to the extent that it is believed). Luther, on the contrary, occupies himself with the person who believes, with the beneficiary of the work of redemption and with the faith by which human beings have access to salvation. Doubtless it would be wrong to speak of Luther's "subjectivism." Unlike certain modern theologians, he did not make the conscience of the believer the supreme theological place. His thought is too "kerygmatic" for that. It follows, as does the biblical witness, the movement by which God draws near to human beings in order to save them. But it does not stop at describing this approach as in some way the internal structure of the acts and being of God. It goes further to the place where the act of God encounters human beings under the form of faith. At the same time, it determines the structure of that faith, by a new attention to human beings and to their religious experience, their relation to the Word and its proper nature, which is distinguished from love or works. Luther places himself then, both in what can be called the *kerygma*—or the proclamation of the acts of God, which he describes in his theology—and also in what can be called the religious experience of human beings, confronted by the wrath of God and in quest of salvation.

More than with St. Thomas, Luther's christology is from the beginning, soteriology, for he reckons that, without a soteriological point, the christological mysteries themselves are falsified. His christology, which is directed toward the Word and faith, toward the union between Christ and believer, is thus distinguished from, without necessarily being opposed to, a christology which is more than ontological, seeking to analyze the mystery itself, to place its different elements, to disentangle its interior logic rather than to emphasize from one end to the other the soteriological theme. Luther knew the thought of St. Thomas very little, but a comparison between two systems of thought is interesting, for it shows that Luther is situated, more than St. Thomas, at the threshold of the modern world, which centers on the subjectivity of human beings.

In that, Luther was certainly influenced by Nominalism, which places the real in the consciousness. At the same time, for him, as for many religious authors of the Middle Ages, the significance of the religious experience itself arises. In a world of great social, cultural, economic, and other upheavals, the religious experience itself occupies a central place, while the well-established cosmological and theological conceptions collapse and human beings are left, in some sense, alone with themselves.

By comparing the positions of Luther's christology with those of the Occamist theologians, we have discovered characteristic differences. While from Occam to Biel, one strove particularly to maintain the separation between the two natures of Christ and one scarcely went beyond the position of St. Thomas on the communication of attributes, Luther much more strongly united the two natures of Christ by speaking of the personal existence which was conferred on the humanity of Christ in the hypostatic union, and by envisaging also a certain kind of communication of attributes, not only to the total actual person of Jesus Christ, but between the two natures themselves. He thus based the ubiquity on the communication of attributes, while Biel seems rather to have postulated it on the basis of the infinite possibilities of the liberty of God.

Luther and His Protestant Adversaries

At several times, we have compared the christology of Luther with the thought of theologians who were opposed to him but who were also situated within the Protestant camp. It appeared clear to us that it is his way of understanding the incarnation and its continuance by outward means that has most of all separated him from the Enthusiasts, whom he reproaches for substituting a Christ as moral example for the Christ who gives righteousness to the believer, and who constitutes the cornerstone of the doctrine of justification by faith.

The controversy with Zwingli showed how much, in Luther's thought, the divinity acting in our favor and present in the Eucharist was inseparably bound to the humanity. To a certain degree, it is possible to affirm that the controversy with Zwingli—and even, much later, that between Calvinists and Lutherans—reproduced the conflict between the Alexandrians and the Nestorians, which led to the compromises of the Councils of Ephesus and Chalcedon.

Luther, Lutheran Orthodoxy, and the Kenotic Theologians

Finally, we must place Luther's christology with respect to later developments of theology.

The theologians who quote Luther as their authority and have been designated "Lutheran" see themselves above all as called on to clarify the Lutheran conception of the communication of attributes, in order to emphasize the indissoluble union between the two natures. They will thus bring a number of refinements to the concept envisaged by Luther, notably by distinguishing different kinds of communication of attributes: *genus idiomaticum, genus apotelesmaticum, genus majestaticum*. It is this last concept, attributing the divine properties to the human nature, which is peculiar to Lutheran theology.

At the same time, however, these theologians will not respect the intuitions of Luther at all points. Thus they recoil before the idea of a *genus tapeinoticon,* which envisages the communication of the suffering of the humanity to the divinity—an idea which was, however, already there in Luther, but will be taken up again only in the Kenotic theories of the 19th century.

In what concerns the saving work of Christ, one can detect in Lutheran orthodoxy, a deliberate return to the system of St. Anselm. In contrast to Luther, the affinities with the early church fade, particularly in relation to the importance of the resurrection.

The spirituality will evolve toward Pietism. At this stage, the person who believes will often replace the religious object itself, i.e., Christ. The comparison between this tendency and the spirituality of Luther helps us to distinguish soteriological christology from the anthropological christology in which human beings—their feelings and their religious needs—make the Christ himself and the mighty acts of God pass into the background.

In the 19th century, the Kenotic theologians such as Thomasius and Franck will appeal to Luther's thought in order to go beyond Luther, in fact far beyond him, in admitting the limitations, freely accepted, of the hypostatic union at the moment of the incarnation. This will be an attempt to get out of the dilemma posed by Lutheran christology, in which the communication of attributes and the divinization of the humanity of Christ make it difficult to consider readily the truly human image of Jesus of Nazareth which we know was rediscovered with such vigor in the 19th century. In fact, this attempt perverted the profound thought of Luther, for whom all was based on the presence—hidden, but real, and not limited—of God in the man Jesus. At the same time, however, these theologians reemphasized, following Luther, the theme of the weakness and historicity, even suffering and death, of God. This theme became extremely fruitful in that period, particularly in Hegel.

This leads us to place the christology of Luther, in a general way, in relation to modern christological tendencies.

Luther and the Modern Evolution of Christology

We have already given a certain number of indications on this subject. The attention given by Luther to the consciousness of Christ will reappear in the 19th century with Schleiermacher and others. We also know from the many biographies of Jesus up to the actual discovery of the "Jesus of history," how much theology will be interested in the concrete details of the life of Jesus, as Luther was, and often for the same reasons. But we have already indicated that Luther's attention to the consciousness of Jesus was not as exclusive as it later became in the 19th century; the importance accorded to the body and flesh of Christ separates him from many modern theologians. And it is not the "historic" Jesus, as such, who interests him. With many modern theologians, christology is often reduced to Christ as an ethical example or the subject of a biography, with the transcendence determined by other means, or in extreme cases, even denied. In relation to such theologies, Luther's christology is really dogmatic, in the sense that it does not limit itself to the consideration of Christ as a human being, but rather that it grasps God in Christ.

Evidently there is a great difference between Luther and the modern theologians. Luther did not know, to the extent that we do, the problem of questioning the very idea of transcendence. For him, the divinity of Christ was given by the scriptural witness and, in his time, God as such was not seriously put in question. For Luther, the problem consisted rather of determining the best relations between God and human beings, of discerning the saving intentions of God, and discovering the way in which to participate in his benefits.

But on the basis of our study, we think it is possible to affirm that,

392 Conclusions and Perspective

in the perspective of christology, a new conception of God took form in Luther, a conception which is repeatedly affirmed by certain modern theologians. It concerns what could be called the "historicity" of God, as opposed to his immutability and impassibility.

In one sense, it can be said that Luther put an end to a long Christian tradition dominated by a Platonic conception of God. In this Platonic view, God appeared as the supreme being by virtue of a certain number of metaphysical properties, opposed to those of human beings. In it, God appeared as impassible. There was in it very little question of his wrath or his suffering. He only touched this humanity by the Word dwelling both in the humanity of Jesus and beyond it. We have seen how closely Luther bound God to the weak and suffering humanity of Jesus. Whatever one may think of the concept of the communication of attributes—particularly in the form of the *genus tapeinoticon*—it is impossible not to recognize the appearance of this theme, passing through the Kenotic theologians and Hegel, to reappear in recent times in the theologians of the "death of God." Of course, with this principal difference, that with Luther, as also with Hegel, the death of God is not a permanent state, but an act which God follows with the resurrection, a transitory situation which can be expressed only in terms of paradox.

Contrasting Luther with St. Thomas, we have already indicated that Luther, by his constant attention to soteriology, proclaimed the advent of the modern world. In fact, modern theologians cannot and will no longer make a theology which studies God without considering human beings. The constant interrelation between these two realities is one of the general characteristics of all modern theology. But what distinguishes Luther from a certain number of modern theologians must also be indicated. For Luther, to consider human beings and their salvation does not mean to neglect God and those mysteries to which faith holds fast. In other words, soteriology does not absorb christology, nor anthropology, theology.

Christ is, of course, a reality *pro nobis* and *in nobis,* but he is also and remains *extra nos.* Many modern theologians, on the contrary, try to make a theology from beneath, in a different sense from Luther, by postulating some sort of reality of the divinity, based on the effects of its presence in human beings. We do not wish here to judge the legitimacy of such a step, but we must say that this is a different theological process from that which one finds in Luther. In him, we meet a kerygmatic thought affirming a certain number of things which concern God and a certain relationship of faith to knowledge *(fideisme)* which places these affirmations in the realm of the religious experience of the believer. Modern theological thought has very often favored the second of these two poles. There then remains only the *fideisme,* the attention given to the person who believes and the attempt to reach transcendence by way of the believer.

To end, we must point out the personal element in the thought and christology of Luther and its importance for modern theology. It is above all the place of the Word that must be emphasized here. The question which is posed is the following: How are human beings saved? The Christian tradition replies by stressing the need for a relationship with Jesus Christ. But this relationship can be conceived in very different ways: as an imitation of Christ, ethically; as a christification of the Christian, sacramentally; as an absorption of Christ, mystically; as a knowledge of Christ, intellectually.

Luther, for his part, emphasizes that the saving relationship between Christ and the Christian is by means of the Word, through which Christ acts today, and through faith, through which human beings accept personally and with their whole being the offer of salvation made to them in this way. A personal relationship is thus established between Christ and believers, a relationship which does not abolish the distance between the persons, but allows them to meet by the Word and by faith. Is it necessary again to stress the historical *(geschichtlich)* dimension of this kind of relationship? Faith is contained within a series of acts: the Word resounds, and human beings respond by putting their confidence in Christ, although this history of salvation is not completed here below.

Modern theology insists on the fact that human beings are not nature, but history, and it describes human relations with the aid of historical and personal categories. In order to describe the movement of faith itself, modern theology could not fail to take over the themes of Luther that we have just indicated. At the same time, one can wonder, for example, about Bultmann, whether such theologians can rightly claim Luther as their authority when they reduce the resurrection of Christ to his resurrection in the *kerygma* or when they reduce Christ to what he is for us in the Word. For our part, we think that this reduction and this identification are not found as such in Luther. Still today, Christ acts by the Word, and I encounter him in all his fulness there, and yet I cannot reduce him to this

394   Conclusions and Perspective

Word. We will content ourselves here to raise this problem, without solving it.

We must conclude. Luther's christology is not systematic. And yet it goes far beyond the stage in which a theologian, fond of sermons and devotions, is content to gather and popularize some christological themes which are more or less current. The thought of Luther is not systematic, for it was elaborated fortuitously from writings which he was called on to draft or from sermons which he happened to give. But, in spite of certain faults that we have pointed out, he was concerned with a christology, i.e., a coherent whole of themes concerning the action of God and human beings in Jesus Christ as well as the salvation brought to human beings. This christology was often elaborated within a matrix of thought which has become strange to us. At the same time, however, the motifs of faith do not cease to come through and grip us: the hidden, but real presence of God in this humanity; the reality of this humanity which is one with ours; the true participation of God in the human condition; the constant call addressed to human faith, inviting us to turn away from ourselves in order to rest entirely on Christ. These are all themes through which Luther wanted to do nothing but translate for his contemporaries the biblical witness on the subject of Christ. Like all thought from the past, that of Luther also needs to be set in the context of the thought of his day, and it needs to be interpreted. So treated, his thought, perhaps more than that of others, reveals a lively reality.

BIBLIOGRAPHY

Works of Luther

Luthers Werke. Kritische Gesamtausgabe. Weimar: 1883-.
Luther's Works. American Edition. 56 vols. Jaroslav Pelikan and Helmut T. Lehmann, eds. St. Louis and Philadelphia: Concordia Publishing House and Fortress Press, 1955-.
A Commentary on St. Paul's Epistle to the Galatians. Philip S. Watson, ed. London: James Clarke, 1953.
The Reformation Writings of Martin Luther. Bertram Lee Woolf, trans. London: Lutterworth, 1952 and 1956.
Unbekannte Fragmente. Erich Vogelsang, ed. Berlin: AKG, 1940.

Other Sources

Aquinas, Thomas. *Summa Theologiae.* Rome: 1894.
Calvin, John. *A Compend of the Institutes of the Christian Religion by John Calvin.* Hugh Kerr, ed. Philadelphia, 1939.
Corpus Reformatum. G. Baum, E. Cunitz, E. Reuss, and others, eds. Brunswick and Berlin: 1863-1900.
Enchiridion Symbolorum: Definitionem et Declarationum de rebus fidei et morum. H. Denziger and A. Schönmetzer, eds. Barcelona and Freiburg, 1967.
Patrologiae cursus completus. Greek. J. P. Migne, ed. Paris: 1857-1912.
Patrologiae cursus completus. Latin. J. P. Migne, ed. Paris: 1844-1890.
Zwingli, Huldreich. *Latin Works and the Correspondence of Huldreich Zwingli, Together with Selections from His German Works.* 3 vols. Macaulay Jackson, ed. New York: 1912.
Zwingli, Ulrich. *U. Zwinglis sämtliche Werke.* E. Egli, G. Finsler, W. Köhler, and others, eds. Leipzig: 1905.

General Works

Realencyklopädie für protestantische Theologie und Kirche. Leipzig: 1896.

Dictionnaire de Théologie Catholique. Paris: 1903-1950.
Die Religion in Geschichte und Gegenwart. 3rd ed. Tübingen: 1957-1965.
Die Bekenntnisschriften der evangelisch-lutherischen Kirche. Göttingen: 1930 and 1959.

Particular Studies

Alanen, K. J. E. *Das Gewissen bei Luther.* Helsinki: 1934.
Allgeier, W. *Der "Fröhliche Wechsel" bei Martin Luther.* Dissertation, Erlangen, 1966. (Typewritten.)
Alpers, H. *Die Versöhnung durch Christus: Zur Typologie der Schule von Lund.* Forschungen zur systematischen und ökumenischen Theologie 13. Göttingen, 1964.
Althaus, Paul. *Die christliche Wahrheit: Lehrbuch der Dogmatik.* Vol. 2. 5th ed. Gütersloh: 1959.
Althaus, Paul. *Die Theologie Martin Luthers.* Gütersloh: 1962. *The Theology of Martin Luther.* Philadelphia: Fortress, 1966.
Althaus, Paul. "Luthers Abendmahlslehre." *Luther-Jahrbuch* 11 (1929): 2-42.
Althaus, Paul. "Luthers neues Wort von Christus." *Luther* 26 (1955): 57ff.
Althaus, Paul. "Niedergefahren zur Hölle." *Zeitschrift für systematische Theologie* 19 (1942): 365ff.
Asendorf, Ulrich. *Eschatologie bei Luther.* Göttingen: 1967.
Asendorf, Ulrich. *Gekreuzigt und Auferstanden: Luthers Herausforderung an die moderne Christologie.* Arbeiten zur Geschichte und Theologie des Luthertums. Vol. 25. Berlin-Hamburg: 1971.
Atkinson, J. "Luthers Einschätzung des Johannesevangeliums." *Lutherforschung heute.* Pp. 49-56. Vilmos Vajta, ed. Berlin: 1958.
Aulén, Gustaf. *Christus Victor.* New York: Macmillan, 1969. Stockholm: 1930.
Aulén, Gustaf. *Den kristna försoningstanken: Huvudtyper och brytningar.*
Averbeck, Wilhelm. *Der Opfercharakter des Abendmahls in der neueren evangelischen Theologie.* Konfessionskundliche und kontroverstheologische Studien 19. Paderborn: 1967.
Baillie, D. M. *God Was in Christ. An Essay on Incarnation and Atonement.* New York: Scribner, 1948.
Bandt, H. *Luthers Lehre vom verborgenen Gott.* Berlin: 1957.
Barth, H. M. *Der Teufel und Jesus Christus in der Theologie Martin Luthers.* Göttingen: 1967.
Barth, Karl. "Ansatz und Absicht in Luthers Abendmahlslehre." 1923. *Die Theologie und die Kirche, Gesammelte Vorträge.* Pp. 26-75. Vol. 2. Zurich: 1928.
Barth, Karl. *Church Dogmatics.* Edinburgh: T. and T. Clark.
Bauer, Karl. *Die Wittenberger Universitätstheologie und die Anfänge der Deutschen Reformation.* Tübingen: 1928.
Beer, Th. *Der fröhliche Wechsel und Streit: Grundzüge der Theologie Martin Luthers.* 2 vols. Leipzig: 1974.

Beintker, H. *Die Uberwindung der Anfechtung bei Luther*. Berlin: 1954.

Besse (Dom). *Mystiques bénédictins des origines au XIIIe siecle*. "Pax" series. Vol. VII. Paris: Lethielleux-Desclée De Brouwer, 1922.

Bizer, Ernst. *Studien zur Geschichte des Abendmahlsstreites im 16. Jahrhundert*. Beiträge zur Förderung christlicher Theologie 2/46. Gütersloh: 1940.

Bizer, Ernst. *Fides ex auditu*. 3rd ed. Neukirchen: 1966.

Bohlin, T. *Den korfästa Skaparen*. Stockholm: 1952.

Bornkamm, Heinrich. *Luthers geistige Welt*. 3rd ed. Lüneburg: 1959.

Bornkamm, Karin. *Luthers Auslegungen des Galaterbriefes von 1519 bis 1531—Ein Vergleich*. Berlin: 1963.

Brandenburg, A. *Gericht und Evangelium: Zur Worttheologie in Luthers erster Psalmenvorlesung*. Konfessionskundliche und kontroverstheologische Studien 4. Paderborn: 1960.

Bring, R. *Dualismen hos Luther*. Lund: 1929.

Brunner, Emil. *Der Mittler*. 4th ed. Zurich: 1947.

Brunstädt, F. *Theologie der lutherischen Bekenntnisschriften*. Gütersloh: 1951.

Buchrucker, A. E. "Nullus Diabolus, Nullus Redemptor: Die Bedeutung des Teufels für die Theologie Martin Luthers." *Lutherischer Rundblick* 16 (1968): 150-160.

Bühler, P. Th. *Die Anfechtung bei Martin Luther*. Zurich: 1942.

Burba, K. *Die Christologie in Luthers Lieder*. Gütersloh: 1956.

Camelot, Th. "De Nestorius à Eutychès." *Das Konzil von Chalkedon*. Vol. 1. Pp. 234-250. Würzburg: 1951.

Congar, Yves. *Le Christ, Marie et l'Eglise*. Paris: P.U.F., 1952.

Congar, Yves. "Regards et réflexions sur la christologie de Luther." *Das Konzil von Chalkedon, Geschichte und Gegenwart*. Vol. 3. Pp. 547-587. Würzburg: 1954. *Chrétiens en dialogue*. Pp. 453-489. Paris: Cerf, 1964.

Dieckhoff, A. W. *Die evangelische Abendmahlslehre im Reformationszeitalter*. Vol. 1. Göttingen: 1854.

Doerne, M. "Gottes Ehre am gebundenen Willen: Evangelische Grundlagen und theologische Spitzensätze in De servo arbitrio. *Luther-Jahrbuch* 20 (1938): 45-92.

Ebeling, Gerhard. "Die Anfänge von Luthers Hermeneutik." *Zeitschrift für Theologie und Kirche* 48 (1951):172-230.

Ebeling, Gerhard. *Evangelische Evangelienauslegung*. Forschungen zur Geschichte und Lehre des Protestantismus 10/1. Munich: 1942. Darmstadt: 1962.

Ebeling, Gerhard. *Luther: Einführung in sein Denken*. Tübingen: 1964. *Luther: An Introduction to His Thought*. Philadelphia: Fortress, 1970.

Ebeling, Gerhard. "Luthers Theologie." *Die Religion in Geschichte und Gegenwart*, 4th ed. 1960. Vol. 4. Col. 495-520.

Elert, Werner. *Der Ausgang der altkirchlichen Christologie: Eine Untersuchung über Theodor von Pharan und seine Zeit als Einführung in die alte Dogmengeschichte*. Berlin: 1957.

Elert, Werner. *Morphologie des Luthertums*. Vol. 1. Munich: 1931. *The Structure of Lutheranism: The Theology and Philosophy of Life of Lutheranism, 16th and 17th Centuries*. St. Louis: Concordia, 1974.

Ellwein, E. "Die Christusverkündigung in Luthers Auslegung des Johannesevangeliums." *Kergyma und Dogma* 6(1960):31-68.

Ellwein, E. *Summus Evangelista: Die Botschaft des Johannesevangeliums in der Auslegung Luthers*. Munich: 1960.

Elze, Martin. "Das Verständnis der Passion Jesu im ausgehenden Mittelalter und bei Luther." *Geist und Geschichte der Reformations*. Pp: 127-151. Festgabe Hanns Rückert zum 65. Geburtstag. Berlin: 1966.

Elze, Martin. "Züge spätmittelalterlicher Frömmigkeit in Luthers Theologie." *Zeitschrift für Theologie und Kirche* 62(1965):381-402.

Franck, F. "Communicatio idiomatum." *Real-Encyklopädie für protestantische Theologie und Kirche*. Vol. 3. Pp. 326-334.

Gennrich, P. *Die Christologie Luthers im Abendmahlsstreit*. Königsberg: 1929.

Gerber, U. *Disputatio als Sprache des Glaubens: Eine Einführung in das theologische Verständnis der Sprache an Hand einer entwicklungsgeschichtlichen Untersuchung der Disputatio und ihres Sprachvollzuges*. Basler Studien zur historischen und systematischen Theologie 15. Zurich: 1970.

Gilson, E. *La théologie mystique de S. Bernard*. Paris: Vrin, 1934.

Gloege, G. *Mythologie und Luthertum*. 3rd ed. Göttingen: 1963.

Gogarten, F. *Luthers Theologie*. Tübingen: 1967.

Gollwitzer, H. "Luthers Abendmahlslehre." *Abendsmahlsgemeinschaft*. Pp. 94-121. Munich: 1937.

Grabmann, M. *Mittelalterliches Geistesleben: Abhandlungen zur Geschichte der Scholastik und Mystik*. Vols. 1-3. Munich: 1926.

Grass, H. *Die Abendmahlslehre bei Luther und Calvin: Eine kritische Untersuchung*. 2nd ed. Gütersloh: 1954.

Greschat, M. *Melanchthon neben Luther: Studien zur Gestalt der Rechtfertigungslehre zwischen 1528 und 1537*. Untersuchungen zur Kirchengeschichte 1. Witten: 1965.

Grillmeier, A. "Das *Scandalum oecumenicum* des Nestorius in kirchlichdogmatischer und theologiegeschichtlicher Sicht." *Scholastik: Vierteljahresschrift für Theologie und Philosophie* 36(1961):321-356.

Hägglund, Bengt. *Theologie und Philosophie bei Luther und in der occamistischen Tradition: Luthers Stellung zur Theorie von der doppelten Wahrheit*. Lund: 1955.

Haikola, L. *Usus legis*. Uppsala-Wiesbaden: 1958.

Hamel, A. *Der junge Luther und Augustin*. Vol. 1. Gütersloh: 1934.

Harnack, Theodosius. *Luthers Theologie mit besonderer Beziehung auf seine Versöhnungs- und Erlösungslehre*. Vol. 2. 2nd ed. Munich: 1927.

Heintze, G. *Luthers Predigt von Gesetz und Evangelium*. Forschungen zur Geschichte und Lehre des Protestantismus 10/11. Munich: 1958.

Held, F. *Augustins Enarrationes in Psalmos als exegetische Vorlage für Luthers erste Psalmenvorlesung.* Kiel: 1929.

Herz, Martin. *Sacrum commercium.* Munich: 1958.

Hilgenfeld, H. *Mittelalterlich-traditionelle Elemente in Luthers Abendmahlsschriften.* Studien zur Dogmengeschichte und systematischen Theologie 29. Zurich: 1971.

Hirsch, E. "Drei Kapitel zu Luthers Lehre vom Gewissen." *Lutherstudien.* Vol. 1. Pp. 9-220. Gütersloh: 1954.

Holl, Karl. *Gesammelte Aufsätze.* Vol. 1. 6th ed. Tübingen: 1932.

Hübner, Hanns. *Rechtfertigung und Heiligung in Luthers Römerbriefvorlesung.* Glaube und Lehre 7. Witten: 1965.

Iserloh, Erwin. "Existentiale Interpretation in Luthers erster Psalmenvorlesung." *Theologische Revue* 59(1963):73-84.

Iserloh, Erwin. "Luther und die Mystik." *Kirche, Mystik, Heiligung und das Natürliche bei Luther.* Göttingen: Asheim, 1967. Pp. 60-83.

Iserloh, Erwin. "Sacramentum et exemplum: Ein augustinisches Thema lutherischer Theologie." *Reformata Reformanda: Festgabe für Hubert Jedin.* E. Iserloh and K. Repgen, eds. Vol. 1. Münster: 1965. Pp. 247-264.

Iwand, Hanns J. *Rechtfertigungslehre und Christusglaube: Eine Untersuchung zur Systematik der Rechtfertigungslehre Luthers in ihren Anfängen.* Leipzig: 1930. Photocopy Munich-Darmstadt: 1961.

Jacob, G. *Der Gewissensbegriff in der Theologie Luthers.* Tübingen: 1929.

Joest, W. *Gesetz und Freiheit.* Göttingen: 1951.

Joest, W. *Ontologie der Person bei Luther.* Göttingen: 1967.

Josefson, R. "Christus und die heilige Schrift." *Lutherforschung heute.* Vilmos Vajta, ed. Berlin: 1958. Pp. 57-63.

Kadai, H. O. "Luther's Theology of the Cross." *Accents in Luther's Theology.* St. Louis: Concordia, 1967. Pp. 230-272.

Kaiser, Ph. *Die Gott-menschliche Einigung als Problem der spekulativen Theologie seit der Scholastik.* Munich: 1968.

Kantzenbach, F. W. "Christusgemeinschaft und Rechtfertigung: Luthers Gedanke vom frölichen Wechsel." *Luther* 35(1964):34-45.

Kantzenbach, F. W. "Kontroverstheologische Methode und Denkform bei Luther (nach der Konzilschrift vom 1539)." *Festschrift für Franz Lau.* Göttingen: 1967. Pp. 154-171.

Köhler, W. *Zwingli und Luther.* Vol. 1. Leipzig: 1924. Vol. 2. Zurich: 1951.

Koopmans, J. *Das altkirchliche Dogma in der Reformation.* Beiträge zur evangelischen Theologie 22. Munich: 1955.

Köstlin, J. *Luthers Theologie in ihrer geschichtlichen Entwicklung und ihren inneren Zusammenhang.* Stuttgart: 1901.

Kroeger, Martin. *Rechtfertigung und Gesetz: Studien zur Entwicklung der Rechtfertigungslehre beim jungen Luther.* Forschungen zur Kirchen und Dogmengeschichte 20. Göttingen: 1968.

Lackmann, M. "Thesaurus sanctorum: Ein vergessener Beitrag Luthers zur Hagiologie." *Reformation, Schicksal und Auftrag:* Festgabe für J. Lortz. Vol. 1. Baden-Baden: 1958. Pp. 135-172.

Landgraf, A. M. *Dogmengeschichte der Frühscholastik.* Vol. 2. "Die Lehre von Christus." Regensburg: 1953.

Lienhard, Marc. "Christologie et humilité dans la Theologia crucis du commentaire de l'épitre aux Romains de Luther." *Revue d'histoire et de philosophie religieuses* 42(1962):304-315.

Lienhard, Marc. "Die Verwerfung der Irrlehre und das Verhältnis zwischen lutherischen und reformierten Kirchen." *Gemeinschaft der reformatorischen Kirchen: Auf dem Weg II: Evangelische Zeitbuchreihe.* Polis 41. Zurich: 1971. Pp. 69-72.

Lienhard, Marc. "La doctrine du Saint-Esprit chez Luther." *Verbum Caro* 76(1965):11-38.

Lienhard, Marc. "Les cantiques de Luther et leur témoignage christologique." *Positions Luthériennes* 20 (1972):234-249.

Lienhard, Marc. "L'humanité de Jésus-Christ et la nôtre dans la pensée de Luther." *Positions Luthériennes* 17(1969):143-150.

Leinhard, Marc. "Notes sur un texte christologique du jeune Luther." *Revue d'histoire et de philosophie religieuses* 49(1969):331-340.

Loewenich, Walther von. *Luther und das johanneische Christentum.* Munich: 1935.

Loewenich, Walther von. *Luther's Theology of the Cross.* Minneapolis: Augsburg, 1976.

Löfgren, D. *Die Theologie der Schöpfung bei Luther.* Forschungen zur Kirchen und Dogmengeschichte 10. Göttingen: 1960.

Lohse, Bernhard. *Der Durchbruch der reformatorischen Erkenntnis bei Luther.* Bernhard Lohse, ed. Darmstadt: 1968.

Lohse, Bernhard. *Lutherdeutung heute.* Göttingen: 1968.

Lohse, Bernhard. "Luthers Christologie im Ablassstreit." *Luther-Jahrbuch* 27(1960):51-63.

Lortz, J. *Die Reformation in Deutschland.* Vols. 1-2. 4th ed. Freiburg-Bremen: 1962.

Lortz, J. *La Réforme en Allemagne.* Vols. 1-2. Paris: Cerf, 1970.

Lubac, Henri de. *Exégèse médiévale: Les quatre sens de l'Ecriture.* Etudes publiées sous la direction de la Faculté de théologie S. J. de Lyon-Fourvière, no. 41-42. Part 1. Paris: Aubier, 1959. Part 2. Paris: Aubier, 1969.

McSorley, H. J. *Luthers Lehre vom unfreien Willen nach seiner Hauptschrift De servo arbitrio im Lichte der biblischen und kirchlichen Tradition.* Beiträge zur ökumenischen Theologie. H. Fries, ed. Vol. 1. Munich: 1967.

Manns, P. "Fides absoluta—Fides incarnata: Zur Rechtfertigungslehre Luthers im Grossen Galater-Kommentar." *Reformata Reformanda: Festgabe für Hubert Jedin.* E. Iserloh and K. Repgen, eds. Vol. 1. Münster: 1965. Pp. 265-312.

Maurer, Wilhelm. "Die Anfänge von Luthers Theologie." *Theologische Literaturzeitung* 77 (1952):1-12.

Maurer, Wilhelm. "Die Einheit von Luthers Theologie." *Theologische Literaturzeitung* 75 (1950): 245-252.

Maurer, Wilhelm. "Kirche und Geschichte nach Luthers Dictata super Psalterium." *Lutherforschung heute.* Göttingen: 1958. Pp. 85-101.

Maurer, Wilhelm. *Von der Freiheit eines Christenmenschen: Zwei Untersuchungen zu Luthers Reformationsschriften 1520/21.* Göttingen: 1949.

Meyendorff, J. *Le Christ dans la théologie byzantine.* Paris: 1969.

Meyer, H. B. *Luther und die Messe: Eine liturgie-wissenschaftliche Untersuchung über das Verhältnis Luthers zum Messwesen des späten Mittelalters.* Konfessionskundliche und kontroverstheologische Studien 11. Paderborn: 1965.

Michel, A. "Communication des idiomes." *Dictionnaire de théologie catholique.* Vol. 7. Col. 595-602. 1922.

Müller, G. "Luthers Christusverständnis." *Jesus Christus: Das Christusverständnis im Wandel der Zeiten: Eine Ringvorlesung der theologischen Fakultät der Universität Marburg.* Marburg: 1963. Pp. 41-57.

Nilsson, K. O. *Simul: Das Miteinander von Göttlichem und Menschlichem in Luthers Theologie.* Forschungen zur Kirchen und Dogmengeschichte 17. Göttingen: 1966.

Obendieck, H. *Der Teufel bei Martin Luther.* Berlin: 1931.

Oberman, Heiko A. "Simul gemitus et raptus: Luther und die Mystik." *Kirche, Mystik, Heiligung und das bei Luther.* 1st ed. Göttingen: Asheim, 1967. Pp. 20-59.

Oberman, Heiko A. *Spätscholastik und Reformation: Der Herbst der mittelalterlichen Theologie.* Zurich: 1965.

Olivier, D. "Le deux sermons sur la double et triple justice." Oecumenica 3 (1968):39-69.

Pannenberg, Wolfhart. *Grundzüge der Christologie.* Gütersloh: 1964.

Pannenberg, Wolfhart. "Neue Wege katholischer Christologie." *Theologische Literaturzeitung* 82 (1967). Col. 95-100.

Pesch, O. H. *Die Theologie der Rechtfertigung bei Martin Luther und Thomas von Aquin: Versuch eines systematisch-theologischen Dialogs.* Walberberger Studien der Albertus-Magnus-Akademie 4. Mainz: 1967.

Pesch, O. H. "Zur Frage nach Luthers reformatorischer Wende: Ergebnisse und Probleme der Diskussion um Ernst Bizer—Fides ex auditu." *Catholica* 20 (1966):216-243; 264-280.

Peters, A. "Die Trinitätslehre in der reformatorischen Christenheit." *Theologische Literatiturzeitung* 94 (1969):561-570.

Peters, A. *Glaube und Werk: Luthers Rechtfertigungslehre im Lichte der Heiligen Schrift.* Arbeiten zur Geschichte und Theologie des Luthertums. Vol. 8. Berlin-Hamburg: 1962.

Peters, A. "Luthers Christuszeugnis als Zusammenfassung der Christusbotschaft der Kirche. *Kerygma und Dogma* 13 (1967): 1-26, 73-98.

Peters, A. *Realpräsenz: Luthers Zeugnis von Christi Gegenwart im*

Abendmahl. Arbeiten zur Geschichte und Theologie des Luthertums. Vol. 5. Berlin-Hamburg: 1960.

Pinomaa, L. "Der existentielle Charakter der Theologie Luthers: Das Hervorbrechen der Theologie der Anfechtung und ihre Bedeutung für das Lutherverständnis." Annales Academiae scientiarum Fennicae. Ser. B. 47, 3. Helsinki: 1940.

Pinomaa, L. "Die Heiligen in Luthers Frühtheologie." Studia theologica, Cura Ordinum theologorum scandinavicorum edita XIII/1. Lund: 1959. Pp. 1-50.

Pollet, J. V. M. "Zwinglianisme." *Dictionnaire de théologie catholique.* Vol. 15. Col. 3745-3928. 1950.

Prenter, Regin. *Der barmherzige Richter: Justitia dei passiva in Luthers Dictata super Psalterium 1513-1515.* Acta jutlandica. Publications of University of Aarhus XXXIII, 2, theological series 8. Copenhagen: 1961.

Prenter, Regin. *Schöpfung und Erlösung.* Göttingen: 1960.

Prenter, Regin. *Spiritus Creator: Studies i Luthers theologi.* 2nd ed. Copenhagen: 1946.

Ratzinger, J. *Einführung in das Christentum.* Munich: 1968.

Roth, E. *Sakrament nach Luther.* Berlin: 1952.

Ruhland, F. Th. *Luther und die Brautmystik: Nach Luthers Schrifttum bis 1521.* Giessen: 1938.

Scheffczyk, L. "Lehramtliche Formulierungen und Dogmengeschichte der Trinität." *Mysterium Salutis: Grundriss heilsgeschichtlicher Dogmatik.* Vol. 2. Einsiedeln-Zurich-Koln: 1967. Pp. 146-220.

Schempp, Paul. *Luthers Stellung zur heiligen Schrift.* Munich: 1929.

Schloemann, M. *Natürliches und gepredigtes Gesetz bei Luther.* Berlin: 1961.

Schwarz, R. "Gott ist Mensch: Zur Lehre von der Person Christi bei den Ockhamisten und bei Luther." *Zeitschrift für Theologie und Kirche* 63 (1966): 289-351.

Schwarzwäller, K. *Theologia crucis: Luthers Lehre von Prädestination nach De Servo arbitrio.* Forschungen zur Geschichte und Lehre des Protestantismus 10/39. Munich: 1970.

Seeberg, Erich. "Die Anfänge der Theologie Luthers." *Zeitschrift für Kirchengeschichte* 53 (1934):229-241. *Luthers Theologie.* Vol. 2. Pp. 4-16.

Seeberg, Erich. *Luthers Theologie.* Vol. 2. "Christus: Wirklichkeit und Urbild." Stuttgart: 1937. Darmstadt: 1969.

Seeberg, Erich. *Luthers Theologie in ihren Grundzügen.* 2nd ed. Stuttgart: 1950. 1st ed. 1940.

Seeberg, Reinhold. *Dogmengeschichte* I-IV. 6th ed. Stuttgart: 1960. 1st ed. 1895-1898.

Seils, M. *Der Gedanke vom Zusammenwirken Gottes und des Menschen in Luthers Theologie.* Beiträge zur Förderung christlicher Theologie 50. Gütersloh: 1962.

Siggins, J. K. *Martin Luther's Doctrine of Christ.* Yale Publications in Religion 14. New Haven: 1970.

Sommerlath, E. "Das Abendmahl bei Luther." *Vom Sakrament des Altars*. Leipzig: 1941. Pp. 95-132.

Sommerlath, E. "Luthers Lehre von der Realpräsenz im Abendmahl." *Ihmelsfestschrift*. Leipzig: 1928. Pp. 320ff.

Staehelin, E. *Das theologische Lebenswerk Johannes Oekolampads*. Leipzig: 1939.

Stange, C. *Der johanneische Typus der Heilslehre Luthers im Verhältnis zur paulinischen Rechtfertigungslehre*. Gütersloh: 1949.

Steck, K. G. "Ablass." *Die Religion in Geschichte und Gegenwart*. 3rd ed. Vol. 1. Col. 64-67. 1957.

Strohl, H. *Luther jusqu'en 1520*. 2nd ed. Paris: PUF, 1962.

Süss, Th. *La communion au corps du Christ*. Neuchatel: 1968.

Süss, Th. *Luther*. SUP "Philosophes." Paris: PUF, 1969.

Tarvainen, O. "Der Gedanke der Conformitas Christi in Luthers Theologie." *Zeitschrift für systematische Theologie* 22 (1953): 26-43.

Thimme, Hanns. *Christi Bedeutung für Luthers Glauben unter Zugrundelegung des Römerbrief, des Hebräerbrief, des Galaterkommentars von 1531 und der Disputationen*. Gütersloh: 1931.

Thomasius, G. *Christi Person und Werk: Darstellung der evangelisch-lutherischen Dogmatik vom Mittelpunkte der Christologie aus*. Vol. 2. Die Person des Mittlers. Erlangen: 1857.

Tiililä, G. *Das Strafleiden Christi*. Helsinki: 1941.

Vajta, Vilmos. *Die Theologie des Gottesdienstes bei Luther*. Forschungen zur Kirchen und Dogmengeschichte 1. Göttingen-Lund: 1952.

Vajta, Vilmos. "Sine meritis: Zur kritischen Funktion der Rechtfertigungslehre." *Oecumenica* 3 (1968): 146-195.

Vercruysse, J. *Fidelis populus*. Veröffentlichungen des Instituts für europäische Geschichte Mainz. Vol. 48. Wiesbaden: 1968.

Vogelsang, Erich. *Der angefochtene Christus bei Luther*. Arbeiten zur Kirchengeschichte 21. Berlin-Leipzig: 1929.

Vogelsang, Erich. *Die Anfänge von Luthers Christologie nach der ersten Psalmenvorlesung*. Arbeiten zur Kirchengeschichte 15. Berlin-Leipzig: 1929.

Vorländer, D. *Deus incarnatus: Die Zweinaturen christologie Luther bis 1521*. Untersuchungen zur Kirchengeschichte 9. Witten: 1974.

Watson, Ph. S. *Um Gottes Gottheit: Eine Einführung in Luthers Theologie*. Berlin: 1952.

Weber, O. *Grundlagen der Dogmatik*. Vol. 2. Neukirchen-Moers: 1962.

Wendel, Francois. *Calvin: Sources et évolution de sa pensée religieuse*. Etudes e'histoire et de philosophie religieuses publiées par la Faculté de théologie protestante de l'Université de Strasbourg. Paris: 1950.

Wolf, E. "Die Christusverkündigung bei Luther." *Jesus Christus im Zeugnis der Heiligen Schrift und der Kirche*. Munich: 1936. *Peregrinatio: Studien zur reformatorischen Theologie und zum Kirchenproblem*. Munich: 1954. Pp. 30ff.

INDEX

Names

Abelard, 178
d'Ailly, Pierre, 29-30, 149, 329, 337
Alber, Matthaeus, 201
Althaus, Paul, 111-112, 171, 181, 260, 341, 345
Ambrose, 64, 68
Anselm, 28, 57, 74, 76, 109, 118, 129, 141, 177-178, 180-182, 374, 387, 390
Apollinarius, 167, 315, 317
Arnoldi, B. von Usingen, 226
Aristotle, 30, 126, 388
Arius, 312-313
Athanasius, 17, 53, 60, 70, 74, 123, 132, 177, 223, 232, 313, 321, 374, 386
Augustine, 17ff., 33, 36, 40-41, 60, 64, 72, 107, 115-116, 164, 170, 183, 211-212, 320, 321-325, 386
Aulén, Gustaf, 290

Barth, Karl, 38
Basil, 323
Bernard, 32ff., 311
Biel, Gabriel, 29ff., 68, 226, 329, 332, 337, 389
Bizer, Ernst, 60ff., 73
Bonaventura, 32, 102, 322, 329
Bornkamm, Karin, 273
Brenz, 202
Bucer, 250, 309
Bultmann, Rudolf, 393

Calvin, John, 38, 170, 203, 223, 336ff., 345, 375, 389
Campanus, 310
Carlstadt, 198ff., 207, 222
Cassiadorus, 310
Cerinthus, 166
Chrysostom, 64, 70, 72, 386
Congar, Yves, 13-14, 22, 24, 26, 37, 44, 67, 195, 234, 290, 296, 318, 375
Crabbe, Pieter, 311

Cyprian, 212
Cyril of Alexandria, 27-28, 233, 317, 335-336, 341

Dionysius the Areopagite, 20, 33-34, 323
Duns Scotus, 29-31, 330

Eckhart, Meister, 34
Elze, Martin, 35
Erasmus, 212, 255, 258, 260
Esnault, R., 269
Eusebius of Caesarea, 310
Eutyches, 316ff.

Faber, Johannes, 324
Faber Stapulensis, 39-41
Franck, F., 173-174, 390

Gerson, J., 116
Gertrude, 33
Gregory the Great, 70, 183
Gregory of Nyssa, 183
Gregory Nazianzus, 336, 364, 386
Greschat, M., 272

Hamel, A., 26
Harnack, Adolf von, 37
Harnack, Theodosius, 11-12, 318
Hegel, Friedrich, 391-392
Heintze, G., 105
Hilary of Poitiers, 212, 324
Holl, Karl, 49, 110, 115, 318
Honius, 196ff., 201

Irenaeus, 17, 177, 212, 223, 386
Iserloh, Erwin, 73-74, 283

Joachim di Fiore, 333-334
Joest, W., 135
John of Damascus, 27, 232-233, 336, 341
John the Grammarian, 27
John of the Cross, 33